Object-oriented SSADM

Keith Robinson and Graham Berrisford

Prentice Hall
New York   London   Toronto   Tokyo   Singapore   Sydney

First published 1994 by
Prentice Hall International (UK) Limited
Campus 400, Maylands Avenue
Hemel Hempstead
Hertfordshire, HP2 7EZ
A division of
Simon & Schuster International Group

Printed and bound in Great Britain by
Redwood Books, Trowbridge, Wiltshire

Library of Congress Cataloging-in-Publication Data

Robinson, Keith.
  Object-oriented SSADM / Keith Robinson and Graham Berrisford.
    p. cm.
  Includes bibliographical references and index.
  ISBN 0–13–309444–8
  1. Electronic data processing—Structured techniques. 2. System analysis. 3. System
design. I. Berrisford, Graham. II. Title.
QA76.9.S84B47 1994
005.1'13—dc20   93–33041
                                                    CIP

British Library Cataloguing in Publication Data

A catalogue record for this book is available from the British Library

ISBN 0–13–309444–8

---

2   3   4   5   98 97 96 95 94

Dedication

Keith Robinson wished to dedicate this book to his father, George. I am happy to do this on his behalf, and sadly I dedicate it also to the memory of Keith himself, who died as the book was nearing completion.

Anyone who uses Keith's software can tell that as a software engineer he was a genius. The better you knew him, the more you were impressed by the breadth of his learning and the depth of his intellect. Physically and mentally, Keith was a giant of a man, yet he carried his gifts lightly, and shunned any form of self promotion.

In several areas, Keith's judgement was so reliable that if he disagreed with you, it was wise to bet on events proving him right. His death was untimely, leaving unfinished work of great promise. I will be pleased to complete any part of this work at half his pace, and can only hope that this book meets his high standards.

Graham Berrisford

Contents

Part Two: The Need for More Than Data Modelling

Part Three: The Need for More Than OO Programming

Part Four: Conceptual Modelling

Part Five: External Design

Part Six: Further Issues

Preface

Why should anyone want to use object-oriented ideas in systems analysis and design? Our starting point is that there are four major business objectives and an apparently minor design problem, which turns out to be a major one after all, which ought to be addressed by these ideas.

The business objectives

First, businesses need to reduce the cost of developing and then enhancing any single information system. One way to do this is to reduce the volume of documentation by designing and reusing common components. This book is very much concerned with reuse of components within a system. Readers learn where object-oriented ideas such as encapsulation and inheritance can help, where they have their limitations, and where other roads to reuse can be just as effective.

Second, businesses need to speed up system delivery. One way to do this is to partition a large information system for delivery via the successive stages of an incremental programme. In assembling a large system from smaller ones, the problem is how to build the first system so that another can be added to it, without significantly reworking or retesting the first system. This book does not fully solve this problem, but it provides the basis of 'software componentry' design techniques which we are developing as the solution.

Third, it is deceptively easy to set up a database structure and populate it with data. The difficult thing is to specify the rules which keep the data under control. The world is full of databases growing harder to use as they become increasingly cluttered with inconsistent and irrelevant data. Where historical data must be retained, amongst other design problems, analysts need ways of working out and specifying what should happen on the logical death of an entity, and how it may be deleted in a controlled way by a later event. Entity behaviour modelling seems the best answer to this need.

Fourth, some businesses cannot afford to implement incorrect systems. They need ways of proving the correctness of a system specification before it is coded. The book outlines practical analysis techniques for specifying business rules in a formal system specification language. The extra effort needed to apply the techniques may be justified by systems which are less error-prone.

Finally, where a single event has effects on several distinct objects, and the implementation environment does not provide automatic support for a 'commit unit', then designers have to design a message passing protocol. This book outlines solutions to this problem, as different implementations of one underlying theory.

The intended readers

The book provides systems analysts and designers with new techniques for defining an information system as a set of reusable components. These techniques integrate the ideas of entity modelling, object-oriented programming and graphical user interface design. They can be applied with current technology and supported by current CASE tools; they do not require an object-oriented database management system; a graphical user interface is helpful but not essential.

Systems development managers and database managers should benefit from the beginnings of answers to questions like: How far can systems be developed by extension of existing components? How do we use corporate modelling and reverse engineering? How can we migrate from old systems to new corporate systems?

Future developments

This book is not the final word; it is a summary of some of the advice Model Systems' consultants are giving to clients at the time of writing. Some of the analysis and design techniques introduced in this book cannot be fully described herein. Further publications are planned, especially in the area of entity event modelling. We are currently developing a 'software componentry' theory to help clients with:

- down-sizing, partition and distribution of systems
- incremental delivery, application integration and regression testing
- planning the systematic reuse of database components and routines.

As part of the consortium working on the European Modelling Languages within the EUASSET project we are developing a meta-model for a methodologies at the 'enterprise modelling' row of the matrix shown on the last page of chapter 32.

Products supporting this book

The text of the book was written in MacWrite II, the pictures were drawn in MacDraw version 1.9.5 and the case study diagrams were drawn or generated using Aut2 version 4.7.3. None of this material may be reproduced without permission. For lecturers wishing to base a course directly on this book, Model Systems can supply a comprehensive set of visual aids on paper and disk.

Aut2 is acknowledged to be exceptionally user-friendly, but its advanced automation features are less well-known. For example, it automates 'object-oriented SSADM' techniques such as the recognition of super-events, the transformation of entity behaviour models into effect correspondence diagrams and event procedures, and the generation of invocation hierarchies in which event procedures call each other.

Extending SSADM

To find out how SSADM can help with software reuse, read part one, then chapters:

12 for reuse of objects in entity data models
14 for reuse of 'methods' in entity event modelling
24 for reuse of graphical user interface components
31 for further software reuse issues and ideas
32 for corporate strategies for software reuse.

If your aim is to find out how SSADM works in the context of prototyping, rapid application development, or graphical user interface design, then read parts one and five. If your aim is to find out how SSADM employs entity event modelling, then read parts one, two and four. If your aim is to find out how SSADM can help with batch function design, then read part one and chapters 25, 28 and 29.

Acknowledgements

This book is the culmination of several years research and development. Chapters 2, 7 to 10, 14 to 19, and 30 are mostly based on material written by Keith Robinson, much of which has been published previously and is listed in the references at the end of the book. Chapters 20 to 29 are mostly based on papers written for the Union Bank of Switzerland (UBS).

We thank Model Systems' clients, especially UBS and the UK Government, for permission to use extracts from papers and reports written for them. Many people have made helpful contributions. We especially acknowledge the support given by the following people, who worked for the organisations shown at the time of their involvement.

Kurt Werli	UBS
Christoph Henrici	UBS
Rudolph Hagenmüller	Siemens Nixdorf
Manfred Pfieffer	Siemens Nixdorf
Peter King	Birkbeck College, University of London
Christian Werdich	In GmbH
Bob Brown	Database Design Group Inc.
Dan Tasker	Westpac
John Hall	Model Systems Ltd.
Liam McDonagh	Model Systems Ltd.
Chris Bird	Model Systems Inc.
Keri Anderson-Healey	Model Systems Inc.

Part One:

Introduction

Chapter 1

Aims and scope

This chapter defines who should benefit from reading this book and describes the division into six parts.

1.1 **The reader**

This book is aimed at systems analysts and designers, systems development managers and database managers. It is the first 'how to' book in its field. It shows how to improve the design of large information systems by:

- designing for software reuse and maintenance
- incorporating object-oriented ideas
- adding a graphical user interface.

The book should prove valuable to anyone who uses entity modelling techniques, whether within SSADM or within a comparable systems development methodology such as Information Engineering, Yourdon or JSD. Readers will find a theory of information systems development which unifies ideas from computer science with the best of business practice.

The people to whom we speak most directly are those in the 'information systems community' who build information systems for commerce, industry or government administration, especially those seeking to reduce the development and maintenance costs of these systems. We use straightforward practical examples, relevant to everyday systems development projects, to illustrate new ways to improve an information system's design. By 'improve' we mean that the system will make more reuse of components, will be more robust in the face of specification changes, and will use less code.

There is a second group who should find the ideas and techniques in this book useful, that is those in the 'computer science community' who are interested in object-oriented ideas or systems development methods.

This is an interesting moment; not only because we can see the confluence of previously distinct streams of thought, bringing the two communities together, but also because we can see real prospects of achieving commercial gain by designing some measure of reusability into information systems, even if this is only a small gain and a small measure.

1.2 **The goal: increased reuse**

Although this book is about adding object-oriented ideas to established entity modelling techniques, this is not in itself a useful goal. The goals are to build information systems better and quicker, and specifically to increase software reuse.

In software development, reusable components have grown slowly from the bottom up. The most generally useful of low-level sub-routines eventually become embedded in higher level programming languages as executable statements. For example, people used to have to write programs to calculate the number of days between two dates, but software manufacturers now provide such components as single instructions in their programming languages.

There are two problems here. First, this is a slow process. It takes a long time for the continual reinvention of a particular processing wheel to be spotted by software manufacturers and for the problem to be solved by extending programming languages. Second, we cannot rely on production software designers to solve the problems for us.

The time has come to look for reuse at higher levels of system design. Each application system throws up chances for designing reusable routines which are specific to the data structures of that system. Application system developers must be made responsible for discovering and designing reusable components of their own.

Helping people design for reuse

An important step in helping people design for reuse is to give names to the various levels at which reuse can be designed into a system. Some of the levels are shown in this diagram, with an indication of where they are discussed in this book.

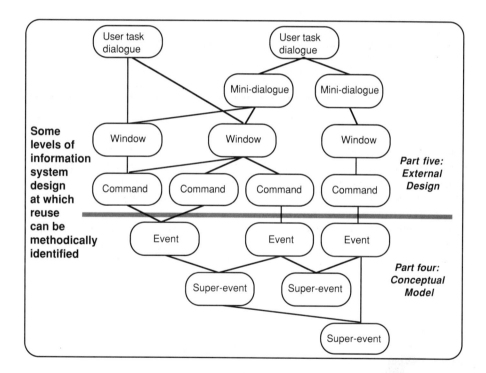

The second step is to define techniques which help in the discovery and specification of these reusable components. Several techniques are introduced in parts four and five. As far as we are aware, these are new techniques. Certainly they are not described in any other book or methodology we have studied. They have the advantage of being closely integrated both with each other and with SSADM4, which is our starting point.

How much reuse?

The question which may be foremost in the mind of a systems development manager is, Just how much reuse can be achieved? Ian Graham has said 'industry commentators have observed that reuse ... could save up to 20% of development costs' (Graham, 1991). Higher estimates have been made elsewhere. Our experience suggests that something around 20% might be achieved, by a combination of the techniques described in this book.

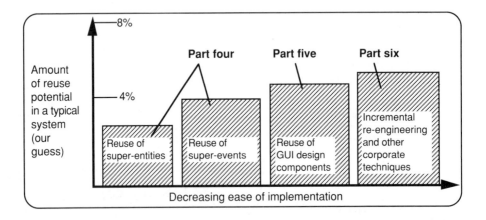

One point made by this graph is the relative strengths of the different approaches. Unfortunately it seems to be true that the techniques which give the largest advantage are the hardest to apply. The relatively straightforward 'application design techniques' described in parts four and five are probably less significant than the harder to manage approaches mentioned in part six.

The percentages are only guesses. Different systems contain very different proportions of reusable components. Lest the percentages shown turn out to be overestimates of the average figure, let us point out that saving 3% of the cost of developing a large system should pay back the effort of reading this book and using the techniques.

Helping the migration from old to new

Since there is enormous investment in old systems, another goal of this book is to help people to migrate from old systems to new corporate systems, which can then be extended by reuse of existing components. There are two sides to this. Parts four and five show how to build new systems better by using analysis and design techniques. Part six discusses methodical re-engineering of old systems using 'corporate modelling' and 'reverse engineering' techniques.

This book is mainly concerned with reuse *within* a system. The planned migration from old systems to new systems, maximising the reuse of old components on the way, involves further ideas. We are developing suitable 'software componentry' techniques in work we are currently doing for the UK Government. These techniques build on the ideas expressed in this book.

1.3 **Part one: introduction**

Part one introduces the goals and structure of the book. The structure is based on a 3-Schema Architecture which divides a system into three interconnected components:

- a Conceptual Model - support of business rules by data storage and processes
- an External Design - support of user tasks by functions, dialogues, windows, etc.
- an Internal Design - physical database design, read and write routines.

The 3-Schema Architecture provides guidance on how best to implement systems in a modular fashion. It is the basis for the systems development methodology presented in parts four and five. The methodology helps analysts and designers to define an information system as a set of reusable components and to develop systems by extending existing components. It employs entity data modelling, entity behaviour modelling, object-oriented programming, prototyping and graphical user interface design techniques.

A little of the background to part one

The methodology is based on SSADM4. We call it simply 'the methodology', but if a name is needed it may be called SSADM4+OO+GUI. Like SSADM4, it covers activities from systems analysis through systems design to database and program specification. It is very important that the system model built during systems analysis can be carried forward into design and then implementation.

There are those who object to the word 'methodology', but it is the right word according to the two definitions given in Chambers 20th Century Dictionary. First, the book describes 'a system of methods and rules applicable to work in a given science or art'. Second, the book gives an 'evaluation of subjects taught and principles and techniques of teaching them'. SSADM4 has grown by integrating what were once seen as distinct methods, rules, techniques and notations. SSADM4+OO+GUI is the result of continuing this process.

The methodology uses notations for system specification which are pictorial and machine-independent, yet also formal. In some areas (notably entity data modelling), the SSADM4 notation offers only marginal advantages over other notations in common use. In other areas (notably entity event modelling), we explain why the notation presented has significant advantages over others proposed.

But the methodology must offer more than notations. It must show how the notations are integrated into a coherent system specification; it must offer reasonably prescriptive techniques for making effective use of the notations; it must be applicable with current programming languages and current database management systems; and it must be supportable by current CASE tools.

1.4 **Part two: the need for more than data modelling**

If you come to this book from a background in database systems development, or if you
think an application generator can meet all your needs, part two suggests why you may
need a broader theory of modelling the real world in systems development. Someone
seeking to study the methodology in parts four and five might at first overlook part two,
but the essays in this part are relatively easy to read. Part two sets the scene for, and
defines terminology used in, the rest of the book.

A little of the background to part two

Beside the shortcomings of data modelling as a theory of systems development,
discussed in part two, it turns out that data modelling offers less than has been hoped to
the designer seeking to increase reuse of system components. Some reasons why entities
are rarely shared between different systems are explored in part four.

Traditionally, programmers and database designers have had separate perspectives, but
neither perspective is enough on its own.

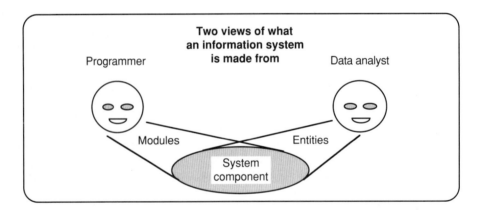

There are now some new ideas coming out of object-oriented programming which can
help us. The main object-oriented idea is to build processing routines around data types,
rather than from the classical programmer's viewpoint. The methodology provides a
theory of systems analysis and design in which each object in a system is viewed from
both data and processing perspectives.

It is true that in important ways the data-oriented and process-oriented views of an
object are both necessary and inseparable. However, there are stages in systems analysis
when one view is dominant. Some of the analysis techniques in the methodology can be
categorised as either data-oriented or process-oriented. In general, the methodology
looks at the data view before the process view; some reasons for this are discussed in
part two.

1.5 **Part three: the need for more than OO programming**

Like part two, part three defines terminology used in the rest of the book. If you come to this book from a background in database systems development, part three introduces you to object-oriented programming ideas. If you come from a background in object-oriented programming, part three highlights the limitations of object-oriented programming languages as tools for building large information systems.

A little of the background to part three

So far, applications which have been implemented in object-oriented programming languages tend to be in the area of what may be called 'production software'. Object-oriented programming languages are strongly biased towards applications with few objects (thousands at most), which are stored in main memory, temporary (that is alive only during the execution of a program) and related in a simple structure of classes and sub-classes. By way of contrast, an information system often contains millions or billions of objects, which are stored on backing store, persistent (that is alive between executions of a program) and related in a complex data structure.

There are other less straightforward differences between typical object-oriented systems and information systems. In part three we list several ways in which the object-oriented approach, as it is revealed through programming languages, must be extended for information system design. The last of these is that an analysis methodology must be developed.

1.6 **Part four: conceptual modelling**

Part four shows how to build a Conceptual Model which captures the essential 'business rules' and is directly implementable as a database and programs at the heart of an information system. In the step-by-step development of a substantial case study, part four shows how analysis techniques can deliver the benefits of reuse.

A little of the background to part four

The general understanding of object-oriented ideas, if there can be said to be one, is heavily influenced by their use in building graphical user interfaces. But the fact that designers may benefit from using object-oriented implementation tools is barely relevant at the level of systems analysis discussed in this book. It turns out that object-oriented ideas are more directly helpful to the analyst in Conceptual Modelling, where their impact is entirely different from their impact on External Design.

Part four shows how entity behaviour modelling can be enriched by the use of object-oriented programming ideas to maximise the reuse of components through the identification, analysis and design of super-events. The unique advantage of the approach is that super-events are detected and designed *during systems analysis*, not introduced as an afterthought at the end of system design, by looking for common code.

1.7 **Part five: external design**

Part five (which is not dependent on part four) shows how to increase reuse in building an External Design around the Conceptual Model, using rapid application development techniques and more systematic design techniques. Continuing the step-by-step development of the case study started in part four, it illustrates new techniques for adding a graphical user interface to an information system, and for designing off-line functions. Reuse of components is a recurring theme throughout this part.

The final chapter, on error handling, is an important supplement to the techniques in parts four and five.

1.8 **Part six: further issues**

Part six (which is not dependent on parts four or five) is aimed more at managers of systems development departments than at systems analysts and designers. This final part rounds up some topics which do not naturally fit in earlier parts, notably:

- what is wrong with current CASE tools and what can be done about it?
- how CASE tools can or do support the methodology
- opportunities for increasing reuse of components (within and between systems)
- corporate strategies for achieving software reuse.

A little of the background to part six

Part six is peripheral to the main thrust of the book. It offers observations on and future directions for CASE tool development. It widens the discussion of reuse beyond that of the specific design techniques which are discussed parts four and five.

For many years the hopes of software developers for increased reuse have centred on modularity. The classical approach to reusability is to build a library of common routines (which may be called modules, procedures, functions, sub-routines or whatever). It was hoped that by keeping modules small they could be independently tested, and that those validated modules could be recombined easily into new programs. This approach, using conventional technology, is generally agreed to have failed. A number of reasons why modular programming is not enough are explored in part six.

1.9 **What the book is *not* about**

This book is not a dry academic thesis. It is directly relevant to everyday systems development projects. The new ideas and techniques introduced in parts four and five are being used today to reduce the development and maintenance costs of large information systems.

It is our explicit aim *not* to concentrate on techniques which depend upon using an object-oriented programming language, or an object-oriented database management system or a user interface management system. However, the design of a graphical user interface is discussed at length in part five, as one possible implementation of the External Design.

How far the methodology might be relevant to the design of production software such as operating systems, database management systems, user interface management systems and so on, is not our concern. Earlier books on the methodical use of object-oriented ideas have included illustrations drawn from these areas, so extending our methodology into these areas can be envisaged.

This book is not aimed at strategic planning, but people engaged in strategic planning might find some of its analysis techniques useful and there is some discussion of 'corporate modelling' in part six. Apart from what may be inferred from chapter 18, the book does not attempt to deal with the analysis of how data and processes might be 'distributed', but the methodology is currently being extended to make the necessary steps explicit.

1.10 **The coming together of ideas**

The coming together of ideas mentioned at the beginning of this chapter can be summarised in a diagram.

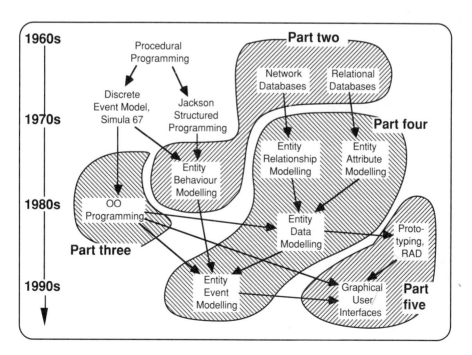

1.11 **Conventions used in the book**

Each key word is included in the index, where the references direct the reader to a definitions, descriptions and illustrations of the word.

To make the book accessible to the general reader we have assumed little if any knowledge of SSADM and we have avoided some of the words and conventions peculiar to that methodology. For example, we have used lower case initial letters for terms like 'function' and 'data flow diagram'. There are some minor differences in terminology, notably:

SSADM term	Our term
Entity Life History	Entity behaviour model
Update or Enquiry Process Model	Event or enquiry procedure
State Indicator	State variable

We have placed the word 'user' in front of 'function' and 'dialogue' where we are talking about a function or dialogue designed to support the user in carrying out a business task, since the term 'system function' which is used in the SSADM structural model is misleading in this respect.

In the main, we've avoided using acronyms. Here is a list of some which do appear.

BSO	Business System Option
CASE	Computer Aided Software Engineering
DFD	Data Flow Diagram
EAP	Enquiry Access Path
GUI	Graphical User Interface
IE	Information Engineering
I/O	Input or Output
JSP	Jackson Structured Programming
LDM	Logical Data Model (same as entity data model)
OO	Object-Oriented
OMT	Object Modelling Technique
PDI	Process/Data Interface
SSADM4	Structured Systems Analysis and Design Methodology version 4
TNF	Third Normal Form
TPMS	Transaction Processing Management System
TSO	Technical System Option
UIMS	User Interface Management System

Chapter 2

Introducing
the methodology

This chapter presents an overview of the methodology. It introduces a rationale based on the things which all information systems and system functions have in common, called the 3-Schema Architecture, and it introduces notations which are universally applicable in information systems development.

2.1 The 3-Schema Architecture

Seen from a sufficiently distant viewpoint, all information systems look much the same and do the same kind of things. They have a general shape or 'architecture'.

The 3-Schema database architecture

In the mid 1970s the ANSI/SPARC committee on database management systems developed an architecture for database systems (Tsichritzis and Klug, 1978) which supplanted the older, more naive, notion of a division between the 'logical' and 'physical' views of data.

In this architecture, the notion of 'physical' data, that is, data as actually stored, was retained in the notion of an 'Internal Schema' which defines the storage structure of the data. However, what was previously thought of as 'logical' data, was now divided between an 'External Schema' and a 'Conceptual Schema'.

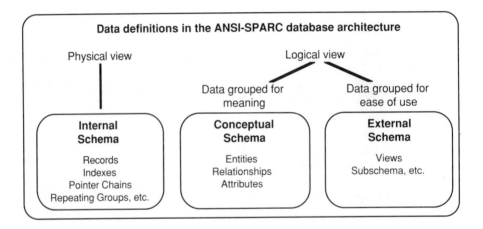

When it was first proposed there was considerable lack of understanding about the role of the Conceptual Schema or 'entity data'. Since then, however, the idea of having a central entity model of the user's business has gained wide acceptance as a way of, among other things:

- understanding the user's business
- gathering data about volumes and driving the physical data design
- mediating between different, co-operating DBMSs
- gaining some portability of design
- providing building blocks for external views to be constructed.

A 3-Schema *processing* architecture

The idea of extending the 3-Schema database architecture into processing was raised by Jim Lucking of ICL, among others on the ANSI/SPARC working party. The main aim was to extend the Conceptual Schema to become a 'Conceptual Scenario' covering both data and processes. At the time, however, no-one knew how to do this.

Recently, a modern form of the 3-Schema Architecture has been developed which extends it into the area of software design and specification (Duschl and Hopkins, 1992). The essential ideas are shown in this diagram.

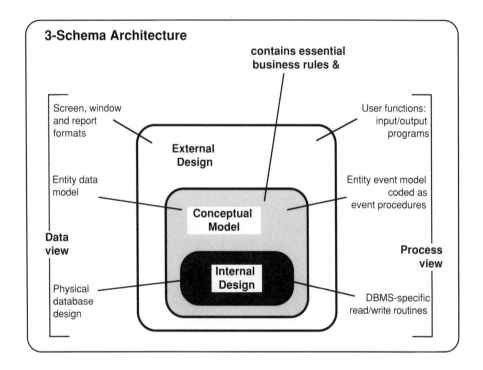

Despite the use of words like 'procedure' and 'routine' to describe the building blocks of system processing, the methodology does not commit designers to procedural language implementation. Some of the end-products may be more readily implemented in a declarative language like SQL, or in an object oriented programming language.

The 3-Schema Architecture is not so much a high-level specification, to be developed by top-down decomposition, as it is a template for software development, to be fleshed out by system-specific detail. The template is based on the assumption that most information systems share the same kind of overall structure, basic components and division between data and processes.

To draw an analogy, before an engineer begins to design a new car there is already a set of assumptions about what needs to be done, based on how previous cars have been built. One can predict that quite separate design effort will be required for the power unit, the chassis, the superstructure and the electrical accessories. This is not top-down decomposition. The car is not being treated as a homogeneous mixture of components. It is being divided into distinct specialist areas, each requiring different expertise and knowledge, each governed by quite different objectives. One can be reasonably confident that the same *separation of concerns* will apply to all cars.

Separation of concerns in systems development

This 3-Schema Architecture can be used to divide system development into three parallel strands.

The **Conceptual Model** comprises the essential business rules and knowledge, expressed in an entity data model and entity behaviour model. This system model is independent of the user interface and portable between implementation environments. It should be coded as logical database processes which apparently read and write entities in the entity data model. (This is the main difference from the old ANSI/SPARC architecture, in which conceptual data was never supposed to be 'materialised'.)

For the Conceptual Model it is possible to believe that there is in some sense a 'right answer'. Through the use of stereotype components and a disciplined approach to entity event modelling, the designer can produce a highly objective procedural specification of the database processing.

The **External Design** comprises the user interface, made up of data definitions for input/output files, screens and reports, and process definitions for dialogue and batch input/output programs. The External Design depends on trade-offs between a number of different things (organisation structure, ergonomics, system efficiency, end-user input-output device technology, arbitrary preferences of particular users, audit principles, security, user politics, etc.). So any method for designing the input and output processes must be creative, that is, it must involve inventing solutions. Heuristic approaches like prototyping clearly have a strong role to play here.

The **Internal Design** defines the physical database design, perhaps tuned for performance reasons, and the **process/data interface** or PDI. The PDI is composed of internal data storage and retrieval processes which deal with reading and writing individual records from the physical database. They are written so that conceptual processes can act as though they read and write entities in the entity data model. An internal process might assemble conceptual data from quite differently structured physical data, and vice versa. The Internal Design also depends on trade-offs between a number of things whose relative importance is subjectively defined: time objectives, space objectives, maintainability. Again, this implies that there is no 'right answer' and that a heuristic, prototyping approach is needed.

Analysis *versus* design

There is another tripartite division, loosely related to the 3-Schema Architecture. Most techniques combine in varying degrees: **analysis**, requiring the discovery of new facts; **design**, requiring judgements and decisions based on facts and rules of thumb; and **transformation** of inputs into outputs. The relationship to the 3-Schema Architecture is shown below.

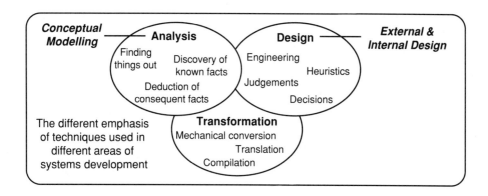

The different emphasis of techniques used in different areas of systems development

The place of prototyping

To some extent the Conceptual Model already exists in the end-users' minds before the analysis starts and only has to be *discovered*. The 3-Schema Architecture separates this part of the system from the part whose properties are subjective and so must be *designed*, the Internal and External Designs.

Prototyping and heuristic methods are needed in systems development, but they are not the whole of the story. Just because they are needed in some areas of systems development, this does not imply that they are needed everywhere. Experience suggests that prototyping methods are more appropriate to design than to discovery, so the Conceptual Model is an area where prototyping is less appropriate; it can even be counter-productive.

This is in line with the views expressed by Vonk (1990) who emphasises that prototyping is most effective in the domain of External Design, and recommends it should mainly be used in this context. See chapter 20 for further discussion of prototyping.

Separation of concerns in implementation

The 3-Schema Architecture is not just a way of viewing systems during analysis. In the end, each view of the system will be coded in distinct programs in the implemented system. Ideally, the code defining the final system will contain three elements:

Program code for	Implements
External Design	the user interface
Internal Design	the physical storage and processing environment
Conceptual Model	the necessary processing semantics

Separating the Conceptual code (that which implements the Conceptual Model) from the rest, and placing all the knowledge about the business rules in that set of code, leads to the advantages listed later in this chapter. One worth emphasising here is: reuse.

The Conceptual code is reusable behind different user interfaces or External Designs. A different user interface can be coded for different users, or even for different user interface management systems (UIMS). Likewise, the Conceptual code is reusable between different physical data storage implementation environments (or Internal Designs); a different process/data interface can be written for different optimised versions of the data model, or even for different database management systems.

Further advantages are modularising the physical code in this way are discussed later in this chapter. Of course there are alternative design strategies in everyday use. For example, instead of coding the Internal Design separately in the form of process/data interface, the designer may code the Conceptual Model processes so that they read and write records in the physical database. The designer may overlook the fact that this increases the dependence of the system on a specific database implementation and reduces ease of maintenance, for the sake of reducing the total number of modules in the system. However, we would argue that alternative design strategies like this are best taught and understood as deviations from the 3-Schema Architecture.

Comparable views

Many others have advanced the importance of separating the three schemas in both systems analysis and systems implementation. The Object Management Group's reference model (as yet unpublished) is based on a similar tripartite division. The equivalence of the OMG reference model to the 3-Schema Architecture is shown here:

Conceptual Model   =   Analysis
External Design   =   Design
Internal Design   =   Implementation

The pyramid below shows an adaptation for our purposes of the ISTEL Application Architecture, annotated with remarks made by John Alexander at a BCS conference (CASE, 1990). The policy is to build an application system out of the three communicating components shown below.

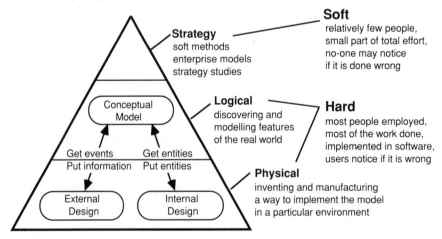

About the top of this pyramid Alexander says, 'no-one ever got called out in the night because a strategy study fell over'. With the increasing need to integrate applications, this may no longer be true. Corporate models are needed for controlling an incremental programme of systems development projects; see chapter 32 for further discussion.

Note two differences in terminology. James Martin might call the top level in the pyramid the 'conceptual' level, but we use the term 'conceptual' to refer to the middle level, that is, the essential data and functions of an information system which may be considered to model features of the real world. Alexander places the External Design within the physical level, but we shall describe both logical and physical design techniques for External Design.

Others who propose a division between the Conceptual Model and External Design include Rumbaugh *et al.* (1991), Jacobson (1992) and Courtney (1991) who opens his paper with three 'principal lessons' one of which being:

- 'the computational processing should be separated from the user interface'.

2.2 **Machine-independent specification**

Part four builds on the idea that an information system is, or rather contains, a 'real-world model'. This is not the only possible starting point. It is possible to start instead from the idea of building a machine-independent system specification and arrive at much the same conclusions. By 'machine-independent', we mean independent of both hardware and software implementation products.

Perhaps the major limiting factor on reuse to date has been that a product-specific component cannot be directly reused under the control of a different database or processing management system. Working system components are limited by the implementation environment in which they are implemented, and constrained to be reused only in the same environment.

One solution is to make everyone use the same implementation environment. This might work in the short term, but the pace of progress makes it futile in the long term. It seems unlikely that a plan could be made for upgrading all systems to each new generation of software environment (new programming language, database management system, windows interface, etc.) as they are installed.

The alternative solution is to step back from the physical implementation level to the logical level. Indeed, one of the most venerable and widely known system design principles is to postpone physical implementation decisions as long as possible. This is why most systems development methodologies are based on a machine-independent form of system specification. The idea is that machine-independent specifications will outlive their product-specific counterparts. Also, there should be greater scope for their reuse, because they are not constrained by any specific database or processing management system.

Machine-independent specification as an abstraction

A machine-independent specification is an abstraction, in two ways. It is general rather than specific, that is it does not predispose the designer towards any specific implementation tool. It suppresses detail, that is those details specific to a physical implementation product, and particularly those details to do with optimising systems performance such as database block sizes.

For machine-independent specification to be successful there must be some kind of agreement about:

- what it should cover
- how it should be documented
- how it should be used.

If this agreement is not reasonably universal or enduring, then the machine-independent specification gives little advantage over a product-specific specification. Chopping and changing specification languages can be as bad as chopping and changing implementation languages.

What machine-independent specification should cover

Given the three separate areas of concern, which of these should be the concern of a machine-independent specification? It is obvious that the prime concern of a machine-independent specification must be the Conceptual Model, capturing the essential business rules and knowledge which might be transferred between system implementations.

It is less clear how far the External Design should be a concern of a machine-independent specification. And clearly, the elements of the Internal Design should not appear in a machine-independent specification. These elements are concerned with the performance of the system using a specific database management system, so they cannot be reusable elsewhere. This level of detail should be suppressed from a machine-independent specification.

How machine-independent specification should be documented

It must be advisable to use languages for machine-independent specification about which there has already been reasonably universal and enduring agreement. Do not worry too much about the syntax of the diagrams which follow; what matters is the semantics, which is expressible in many different notations.

Languages for specifying the Conceptual Model

There is widespread agreement about how to specify the stored data of the Conceptual Model in a machine-independent way. An entity data model is documented as an entity relationship model supported by the data items for each entity (conventionally in the form of a third normal form relation for each entity).

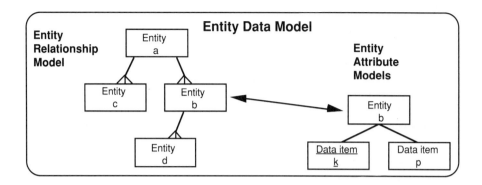

Entity data modelling is further described in part four. Several different notations are in common use, but most of the differences between them are cosmetic or syntactic; the semantics are widely agreed and understood.

There is less than universal agreement about how to specify the processes of the Conceptual Model in a machine-independent way. We see data flow diagrams, action diagrams, Jackson structures, fence diagrams, state transition diagrams and Petri nets used in a variety of contexts. This confusion arises partly because the concerns of the Conceptual Model have not been clearly separated from the concerns of the External Design.

Of many methodologies proposed, the strongest in the area of modelling the processes of the Conceptual Model is SSADM4. It offers relatively advanced entity event modelling notations which will be used in the methodology described in part four.

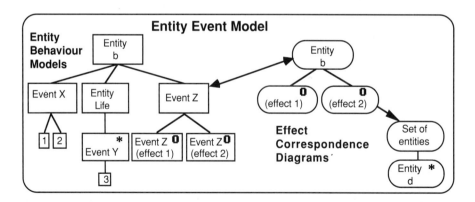

The entity event model is made up of entity behaviour models (known in SSADM as entity life histories) and effect correspondence diagrams. The relevant modelling notations have long been tried and tested. They are based on Jackson's notation for describing regular expressions, see Jackson (1975). Most of them have been employed in entity event modelling for a decade or more, see Robinson (1977).

An **entity behaviour model** shows all the effects of events upon one entity (or object), the valid state transitions between event effects, and for each effect the 'operations' acting upon properties (attributes and relationships) of the object. In an OO environment this is the encapsulated specification of the processing attached to one object, though we shall see in part four that some 'methods' only shown only indirectly in an entity behaviour model.

An **effect correspondence diagram** is a model showing all the effects of one event, on several entities or objects, co-ordinating these effects via 'correspondence arrows'.

As we shall show, there are various ways to implement the processing specified in an effect correspondence diagram. In an OO environment the correspondence arrows on the effect correspondence diagram might be implemented as messages passing between objects. In a conventional programming environment, an **event procedure** may be mechanically generated from an effect correspondence diagram. There is an analogous technique for defining an **enquiry procedure**. Many event and enquiry 'procedures' can be implemented in a non-procedural language such as SQL.

To summarise, the Conceptual Model is an **entity model** composed of several parts and carried forward to implementation as shown in the diagram below.

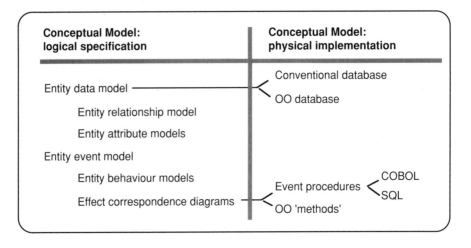

Some people are surprised at the inclusion of event procedures under the heading of the Conceptual Model, because they imagine that the division between Conceptual Model and Internal Design is the same as the old division between logical and physical in SSADM. Even when the event and enquiry procedures are coded in a specific language (say SQL or COBOL) they are still part of the Conceptual Model. Likewise, when dialogues are implemented as screens or windows, they are still part of the External Design.

Maintaining a continuous three-way separation of concerns from analysis and design through to implemented code is one of the advantages of the methodol ·y.

Languages for specifying the External Design

Part five shows how to specify the data flows of the External Design in a machine-independent way. There is a formal theorem (Kleene, 1956) which assures us that any data recognisable by a program can be specified as a 'regular expression'. So you can always document the data items in a data flow, using a diagrammatic form of regular expression, such as a Jackson structure.

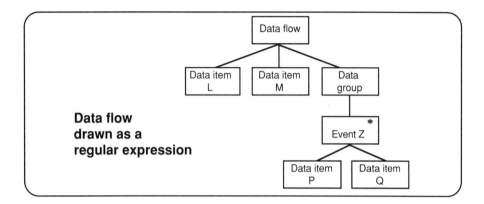

However, such structures need not be used everywhere. Where I/O design is simple, the specification of dialogues, screens and windows may be made directly using the tools of a specific product (see part five).

Part five also shows how to specify the processes of the External Design in a machine-independent way, using products such as Data Flow Diagrams and Specific Function Models to illustrate the aggregation of system processes to support 'user functions'.

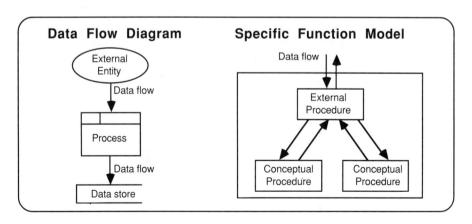

Languages for specifying the Internal Design

The Internal Design is specified in the form of a physical database design and internal database procedures, that is, routines which enable the processes of the Conceptual Model to act as though they read and write entities in the entity data model.

The concerns of the Internal Design are partly machine-specific, but there is room for generalisation. We have presented courses on the universal principles of database design which link all popular database management systems, and something along the same lines appears in a reduced form in stage 6 of SSADM version 4. There is no space here to include all our material on this. What we have to say about Internal Design in this book is mainly restricted to chapters 12 and 18.

How machine-independent specification should be used

Machine-independent specification is used in two ways, in forward engineering and in reverse engineering. Forward engineering should not and need not be an aimless uncontrolled activity. Several systems development methodologies have been developed to provide guidance and tools for forward engineering of an information system. This book adds some new forward engineering techniques to existing methodologies.

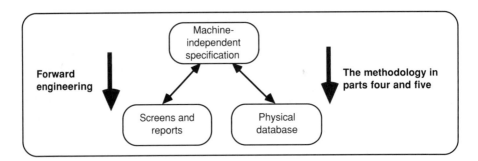

Most of this book is about forward engineering. However, reverse engineering, abstracting a machine-independent specification from an existing system, is discussed in chapter 32.

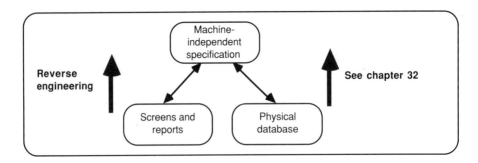

2.3 A methodology of analysis and design techniques

First of all, if a methodology uses several specification languages, they must relate to each other. It should be possible to build a metamodel, or at least an illustration like the one below, showing how the objects in the different languages are related.

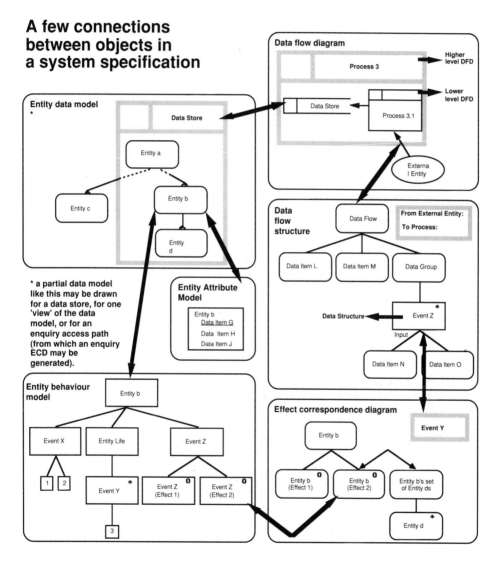

At this level of overview, the methodology's notations are like those of SSADM4, but at lower levels some differences will be revealed.

A methodology for forward engineering must offer more than specification languages and diagrammatic notations, it must help the analyst to discover and organise the objects which are to be modelled. It must offer analysis and design *techniques*. The following diagram shows an overview of how our methodology connects various systems analysis and design techniques, within a framework defined by the 3-Schema Architecture.

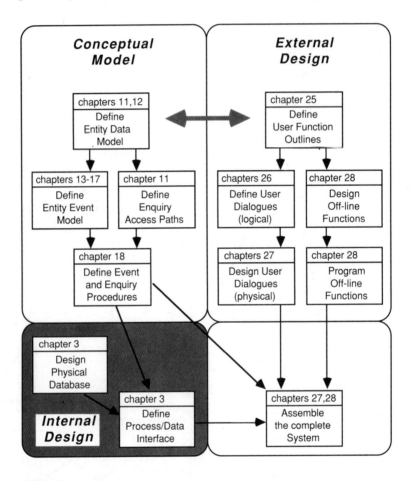

The broad arrow here stands for the many interactions between the Conceptual Model and the External Design which cannot easily be represented in such a diagram. As presented above, the methodology has a lot in common with SSADM4, but is less constrained, by historical precedent or by a project management control structure. We describe no formal stages and steps in this chapter beyond those implied by the sequential arrangement of techniques in the above diagram.

Readers who need a more formal management structure for the methodology in this book may superimpose the SSADM4 'structural model' on it, as we shall demonstrate in the next chapter.

2.4 **How the methodology meets system design objectives**

In building any methodology, you should keep the objectives in mind. The list below is not a summary drawn from a comprehensive survey of work done in the field of defining objectives for systems design, but simply an expression of the aims we have felt to be most important. We are looking for:

- Minimal development effort
- Minimal amendment effort
- Portability between platforms
- Rapid response to users
- Understandable design objects
- Reusable design components
- Incremental path from design to implementation
- Complete knowledge acquisition
- Zero-defect implementation
- A learnable design process.

Minimal development effort

To develop systems with the minimum development effort, you should use design techniques which are appropriate and relevant and which minimise the number and size of data and process objects to be defined, by avoiding duplication.

How the 3-Schema Architecture helps

In the External Design you can make use of RAD and prototyping techniques. In the Internal Design you can make use of prototyping for the improvement of a first-cut database design into an optimised design. Most of the 'structured' development effort must be directed into building the Conceptual Model, where entity data and entity event modelling provide a direct way of specifying the system.

The addition of super-events to entity event modelling enables a kind of 'normalisation' of processes, so no redundant code need be specified or implemented. If applied from the start, it takes less effort, though attempting to apply it after implementation requires a horrendous amount of effort.

Minimal amendment effort

There are two ways in which designers need help to change the system in response to a new or revised user requirement. First, they need help to locate the relevant components of the system; each business rule, each user requirement, should be handled by a distinct component of the implemented system, so that where to effect a change is readily understood. Second, they need help to predict side-effects caused by changes; it should be clear what the effect of change will be, so that no undesirable side-effects are accidentally triggered by a change.

How the 3-Schema Architecture helps

The 3-Schema Architecture helps the designer first to locate where an amendment must be made, and then to localise the scope of its effects. It explains which changes are difficult and which can be effected swiftly.

Maintenance and amendment requests tend to come from three directions. First, users want mistakes corrected. Errors may be divided into errors in the business rules (Conceptual Model) and mistakes in the way the user interface works (External Design).

Second, users want changes in functionality, perhaps as a result of a legislative change. These will mean first changing the Conceptual Model and only then making the consequent changes to the External Design.

Third, users want faster system performance. This will almost certainly be met by amendments to the Internal Design alone. Individual corrections and changes in functionality normally have no effect on the Internal Design, because they rarely raise significant performance problems. However, performance may need attention after several corrections and changes have been made.

The External Design and Internal Designs can be adapted via prototyping. The Conceptual Model can be adapted by restructuring the entity data model and entity event model. How easy or difficult this is in practice depends on how readily the Conceptual Model can be separated from the other schemas in the given implementation environment.

In general, separation of concerns helps the designer to predict the side-effects of any amendment. In particular, entity behaviour modelling can be used to predict what impossible states the database may get into as a result of changing the Conceptual Model.

Portability between platforms

Portability means we can build systems which can survive longer than the platforms on which they are based. Design techniques should help the designer to transport a system or its essence, from one implementation environment to another.

How the 3-Schema Architecture helps

The essential code (the Conceptual Model) should be portable between different user environments and different physical implementations.

The Conceptual Model can be implemented within a variety of External Designs, that is, event and enquiry procedures can be invoked from many different user functions. Only the External Design will be dependent on the user interface management system. So only the External Design will need tailoring for a new user interface management system.

The Conceptual Model can be connected to a variety of Internal Designs, that is, physical read/write routines can be written for any database management system or any optimised version of the entity data model. Only the Internal Design will be dependent on the database management system. So only the Internal Design will need tailoring if we decide to optimise resource usage via a new database management system.

Rapid response to users

A rapid response to a user request is not always possible, some requirements are difficult to meet, but design techniques should help us meet a stated requirement with the amount of effort which is natural to it. The effort should roughly correspond to the user's perception of how difficult the problem is.

How the 3-Schema Architecture helps

The designer can identify which processing components are to be heuristically designed (suitable for fast-path development, or prototyping) and which need to be discovered by careful analysis of the business rules and requirements.

Reuse of existing data and process objects should help us to respond more rapidly to user requests. New systems can borrow from old ones. Clearly this depends on a substantial investment in the design of existing systems to facilitate reuse.

Understandable design objects

Design techniques must result in definitions of data and process objects which are understandable and amendable. This means defining them in a formal way, using diagrams rather than narrative text, since the latter is notoriously ambiguous.

How the 3-Schema Architecture helps

In the External Design, to begin with the analyst may represent processes using data flow diagrams, but this is not carried through to process design. Instead the designer uses the technique of user function definition to parcel up the processing into programmable units. The data flows between processes in a user function are clearly represented, using well established program design notations.

In the Conceptual Model, entity event modelling provides two views of database processing; these are the entity behaviour model view and the effect correspondence diagram view. Entity behaviour modelling helps the understandability by 'encapsulating' data and process definitions together. The event or effect correspondence diagram view is necessary because entities will be stored as records under a database management system, and database processes will be based on events rather than entities. Database event and enquiry procedures are developed directly from the effect correspondence diagrams, using well-established program design notations.

In the Internal Design, the internal database procedures can also be represented using the same structured notations.

Reusable design components

Design techniques should enable proven system components to be reused in developing a new system, or amending an old one.

How the 3-Schema Architecture helps

Despite some of the claims, methodologies like Information Engineering and SSADM do not offer much help to the analyst in detecting reusable components, or specifying them.

Reuse is, however, very much the concern of the object-oriented school. Perhaps the best-known object-oriented ideas are encapsulation and inheritance. At the end of part three we show how these ideas apply at different points within the methodology.

In the External Design, at both low and high levels of abstraction, there are many opportunities for reuse. These are fully described in part five.

In the Conceptual Model, event and enquiry procedures can be embedded in many different functions of the External Design. At a lower level, design techniques for discovering and designing reusable components in the Conceptual Model are very much the concern of part four, where we shall show how to discover and record reusable objects (or super-entities) and more importantly, reusable methods (or super-events).

In the Internal Design, if the designer follows the simplest (unoptimised) strategy for writing internal database processes, that is one to read each entity and one to write each entity, then these modules will be reusable across all the event and enquiry procedures. However, system performance targets may require the internal database procedures to be designed in a less reusable way.

Incremental path from design to implementation

Design techniques should provide a step-by-step route from analysis through design to implementation with no missing pieces, requiring no large intuitive leaps. As many steps as possible should be mechanical and able to be automated.

How the 3-Schema Architecture helps

In the External Design, the methodology provides data flow analysis and user function definition as techniques for system decomposition. This is a user-oriented approach to identifying the functions or programmable units, within a system. A function can be viewed as a group of logical processes which are to be executed together. To each function the programmer can apply well-known design principles to define it as a series of simple communicating programs.

In the Conceptual Model, the methodology enables an entity-by-entity description of processing to be built up in a step-by-step fashion, then transformed into an event-by-event set of database update programs. In the simplest implementation, a component of the Conceptual Model (say, an event procedure) can be embedded directly in a component of the External Design (say, a dialogue procedure). Super-events shorten the incremental path.

You could choose to play down or ignore the Internal Design; in other words, choose to implement the entity data model directly in the form of a physical database structure. Where it is possible and desirable to map logical objects one-to-one onto physical objects, then each event and enquiry procedure in the Conceptual Model can be implemented directly, bypassing the need for any Internal Design (any internal database procedures).

Otherwise, for the Internal Design, the methodology assumes the definition of a process/data interface (or internal database procedures) for mapping the Conceptual Model onto the Internal Design.

Complete knowledge acquisition

Design techniques should provide some assurance that all the relevant knowledge or business rules have been analysed and defined.

How the 3-Schema Architecture helps

The External Design is a part of the system which must be designed rather than discovered. It is not so much a matter of knowledge acquisition as a matter of negotiation with the user, balancing different objectives

In the Conceptual Model the methodology provides a repository for business knowledge, separate from the External Design and Internal Design. It also provides, through various entity modelling techniques, prescriptive step-by-step techniques for knowledge acquisition. Inadequate analysis of user requirements is all too common. Entity behaviour modelling is the only technique we know which provides an incremental approach to discovering the Conceptual Model processing. Without it, much of this knowledge acquisition is left to chance. A measure of this is that, in our experience, entity behaviour modelling always triggers many corrections and revisions to the entity data model.

The Internal Design is a part of the system which must be designed rather than discovered. It is not so much a matter of knowledge acquisition as a matter of balancing different performance objectives and measuring the performance of a variety of different designs.

Zero-defect implementation

The more thorough the analysis and design techniques, the more likely they will lead towards a perfect implementation, 100% correct in the sense that it works first time and does what the user wants.

How the 3-Schema Architecture helps

The methodology helps to ensure correctness of process design by:

- separation of concerns into Conceptual, External and Internal Designs
- cross-validation of these different views of a system
- automated or JSP style implementation of procedures.

In the Conceptual Model, the methodology provides prescriptive step-by-step techniques for knowledge acquisition, helping to ensure all user requirements are analysed and documented. When it comes to program design, some procedures can be generated automatically in SQL, but for others an approach based on JSP is used. JSP is probably the most successful of program design techniques in generating programs which work first time, though it does not help us to know whether the program is doing what the user wants.

A learnable design process

Design techniques must be understandable, based on objective criteria rather than subjective judgement. Detailed rules and guidelines should be available on when and how to use the techniques.

How the 3-Schema Architecture helps

The methodology distinguishes processes which can be discovered objectively, from processes which require invention and design.

The Conceptual Model is the part of the system which is objectively constrained and so must be discovered. The methodology provides learnable techniques for discovery of the requirements. But note that the entity event modelling technique is a new way of doing things, a new paradigm, which requires training.

The Internal and External Designs are more subjective and so must be designed.

2.5 Stereotype components

In the course of developing several information systems, it is possible to identify standard design components which can be reused over and over again. These stereotype components are universal models (like the 3-Schema Architecture) but they are concerned with a smaller area of functionality and a lower level of detail. In fact they may be already specified at the lowest possible level of detail, requiring amendment rather than more detailed specification.

Stereotype components in physical design

What application generators and 4GLs do best is provide stereotype components for the system builder. Popular stereotypes offered by application generators and their limitations are discussed in chapter 21.

Stereotype components in logical design

There are also logical components which can be copied and tailored to meet specific requirements, especially within the Conceptual Model and External Design.

Part four, on Conceptual Modelling, shows we have made progress in identifying stereotype models for describing common business rules used in the updating of a database. Some of these stereotypes reflect the rules commonly applied in application generators such as 'cascade' or 'restrict', but by attaching these rules to process objects (events) rather than data objects (entities) we are able to produce a richer and more flexible system specification. It is also possible to develop stereotype entity data models for handling common kinds of information requirement.

Part five, on External Design, shows it is possible to develop stereotypes for dialogue design, both for the design of interface components (windows, lists, etc.) and standard code routines for controlling the interface to the Conceptual Model.

Chapter 3

Using the SSADM4 structural model

In this book we present ideas and techniques which are relatively independent of any specific IT methodology. This chapter is different in that it concentrates specifically on SSADM4, on how its structural model can be used as a management structure imposed over the techniques. It offers insights into when and how the SSADM4 structural model may be tailored, based on knowledge of the compromises which lay behind its development.

3.1 Decisions to be taken within an IT methodology

Information system development decisions must be taken in the context of the contribution which the system will make to the solution of business requirements. In the light of this, we can identify six major types of decision within the scope of a system's development. Each type of decision provides a context for the next.

Agree scope
Developers must agree with users the scope of development, perhaps as a result of a feasibility study or by identifying a project in the context of a wider strategy.

Agree business problem situation
Developers must agree with users the operation of current system, problems in the operation of current system, functional and non-functional requirements for new system.

Select solution to business problem situation
Developers must choose with users an information system solution to some or all problems and requirements at a price acceptable to the users.

Agree detailed requirements specification
Developers must agree with users in detail the information to be managed by the new system, the business activities to be represented in the system and the information management and access facilities to be made available to end-users and other systems.

Select implementation environment for requirements specification
Developers must choose, with users' agreement, the hardware and software platform for running the new system.

Agree computer system design
Developers must agree with users a computer system design which implements the requirements specification on the chosen platform.

   Methodologies can be compared by assessing which of these decisions are included within their decision structure. For the purposes of project management, these decisions may be applied within a 'waterfall model' or 'spiral model' as we shall see.

3.2 The SSADM4 structural model

The SSADM4 structural model may be divided between stages to do with analysis and design (1, 3, 5 and 6) and stages to do with making decisions (2 and 4). Here are the first five stages and steps, reflecting this division.

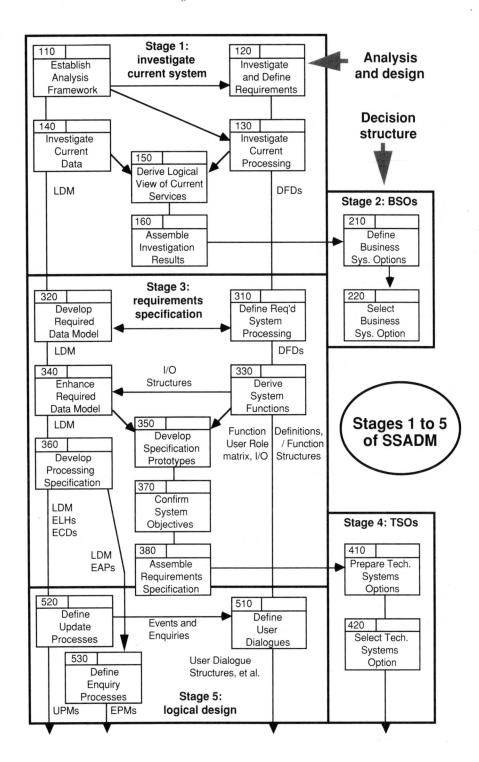

3.3 **Understanding and tailoring the structural model**

Does SSADM need changing to accommodate OO ideas?

SSADM is probably the most object-oriented of all the information systems development methodologies designed in the 1980s. A flexible view of the SSADM structural model is encouraged in the 'Accelerated SSADM guide' (yet to be published), but it turns out the default structural model does not require any alteration to accommodate object-oriented ideas. It is interesting to note that at least one other internationally-used methodology has had to be changed towards the SSADM model.

However, we shall see in parts four and five that some tinkering with individual analysis and design techniques is necessary. And this chapter discusses a number of practical reasons to bend the structural model. This may seem surprisingly negative for a book on SSADM, so let us make it clear that we regard SSADM as the best-engineered methodology around. Its current structural model has been remarkably successful in wide variety of different circumstances. The fact that it requires very little adaptation is a tribute to its designers.

What this chapter does

This chapter does not offer a tailored version of the structural model; it provides an understanding on which tailoring can be based. To begin with, the structural model is not a model in the sense of 'entity data model'; it is a model in the sense of 'role model' or 'example'; it is an invention purposely constructed to:

- arrange analysis and design techniques in a rational sequence
- enable management decisions to be taken when they are needed
- minimise the need for iteration and revision
- produce an outline system specification as early as possible
- keep the system specification machine-independent as late as possible.

The structural model makes a delicate balance between the needs of different people, between managers, outside suppliers, analysts and designers. To any one of these the balance may seem arbitrary, but it is not, it is a compromise which cannot suit everyone or every project. We have gathered from members of the SSADM4 development team, some observations on how these compromises were arrived at, and suggestions about how to resolve practical difficulties.

Structural model as waterfall model or spiral model

In practice, almost every task may reveal something new and thereby trigger revision of earlier products and earlier decisions. But it is impossible to manage a structural model which says earlier decisions (the choice of a business option or technical option) must be revisited after each step. It is impossible to draw a picture of a structural model which says all products (e.g. the requirements catalogue) are amended at every step.

Two models have been proposed to help the manager control iteration. Boehm proposed the **spiral model** which looks something like this:

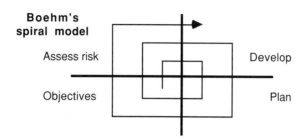

The spiral model is too generic to be very helpful. You must know in advance what the end product is supposed to be each time around the spiral. Royce proposed the **waterfall model** as means of limiting the possibilities for iteration. Strictly SSADM does not follow the 'waterfall model', but this is near enough true to justify saying so here. The structural model includes four passes through systems specification, adding more detail at each pass:

Stage 2: business system options
Stage 3: requirements specification
Stage 5: detailed logical design
Stage 6: implementable physical design.

There are two views of how the spiral model might be supplemented or combined with a waterfall model.

Waterfall model as spiral model
First, we can wind up a waterfall model into the form of a spiral model. The four passes through systems specification can be represented using the spiral model.

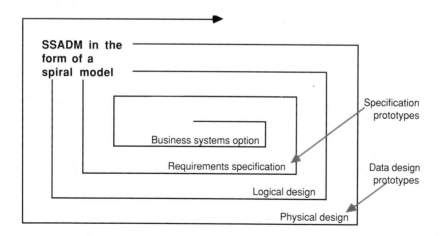

It's hard to imagine a method which tried to handle iterations which involve redoing more than one stage, or represented the multitude of smaller iterations within each stage. The SSADM4 structural model emphasises the four iterations shown above.

Evolutionary development model as spiral model

Second, we can place the whole of a waterfall model such as that of SSADM within the quadrant of the spiral model called 'Develop'. In this way the spiral model represents 'evolutionary development' whereby each version of a system replaces the last.

Three chronological divisions

SSADM is divided into six apparently consecutive stages. There are three major divisions:

> current system / required system
> logical design / physical design
> requirements specification / detailed design.

Between stages 1 and 2 there is a division between current system and required system specification. Between stages 5 and 6 there is a division between logical (or machine-independent) and physical specification.

Between stages 3 and 5 there is a division between requirements specification, to be signed off by users and published for procurement of further system development, and detailed design (the name 'logical design' is not entirely correct). This division is more artificial than the others. The role of stage 5 is reconsidered later in this section.

Stage 1: Investigate the current system

The SSADM4 development team made a conscious decision to limit the amount of time spent investigating the current system in stage 1. In earlier versions of the methodology people often spent too much time and effort at this stage, before preparing business systems options and choosing one.

In practice: if you want to extend the products produced from stage 1 techniques (say extend the User Catalogue to include more formal user descriptions, or extend the Requirements Catalogue with performance measures and usability requirements), then do these things at stage 3. If you extend the products at stage 1 you will have to apply these techniques to the current system, or for each business systems option, neither of which is sensible.

Stage 2: Business systems options

The preparation of and choice between business systems options is done at the last possible point in the methodology, just before detailed requirements specification. One reason for this is to discourage decisions from being made before a proper investigation of the current situation. Another reason is to minimise the risk of the chosen option becoming dated.

In order to make a fully informed choice between business system options, it would be necessary to complete the analysis and design of each of them. Obviously, the compromise must be to do only a percentage of the analysis work for each option. The size of this percentage, the amount of effort to be expended, will depend on cost and risk factors; it may be greater or smaller than SSADM4 implies.

In practice: of course, if there is only one business systems option, then this stage is partly redundant. If you can make a choice earlier than stage 2, because it is easy to do so and there is no significant risk of the choice being mistaken, then you should do so. However after stage 1 it will usually still be necessary to cost the chosen option and seek authority to proceed with system specification.

Stage 3: Requirements specification

Stage 3 is designed to produce a requirement specification. Since an IT department may tender for physical systems design and implementation from many different suppliers, using different hardware and software, the SSADM4 development team considered it important to make the requirements specification as machine-independent as possible.

In practice: almost all of the practical problems in stage 3 are to do with the desire or need for a machine-independent specification of the user interface. This is where SSADM4 must often be tailored. Three more specific points can be made.

The need for machine-independent dialogue design techniques

The SSADM4 development team knew (in 1988) that many SSADM users would build systems with old-fashioned, difficult-to-use, user interface technology. These users need a paper and pencil way of planning their user interface.

But more than this, they considered it unreasonable to omit logical dialogue design altogether. It *is* reasonable to do something before switching on the prototyping tool, to plan on paper what dialogues will be included in the scope of the design, what windows will appear in each dialogue, and what the navigation path through each dialogue will be. If a machine-independent procurement specification is required, then it *is* necessary to have notations for specifying each of the user dialogues. Prototype screens are not the whole answer to this need.

User procedure design is not fully within the scope of SSADM4. However, practitioners may use DFDs for user task modelling (see chapter 25) and I/O structures to specify the data items which are included in the I/O data flows of a user dialogue (see chapter 26). We have seen several alternative notations proposed in these areas, but none seem to be an improvement (more understandable, more formal, more generic).

The need for earlier dialogue design

Although the dialogue design technique does not appear until stage 5, the SSADM4 development team expected people to anticipate tasks from later modules. They assumed that if good user interface design tools are available, then they would be used directly to support the techniques of Function Definition and Specification Prototyping in stage 3. Any useful results can be included in the prototyping log or the requirements catalogue.

The need for user involvement and agreement
Crudely, the sequence in the SSADM4 structural model is:

	Conceptual Model	External Design
Stage 3 machine-independent	logical data model	logical I/O structures
Stage 4 choose machine	choose DBMS	choose TPMS or UIMS
Stage 5 machine-independent	logical data routines	logical dialogues
Stage 6 machine-dependent	physical database	physical user interface

Everyone (users included) can understand a data model better than a database design, so it is reasonable to ask users to sign-off a Conceptual Model specification which stops before physical design. But few people (certainly not users) understand logical I/O structures better than screen or window designs, so it is unreasonable to ask users to sign-off an External Design specification which stops before physical design.

In practice: given these three points, there is a strong case for moving dialogue design back from stage 5 to stage 3. User procedure design should proceed in parallel with stage 3 and inform the definition of user functions and dialogues. And of course users should be discussing and agreeing the user interface design at this stage. So it is clear that work should start on designing, or at least prototyping, a physical user interface at this stage.

The purpose of Specification Prototyping
The SSADM4 development team considered whether dialogue design might be included within the Specification Prototyping step of stage 3, but in the end decided it was better to keep the systematic dialogue design techniques apart from prototyping. Specification Prototyping was intentionally restricted to one purpose, that is validation of the requirements specification.

Stage 4: Technical systems options
Given that architectural principles should be in place before an SSADM project begins, the preparation of technical systems options is done, and choice between technical systems options is made, at the latest possible point in the methodology, just before detailed physical design. One reason for this is to minimise the risk of choosing out-of-date technology. Another reason is to encourage a machine-independent design to be carried as far as possible.

But of course the notion that people do not have to examine technical systems options or choose an implementation environment before stage 4 runs counter to the need to do some physical user interface design, or at least prototyping, during stage 3. It also makes it harder to make decisions at the business systems option level to do with distribution of data and processing.

In practice: of course, if there is only one choice of hardware and software, then this stage is largely redundant. If you can make a choice earlier, because it is obvious or there is no significant risk of the choice being mistaken, then you should do so. Often you may choose an implementation environment within or after stage 2. At the very least you ought to choose tools for prototyping. You might choose one tool for prototyping the user interface, another for prototyping the database design, and yet other tools for the final implementation. However after stage 3, it will usually still be necessary to estimate sizing, timing and costs. This must be done to ensure that the chosen 'machine' has sufficient capacity and can be afforded.

Stage 5: Logical systems design

There are three design steps in stage 5, all of which could be placed elsewhere. Step 510 is about logical dialogue design; this a requirements specification step and it really belongs in stage 3. Steps 520 and 530 are about transforming effect correspondence diagrams and enquiry access paths into pseudo-code; since this transformation is oriented towards procedural languages, it is more physical than logical and it may be placed in stage 6 (and if so, then effect correspondence diagrams should be supplemented with operations in stage 3).

The SSADM4 development team considered getting rid of stage 5 altogether, moving its techniques into other stages, but they had two very good reasons to keep stage 5. First, they promised Government departments 'stability and protection of investment', that is to say SSADM4 would be backwards-compatible with SSADM3. Second, they wanted to ensure that a requirements specification for competitive tender did not imply any specific target implementation environment.

The first reason is becoming out of date. The second reason is not relevant to most users and has often proved unhelpful, since the result is that procurement specifications produced out of stage 3 tend to be too light in the area of the user interface specification. It is now possible to move SSADM4 forward in this area.

In practice: we recommend renaming stage 5 as 'Physical Design of the Conceptual Model and External Design', moving something like the old step 510 (see chapter 26) into stage 3, and adding a new step 510 (see chapter 27) called 'Design the User Interface'. Part five of this book introduces new machine-independent window and dialogue design techniques which can be used at stages 3 and 5.

Stage 6: Physical design

This stage is to do with implementing the logical design in a specific implementation environment. It is divided into data and physical process specification techniques. The data design techniques are fine (behind them there was a great deal of detailed research into general principles of database management which was not published in the manuals), but the process specification techniques could be better organised.

In practice: for the Internal Design (physical database design and process/data interface), we say nothing in this book beyond what SSADM4 already says. But we recommend replacing the physical process specification steps in stage 6 by advice on how to assemble a full system, by invoking code for the Conceptual Model from within the External Design. This advice is to be found at the end of the techniques for External Design in part five.

3.4 **More general problems with the structural model**

More general problems with the structural model include the following.

Parallelism is not encouraged enough
In reality, there are fewer sequential constraints than is implied by the structural model. Many of the tasks may be carried out in parallel, one informing the other. We ought to reshape the structural model to represent more of the parallelism which is allowable.

Management decision points are inflexible
As discussed above, there are good reasons why stages 2 and 4 might be done earlier than is suggested in the SSADM4 manual (that is, the latest possible points).

Analysis and design is mixed up with project management
The structural model contains steps which are more or less formal analysis and design techniques, mixed up with steps which are to do with assembling documentation for management review.

The logical/physical divide is too naive
Many of the 'in practice' points above are related to the logical/physical divide. We need is a more sophisticated rationale, more capable of representing parallelism.

Solving these problems
It is interesting and helpful to divide SSADM into strands which may be organised in parallel, and perhaps carried out by different people.

Analysis versus management
The division between stages to do with analysis and design (1, 3, 5 and 6) and stages to do with making decisions (2 and 4) has been shown in a diagram earlier in this chapter. We need to further sub-divide the analysis and design techniques.

Data versus process
It used to be said that systems analysis and design in SSADM had three facets: data, process and time. You might try to divide SSADM between parallel strands of *data* and *process* specification, but this doesn't work, because most steps are about both data and process specification. DFDs and Functions specify the processing of input data flows against stored data, producing output data flows. The data model specifies the stored data, but it must be validated and supplemented by the specification of database processes (in enquiry access paths and effect correspondence diagrams).

   Process specification in SSADM is a source of confusion to many people. Some are not sure how far database processing should or can be specified using DFDs and Function Definitions. Some think that Dialogue Design is the prime activity. Some are not sure why they need effect correspondence diagrams and enquiry access paths at all. A clearer separation of concerns is needed.

Conceptual versus external

Using the 3-Schema Architecture, SSADM analysis and design clearly breaks into two streams. One is driven from the data model: enquiry access paths and EPMs, entity life histories, effect correspondence diagrams and UPM. The other is driven from the DFDs: function definitions, dialogue designs, specific function models.

It may be thought that this division is an accident, or a *post-hoc* rationalisation, but it is not. It was in the minds of the SSADM version 1 development team and in the minds of the SSADM version 4 development team, but it was not given a face or name until more recently.

We can call the data model strand Conceptual Modelling and the DFD strand External Design (Internal Design appears only within stage 6). And we can look at reshaping the structural model to match the 3-Schema Architecture more closely.

3.5 A more flexible structural model for SSADM4

The next page shows SSADM4 arranged in three columns, to do the following.

Encourage activities in parallel

Within one of the columns, the sequence of steps is important. We do not advise changing this sequence (though a follower of JSD might do step 360 before step 320 in the Conceptual Modelling column). However, imagine that each of the two shaded columns can slide up and down. This image encourages us to work on the Conceptual Model and External Design in parallel, using whichever progresses faster to inform the other, and whichever progresses slower to validate the other.

Make the management decision points more flexible

Imagine the decision structure column can slide upwards. This image encourages us to be more flexible about choosing business and technical systems options earlier, as indeed we may have to do in practice.

Clarify the interface from analysis and design to project management

The three columns separate the steps which include more or less formal analysis and design techniques from the steps which are to do with assembling documentation for management review. The two shaded columns separate the analysis and discovery of the Conceptual Model from the more intuitive and pragmatic design of the External Design.

Update the logical/physical divide

The logical/physical divide has been replaced by the 3-Schema Architecture. Some physical design is considered appropriate earlier in the methodology, especially physical user interface design, though we have preserved the old step number (510).

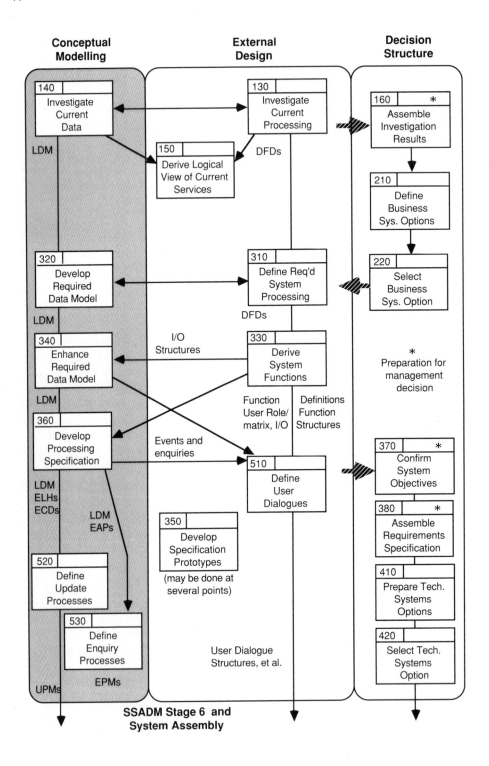

Conceptual Modelling

External Design

Decision Structure

| 140 |
| Investigate Current Data |

LDM

| 130 |
| Investigate Current Processing |

| 160 | * |
| Assemble Investigation Results |

| 150 |
| Derive Logical View of Current Services |

DFDs

| 210 |
| Define Business Sys. Options |

| 320 |
| Develop Required Data Model |

LDM

| 310 |
| Define Req'd System Processing |

DFDs

| 220 |
| Select Business Sys. Option |

| 340 |
| Enhance Required Data Model |

LDM

I/O Structures

| 330 |
| Derive System Functions |

*
Preparation for management decision

| 360 |
| Develop Processing Specification |

LDM
ELHs
ECDs

LDM
EAPs

Function User Role/ matrix, I/O

Definitions Function Structures

Events and enquiries

| 510 |
| Define User Dialogues |

| 370 | * |
| Confirm System Objectives |

| 380 | * |
| Assemble Requirements Specification |

| 350 |
| Develop Specification Prototypes |
(may be done at several points)

| 520 |
| Define Update Processes |

| 410 |
| Prepare Tech. Systems Options |

| 530 |
| Define Enquiry Processes |

| 420 |
| Select Tech. Systems Option |

UPMs

EPMs

User Dialogue Structures, et al.

SSADM Stage 6 and System Assembly

3.6 **Adding techniques to SSADM4**

The structural model needs further attention to deal with things missing from SSADM4, partly because of the passage of time since its scope was planned.

Off-line function design techniques

Apart from the Universal Function Model in stage 3 and Specific Function Models in stage 6, there is much to be said about off-line function definition which is missing from SSADM4. Some explanation is needed of how to design data collection, data distribution, input and output sub-systems. It turns out that this is a bigger issue than we can cover fully in this book, but chapter 28 outlines the techniques needed.

Rapid application development techniques

Many, perhaps most, people 'out there' are using application generators to bash out systems as quickly as possible based on an entity data model. These systems do satisfy limited kinds of business requirement. Some explanation of how rapid application development sits alongside the development of more complex systems is needed. This is given in chapters 20 and 21.

Prototyping techniques

SSADM4 already has a step for prototyping intended to test the requirements specification and discover new requirements, but it can be expanded, or rather divided into distinct steps carried out in parallel with those steps in the core of SSADM4 which it is intended to support. Various techniques to support prototyping are described in part five.

GUI design techniques

Finally, there is a need for advice on GUI design. In part five we modify the following SSADM4 techniques as is necessary to accommodate GUI design:

Step 350: Specification Prototyping   (chapters 21 to 23)
Step 510: Define User Dialogues   (chapters 24 to 27)
Step 650: Complete Function Specification   (chapters 24 to 28).

So here is a version of the structural model, with extra techniques for:

- testing requirements specification
- prototyping user dialogues
- rapid application development
- designing a GUI.

Adding supplementary techniques to SSADM

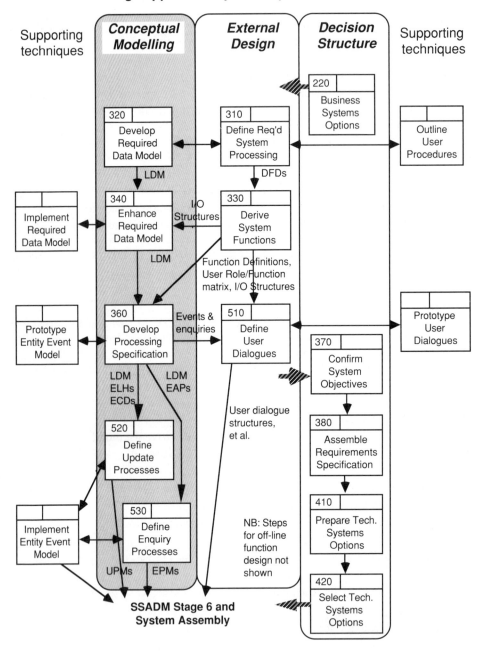

Supplementary, optional and parallel, steps

When it comes to tailoring SSADM4, the extra steps do not have to be included within the SSADM4 structural model. Instead they may be placed alongside as optional and parallel techniques.

User procedure design

Purposes: to lead to the specification of a User Procedure Manual (outside of SSADM4), to inform the systems development process. Inputs: the results of stages 1 and 2, user interviews and discussions. Technique: not within the scope of this book, but see chapter 25.

Implement entity data system

Purposes: to develop a 'data fixing system', to make the data model visible to users, to test the model against user expectations, to refine the definition of *attributes* for each entity. Other purposes are listed in chapter 21. Inputs: the data model. Technique: see chapter 21.

Prototype entity event system

Purposes: to make the entity event model visible to users, to test it against user expectations, to refine the definition of *events* for each entity. Inputs: the data model, event and enquiry triggers. Technique: see chapters 22 and 23.

Prototype user dialogues

Purposes: to make the on-line functions visible to users, to test them against user expectations, to design a user-friendly display of the data retrieved from the database in response to events and enquiries, to experiment with navigation paths through events and enquiries. Inputs: Function Definitions, I/O Structures and perhaps an event-driven interface design. Technique: informal, but the techniques in chapters 23 and 27 may help.

Implement entity event system

Purposes: to generate a working system as swiftly as possible (but with a naive user interface), to provide reusable components for assembly into the full system. Inputs: the data model, event and enquiry triggers, event and enquiry responses, event and enquiry procedures. Technique: see chapters 22 and 23.

Implement physical dialogues

Purposes: to implement the full system, complete with user dialogues which support user tasks by invoking the events and enquiries in a user-friendly defined sequence. Inputs: all the products of the above steps, plus event and enquiry procedures. Technique: see chapters 26 and 27.

3.7 **Viewing our methodology in terms of SSADM4**

Though there are some differences in detail, the analysis and design and techniques in this book are closely related to those in SSADM4. A comparison can be drawn by placing SSADM4 step numbers on the diagram from chapter 2.

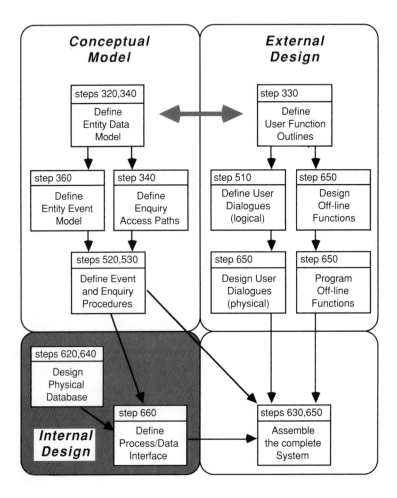

Note that a significant portion of our methodology can only be placed in step 650. SSADM4 gives little relatively attention to the things which need to be done in physical design, especially the design of the user interface, off-line functions and program modularisation. There are no SSADM4 equivalents to the rapid implementation techniques described in part five.

3.8 Adding JSP to the methodology

The methodology, by which we mean SSADM4 as modified in this book, is about completing a formal system model ready for programming, comprising data specifications (data flow structures and database structures supported by record and data item definitions) and process specifications (specific function models of connected procedures, supported by program structures with conditions and operations). JSP is a technique which carries forward the design of each programmable unit into procedural pseudocode.

Despite our frequent use of the word 'procedure' to describe a programmable unit of system processing, Our methodology does not commit designers to procedural language implementation. However, it uses JSP techniques to decompose off-line functions into procedures and to specify each procedure, so programmers may naturally go on to use JSP to design and implement each procedure in a procedural language. The methodology provides the most complete definition yet of how to move from a systems methodology into programming.

Advantages

For a systems development organisation, aligning the methodology with JSP and teaching people how to use JSP principles in program design may give these several advantages on top of the design objectives outlined earlier:

- For the first time, systems analysts and programmers will be given cohesive methods, so that they will share skills and communicate using the same specification and design language.

- Programmers trained in JSP will be well prepared for further training in the methodology.

- Programmers trained in JSP will be able to move more naturally up the career ladder from program coding, then to program design, then to program specification, then to using the process modelling techniques in the methodology.

- JSP principles can be used to explain the theory underlying some of the methodology techniques and extend them further into programming.

- JSP principles bring a greater discipline and formality to some of the methodology techniques (notably to the use of 'quits' and 'state variables' in entity behaviour modelling).

Methodologies have been slow to make effective use of JSP. Although Information Engineering provides equivalent process modelling notations, it doesn't provide any equivalent techniques.

3.9 **Adding the methodology to Information Engineering**

Information Engineering is more like a tool-box than a prescriptive methodology. It concentrates on end-products and is less concerned with techniques and methods by which the end-products are produced and validated. So it is possible to use the methodology in this book with Information Engineering tools, or to produce Information Engineering end-products. This table expresses some end-products in the language of Information Engineering.

The methodology end-product	IE end-product
Entity data model	Data model
Specific function model	Process flow diagram
Event or enquiry procedure	Action diagram

Information Engineering offers several diagrammatic notations for process modelling and specification, such as fence diagrams and state-transition diagrams. But it expects all these diagrams will be transformed into **action diagrams** within the final system specification.

All the process model diagrams used in our methodology can be transformed into action diagrams. At least one CASE tool will perform this translation automatically. This fact may prove important if a CASE tool like IEW or Excelerator is to be used for code generation.

James Martin has suggested that entity behaviour models can be represented using state-transition diagrams. While this is true, several reasons to prefer entity behaviour models to state-transition diagrams are given in chapter 13. Both can be transformed into action diagrams.

3.10 **Concluding remarks**

In summary, readers who need a formal management structure for the methodology in this book may superimpose their own decision structure upon it. In practice, we normally employ a variant of the SSADM4 structural model.

This chapter has described some reasonable ways to vary from the full or default structural model. We have been working on an 'Accelerated SSADM' guide for the UK Government which goes further than this. It describes more dramatic variants, especially for situations where the system to be developed may be regarded as in some way 'small' or 'simple'. Readers of this book may be surprised to find that one of the proposed variants is to omit entity event modelling altogether! However, this variant of SSADM has too little connection with object-oriented ideas to be of concern here.

Students of SSADM4 and Information Engineering, eager to learn new techniques, may find the next two parts the book to be an irritating diversion into philosophy. These readers may skip directly to parts four and five.

Part Two:

The Need for More Than Data Modelling

Chapter 4

Basic ideas about modelling the real world

For those coming to this book with little experience of modelling techniques, this chapter is an introduction to modelling the real world within information systems. The terms introduced in this essay, especially abstraction, identity, association, composition and generalisation, are taken for granted in later chapters.

4.1 Introduction

Most of us who work in computing see the world through the narrow window of the implementation mechanisms we are familiar with. Relational database designers may see the world as composed of data groups in 'third normal form'. Object-oriented programmers may see the world in terms of 'inheritance trees'. Programmers who use procedural programming languages may see the world in terms of sequential processes.

There are many implementation mechanisms which have been successful in some way, but none has been entirely successful on its own. It would be foolish to rely on just one of them as a source of inspiration. Each implementation environment has been manufactured to suit a sub-set of the various kinds of computer system which have to be built; each may fail when faced with a different sub-set.

The relational view may fail when faced with the problems of sending messages from one part of a distributed database to another. The object-oriented view may fail when faced with large volumes of persistent data. The procedural programming view may fail where parallel processing is needed, whether within the database or at the user interface.

The difficult but necessary thing is to step away from the implementation mechanisms to look at the world more directly. We need at least to look through a much wider window, one which will accommodate all the above points of view and integrate them into a more complete picture.

Ideas before notation

Methodologists (a title awarded to themselves by authors of books like this one) are sometimes blinded by a different kind of implementation mechanism, diagrammatic notations. Once we have become familiar with a notation, we find it difficult to envisage things which the notation doesn't already represent, or to accept other notations. If our notation permits an idea to be modelled, we don't question whether the idea should be modelled at all. If our notation allows one idea to be modelled in different ways, we may not perceive that there is a single underlying idea.

Many authors introduce their diagrammatic notation first, then fit their ideas to them. What we want to do in this chapter is introduce ideas; the notation is a secondary concern. The main ideas are to do with real-world modelling. But keep in mind that the models are very, very limited. They show only a tiny part of the real world, and a restricted view of that part.

The primacy of data in knowledge acquisition

Later we shall define 'objects' in terms of both data attributes and processing behaviour. In important ways these two perspectives of an object are both necessary and inseparable. However, for many purposes it is helpful to consider data and process perspectives separately. There are stages in systems analysis when one view is dominant, and most of the analysis techniques included in this book can be categorised as either data-oriented or process-oriented. Throughout this book the data perspective will be considered before the process perspective. We go as far as to make this a principle and call it 'the primacy of data'.

Input-output driven design

To a programmer, 'modelling the world' means modelling the input and output data of a program. Here 'the primacy of data' means that the design of program naturally starts from the data it consumes and produces.

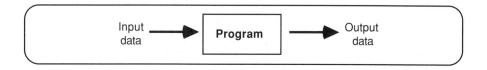

This idea, of starting from the input and output data, can be seen in many views of programming. A program specification usually begins with a definition of the input and output data structures which the program handles. In a COBOL program, the Data Division is written before and placed above the Procedure Division. Jackson founded a very effective program design method on the principle that the structure of a program should be built by first defining its input and output data structures (in the form of regular expressions), then combining these data structures into one processing structure. Declarative programming languages are based in the idea that processing rules can be attached to input and output data elements.

The idea of output-driven design may seem old-fashioned, but it should not be cast aside. The case for it was well argued by Ken Orr (1981), and his arguments still carry some weight. In chapter 3 we discuss the need to address SSADM's lack of emphasis on the user interface.

Having said this, it is true that most modern systems development methodologies have a different emphasis. No-one (except Mike Woodger, see chapter 8) would dream of starting a program design from the middle. But this is exactly the idea behind methodologies such as Information Engineering and SSADM.

Database-driven design

To a systems analyst, 'modelling the world' means modelling the core of a system. Here 'the primacy of data' means that the specification of a system starts with the data it maintains, called from now on the 'database'.

How come information system design is supposed to start from the middle? Why is the specification of the database considered to be more important than that of the input and output data? Perhaps we ought to answer a basic question first. What is a system?

The difference between program and an information system

In the broadest sense of the word, a 'system' is something around which a boundary can be drawn. Any system can be viewed in two ways. It can be viewed as a black box consuming inputs and producing outputs, without any thought as to its contents. Or it can be studied in terms of what is contained within its boundary. It is instructive and useful to think of information systems in both of these ways.

External view of an information system

From an external view, nothing can be seen of a system's workings. All that can be seen is data streaming into and out of the system. To its immediate users, what matters about a system is what it produces and what it consumes in order to do it, rather than what it contains. The purpose of an information system is no different in character from the purpose of a program; it is to produce the required output data from the available input data.

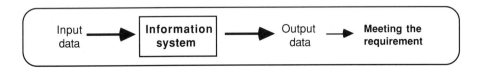

Given this external viewpoint, at first glance it seems hard to distinguish an information system from a program. But looking more closely at how well the input and output data streams correspond to each other, we find a way to distinguish information systems from programs. Generally:

- a program's outputs correspond strongly to its inputs
- an information system's outputs correspond only indirectly to its inputs.

A program is usually able to generate output data immediately from its input data, or at least without a significant delay. An information system usually has to resolve several structure and scheduling clashes between its input and its output data. To do this it has to store a considerable amount of data internally, in its database.

Internal view of an information system

The internal view of a program and of an information system may be compared in terms of three major components, as illustrated below.

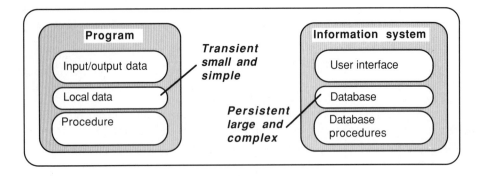

The marked differences between the local data of a program and the database of an information system provide a second scale on which to distinguish an information system from a program.

The local data of a program is usually small and simple in structure. It is also transient, that is, thrown away at the end of the program. The design of this local data is rarely a significant task; it usually happens as a by-product of program design. In contrast, the local data of an information system is organised in a potentially very complex data structure, and is stored with some degree of permanence in its database.

The primacy of the database in information systems design

One of the weaknesses of OO approaches to date has been that they tend to underestimate the analysis and design effort required to specify the storage and retrieval of persistent data in a multi-user environment.

In conventional information systems design, there are three main reasons why so much attention is given to designing the system's database, and why it is often considered to be the primary job of the systems analyst. The reasons are: efficiency, stability and amendability.

Despite the growth of machine power, efficiency remains an important consideration in systems design. The overall efficiency of a large information system depends first and foremost on efficient data storage and retrieval. This is the reason why systems development methodologies place a lot of emphasis on activities which minimise accesses to the system's database. For example, SSADM includes:

- relational data analysis, to minimise update accesses
- enquiry access path analysis, to minimise enquiry accesses
- first-cut physical database design rules, to optimise record clustering.

In an attempt to maximise stability and flexibility, systems development methodologies emphasise building the database around a *model of the real world*.

Stability is important, not only because restructuring and reorganisation of a database are very expensive activities in themselves, but because they imply a certain amount of reprogramming as well. The idea is that a database structure which models the real world should remain more stable than a database structure designed with performance or other machine-dependent considerations in mind.

Amendability is important because systems must evolve, perhaps over many years, to meet changing requirements. A database structure which models the real world should be more naturally amendable and flexible; it should be clear when the real world changes which is the corresponding part of the system to be altered.

The idea of real-world modelling is closely related to the idea of **abstraction**. As Dijkstra pointed out (Dahl, Dijkstra and Hoare, 1972), abstraction is such a fundamental idea, running through almost every aspect of computer science, that it is hard to draw a line around any discussion of it. But we can look at some specific meanings and uses of the word.

4.2 **Abstraction from the system towards the real world**

It is possible to abstract some kind of conceptual model from an implemented computer system. For example, you would normally expect to be able to abstract an entity data model from a specification of a working system, either from the database, or from input and output designs.

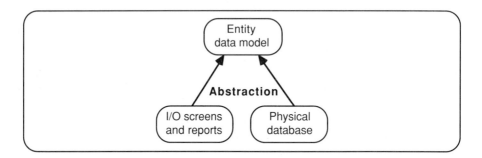

An entity data model is derivable from an analysis either of the input and output data or of the physical database and other file storage. This derivation may be done using the relational data analysis technique briefly mentioned in chapter 11.

Machine-independent specification as real-world model

Some readers may be unhappy with the notion that an entity data model is a model of the real world (the start of chapter 5 amplifies this point). But these same readers will probably go along with the notion that an entity data model is a 'machine-independent system specification', and we would hope to convince them that the two ideas are very much related. When you have removed machine-dependent elements from a specification, what remains must be to do with the real-world problem you are trying to solve, so a machine-independent specification may also be regarded as a model of the real world.

Entity data modelling is now the cornerstone of many methodologies and indeed the techniques in this book. An entity data model is clearly a machine-independent specification of a database. There is now little disagreement with the idea that an entity data model represents concepts which users of a system understand in the real world.

Beyond entity data modelling

Later chapters are very much concerned with entity *process* modelling techniques. These may be thought of as abstractions towards the real world from the specifications of input data and database update processes. We shall model the behaviour of an entity over time, as though it were a long-running program. However, for the purposes of this chapter, it is sufficient to draw on ideas to do with modelling the data-oriented view of objects.

4.3 **Abstraction from the real world towards the system**

Coming from the opposite direction, an information system may be viewed as a model of the real world. But it is a very, very limited model of the world, after it has been reduced through two filters as shown below.

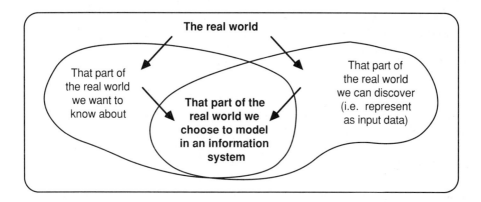

Systems engineers are not interested in modelling the real world *per se*. They model only the things the users care about and can represent as input data to the system. They are not interested in building a model for its artistic or scientific merit (for which painting, sculpture, or quantum mechanics may be preferred). They build a model to specify the achievable requirements of an information system. They are concerned with the meeting point between the two opposing directions of abstraction, shown below.

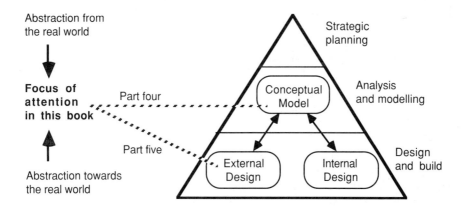

The pyramid, which was introduced in chapter 2, is deliberately drawn to resemble one used by James Martin in presenting Information Engineering and by John Alexander in presenting the ISTEL Application Architecture. It is time to focus more closely on the middle level, the notion of a Conceptual Model.

4.4 Object types and instances

Before we start to build a model of the real world around the objects of interest, there are two rules to be understood which are invisible in any object model diagram.

For each object type there may be many object instances.

The models show object types (in the case study, Employer, Vacancy, Applicant and Interview). They do not show object instances. It is assumed that for each object type shown in the model there may be any number of object instances (any number of Employers, Vacancies, Applicants and Interviews).

An object instance must have a unique identity.

Identity is a concept missing from the diagrams, but vital in understanding modelling. There are two reasons to identify each individual object instance: one is the need to distinguish one object from another, the other is the need to map instances within the system onto instances in the real world.

If you cannot distinguish between instances of an object type, you should not model it as an object class. In the case study there are many Posts for a Vacancy, but since one Post cannot be distinguished from another, this object type does not appear in the data model; it appears only indirectly as an attribute of Vacancy called Total Number of Posts.

If the instances of an object type cannot be mapped onto things in the real world, the system cannot tell us anything useful about that world.

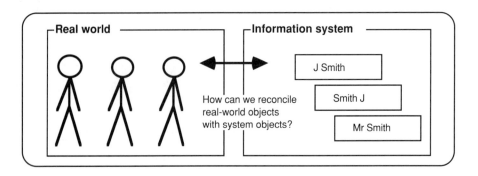

The two roles for an object's identity, to distinguish one object from another and to identify objects in the system with their counterparts in the real world, will be further discussed in chapter 11. The way that the identity of an object is determined and recognised in an information system is usually by means of a unique key. Keys are not of interest here; they will be discussed later.

After its identity, an object may have many other properties. Following the 'primacy of data' principle, having found some identifiable objects of interest, the next step is to define the data properties of these objects, and the constraints upon them.

4.5 Object aspects

For each object type in the model, the analyst will define its data aspects and the processing constraints upon these. An object's data aspects may be divided into attributes and relationships to other objects. However, attributes and relationships are not completely distinct from each other. In some ways, attributes and relationships may be regarded as equivalent or interchangeable.

Attributes of an object

Different authors have different opinions about the scope of relational theory. Does it include integrity constraints? Does it include relational query languages? But one thing they agree on is that it provides a description of how an object in 'third normal form' has an identity and a number of attributes (no more than one of each type) dependent on that identity. For example, see the diagram below.

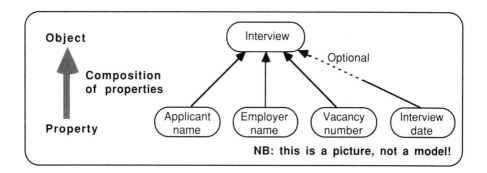

Note that the diagram is only a picture, not a model of relationships between objects. The attributes of an object are not independent objects, with identity of their own, and will not normally be shown as objects in an object model.

This is an oversimplification. There are reasons why attributes might become objects of interest in their right. Later chapters will discuss several ways in which this might happen: by division into parallel aspects of an aggregation, by inversion into a master object, by mutual exclusion into sub-type objects. One of the weaknesses of relational theory is that it does not account for parallelism or mutually exclusion of data properties; we shall attempt to build a broader theory.

Relationships between objects

The relationships in a data model always connect two object types. A relationship between two objects can never be perfectly symmetrical. In the French methodology MERISE, it is said that one of the objects 'dominates' the other (Rochfield, 1987). The rule in our methodology is that the dominant object type is called the 'master' of the relationship, the other is called the 'detail'. To decide which is which, see chapter 11.

4.6 **Object associations**

This and the following sections explore the ideas which underlay the concept of, and are the reasons for, a relationship between objects. An **association** is a relationship between two independently identifiable objects. In the loosest form of association, an object of type A may be associated with many of type B and *vice versa.* For example, one Doctor may see many Patients, one Patient may see many Doctors.

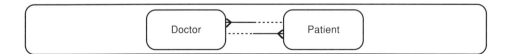

But this is not a very helpful idea. The trouble is that between any two independently occurring objects there is the possibility of such a many-to-many relationship. The job of the analyst is find out why two objects are related and to *constrain* the model of the real world so that it explains this relationship.

In building a model, we show only those associations which are constrained so that in one or both directions the number of objects is limited to one.

So the analyst must search for the reason why two independent objects are related and give an identity to this reason. In other words, the analyst must make sure that reasons are recorded as identifiable objects. This means refining a many-to-many relationship between two objects in the model, by identifying the independent object which links them via one-to-many relationships. For example, the object which links Doctor to Patient might be Appointment.

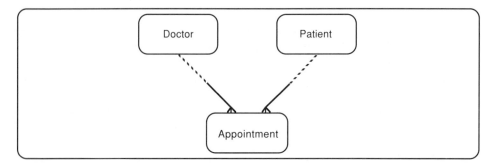

Some people think that an object in a model of this kind must be something you can touch. This is wrong. Many, even most, objects cannot be touched, except in so far as they might be represented (or modelled) as information on a piece of a paper. Objects which seem tangible at first often evaporate on closer examination. You cannot touch a Doctor, you can only touch the person who plays the role of Doctor, or the certificate which qualifies them for this role.

Some people make a distinction between kernel objects (say, Patient and Doctor) and associative objects (Appointment), but such a distinction has little meaning outside of the scope of a defined model. What appear to be associative objects in one model may be the kernel objects in a different model, and vice versa.

Often, to represent the partial view of the real world which is of interest to system users, the analyst must constrain the model to show only one side of a relationship between two independently identifiable objects. And since users understand the world in different ways, even a single, named object may appear in different forms in different models.

Every model is incomplete and biased

It would be foolish to imagine that it is possible to build a model of everything in the real world, of every perspective. Each system model is very much constrained by the perspective of the system's users, and by the view of the analysts and designers about what is important and what the system can do for the users.

In the Doctor's model below, the Appointment object represents the actual visit of a Patient to a Doctor. Let us say that Doctors do not register Symptoms which they cannot attribute to a Medical Condition (or cause of complaint), so a Symptom is only ever identified and recorded by the Doctor as the link between a Patient and a Medical Condition.

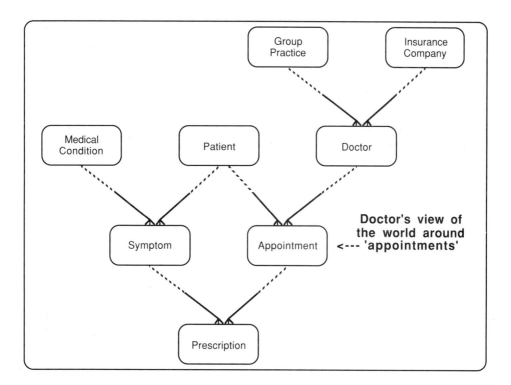

The receptionist's world view is significantly different, as shown below.

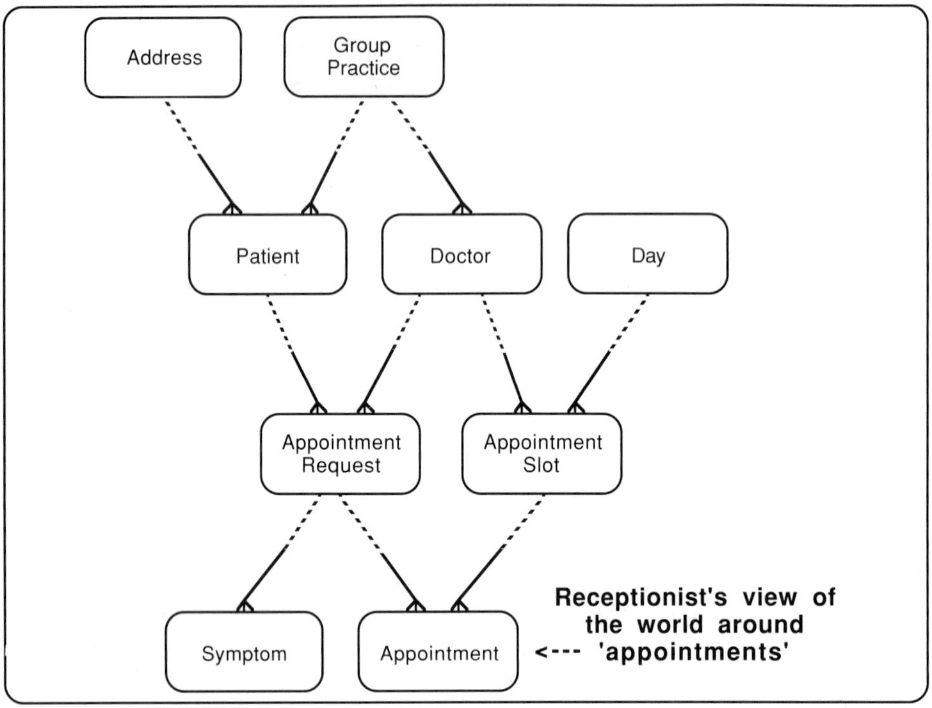

In the receptionist's model, an Appointment represents the matching of an Appointment Request (which the receptionist takes a note of) to an Appointment Slot (an entry in the appointment book). An Appointment Request may be swapped between Appointment Slots. A Symptom now appears as an incidental detail, noted by the receptionist under Appointment Request.

So, any model is constrained by needs of the user. One important requirement to be investigated and expressed is how much historical information is needed. Although the doctor is entirely uninterested in the process by which an Appointment is made, the receptionist (let us say) wishes to keep track of all the Appointment Slots an Appointment Request has been assigned to since it was first made.

4.7 Two more kinds of abstraction

We have already discussed two kinds of abstraction, away from and towards the real world. The word 'abstraction' can be used as a label for other ideas in the world of information systems analysis and design. Abstraction is sometimes used to express with the shift of attention from a low level or detail object, to a higher level or master object.

We can distinguish ways to abstract upwards to a master object from detail objects, leading to two different kinds of model:

- Composition, giving rise to a higher-level or composite object
- Generalisation, giving rise to a class hierarchy.

It is not a trivial matter to understand the differences between association, composition and generalisation. There is, confusingly, an overlap between the ideas. This illustration may help to introduce these ideas.

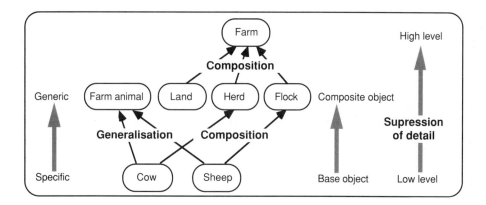

All the notions in this diagram are used throughout information systems specification and appear in various guises within well-known methodologies and implementation mechanisms.

Generalisation underlies the notion of class hierarchies, which predominate in the world of object-oriented programming. Association and composition underlay the notion of more complex data structures and functions which predominate in the world of large database systems. One other idea shown in the diagram, suppression of detail, underlies top-down approaches to systems development.

4.8 Abstraction by composition

Composition is the process by which large objects are made out of smaller ones. For example, a Flock is made up of Sheep, a Polygon is made up of Points (the lines between them being implied), an Invoice is made up of Debit Items and Credit Items.

Suppose a system is to be built to display the current state of a tennis match and record forever the full progress of whole match. The tennis match can be seen as a hierarchy of compositions.

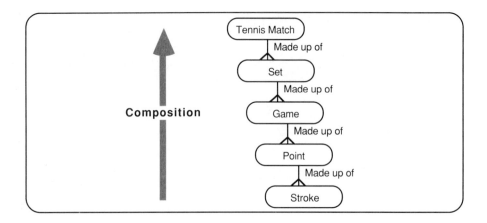

The analyst must decide how many levels of composition are to be recorded in an information system. At which level of abstraction will the system will operate? Will it record each set? each game? each point? each stroke of a rally? Ultimately this question is answered by defining the user's requirements (or potential requirements) for output information. If a scoreboard is the only requirement, then strokes need not be recorded.

Player	Server	1st Set	2nd Set	3rd Set	Game Score
M Frost		7	2	4	40
S Baddely	■	6	6	4	30

Aggregation and aggregate objects

We have been careful to use the terms composition and composite object rather than aggregation and aggregate object, because we want to save the term 'aggregation' for a very restricted kind of composite object, one which cannot include lists or repeating data.

We find two kinds of composition to be useful in the methodology:

- aggregate data objects (c.f. a third normal form relation)
- composite process objects (c.f. a computer program or routine)

Composition and aggregation are further discussed in chapters 9, 12 and 13.

4.9 Abstraction by generalisation

Generalisation, which might also be called 'abstraction of type from instance', is perhaps the single most important idea in software engineering. Data objects and executable processes are only useful in an information system because they are instances of a type which can be reused many times.

Arguably the most important job of the software engineer is to identify the data and process types which can be reused most widely and most efficiently. The title 'software engineer' here is meant to cover all roles in systems development, since generalisation is carried out by many different people. Generalisation is the process by which class hierarchies are created. Class hierarchies are introduced here and further discussed in later chapters.

Class hierarchies

We need a way of defining a class hierarchy which doesn't limit it to data modelling. To a mathematician, a 'directed graph' is a structure of nodes connected by lines, where the the lines are directional or asymmetrical. So a class hierarchy can be defined as a directed graph in which super-type nodes are divided into sub-type nodes. The super-type node provides a place to record properties common to all its sub-types.

The main benefit that analysts should gain from discovering or specifying class hierarchies is less redundancy in the system specification by greater reuse of common components. The first two class hierarchies shown below generalise from the level of object instances. Later illustrations of class hierarchies start from a higher level of abstraction, showing only types.

Common domains in data item definition (see chapter 29)

Where two or more data items (whether attributes of entities or items in an I/O data flow) share the same definition, then it is sensible to create a common domain or data type to record this. Here is a simple class hierarchy, developed by generalisation from the lowest level instances of data items.

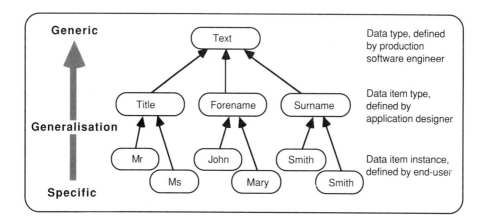

The highest level of abstraction (called data types in the diagram above) has already been defined by production software engineers. The designers of compilers, database management systems and application generators define a set of data types such as text, integer and date. All data items declared to be of a given data type will inherit the properties of that data type. For example, all numeric data items given a PIC 9 clause in COBOL will share or reuse the same validation processes.

The job of defining the middle level of abstraction (called data item types in the diagram above) remains in the domain of information systems analysts and designers. But you can imagine production software in which 'surname' was provided as a distinct data type, and various 'titles' were offered as pre-defined sub-types of this type.

Where not enough data types are provided by the software implementation language, designers may have to define their own data types, specific to the system being designed. A deep and complex structure of data types or domains could be created (see chapter 29 for further discussion).

Data types are usually thought of as applying to individual data items, but what about groups of data items, or record types?

Common data groups in data flows (see chapter 26)

Where two or more data flows share the same data group, then it is sensible to create a common data group to record this. A deep and complex structure of data groups could be created. In practice, it is often convenient to define the bottom level of common data groups in terms of components of the Conceptual Model:

- input data flows   data groups are usually events and enquiry triggers
- output data flows   data groups are often entities.

Super-type records in a database (see chapter 12)

Where two or more record types share data items, then it is possible to create a super-type record in the database to record these common properties. Who defines the most generic record type in the example below?

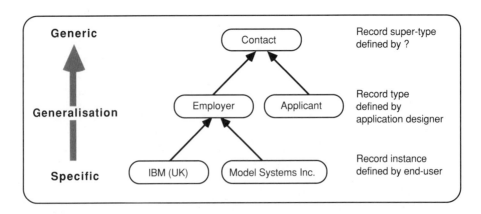

In this example, the systems analyst defines the record types Employer and Applicant. The systems analyst may also define the Contact super-type record to accommodate data and processing common to both Employer and Applicant. But if the Contact super-type record might be reused over more than the narrow scope of one application, perhaps the job of designing this reusable component would better be regarded as a job for the database manager. And perhaps database management systems will move in the direction of providing standard master objects, such as a Contact record, for reuse in any system, just as they provide standard data types for data items.

When and how to make super-type records in the database, to minimise redundant data and processing and maximise reuse, is further discussed in chapter 12. There is an overlap between the notions of a common domain and a super-type record. Chapter 29 suggests that whether the analyst defines the former or the latter depends largely on whether or not the user is allowed to update the value of the domain while the system is running.

Generalisation of process components

Given the primacy of data, generalisation in process design follows generalisation in data design. Thus processes are generalised to handle the differences between repeated instances of a data structure type. Thus each iteration of a loop in a computer program is an instance of a type, designed by the programmer to handle serially repeated instances of a data object. Thus each execution of a larger program or routine is an instance of a type designed by the programmer to handle multiple instances of larger data structures.

Generalisation of executable statements

A class hierarchy may be imposed on the executable statements of a programming language, as shown in the following illustration.

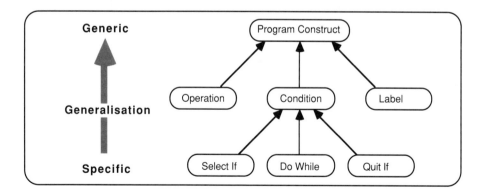

Every programming language is composed of statements which are reusable components. The programmer is provided with a set of reusable objects pre-defined by the production software engineer. At a higher level of system specification, SSADM provides analysts with a limited and highly generalised set of data manipulation operations ('not generalised enough', some people have said).

Super-events in entity event modelling (see part four)

Where two or events share the same effect on one or more entities, then it is sensible to create a common component (or super-event) to record this. An event class hierarchy is normally drawn upside-down, as shown below.

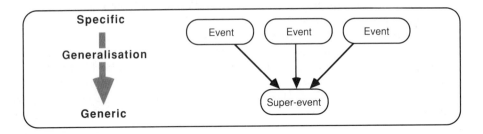

The super-event concept saves some process specification. A common routine is created for the super-event. The super-event really pays off where it can be treated as an ordinary event in the behaviour models of related entities, saving further redundancy of specification. Chapter 17 shows that a relatively complex network of common routines can be developed using this idea.

4.10 Mixing up association and generalisation

We must plead guilty to the charge that our models sometimes confuse association and generalisation. The models can be used to show two very different kinds of relationship: association relationships (connecting distinct objects with distinct identities) and class hierarchy relationships (connecting various sub-types of a single object).

Despite the potential for confusion, there are reasons to allow analysts to record both association and generalisation in the same model. First, generalisation of type from instance can be modelled in either way, as shown in the diagram below.

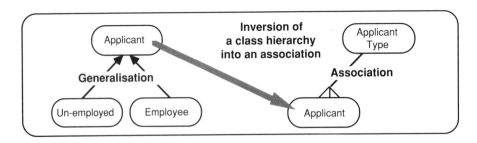

Second, each object type in a class hierarchy may have associations to other object types.

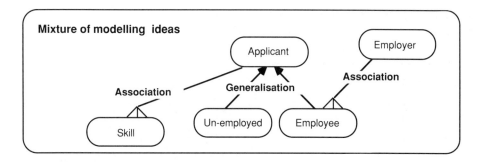

In modelling a system, analysts may have to use association, generalisation, or both. Some degree of confusion cannot be avoided. Both ideas, association and generalisation, must be understood, recognised and manipulated by the analyst to specify the requirements of an information system.

Guidance on when to mix up associations and generalisations and when to separate them into distinct data models is given in chapter 12.

4.11 Networks of objects

Note that large systems always require a network of types, not just a hierarchy, as we can see by combining two of the earlier examples.

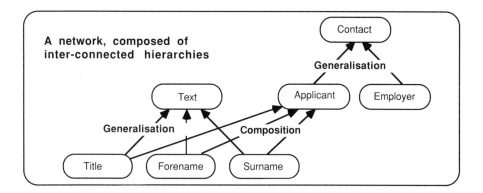

A system contains a range of data and process specifications, from high level to low level. The higher levels are clearly compositions of more basic components. By simply adding together objects in different combinations, it is possible to make a very complex network of objects.

Data structures as composites
Complex data structures may be thought of as composites.

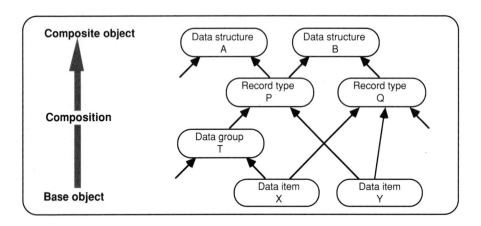

Processing functions as composites
Composition is as common in processing as it is in data structures.

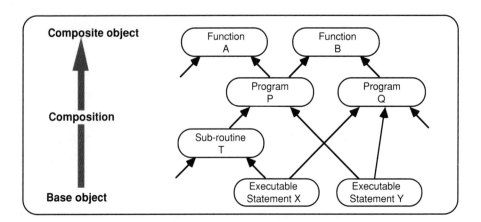

Compare this diagram with the similar one at the start of chapter 1. In both, components are reusable because they are connected in a network structure. Components arranged in a simple hierarchy cannot be reused at all, as noted in the discussion of data flow diagrams in chapter 25. A further discussion of reuse in chapter 31 suggests that reuse of components gets harder as you move upwards from base objects to composite objects.

4.12 **Abstraction by suppression of detail**

Abstraction by **suppression of detail** and its relationship to composition, are perfectly illustrated by a hierarchically organised set of data flow diagrams.

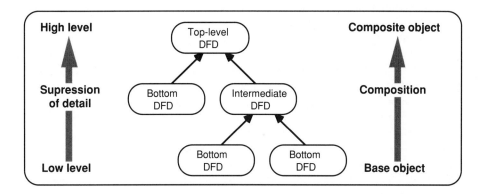

Three more examples of suppression of detail are commonly found in system specification. An entity data model suppresses detail by hiding the attributes of each entity (unless these attributes are inverted to become entities in their own right). A corporate data model may further suppress detail by rolling up one-from-many compositions (so that only the master objects or master entities are seen) and rolling up sub-types (so that only the super-types of a class hierarchy are visible). Data flow diagrams and other kinds of system flowchart suppress detail by showing only the labels of processes and the data flows between them.

Suppression of detail is not the same as composition

Composition does not by itself help reuse. A master object contains lower level objects, but it cannot be separated from them. To put it another way, you cannot win a tennis match without playing every point.

But when looking at the *specification* of a master object, the definition of the base objects may be taken for granted. Such suppression of detail gives some limited opportunities for reuse of high-level specifications. By suppressing the detail of each point from the *description* of a tennis match, the same score might be applied to different matches.

Suppression of detail is not the same as generalisation

A high-level specification may be either specific or generic; for example a top-level data flow diagram may be descriptive of only that system, or applicable to other systems as well. A low-level specification may be either specific or generic; for example the generic design in part six is clearly low-level.

Unfortunately there has in the past been confusion between the notions of generalisation and suppression of detail. This confusion may even have hindered the development of better theories of systems development. It may explain why many good people have been lost for years down the blind alley of top-down decomposition.

Top-down methodology?

We do use data flow diagrams, as discussed in chapter 25, but this does not mean we propose or recommend a top-down methodology. Meyer (1988) gives many reasons why top-down systems decomposition is no longer considered a viable approach for developing large information systems. He is especially concerned to make the point that top-down decomposition is anti-reuse. It doesn't help you discover reusable components, because it acts in the direction of specialisation rather than generalisation.

We take it for granted that top-down decomposition is no longer used as a primary systems development technique, offering no more than this short analogy by way of explanation. Suppose a tennis player's coach is asked to predict the score by which the player will win a match. Although the score may be seen as high-level abstraction from reality, this is not to say it has any predictive value. The coach would be foolish to bet on the predicted score being correct, egotistical to think that predicting the score will significantly affect the play, and mistaken to take much credit for winning the match.

Yet systems managers often place such a foolish, egotistical and mistaken faith in top-level design documentation they hand over to their staff for further development. By all means draw a top-level diagram to get the analysis started, but don't think you've achieved much, that you can force the later work to follow your high level plan, or that you can take the credit if your top-level diagram turns out to be correct after all the real work has been done!

Chapter 5

The need for more than relational data modelling

Some have proposed that data modelling techniques and notations can be extended to capture every kind of 'business rule'. This chapter looks at the background to entity data modelling and points to the inadequacy of the data modelling as a theory for systems development. One conclusion is that to capture the full semantics of an information system, the business rules should be attached to events rather than data records.

5.1 **Is there a real-world modelling theory?**

A counterweight to chapter 4 is needed, a counterblast to the prevailing wind in books of this kind. It is important to realise that entity data modelling is not an academic exercise based on abstract theories. To be useful, the entity data model must lead to the specification of a system's database. Entity data modelling techniques were first developed by generalising backwards from proven data storage mechanisms to formulate appropriate modelling techniques.

   In fact, in the early days of systems development methodologies there was reluctance to acknowledge that the 'logical data model' was an entity model; it was a commonplace to refer to 'data groups' rather than 'entities'. And it is said that for many years Charles Bachmann did not accept that Bachmann database diagrams could be thought of as models of the real world.

   We want to stress this 'reverse engineering' view of entity data modelling. Partly because this is why entity data modelling works in practice. And partly because adopting a reverse engineering frame of mind acts to constrain the excesses of real-world modelling which are too frequently indulged in.

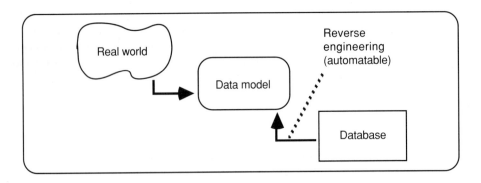

There are those who propose that data modelling is about modelling the real world, as though it is an esoteric or abstract activity, independent of the information requirements of systems users and independent of database design. There are also those who see entity data modelling as a top-down technique, not requiring definition at the level of data items. These are mistaken emphases and they have in practice led to four problems.

   First, some people draw entity data models which are only graphical representations of their ideas about the world, which are ambiguous and informal. The problem is in supposing that these models can be used as the basis of systems development. Such models may give the appearance of progress towards system specification, but are usually of little practical use. The quality assurance of what is presented as a data model is a much bigger problem in practical systems development than is generally admitted.

   Second, some people draw entity data models for specific purposes for which they are not well suited, for example, as the basis of window design (see part five for a more appropriate method for window design).

Third, people have been wrongly persuaded an entity data model is the right or only vehicle for specifying all the 'business rules' they need to express. This is a mistake we shall return to later in this chapter and many other times.

Fourth, people waste time arguing about what an entity or relationship is from an abstract point of view. There is no grand 'modelling theory' to appeal to, beyond what is discussed in part four. Ideas from psychology and general systems theory are of very limited value. What an entity is and what a relationship is are more readily understood in the light of what information a user needs to extract from a system, and how data objects must be stored and processed to achieve this.

Why should anyone spend time modelling a part of the real world? There is no reason to unless they're aiming to implement the model as data and processes in some kind of business information or process control system. The model is only useful if it is an abstraction from implementable specifications of data and processes.

Of course any feature of the real world which can be implemented as data and processes in a computer can also be modelled using the notations in this book. This is no surprise. It has to be true of any notation which is an abstraction from implementable specifications of data and process objects. But designers need no theory of real-world modelling which is independent of the information systems they have to build. There is no purpose or value to it. Designers *do* need a theory of real-world modelling which is clearly related to system design, to the way that programming languages and database management systems work.

So far there has been rather too much reliance on what is sometimes called the relational model. Even if one could say the relational model has a completely mathematical basis, and some doubt this, there are reasons to suggest we need a more general theory.

5.2 An entity data model is a reverse-engineered database

So if not from a real-world modelling theory, where did entity data modelling come from? Entity data modelling techniques were first developed by people who understood the nature of proven physical database management systems, then generalised backwards to formulate appropriate modelling techniques.

Looking at successful implemented systems, it is immediately apparent that there are two main kinds of proven database management system: relational and network. It doesn't matter which kind of database management system is to be used, because entity data modelling techniques were developed backwards, by generalising the properties shared by a range of successful physical database management products, both relational and network.

The word 'database' is used in many ways. We don't want to be too particular about how a specific database system works, but do need to make some general statements, so that we can see how entity data modelling techniques work.

Relational model

The relational model was conceived by Codd in a series of papers starting in 1970. Much is made by others of the sound theoretical foundation of the relational model in mathematical theory. But we are wary of overplaying the mathematical heritage and we shall deliberately avoid using mathematical jargon.

A comprehensive description of the theory is provided by Graham (1991); we shall pick out only salient features. The basic ideas behind relational database design, stemming from the work of Codd, Date and others, may be summarised as shown below.

Relational Data View

The data of a system can be reduced to
a network of simple relations,   after
related via their keys.   Codd, Date and others

According to the relational view of entities, each entity is a relation, where:

- a relation comprises a key and any number of other data items
- the value of each data item is dependent on the value of its key
- two instances of a relation with the same key are not allowed
- there cannot be several instances of a data item in a record.

In a relational schema each relationship has a detail end and a master end. Taking the relational view, a relationship between two relations is represented from the *detail* end. The detail relation holds the key of the master relation.

On top of the relational model, relational theory includes **relational calculus** (which may be regarded as providing non-procedural statements of ways in which the data model may be manipulated) and the more procedural expression of this in the form of **relational algebra**. Relational algebra is based on four primitive operations: Selection, Projection, Union and Join.

Omissions from relational theory

Relational theory does not include SQL, which is a language incorporating most of the ideas of relational algebra. Nor strictly does it include the theory of normal forms mentioned in chapter 11.

More importantly for us, relational theory includes neither a theory of class hierarchies (indeed there is no explanation of any kind of optionality in data), nor a theory of business rules or integrity constraints; 'the relational model is a purely syntactic model; it contains no intrinsic support for any kind of semantics' Graham (1991).

Part four is concerned with filling these gaps, with extending entity data modelling to handle class hierarchies and with adding a theory of entity event modelling for the specification of semantics (business rules or integrity constraints).

Network database view

The network view of database design, stemming from the work of Bachmann, Dodd and others, may be summarised as shown below:

Network Database View

The data of a system can be reduced to
a network of simple records,
related via pointer arrays (tables)   after
or pointer chains (lists).   Bachmann, Dodd and others

Taking the network view of entities, each entity is a record. This is more relaxed than the relational view. Comparing records with relations:

- two instances of a record with the same key *are* allowed
- there *can* be several instances of each data item in a record.

In a network database each relationship has a detail end and a master end. Taking the network view, the main emphasis is on representing the relationship between two records from the *master* end. There are two common implementations; the master record either:

- holds a table (or pointer array) of the keys of its detail records
- is connected via a list (or pointer chain) of the keys of its detail records.

However, a relationship can be implemented by a storing a foreign key in the detail entity, in the same way as in the relational view.

Entity data modelling view

Many think that entity data modelling is a development of the relational model, but entity relationship modelling techniques were mostly derived from the network view. Entity attribute modelling techniques derived from the relational model were grafted on later.

Entity Data Modelling View

The data of a system can be reduced to
a network of simple entities,   after
related via master-detail relationships.   SSADM and other methods

---

In entity data modelling techniques, an entity is normally constrained to be like a relation in a relational database, that is, more constrained than a 'record' in a network database. In particular:

- two instances of an entity with the same key are not allowed
- there cannot be several instances of a data item in a record.

But there have been questions raised about the second of these constraints. Must an entity always be in first normal form? In the network view, a master record may hold a list of the identifiers of its details. Such a list may prove essential in a theory in which objects are stored in distinct locations; in order to send messages to each other, objects need to know (or be able to find out) where the related objects are.

While entity attribute modelling is normally constrained by the same rules as relations in a relational database, entity relationship modelling has developed more from the network database school of thought. Entity relationship modelling in this book is based upon three principles:

- every kind of relationship can be implemented as a master - detail relationship (not just associations, but also class hierarchies)
- there is a way to decide which entity in a relationship is the master and the detail
- each relationship models a real-world association which is asymmetrical.

In both relational and network views, a relationship between entities is asymmetrical; it has a master end and a detail end. Many different kinds of relationship can be distinguished in an entity data model, but there are also many things which cannot be shown.

5.3 Relational databases are no better than network databases

So far in this chapter we have put up ideas from relational and network databases side by side. Surely relational databases are more advanced than network databases? This seems to be the conventional wisdom; certainly there is a large body of opinion which favours the former over the latter.

Graham (1991) argues for the primacy of the relational view. He is authoritative, erudite and informative about not only the relational model, but a wide range of subjects such as expert systems, prototyping and fuzzy objects. However, in parts three and four we show why we think he is wrong to emphasise the object-oriented idea of 'inheritance' since we have not found it very useful in the Conceptual Models of large information systems. And in this chapter we suggest he is mistaken to promote relational over network databases.

At the implementation level, we are very little concerned with which kind of database management system might be used to implement a system model. But at the modelling level, we are very much concerned to point out that relational theory does not provide a sufficient theory of systems development. One way to do this is to consider some of the points made by an expert like Graham who promotes the relational view.

'The relational model was the first formal data model. Relational databases based on it were more flexible than earlier … network systems.' Graham suggest that relational databases are superior because the relational model:

- makes databases easier to restructure
- facilitates non-procedural programming
- is based on set theory.

We are drawn more to the view that the relational model is like the network database model, but optimised from a data storage point of view and horribly unoptimised from a processing point of view. Let us challenge the three points above.

Network databases can be as easy to restructure

The network database designer seeking a 'flexible' database can store foreign keys, provide for direct access on keys (as well as via pointer chains or lists) and use SQL, just like a relational database designer. It may seem quicker and cheaper to specify a 'join' in language like SQL than to build the relationship into the database schema, but note that the former carries hidden costs in terms of extra processing.

Network databases can facilitate non-procedural programming

It may be true that relational calculus and successful non-procedural languages were first developed by those working with the relational model, but the benefits of non-procedural programming are not restricted to relational databases, and the SQL most people use is only loosely based on relational calculus.

Graham points out that 'concerning the relative efficiency of relational query languages compared with approaches based on object identity … it is almost ironic that this property is possessed not only by object-oriented databases but also by early network systems'.

Network databases are no less mathematically sound

Words like 'calculus' and 'algebra' lend a quasi-mathematical credibility to relational theory which gets in the way of serious debate. Even if the relational model does have a sound mathematical basis, there are two reasons why this is of little importance. First, to make relational databases efficient enough to be useful, they are in practice underpinned by CODASYL style indexes and pointer chains, so in what sense are these systems any more 'relational' than a network database?

Second, who is to say that there is not an even better mathematical basis for a network database, one which has yet to be discovered or developed? Graham talks of *post facto* rationalisation of the network database, and mentions an example. We believe a mathematical formulation of the entity event modelling theory in this book is possible, based on regular grammars, finite state automata and Turing machines, and using 'formal methods' to represent the entity event model. But it is debatable whether such mathematical reasoning will help the system analyst.

5.4 **Relational theory is known to be inadequate**

Graham says 'I was one of the people in the late 70s and early 80s who proselytized on behalf of the relational gospel' but suggests the relational gospel is now being supplanted by what he calls the 'Entity-Relationship model' and is surprisingly like the network view. He identifies several weaknesses in the relational model. We will begin with two of his, then add two of our own.

Masters don't know where their details are

The first big weakness of relational theory is that it suggests that a master entity should not 'know about' its details. In the relational view there are no tables or lists, only foreign keys. This minimises data redundancy, but access from master to detail involves a great deal of processing redundancy. This is a very large factor in slowing down system performance. Where a database is distributed it is almost inconceivable that a master entity should not somehow know where its details are.

In the network view, tables and lists are allowed, especially for storing relationships. Thus, while data redundancy is thus permitted, access from master to detail involves no redundant processing. In entity modelling, it is largely irrelevant how access from master to detail is achieved. The designer may choose to implement any given relationship in the relational or network style, assuming the choice is not dictated to him/her by the chosen database management system or by standards for programming of database accesses.

Composite objects cannot be stored

Graham suggests composite objects are problem for the relational model because relations must be in first normal form, with no repeating data. In the network view, the master record of a set is at least akin to a composite object where it is connected to a pointer chain or a list of it details. We define composite objects in process modelling rather than data modelling, so Graham's concern is not important to us

Objects are key-oriented rather than type-oriented

Relational theory does not account for mutually exclusive or optional data. Chapter 12 looks at this topic in some detail.

Database semantics are not handled

The second big weakness of the relational model is that it makes no provision to support business rules. Chapter 29 draws a distinction between business *policies* and business *rules*, but here we are talking only of business rules.

People have attempted to extend the relational model to accommodate business rules. These approaches are sometimes called 'semantic data modelling'. The approach described in chapter 11 might be seen as one of these, except that we make the assertion up front that all business rules cannot be recorded in an entity data model.

5.5 **Not all business rules can be recorded in a data model**

It has become fashionable to talk about recording business rules in the entity data model. Information system builders are all too well aware that referential integrity rules do not capture all the kinds of business rule which need to be implemented.

Business rules which *can* be recorded in an entity data model

Of course there are some rules which can be expressed by distinguishing different kinds of relationship between entities, notably the following.

Dependence of an entity on a relationship

Most entity data model notations provide for the specification of a relationship being mandatory or optional from the point of view of one entity type.

Cardinality of a relationship

Most entity data model notations provide for the specification of some special cases of limitations to cardinality, such as where relationships are limited to one at most, and whether 'many' includes zero or not. Rules normally expressed in an entity data model include:

Rule	Case study example from chapter 11
one: to zero, one or many	Employer to Vacancy
one: to one or many	Applicant to Skill
one: to zero or one	
zero or one: to zero, one or many	Placement Consultant to Applicant
zero or one: to one or many	

These are very primitive business rules, not at all sufficient for more than simple record-keeping systems.

Business rules which *cannot* be recorded in an entity data model

There are many rules which cannot be shown. To begin with there are kinds of cardinality which are not distinguishable in most entity data modelling notations, viz:

one: to zero or many, where many excludes one
one: to many, where many excludes zero or one
zero or one: to many, where many excludes zero or one.

Maybe these are too rare to worry about, but there are other varieties of relationship we find it difficult to distinguish in an entity data model. For example, chapter 11 identifies these concepts:

- fixed master   (a Vacancy may not swap between Employers)
- changeable master   (an Applicant may swap between Placement Consultants)
- monogamous detail   (Applicant has one Interview at a time, many over time)
- polygamous detail   (Applicant has many Interviews arranged in parallel).

Further, where a relationship is optional, this can mean many different things. Suppose a detail entity may exist without a master entity, this might mean that the master of the relationship:

- is missing until found, and fixed thereafter
- is present until deleted, and absent thereafter
- is changeable and optional.

We've only scratched the surface here. It is impossible to extend the entity data modelling notation to record all business rules. To formally define a business rule, we need a way to record how entities are changed by an event from one valid **state** to another. To implement a business rule, we need a way to specify the valid prior state of an entity in the **preconditions** of an event. The techniques described in part four give us what we need.

5.6 The record-based view of systems is too naive

There is a common view of system specification, adequate up to a point, which is record-based. This view arises out of the relational model and is embodied in many 4GLs or application generators. Typically, an application generator is based on some kind of relational database, where each database record is a third normal form relation containing a unique key and the foreign keys of related records, and it is expected that system specification is based on the definition of these database records.

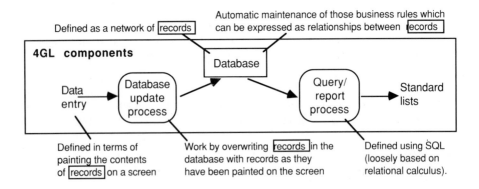

There are many 'record-keeping' systems where this naive view of an information system is sufficient, or almost sufficient. Chapter 21 suggests it is possible to gain enormous productivity benefits by using an application generator for this kind of system. But this book is concerned with how to define and implement the business rules of more complex systems. In these systems, while relational database packages and application generators based upon them are fine for retrieval, they turn out to be seriously flawed for updating.

Application generators try to model reality by hanging activities directly on data. This may be done either non-procedurally (by specifying some relational integrity constraints such as restrict and cascade) or procedurally (by coding some database procedures). Either way there are some problems for which the approach fails.

The moral tale in chapter 30 shows that for a given record type, both 'restrict' and 'cascade' delete rules may be reasonable, under different circumstances and triggered by different events. What we want is for the behaviour of the system to be determined by the event which occurred, not by the invariable rule defined in the database for that record type. More than this, we want the rules to be fired by any state-change we may specify in the Concepual Model, not by physical data management operations like 'delete record'.

Missing: the event

SSADM and MERISE do both have some notion of business events. There's a growing awareness in IBM that AD/Cycle needs to address business events. There's much less agreement as to how to represent events and their interaction with the rest of the system. But events are necessary to understanding what a system is about.

There's a reasonable consensus that implemented systems are models of important real-world concepts. A database record models a real-world thing. A process models a real-world activity. But what in the world does a commit unit model?

Broadly speaking a commit unit represents a collection of processing that must succeed or fail as a whole (e.g. a transfer of funds cannot be complete unless the funds have both been moved out of one account and moved into another). This isn't a data processing concept; this is an end-user concept. Business events represent the atomic changes in reality the system must model.

5.7 Further limits to the usefulness of entity data models

Although building an entity data model to reflect the real world is a large part of what this book is about, it is worth giving further reasons why modelling is not in itself a solution to all the problems of information systems development. In addition to the fact that the concept of the event has been missing, three more points may be made to restrain those who get carried away with modelling the real world, or 'enterprise', divorced from any analysis of a system's place in the user's business. To begin with, it is obvious that a considerable amount of design effort is needed to build the external and internal views of the entity data model.

The need for External Design

A database is useless on its own without a user interface. An information system is only useful when it produces outputs. The end-users' ultimate requirement of a system is output information and the end-users' main task is data entry. This is why most end-users are most comfortable expressing their requirements in the form of input and output data, and prototyping the user interface is such a valuable part of systems development.

The difficulty of identifying entities

People get upset with organisations such as banks which don't recognise the possibility of a person with many accounts, or at many branches; who treat people only as account numbers. We have heard people propose that this is a problem which modelling of the real world will solve; they put up a data modelling solution of the kind shown below.

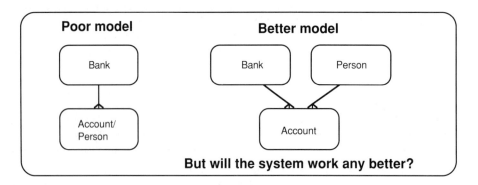

But the entity data model does not in itself solve problems to do with identity. Introducing a person as an entity in the data model does not help. This is really a business problem to do with the difficulty of attaching identifiers to people. The solution lies in the design of an user interface which forces system users to recognise whenever they are dealing with the same person. This is not a problem solved by entity modelling techniques.

The need for Internal Design

An entity data model may have to be considerably distorted for efficient system performance. An entity data model is not always the best database structure. The database does not have to be in third normal form; it does not even have to be implemented using a database management system. This is notably true of systems which are based on producing large volumes of a specific output. Consider an electricity billing system, the main function of which is to print ten thousand bills each day. The business is so dominated by the object 'electricity bill', that everything else fades into insignificance. The database might reasonably be maintained in the form of a serial file of billable accounts (composed perhaps of one or more electricity meters).

Chapter 6

The need for
process modelling

Some have proposed that process modelling will in future be supplanted by data modelling. This chapter raises the profile of modelling of a system's processes, as well its data.

6.1 **Processes weigh more than data**

For the kind of system we are concerned with, it is the job of the systems analyst to specify the contents and structure of the database. It probably goes without saying that the data items in the database will represent objects and features of the real world, and should be organised in such a way as to reflect the organisation of these real-world objects and features. For example, in the database of our case study there are records which are in one-to-one correspondence with entities in the real world such as an Employer, Applicant or Interview.

Following almost any systems development methodology, an analyst will employ entity data modelling techniques to organise stored data into the correct data structure. This is often seen as the main job of the analyst, and much of his/her time is allocated to this task. Yet, if you look at the implemented code of almost any information system, you will find that the database definition is far outweighed by the listings of the programs. Where did all this program code come from?

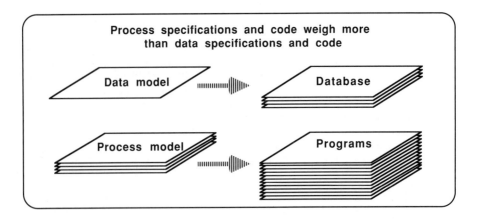

It is misguided to suggest that all is needed is to extend data modelling notations until they capture all of the semantics currently expressed in programming. At the end of this path lies a data model so large and complex it is unusable. If process modelling techniques which are equivalent or comparable with data modelling techniques are developed, then it must be true (since the models are just an abstraction from the implementation) that many pages of process models must be developed for one page of data model. Indeed, it turns out in practice that process models take longer to develop, and are significantly more complex, than data models.

Unfortunately, less help is offered where more is needed. Methodologies have been less successful in providing techniques for process modelling than for data modelling. Two quite different problems for a methodology to solve in process modelling are:

- the specification of each programmable unit
- the decomposition of a system into programmable units.

6.2 **The specification of one programmable unit**

Following the example of data modelling techniques, it is likely that successful process modelling techniques will be developed backwards from an understanding of proven program design principles. A lot of progress has been made in helping the designer with the problems of designing and specifying an individual procedure. Some developments, more closely related than might at first be thought, are briefly mentioned here.

Jackson structured programming (JSP)

Jackson (1975) provided techniques for ensuring that the structure of a program is based on the structure of the problem it solves. Its basis in mathematics is the idea that programs are algorithms which have the task of 'parsing' type three regular grammars, or regular expressions. Briefly, the program designer:

- models the input and output data structures as regular expressions
- merges these data structures to create a single program structure
- adds executable program operations and conditions to the program structure
- mechanically transforms the result into procedural code.

Jackson's two big contributions were to show how to solve specific design problems using the techniques of 'backtracking' and 'inversion'. JSP is remarkably successful in its domain. It takes you about as far you can go with a procedural program design theory. In two decades we have needed only to tweak at the edges of the basic program design method.

It is possible to view the initial steps of JSP as a declarative specification of what the program should do, and the later steps as a relatively mechanical transformation of this into procedural pseudocode. You can imagine an application generator which turned JSP (usually viewed as an old-fashioned 3GL approach) into a declarative specification method.

Declarative languages

In recent years, significant productivity achievements have been achieved by the adoption of languages which might be called:

- declarative languages
- non-procedural languages
- fourth generation languages (4GLs)

At the level of implementation, we don't care whether a specified process is written in a third or fourth generation programming language. We propose that languages like SQL are well suited to implementing some design products, but they are not the only implementation path and they cannot be used for all design products.

At the level of system modelling, some people believe future methodologies will drop procedural specification altogether in favour of languages such as SQL. But we do not think that declarative specification can entirely replace procedural specification. There are several reasons why SQL cannot be used as the basis of any comprehensive systems methodology.

Rumbaugh *et al.* say 'SQL is far from ideal... has any technical flaws... violates modern principles of programming languages... scope is small and incomplete... does not address important issues'. It is recognised that there are procedures for which SQL is unsuitable, or no better than a procedural language. SQL does not provide a means of specifying:

- error detection (except for limited kinds of database integrity rule)
- error response, error handling
- the output from a successful event or enquiry
- a user dialogue composed of several events and enquiries.

We *do* recommend using SQL for most database enquiry processes. But note that coding in a procedural language is sometimes easier, especially where the enquiry requires:

- input data to be merged into the output data
- a 'complex' calculation
- a 'complex' database access path (e.g navigating a relationship more than once).

The long-awaited SQL2 standard turns out to be mainly concerned with 'embedded SQL', meaning that some kind of host procedure is still required. Since SQL is limited in all the ways mentioned above, application generator vendors must add extra features to and around it. These features may introduce further constraints as to what the systems analyst can specify. A system modelling methodology cannot commit itself to any manufacturer's variant of SQL, or be limited to the kind of record-keeping enquiry system for which it works especially well.

Procedural and declarative specifications both have a place

There are roles for procedural as well as declarative specification in systems development. Above the level of coding, it is natural to model a real-world process (a sequence of events which takes some time to complete) using a procedural form of specification, such as a flowchart or regular expression. Part five shows how the short-term sequence of events in a user function or user procedure is naturally modelled using an 'I/O structure' or 'dialogue structure'. Part four shows how the long-term sequence of events in a business thread or business process is naturally modelled using an 'entity life history' (comparable in the GRAPES methodology to a 'business transaction').

In this context, it may be noted that the state-transition diagrams often used in books on object-oriented design are just as procedural as the Jackson Structures or regular expressions used in this book.

Procedural and declarative implementation languages are both valid

In our methodology, event and enquiry procedures are logical specifications in that they do not predispose the designer to any specific implementation language. However, it is true that they are essentially 'procedural' specifications, and therefore may be considered as past the point where a choice might be made between a procedural or non-procedural implementation language.

Event and enquiry procedures could stand as specifications for implementation in a non-procedural language. But SSADM includes non-procedural specification diagrams, ones which do not have the sequential nature and all the processing detail of an event or enquiry procedure. You can specify an enquiry process using an enquiry access path (see chapter 11). You can specify an update process using something like an effect correspondence diagram with operations on (see chapter 18).

Given such a specification, you can implement it in any language you choose. An SSADM guide for taking such specifications and writing event and enquiry procedures in SQL has been written, but is yet to be published. It reinforces the message that there are some event and enquiry procedures which must be coded procedurally, and there are others which are more easily coded procedurally.

Program generation

Some individual procedures or programs can be generated from specifications of their input and output data by application generators. But if this was enough, then application generators wouldn't need to provide you with any programming language. In practice, while application generators are very good at helping you create a database and generate database enquiry programs, they are not so good at generating programs in what designers regard as the more difficult areas:

- database updating
- data entry dialogues
- off-line functions

Application generator manufacturers have to provide you with both procedural and declarative languages for doing things like this. It is recognised that they both kinds of language have a role to play.

So, for the specification of a single programmable unit we have many procedural and non-procedural design methods, techniques and languages. This brings us to the question of how to break a complex system down into the units which can readily be programmed.

6.3 **The decomposition of a system into programmable units**

There is no sharp distinction between a program and a system. Essentially, both consume input data and produce output data. But systems are more complex in that there is no direct way to transform the input into the output. So the software engineer is faced with the problem of how to identify the simple programs from which the system can be composed.

JSP offers a little help in system decomposition, by defining different kinds of 'structure clash' and their resolution, but it turns out, not enough. STRADIS, Yourdon and MASCOT are three methodologies which started out in life in the 1970s as system decomposition techniques, using variations on the themes of top-down decomposition and data flow diagrams. But while top-down decomposition and data flow diagrams are strong tools for systems investigation, they are weak for system construction.

Data flow diagram-based methods are notorious for having difficulty in providing systematic ways of deciding how to move from data flow representations to program-like representations. There is a famous cartoon (first, we think, shown by Bergland, 1981) where the designer explains how this gap is filled. The cartoon is something like this.

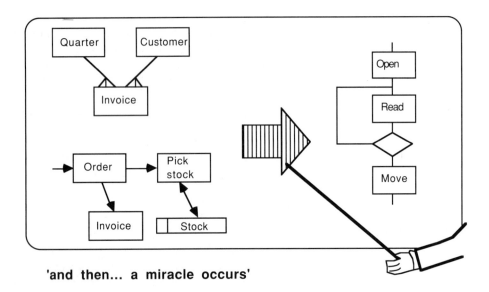

'and then... a miracle occurs'

Reasons why top-down approaches and data flow diagrams are inherently flawed are given in chapter 25. What better theory is there for systems decomposition? The 3-Schema Architecture looks very promising in this respect. The thing it makes obvious is that the processes of a system may be divided into entirely separate process types, dealing with different areas of concern. One of the breakthroughs needed is to realise that these different kinds of processes require different kinds of modelling.

6.4 **Different kinds of process to model**

Using the 3-Schema Architecture, we can identify several different kinds of process in an information system. To illustrate this, it is convenient to borrow a model of an off-line function from chapter 28.

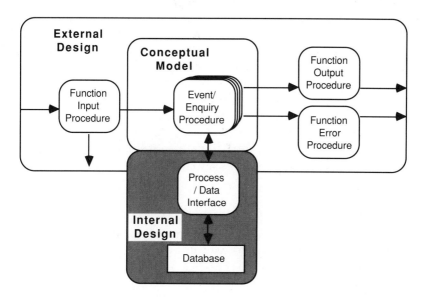

It does indeed turn out that these different kinds of processes in a system will require different kinds of modelling. Looking at a **Conceptual Model**, you may see that each database update process models an event in the real world. For example, a program may be written to model the receipt of a payment from a customer. You can build database update programs on the basis of an entity event model which describes how 'events' affect the 'entities' of the system.

But it would be a mistake to build a report program in the **External Design** around the basis of an entity event modelling method. Such a program should reflect the output data structure. Part five is concerned with the processes of the External Design, with the design of the user interface. At this point in the book, in these essays on modelling, we are more concerned with what might be called the processes of the Conceptual Model.

If the Conceptual Model is to be useful, if the system is to be successful, it is not sufficient to have a correct database structure. The data must be maintained so that it is up-to-date and in a consistent state. The user must be given accurate information in response to enquiries. So it is vitally important that the database update and enquiry processes are specified correctly.

Database enquiry processes

The specification of a database enquiry process is not too much of a problem for an analyst, for six reasons:

1 The specification is mainly composed of descriptions of the required output data and the available input data or database. These are models of **static** data.
2 If the program is run twice in succession, it will produce the same results, because the data it works on is static.
3 Much of the programming work can be automated (using SQL or the like), the remainder may be done using a process modelling and design technique such as JSP.
4 The results of the process are immediately visible and since the output should be designed to make sense to a user, most errors are easily spotted.
5 If the program does not work, relatively little harm is done. The database remains intact, no other program is affected and one knows which program is at fault.
6 In specifying the program, the analyst need not consider how other programs work. Each enquiry program is independent of any other enquiry program.

Database update processes

Someone who is used to specifying database enquiry processes may approach the specification of a database update process with misplaced confidence. It is all too easy to specify a program which looks plausible on paper and seems to work when tested in isolation. But:

1 Where does the specification come from? How does one ensure its correctness? What model is it based on? We need a way to model the **dynamics** of a changing database.
2 If the program is run twice in succession, it will produce different results, because the data it works on is dynamic.
3 Application generators are positively dangerous. They swiftly generate programs which reflect only the most naive of updating requirements and do not contain the necessary validation constraints.
4 The results of the process are invisible. Even when made visible, who notices if a secondary state indicator is set to the wrong value?
5 If the program does not work, it will act like a virus, corrupting the stored data and mysteriously causing other programs to fall over.
6 In specifying the program, the analyst must consider how other programs work. Each update program must act in co-ordination with all other update programs.

In a sense we shall be introducing a top-down approach to dynamic modelling, since the entity data model will be used as the starting point for the definition of a more elaborate entity event model.

Chapter 7

The need for
dynamic modelling

This chapter proposes that it is desirable and possible to model the dynamic aspects of the real world (as well as the static aspects) and to use this model to specify the database processes of a system (as well as the database). In doing this, the chapter introduces some entity event modelling concepts.

7.1 **Static and dynamic models**

An entity data model represents objects and relationships between objects, but only as they are seen at a given moment. The accepted view that if an entity data model is realised in a database, the database is a model of the real world is not strictly true.

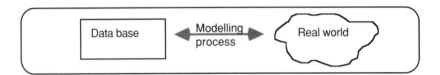

A database is only a snapshot of the world at a particular point in time; it is a model of a time slice of the real world. A full model of the real world would include all of the relevant time slices. As events happen at particular points in time, new versions of the database come in to existence corresponding to new states of the real world.

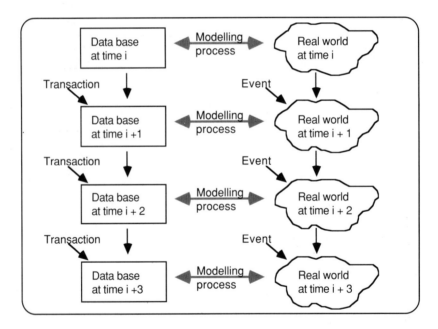

A system must change as the world changes. The programs which update the database must reflect the events which take place in the real world. A system is more than a **static** model; a system is also a **dynamic** model.

What is needed is some clear way of representing the permissible changes of state and the circumstances in which they come about. The traditional way of defining these things is to concentrate on the agents which cause the changes of state: the transactions.

Clearly, transaction handling has to be specified, but if the effects of time on the system are not taken into account very explicitly, the system will not operate correctly.

One simple example is a well-known savings bank which assumes in its system that all withdrawals occur at the beginning of the day, and all deposits at the day's end. How irritating it is to make a deposit of £200 in the morning to an account a few pounds in credit, only to be told that your account is overdrawn if you draw out £150 after lunch!

7.2 **An analogy**

A simple analogy may help to illustrate how significant improvements can be achieved in our level of understanding of a system's dynamics.

Consider a database as a snapshot of the real world at a particular point in time. Suppose this is literally true, that we want to record the position of physical objects in relationship to each other, and so we take a photograph of the objects in question. That photograph is then our database at time i, representing the objects we are interested in as they are at time i. Suppose our subsequent snapshots are all taken at very short regular intervals (time i+1, time i+2, etc.). If all of the snapshots are taken on movie film, we can run the film through a projector and watch the movie.

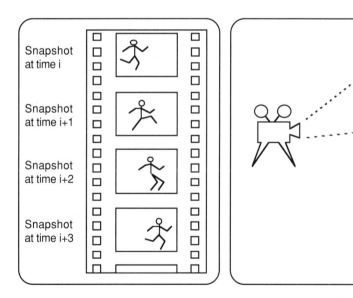

It must be easier, by several orders of magnitude, to understand what is going on in the film by watching the movie instead of by looking at each individual frame in succession and trying to understand the tiny differences between successive frames. An individual frame provides no description of the context in which it occurs. Looking at one frame it may be difficult to decide whether the man is running forwards or jumping back in surprise. Looking at the movie leaves us in no doubt.

Similar problems occur in data processing. If information about an entity's current state is not stored very explicitly, it can be quite difficult to decide whether the entity is in a valid state to be affected by a particular transaction.

Just as an actor cannot successfully act in a scene without first understanding the script of each character (both before and after that scene), so a systems analyst cannot specify a process to update a database without understanding how each entity is progressing through its own life history. Both the actor and the analyst need to understand the **context** in which they are working.

7.3 **The movie**

What is needed is a level of systems analysis akin to watching a movie rather than one akin to looking at individual frames. Or rather we need a level of systems description corresponding to writing the script for the movie instead of one corresponding to specifying the differences between two successive frames.

Continuing the analogy, imagine that you are watching a movie. Sit down and watch the movie. See how it turns out.

In the first scene of the movie, the heroine is shopping in a store.

In the next scene the hero, while walking down the street, is accosted by the villain who forces him at gunpoint to hand over his wallet. The villain is making his escape, clearly worried that the hero is going to give pursuit, when the heroine comes out of the nearby store. The villain takes her hostage and they escape in a car which he steals.

The hero runs after the villain's car. The villain is shown driving his car with the heroine sobbing beside him. The movie cuts to a scene of the hero running and then back to a scene of the villain driving and sneering while the heroine sobs. Several of these scenes follow, one after the other.

In the next scene the villain, having stopped his car, is shown tying the heroine to a railway line.

The movie cuts to a scene of the hero running and then to a scene of a train leaving a station. The movie keeps cutting between scenes of the hero running and scenes of the train puffing nearer and nearer. After this, there is a scene of the train entering a tunnel and then another scene of the hero running, and a scene of the train leaving the tunnel.

Now the hero arrives at the railway line, sees the heroine's predicament and sees the villain in easy reach. While this confrontation is taking place, an inset in the corner of the screen shows the train hooting. The heroine screams and the hero decides sadly that he cannot follow the villain and get his wallet back. He must try to save the girl! While the hero is distracted, the villain pushes him down a steep slope at the side of the road and escapes.

The hero starts to climb out. He slips back on the muddy bank. With awful suspense, we see that each scene of the hero climbing out is followed by a scene of the hero slipping back. Between climbing scenes and slipping scenes the heroine's plight is underlined by scenes of her struggling, scenes of her screaming and scenes of the train drawing nearer and nearer. From time to time, we see a scene of the villain running away.

Then, to our great relief, a scene of the hero climbing out is followed, after an intervening scene of the heroine struggling, by a scene of the hero now successfully at the top of the slope. This is followed immediately by a scene of the train inexorably coming nearer and nearer and nearer. Can our hero rescue our heroine? Is there still time?

No there isn't. In the penultimate scene the train decapitates our unfortunate heroine: the villain is seen in an inset gloating; the hero is grieving (but more for his stolen wallet than for the poor girl).

A final scene shows the villain reclining beside a swimming pool in the grounds of a luxury hotel, enjoying his ill-gotten gains.

Those of you watching the movie (those of you who resisted the temptation to read ahead) probably didn't expect that the movie would turn out this way. The conventions of the genre are such that you expected the girl to be rescued and the villain arrested. Some of you might have left the movie theatre if you had known that the story wasn't going to end happily.

If you are interested in the movie, you must be emotionally involved in its plot. This involvement takes the shape of caring about what happens to the individuals in the movie and being interested in how the plot will turn out. In fact, you usually have expectations about the way the movie will turn out; the emotional tension comes from matching the actual story to what you expect.

Just as the audience at a movie has expectations of how a given set of events in the movie will lead to future events in the movie, so a user of an information system has expectations of what the system will be doing at some future date as a consequence of what is happening now. For example, if a television rental agreement is taken out it is expected that the television set will be delivered to the customer and that the rental amount will be paid on the due dates.

Some of these expectations are so obvious to the user that he will think that they will be obvious to any person with common sense, and it will not occur to him to tell the systems designer about them. But 'common' sense is exactly what the systems designer and user have not got; they do not have a common understanding of the system until the systems analysis is complete!

What is needed is a tool which forces out an explicit representation of what the user's expectations are and of what divergences from those expectations are possible.

7.4 Similarities between the movie and a system

Several similarities exist between the movie and an information system. In both the movie and a system there are *entities*. In the movie, the entities are hero, heroine, villain and train. In the system, the entities are things like customers and appliances. In both the movie and a system, *things happen* causing the states of entities to change. In the movie, heroes get robbed, chase villains. In the system, customers make rental agreements, pay instalments. In both, there are expectations about the ways in which things will happen.

In the movie, heroes will rescue heroines. In the system, customers will pay rentals. These expectations may or may not be justified!

In both, the patterns of things which are happening are all jumbled up. In the movie, the hero is chasing the villain quite independently of the train which is puffing along (he has no idea that the heroine is being tied to the lines). In the system, a customer is paying his rental quite happily, unaware that another customer is not. But if we separate the threads of the action, we can see what is going on. In the movie, the hero is running because he has been robbed. In the system, the customer is paying his rental because the due date has come.

In both, things can happen which are not captured, and which cannot be captured, in the model. In the movie, what happens to the train while it is in the tunnel? In the system, is a customer watching the television set he has rented?

In both, some happenings are independent, even though they take place at roughly the same time. The hero giving chase scene involves only the hero and does not affect any other entity (the villain doesn't know he is being chased). The train puffing scene involves only the train. In both, some things affect several entities at once. In the confrontation scene all of the entities appear. The way one entity behaves in a scene affects how another one behaves; the heroine screams, the hero stays to rescue her and the villain escapes all because the train hoots. In a computer system similar interactions occur, for example a rental agreement may be terminated when a customer dies.

7.5 **Differences between the movie and a system**

Several differences may exist, but further similarities lie behind them. Information systems have a coarse time grain. The movie models reality using a very fine time grain; the model changes several times per second. Information systems generally have a very coarse time grain. They work in terms of significant changes in circumstances (perhaps like each change of scene in the movie), rather than in terms of changes occurring at regular small intervals. However, process control systems (for whose design this method can also be used) work at the level of the movie; regular readings are taken from sensors to monitor the flight of a missile or the progress of a chemical process.

Information systems have several instances of an entity type. The movie has only one entity of each important type. In the information system several entities of each type exist. However, in a process control system there may be only one entity of each type. And in a movie, in a crowd scene, there may be several minor entities of the same type.

Information systems have no pre-destination. In a movie, the life of an entity is pre-destined. The hero is forever doomed to lose his wallet and forever fails to save the heroine no matter how many times the movie runs. In an information system several outcomes of an individual entity's life may be possible; a rental payment may be made on time, or it may be necessary to repossess the rented goods.

Even this difference is not absolute, however. In some movies (e.g. *The French Lieutenant's Woman*) several alternative outcomes are shown. Several versions of a movie may be made with different outcomes. The apparent difference is tied up with the fact that there is only one entity of each important type. Where there is more than one entity of a particular type, there is less pre-destination. In a crowd scene, one member of the crowd may get trampled to death, another may survive.

Finally, stepping back from the movie and considering the audience, an audience member may imagine several potential lives for each of the entities.

7.6 **Characters in the movie**

The train

The way in which user expectations can be captured is by taking each of the entities in the user's system and outlining what happens to it. We can see how this is done in the movie by outlining the scripts to be followed by each of the actors, and by the train.

Taking the train's script first, it appears, in sequence, in a number of scenes in the movie. The scenes in which the train appears are as follows:

- The Leaving Station Scene
- The Train Puffing Scenes
- The Tunnel Entry Scene
- The Tunnel Exit Scene
- The Confrontation Scene (it hoots)
- The Train Nearing Scenes
- The Decapitation Scene (it kills the girl).

These scenes can be organised to form the train's script.

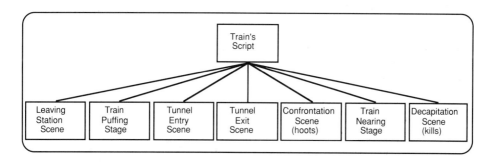

Train Puffing Scenes are not shown in this diagram as individual components of the sequence because there are very many of them and they are all of the same type of scene. Instead, what has been represented is a Train Puffing Stage which we know consists of a series of Scenes. We can represent how a Stage is made up of Scenes by extending the diagram, using an asterisk in the corner of a component to say that the thing it represents occurs many times, making up the component above it:

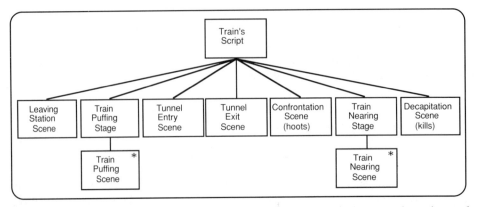

Such a diagram is called an *entity behaviour model*. Note that it does not show the total life of the entity; it doesn't show the train being built or being scrapped. It only shows the period of interest from the time the train comes on screen until its last appearance.

The villain

The villain appears in a number of scenes in the movie. In some scenes he appears by himself, in others he appears with other actors. Spelling these scenes out:

- The Robbery Scene (he commits it)
- The Villain's Car Scenes (he sneers) - Escaping with Hostage
- The Tie Girl to Line Scene (he ties her)
- The Confrontation Scene (he escapes)
- The Villain Running Scenes - Final Escape
- The Decapitation Scene (he gloats)
- The Swimming Pool Scene.

The diagram below shows how the villain's script is made up from all of these things, in the appropriate sequence in time. Again, there are two 'Stages' in the script, each composed of several 'Scenes'.

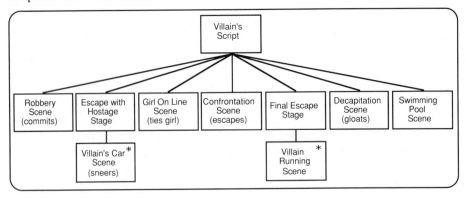

The hero
The hero, too, appears in a number of scenes:

- The Robbery Scene (he is robbed)
- The Chase Scenes
- The Confrontation Scene (he is pushed down the slope)
- The Climb Scenes
- The Slip Scenes
- The At Top of the Slope Scene
- The Decapitation Scene (he grieves - though only for his wallet).

When we try to draw the sequence of individual scenes and compound stages the hero goes through, we see that there are two stages concerned with Climb Scenes, one stage where the hero is failing to climb up the slope, and one where he succeeds.

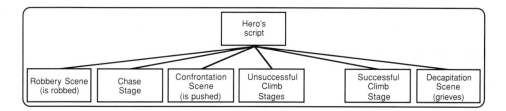

The Chase Stage can be further defined as consisting of many Chase Scenes, just as the Escape with Hostage Stage was defined as consisting of many Villain's Car Scenes.

The Successful Climb Out Stage can be defined in terms of a further sequence of a Climb Scene (destined to be Successful) followed by a Stand At Top of the Slope Scene. The Failure to Climb Out Stage is more complex, consisting of many Climb Out Failures each comprising a Climb Scene (doomed to be Unsuccessful) followed by a Slip Scene.

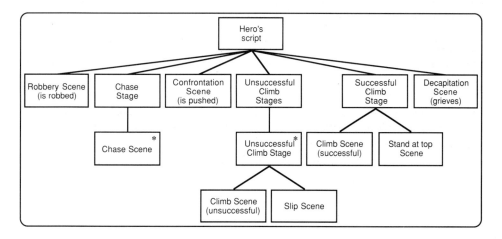

This diagram features an iterated sequence as part of what is called an N-plus-one iteration (since there are N cases followed by one special case).

The heroine

We can similarly list the scenes in which the heroine appears:

- The Shopping Scene
- The Robbery Scene (she is taken hostage)
- The Villain's Car Scenes (she sobs)
- The Tie Girl to Line Scene (she is tied)
- The Confrontation Scene (she screams)
- The Scream Scenes
- The Struggle Scenes
- The Decapitation Scene (she is killed).

Again, when we define the sequence of scenes in the heroine's script we find that we need to introduce some compound stages during which several scenes may occur. We need an Escape with Hostage Stage consisting of several Villain's Car Scenes in which the heroine Sobs. We also need to aggregate the Scream Scenes and Struggle Scenes into a Heroine in Distress Stage.

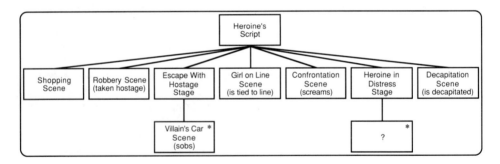

However, the diagramming tools introduced so far are not adequate to define exactly how the Heroine in Distress Stage is made up from the Chase Scenes and Struggle Scenes.

Leaving aside the interleaved Train Nearing Scenes (which do not feature the heroine), Scream Scenes and Struggle Scenes do not occur in any recognisable sequence (unlike Climb Scenes and Slip Scenes which always occur in sequence in the Hero's Script). A Scream Scene may be followed by another Scream Scene, then a Struggle Scene occurs, then another Scream Scene, then three Struggle Scenes in a row, and so on.

Consider a generalisation of the ideas of a Scream Scene and a Struggle Scene: a Heroine in Distress Scene. This is implied by the notion of a Heroine in Distress Stage, which we can now describe simply as consisting of many Heroine in Distress Scenes. Now all we need to say is that a Heroine in Distress Scene is always either a Scream Scene or a Struggle Scene.

We do this by showing the Heroine in Distress Scene component as being composed of one of the components underneath it. We label the corner of such a component with an 'o' to say that there is an option as to whether it is present; one and only one instance of all such components occurs for each individual Heroine in Distress Scene.

The full version of the diagram for the Heroine's Script is shown below.

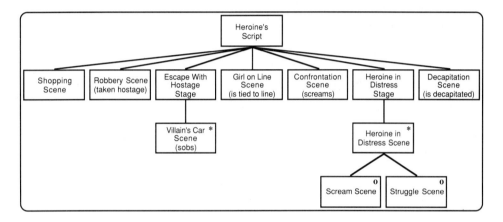

This diagram features an iterated selection, which is always used to describe a random mixture of events.

7.7 Scenes in the movie

Imagine that you are directing the production of the movie. You would ensure that every actor had his or her script. You would want to be sure that when it was time to shoot a scene everyone involved was present. You might have a cast list for each scene identifying the participants and what they do.

So, there are two views of the movie. From the view of the Cast there are many Characters, and each Character makes many Appearances (in Scenes). From the view of the Story there are many Scenes; in each Scene there are many Appearances (of Characters).

The Scene by Scene view is specified below in a diagram showing, for each scene, the characters which appear in it.

Shopping Heroine	**Scream** Heroine	**Struggle** Heroine	**Tie Girl To Line** Villain (ties girl) Heroine (is tied)	**Robbery** Hero (is robbed) Villain (commits) Heroine (hostage)
At Top Hero	**Chase** Hero	**Slip** Hero	**Villains Car** Villain (sneers) Heroine (sobs)	**Climb** Hero (unsuccessful) Hero (successful)
Tunnel Entry Train	**Tunnel Exit** Train	**Train Nearing** Train	**Train Puffing** Train	**Confrontation** Hero (is pushed) Villain (escapes) Heroine (screams) Train (hoots)
	Swimming Pool Villain	**Villain** Running Villain	**Leaving Station** Train	**Decapitation** Hero (grieves) Villain (gloats) Heroine (killed) Train (kills)

Both viewpoints are shown in the entity data model below. Notice the many-to-many relationship between Character and Scene is resolved by the link entity Appearance.

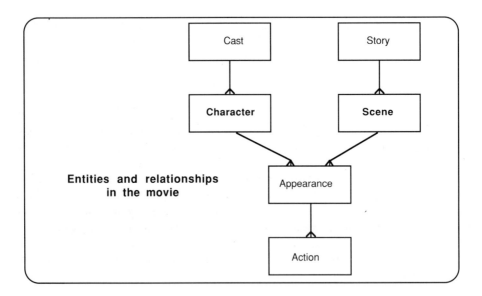

Entities and relationships in the movie

7.8 **Entities and events in an information system**

The main point to be derived from the movie/system analogy is this: just as a film director cannot successfully plan a scene without first understanding the script of each character (both before and after that scene), so a system analyst cannot specify a process to update the data in an entity data model without understanding how each entity is progressing through its own life history.

Character = Entity

Given the full story, we have drawn an entity behaviour model for each character in the movie (Train, Villain, Hero and Heroine). Likewise, given the entity data model of an information system, we can draw an entity behaviour model for each of the entities in it. But we do not produce an entity behaviour model for each individual entity instance (for example, Fred Smith who has rented a television). We produce an entity behaviour model for each entity type (for example, Customer).

The purpose of producing entity behaviour models is twofold. During *analysis* they help us understand the entities better (we often have to change our entity data model or our Data Flow Diagrams as a result of the analysis of some fairly trivial entity behaviour model). They also enable us to pin down how the user expects the system to work and how exceptions to the normal operation of the system arise.

During *design* they give us a formal method for constructing effect correspondence diagrams, from which we can code database update routines. The effect correspondence diagrams may be cross-checked against the more intuitively produced user function definitions, perhaps derived from the DFDs. The results are used to produce program specifications.

Scene = Event

For each scene in the movie, we have produced a cast list. For each event which can occur in an information system we can produce a process specification, or effect correspondence diagram.

Part four of this book describes the formal technique by which effect correspondence diagrams are produced as a by-product of analysing entity behaviour models.

7.9 **Entity event modelling concepts and terminology**

We can use an entity data model to build a meta-model of the main concepts in entity event modelling. Notice the resolution of the many-to-many relationship between entity and event by the 'effect' entity. At a lower level of detail, within each effect, an entity experiences a number of operations.

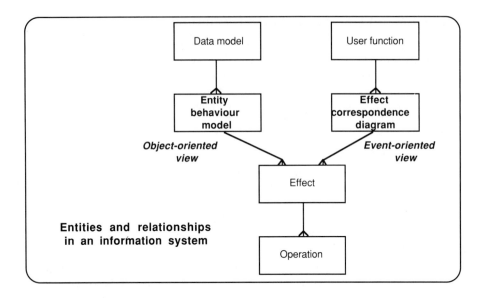

An **entity behaviour model** defines the behaviour of a single type of entity from the moment it becomes of interest to the system, to the moment it ceases to be of interest. It defines what happens to the entity and what the entity does. It shows those events affecting (or affected by) an entity and the pattern of these events. The pattern is composed from sequences, selections and iterations of sub-patterns and of effects of events.

An **effect correspondence diagram** defines the effects of one event type on entities of several types. An event:

- changes the system, from one consistent state to another
- must succeed completely, or else fail (it is a commit unit)
- must update one or more entities
- may refer to an entity without updating (if that entity's state influences the event).

It is meaningless to look at the states of entities during the processing of an event, because the system will be inconsistent. For example, half-way through processing a Stock Transfer event, when the total Stock Items at one Warehouse has been reduced, but the total at the other has not yet been incremented, an enquiry on the overall total of Stock Items will show one less than it should.

An event **effect** is the appearance of an event inside an entity behaviour model. One type of event may have several alternative effects within one entity behaviour model. For example, a Payment may simply reduce the amount outstanding on an Instalment, or be the one which is sufficient to pay it off completely. It is meaningless to look at the state of an entity while an effect is being dealt with. For example, the Amount Outstanding may have been reduced but the 'Number of Payments Made may not yet have been increased.

An event may have different effects on different instances of the same type of entity. That is, the entity plays different **roles** with respect to the event. For example, a Stock Transfer affects two Warehouses, reducing Stock in the Warehouse [old] and increasing Stock in the Warehouse [new].

An **operation** is an action done to an entity as part of the effect of an event on that entity. An operation is at or close to the level of an implementable statement. For example, Subtract Amount of Payment from Amount Outstanding.

These and other concepts are illustrated in chapter 13.

Entity event matrix

The processing at the heart of a database system can be summarised in the form of an entity event matrix, as shown below.

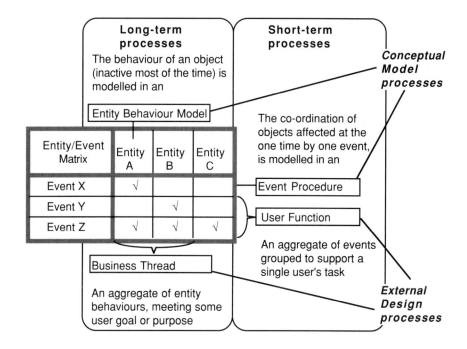

In this diagram we have introduced two ways of aggregating elementary system processes into higher level concepts.

A **user function** can be thought of as an aggregate of events and enquiries, triggered by a primary input to the system, or leading to a primary output from the system.

A **business thread** is a less formal concept, useful in system testing. It may be likened to the behaviour of a very important entity in the system, but it is a kind of unnormalised entity behaviour in that it includes elements of the behaviour of related (master and detail) entities.

7.10 **Aside on meta-modelling**

In this chapter we have used an entity data model to explain concepts in the methodology such as entity, event and effect. This kind of model is often called a meta-model. We use another one in chapter 25 to clarify the difference between various user-oriented concepts, and the relationships between them.

Can the methodology be applied to itself? In methodology development it is usually a good idea to build a meta-model of how the concepts relate to each other, and this meta-model may be a valuable teaching aid.

In the future, we think that a meta-model of information systems will be built and will be the way to control and integrate the development of methodologies and CASE tools. However, we are have many doubts about the meta-models we have seen to date. The task of building and validating the meta-model is proving harder than many have hoped. We are involved in Europe-wide initiatives to make further progress.

The full meta-model of this book (or even one chapter of it) is very, very complex; far too complex to be much help in teaching people to understand the concepts. It is also too complex for implementation as an efficient database structure. If it is to be used for teaching purposes or CASE tool implementation, the meta-model has to be simplified and thereby distorted.

We now turn from introducing data and process modelling in the world of information systems to the world of OO programming, from which comes an apparently very different set of ideas.

Part Three:

The Need for More Than OO Programming

Chapter 8

The need for
OO modelling

The goals are to build information systems better and quicker, and specifically to increase software reuse. This chapter suggests that approaches based on entity data modelling and OO programming languages have got us within shooting distance of these goals, and highlights the need to bring them together in a single methodology.

8.1 **Introduction**

It has long been realised that the development of an information system is a difficult and time consuming task, prone to error and delay. There is clearly a problem to be solved, or rather two problems, which can be expressed as two goals.

To build systems better
One goal is to learn how to get it right first time, to produce systems and programs which are self-evidently correct, which are intuitively obvious in their definition and operation, and so are easy to maintain.

To build systems quicker
Another goal is to learn how define and build such a system in a time span which approximates to the time span that a not-too-naive user would expect to have to take to build, given a reasonably well-formulated statement of requirements.

For twenty years or so, people have been developing and improving techniques for analysing, designing and implementing information systems. We believe we are now within shooting distance of these goals.

8.2 **How to build systems better**

A system should be cost effective. It should use the minimum of resources, by which we mean labour and machinery. While machine costs are plummeting, labour costs are escalating. This was recognised way back in the 1970s and it is still true today. Saving manpower was and is the main aim of a systems development methodology.

It turns out that a disproportionate amount of time is spent, not on running systems or even on first programming them, but on debugging, amending and maintaining them after they have been implemented. Experience tells us that wrong systems are expensive.

The most cost-effective system is normally the *correct* one, one that produces accurate output information every time, and in time for the user to use it. If we can guarantee the correctness of a system specification, we will save money. There are at least three approaches directed at doing it this.

Prototyping
This (not to be confused with rapid application development) is discussed in chapter 20.

Formal methods
To prove correctness, you can specify a computer program or system using a formal language then prove that mathematically speaking the implemented code is a valid transformation of this formal specification. There are three points to make here.

First, the products of the methodology in this book are intended to be formal, in the same sense as a 'formal method' is formal; the aim is to build a complete and formal system model which can be directly implemented.

Second, this is not enough. A methodology must provide more than a formal system model, it must help you to build the model.

Third, if the formal specification and implemented code are transformations of each other, then the old question rears its head again. How do we ensure the correctness of the specification? Where did the specification come from?

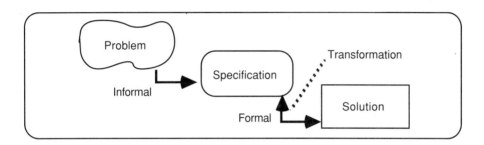

Ultimately, there is no way to be mathematically formal about derivation of the specification from a verbal problem description, or a textual requirements catalogue. The best we can do is to raise the formal specification language to the highest possible level, so that we can validate the system specification against a common-sense understanding of the problem or system requirements. In this book we are concerned with raising the system specification language to a high level, expressing it in the form of diagrams, while maintaining the formality of the specification.

Entity data modelling

The most successful of diagrammatic information systems analysis techniques, that is those which have worked best within systems development methodologies (like Information Engineering and SSADM) might broadly be called entity data modelling techniques. Although there is no single authority to appeal to, it is remarkable how similar are the entity data modelling techniques which have been incorporated in various systems methodologies.

An entity data model is an abstraction by generalisation from different possible physical database designs. It is also an abstraction by suppression of detail of physical design characteristics, and by selective modelling of the real world. It represents the essence of the system's stored data, without the clutter of detail associated with a physical system description.

Entity data models are discussed further in part four, where we are also concerned to extend entity data modelling with entity behaviour modelling techniques. However, while entity modelling techniques have proved to be rather good at helping us to build systems *better,* they haven't really helped us to build systems *quicker*.

8.3 **How to build systems quicker**

Over the last twenty years or so, more and more of the administration of business products and services has been vested in computer systems. In some industries, such as banking and insurance, for all practical purposes the administration of the services *is* the product. In such industries, the single biggest constraint on the introduction of a new service is the time and effort it takes to develop the information system. Three developments should be helping analysts to save time and effort.

Rapid application development techniques
These are discussed at length in part five.

CASE tools
Although the specification language we use in this book is diagrammatic, it is also precise and unambiguous. So many laborious design tasks (especially what might be called transformations) can be delegated to a machine. Current CASE tools may be rather disappointing, but there are real prospects for automating more design and implementation tasks within a CASE tool, as discussed in chapter 30.

OO programming languages
The second major development is that of OO programming languages such as Smalltalk, and C++. These programming languages have primarily been used by people who are interested in designing software to support professional workstations, such as graphics packages and CASE tools.

So why are OO concepts gaining a foothold in the information systems community? Why should those involved in the design of information systems be interested in OO programming languages? Why are OO techniques seen by many people as holding the solution to the problems of system building? The reason can be given in one word: reuse. The hope is that the designer can build systems by pulling together components which have already been defined in other programs or systems. Clearly this should help us to build systems quicker as well as better, since the components should already be tried and tested.

How do we know OO works?
There is now more than ten years of experience of this style of programming, and we can see the results. For example, there exists an integrated word processing, spreadsheet and graphics system where a spreadsheet can be developed, pasted into a word processing document and still be modified even while it is inside the word processing document.

For example, a few years ago, everyone developing a new Apple Macintosh application had to start from scratch, because even though all of the window and menu management looked much the same from application to application there were sufficient differences that programmers found it more convenient to build such management routines out of lower level primitives. Since the provision of MacApp, which implements windows and window controls as objects, most people's convenient development path is just to add a few of their own routines to MacApp.

Here is a new user of MacApp talking: 'This is the first time since I discovered the Macintosh and switched from FORTH to C that the *feel* of programming has been completely transformed for me'. 'The learning curve is long and steep [but] absolutely worth it' (Johnson, 1993).

Does OO work with large systems?

Later in the same article, Johnson hints at the kind of difficulty which is enormously magnified in the development of large information systems, involving many people.

'It used to be that when I'd think of doing something I'd just do it … like building a machine from scratch, piece by handcrafted piece. Now, using MacApp, when I think of something that needs doing I conduct massive searches through megabytes of source code to figure out where its already been done, because no doubt somebody already thought of it, or something very much like it, and implemented it better than I ever could. Often I've spent an hour hunting around for the right place to insert some code, only to discover that I need [only] to set the value of some out-of-the-way Boolean deep inside an object's remote ancestor'.

The difficulty of using very large libraries, discussed in chapter 32, is but one of many barriers to using OO ideas in large systems. Although OO concepts have been proven in limited kinds of application, what has been lacking to date is a practical systems analysis and design methodology, supported by CASE technology, which shows how these concepts can be applied to the design of large information systems.

Our aim in the remainder of this book is to provide a systems development methodology for defining large database systems, which integrates the ideas of entity data modelling, entity behaviour modelling and OO programming, and thereby helps information systems analysts and designers to:

- define an information system as a set of reusable components
- develop a system by extending the use of existing components.

In terms of the 3-Schema Architecture, the systems development methodology is mainly concerned with the analysis of the conceptual model, leading to the design of the central database and database update routines.

Is an object the same as an entity?

Almost. Many people in the information systems community have taken the view that an object is exactly the same as an entity, but this is not quite true. We shall start off with this simple view, though it turns out that an entity may be decomposed into several parallel objects.

In part four we look at how to find the objects, define the relationships between objects, and extend well-established entity data modelling techniques to discover and record reusable objects or super-entities.

OO is like an extended entity modelling technique

Just as entity modelling cuts up a system's data into small packages based on data centred around real-world objects, OO programming cuts up a system's processing into small packages centreed on real-world objects, or on system-defined objects.

OO programming can be thought of as taking an entity model-like definition of what a program's data is and cutting up the program's processing, so each piece of code is tightly bound to the piece of data it relates to.

Almost all of the OO programming technology currently in use operates at the programming level. But it is at the analysis and design levels that the real end-user payoffs occur. However, even at the analysis and design levels, there are a number of design methods which make use of OO programming ideas to extend entity modelling.

In the UK, entity life history analysis in SSADM and JSD is an OO programming technique, although it needs to be extended to differentiate the methods (defined later) from the reasons why those methods are called. In the United States, Bob Brown has defined extensions to the IDEF entity modelling method with a notation to show entities, attributes, relationships and methods.

8.4 Two paradigms for OO design

OO design is characterised by not separating data and procedures; it regards them both as aspects of underlying constructs called 'objects' and it partitions the procedures and data in the system or program according to the objects which they describe.

OO ideas have their origins in the 1960s. They can be seen in the development of the notion of 'co-routines' (for example, Conway, 1963) and in informal ideas about the necessity of starting some programs 'in the middle' advanced by Mike Woodger in his contributions to the ALGOL-60 report (Naur, 1963). The earliest true OO programming system was SIMULA 67 (see Dahl 1966, also Dahl, Dijkstra and Hoare 1972). There are two modern OO approaches, both of which spring directly from SIMULA 67.

OO programming paradigm

This paradigm originated with Alan Kay at Xerox PARC. Its best known exemplar is Smalltalk-80 (see Goldberg, 1981). The key ideas are outlined in the next chapter .

OO programming is characterised by the code's being separated into a number of loosely coupled 'methods' which are invoked by message passing, and by the ability to classify objects and organise the object classes into a hierarchy with methods definable at any level in the hierarchy.

Its major advantage is that, since an object belongs to a whole hierarchy of classes, data and methods defined for classes at any level in the hierarchy are available for 'inheritance' by an object. The OO environment just needs to be told that such-and-such a method needs to be invoked on an object and it will work out which classes the object belongs to and find which method is actually to be used. Programs built this way seem very maintainable and extensible, and have large amounts of reusable functionality.

Control-structured paradigm

The control-structured paradigm is the basis of entity behaviour modelling as it is advanced in this book. This paradigm was first advanced by Jackson (1975) as a way of resolving what he called **interleaving clashes**. It has been very successful in Europe, initially in the programming domain and latterly in the systems domain. It is the main theme of JSD, and one of the main analysis components of SSADM. JSD is usually considered to be more suited to the development of real-time software, but SSADM is clearly aimed at information systems.

(This paragraph has been inserted after Keith Robinson's death. It may surprise some readers to learn that the entity event modelling techniques in SSADM and JSD were developed completely independently, without reference to each other. In 1977 Keith Robinson set out to combine JSP with principles of database design and to extend the 3-schema database architecture into software specification. By the time he presented an 'advanced systems design' course in 1979, Keith had already developed a recognisably 'object-oriented' analysis and design method, including a starvation and deadlock-free message passing protocol for inter-object communication. Something of Keith's control-structured approach to entity life history analysis was included in SSADM version 1, but almost a decade passed before a simplified version of his object interaction diagram was included in SSADM version 4. We developed these 'effect correspondence diagrams' for specifying database update routines where it can be assumed that a database management system will handle the roll-back of commit units and the prevention of deadlock. Where these assumptions are invalid, in some kinds of OO or distributed environment, designers may be better advised to employ something like Keith's original theory! This theory informs the discussion in chapter 18.)

Under the control-structured paradigm, the procedure body for an object is a single block of code structured using sequences, selections (IF THEN ... ELSE ... constructs) and iterations (DO WHILE ... constructs). This code communicates with the outside world only by reading and writing messages. The major advantage of the control-structured paradigm is that the **context** in which any part of the code is executed is extremely visible.

Control-structured or OO programming?

Looking at a stack entry object programmed via entity behaviour modelling, one knows almost without thinking about it that it cannot be popped unless it has been pushed.

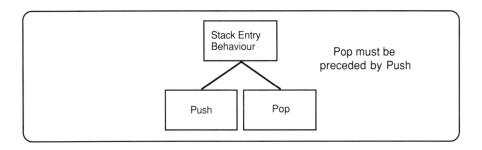

This diagram is not a full specification of stack behaviour. The nature of such a diagram is that it shows only valid events, so it should not include erroneous out-of-sequence pushes and pops, but it is too simple in that it records only one level of the stack and it shows no exceptional conditions. The need to model more complexity merely reinforces the following point.

OO programs are not as immediately understandable as programs built using the control-structured paradigm. You have to study the object state setting and testing to work out that you can't pop unless you've pushed.

This may sound trivial. And, indeed it is, if you're only looking at one object. If you only have to keep track of two or three facts, then doubling the number to four or six is fine; you can keep them all in short term memory; you don't cross a Miller number boundary (Miller, 1956).

But if you have to keep track of five or six facts simultaneously, you'll be killed by the extra complexity which is caused by having to work out what object coupling the state management implies. You haven't enough short-term memory.

When we're involved in systems design, we have often to keep track of several facts at the same level of discourse. Anything, no matter how trivial, which improves how we understand a single fact will have a disproportionate effect on our problem-solving ability.

Our claim is modest; it is that sometimes the control-structured paradigm is superior in this way. For a certain class of problem, namely those problems involved in analysing systems behaviour, it lets you think bigger thoughts than the OO programming paradigm does.

But the OO programming paradigm is also superior for some classes of programming and specification problems. The class hierarchy lets you think bigger thoughts in a different direction, because you only need concentrate on what's different between a new object class and one you already know about.

Chapter 9 looks in detail at OO programming ideas. Chapter 10 outlines where we shall be using OO ideas to inform the development of various system specification techniques.

Chapter 9

Object-oriented modelling ideas

For those new to object-orientation, this chapter outlines the key object-oriented ideas. It also begins to point to the extensions which are required before they can be brought together in a productive way with entity modelling ideas, for use by information system analysts and designers.

9.1 **Introduction**

This chapter is about general ideas and principles of object-oriented design. It is not about any specific object-oriented programming language (or OO environment, as we shall call it), nor does any one OO environment necessarily support all of the principles here. It prepares the ground for a synthesis of the two schools of thought, entity modelling and object-oriented design.

OO environments are mainly used by people designing 'production software' especially graphical user interface tools of one kind or another. One of the first authors in the field, Meyer (1988) drew on his experience in developing his own OO environment (Eiffel) to discuss a wide range of production software design issues. OO environments have also become popular in academic circles where students of computer science can borrow classes from each other.

Information systems designers do not view themselves as part of the production software community; most are unfamiliar with the language in which academic computer scientists converse. Nevertheless OO environments are gaining a foothold in the information systems community too. This is partly a result of the widespread adoption of graphical user interface tools which have been built in an OO environment. However we shall show in part five that the use of such tools in External Design is entirely separate from the concerns of the systems analyst building a Conceptual Model.

Scope

A systems analyst studying the object-oriented programming world may have difficulty distinguishing the ideas which are fundamental and helpful from those which are peripheral or unhelpful. Information systems have design characteristics which are unlike those of production software; in particular they store large volumes of persistent data; the result is that some object-oriented concepts turn out to be unimportant in information system design.

We shall find that some object-oriented ideas are indeed helpful to the analyst in building a Conceptual Model (see part four), but here they are used in a very different way from how they are used in programming GUI software. This chapter concentrates on introducing those object-oriented ideas which are the most important or the most relevant to information systems design, notably those to do with:

- Classes and their properties
- Class hierarchies and inheritance trees
- Object instances and their storage
- Inheritance and delegation mechanisms
- Aggregate objects and propagation of methods.

9.2 **A summary of object-oriented terms**

This section contains brief overview of the OO terms we use in this book.

Class

A class is a set of object instances which share the same properties. There are two basic kinds of property, 'instance variables' and 'methods'. To completely define a class, we must define its data view (all its instance variables) and its process view (all the methods which operate upon those attributes).

Suppose class has ten properties, four instance variables (labelled **v** below) and six methods. Here is an attempt to represent an object of this class by an informal picture.

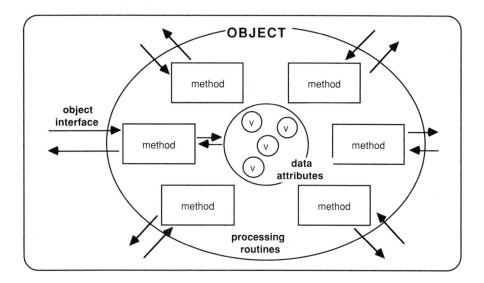

Instance variables or attributes

An object instance variable is simply a data item which represents an attribute of the object. There is little difficulty in defining what an instance variable is, because a data item is at the atomic level of specification, at the lowest level of reusability.

Methods

A method is a processing routine which belongs to an object; it acts on an input message, processes the instance variables and produces a response. Specifying an object's methods is relatively difficult. An unsolved mystery of object-oriented programming is how best to discover what the methods of an object are, and to define methods at the 'right' level of reusability. Part four of this book sheds some light on how this mystery may be resolved.

Encapsulation: of data and processes in an object

Perhaps the fundamental object-oriented idea is that the data and processing perspectives of an object are inseparable. This is called 'encapsulation'. The boundary around an object separates the processing of the object from its interface to other objects.

Encapsulation is related to the more general idea of 'information hiding', which means that the processing routines which access the data attributes of an object are somehow enclosed with that data. The only way to get at the data of an object is through its processing routines. The data and the processing routines together make up the object.

Encapsulation in system specification

Encapsulation can be represented in the way a system is specified. This view has taken hold of methodologists in recent years. It is widely proposed that all the processes which enquire upon or change a data object should be specified along with that object. So the main idea behind an object-oriented analysis and design method is that a system should be constructed by specifying (in co-ordination) both the data-oriented and process-oriented views of the objects in the system. Encapsulation in system specification is fundamental to the approach described in part four.

Encapsulation in system implementation

Encapsulation can be implemented in the way that objects in a system behave at run-time. It means the data items in the data area of an object can only be created or changed during calls to the object. These data items cannot be created or changed between calls to the object, by any other object. There is no way in which an object can look at the data area of another object directly, but there is an indirect way, one object can send a message to another asking it for information.

Encapsulation in system implementation requires some kind of OO environment and has little impact on this guide outside of chapter 18, where implementation mechanisms are discussed.

Objects as long running processes

The view of an object as a long running process (or 'finite state automaton' to be exact) is a very important idea. It means that given the current state of an object and the input message it is to process, it is possible to specify or predict the new state of the object and any output message it will produce. Each object must be in one of a finite number of states. You can specify all the possible states of an object and the transitions between them. Each method invocation occurs in the context of the long running process; it must have a prior state and a successor state. States are not discussed further in this chapter, but feature strongly in chapters 13 to 18.

Composite and aggregate objects

There is a set of OO ideas to do with modelling groups of closely related objects and implementing them. The main purpose for specifying an aggregate object is to automate the propagation of a method from the aggregate object to its component objects. See the end of this chapter for more detail.

Method specification

Method specification is not straightforward. Some relevant concepts are listed below and explained later using examples.

Method body step

The method body is a procedure composed of method body steps, or distinct executable operations and conditions. See 15.3 for what a method body looks like.

Propagation of methods

Propagation is a mechanism whereby when one object is invoked to perform a method, the same method is automatically invoked in related objects. Propagation of methods is commonly associated with composite objects. If a normalised relation (an aggregation of attributes dependent on the same key) is implemented as one object type, then it is clear that physical database operations like create, read, write and delete object will effect all the attributes at once.

However, we are more interested in specifying propagation of methods among larger composites of objects in the Conceptual Model. For example, if Order is a composite object made up of several Stock Item Reservation objects, then the method to cancel an Order must cancel all the Stock Item Reservations. This kind of composition is very short-lived compared with the long life of the stored data. In fact it lasts only for the duration of the event which triggers the methods. It is better to model the propagation by specifying **composite methods** in the process model rather than composite objects in the data model. See the end of this chapter for more detail.

Composite method

A set of methods operating on one or more object types, all triggered by the same event or super-event.

Preconditions

The preconditions of a method define the state an object must be in for that method to work correctly. They may be specified in terms of valid prior states. They are usually coded at the start of a method body as some kind of fail test or quit condition.

Obligations

The obligations of a method are what a 'client' of the object must do before invoking the method. They usually include validating the syntax of the message or parameters the method needs in order to function correctly. They may include ensuring the object is called only after some other object within a defined sequence of object invocations. They are a function of the code which invokes a method rather than the method itself.

Equivalent and polymorphic methods

These are ways of redefining a method in different ways, either to do the same job more efficiently or to do variations of a job. They are discussed in section 9.6.

Class hierarchy ideas

There is a set of OO ideas to do with modelling super-type and sub-type object classes and implementing instances of a class.

Class hierarchy

A directed graph in which super-type nodes are divided into sub-type nodes. The super-type node provides a place to record properties common to all its sub-types. It is assumed that a type lower down in the hierarchy has all the properties of super-types above it in the hierarchy.

Inheritance tree

Same as Class Hierarchy. The idea of a class hierarchy or inheritance tree is important in systems specification.

Inheritance mechanism

A specific implementation mechanism by which an OO environment may avoid storing instances of super-classes. The OO environment implements an object instance as the lowest sub-type it can be matched to, extended with properties inherited from its super-types.

   The idea of the inheritance mechanism is relatively unimportant. Chapter 12 defines alternative implementation mechanisms for conventional database management systems such as 'reverse inheritance' and 'delegation'.

9.3 An example of a class

The example in this section is not meant to be representative of typical objects in an information system. Plenty is said about information systems later. The example is intended to illustrate some object-oriented ideas in a simple way. Not all of these ideas are as relevant to information systems as they are to the example which follows.

   Suppose a graphics application is to be programmed, to help users create and move quadrilaterals around on a screen. To create a quadrilateral the user will:

   select a tool for drawing quadrilaterals
   point to where the first corner (a) should be, click
   point to where the second corner (b) should be, click
   point to where the third corner (c) should be, click
   point to where the fourth corner (d) should be, and click once more.

   It will be necessary to define a class of object Quadrilateral. This means defining both its instance variables or attributes and its methods.

Instance variables or attributes

An instance variable is a data item type associated with a specific class. In the entity modelling world, instance variables are often called 'attributes'. As the first step towards harmony with entity modelling, we are going to use the term 'attributes'.

Amongst the object's attributes is its 'identifier'. The identifier of an object instance cannot be altered, since it maintains the continuity of identity of the object, distinguishing one instance of an object from another.

Illustration

For example, we could define a Quadrilateral in terms of an identifier and eight attributes:

    Quadrilateral attributes
        Quadrilateral identifier
        Corner a, x and y coordinates
        Corner b, x and y coordinates
        Corner c, x and y coordinates
        Corner d, x and y coordinates

Other attributes which can be calculated from the above (such as the length of side a, the angle of side a-b, the perpendicular height from one side to the opposite side) are known as 'derived data' and need not be stored.

Methods

A method is a tiny process, associated with a specific class. There are two kinds of method: enquiry methods (which do not change the object instance in any way) and update methods (which alter the value of one or more attributes of the object).

Illustration

In our example, to allow the user to manipulate Quadrilaterals we might define three update methods and an enquiry method:

    New (a,b,c,d)
        creates a quadrilateral object with corners at points (a,b,c,d)
    Move (x,y)
        tells a quadrilateral object to move itself x units horizontally and y vertically
    Draw
        asks the object to draw itself
    Area
        asks the object to calculate and return its area.

Method invocation

A method is invoked by sending a message to an object instance. Object 99, a quadrilateral, sent the message Move (-3,+2), will relocate its corners and redraw itself.

Method body

The procedure defined to implement a method is called the method body. The various method bodies of an object *are* the definition of the object, much more so than the instance variables. The method bodies specified for a quadrilateral define (or encapsulate) what it means for an object to be a quadrilateral.

In defining a method body, we must define all the data items involved. We can zoom in on part of the earlier picture to show the kinds of data item which may be associated with an individual method.

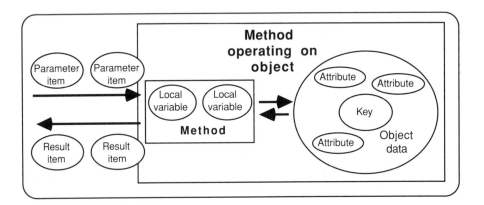

Four kinds of variable

A method always refers to or updates one or more **attributes** of the object. One or a group of the attributes is its 'key', the identifier which distinguishes one instance of class from another. A method always produces one or more **result items**, if only 'OK' or 'Fail'. A method may require one or more **parameter items** to be input, but it may require no parameters, only a trigger, especially if it is an enquiry method. A method might need one or more **local variables**, private to the method; but it turns out that very few of the methods defined for maintaining an information systems' database require any local variables.

Information hiding

How a method works should be invisible to the user of that method. This accords with the principle of 'information hiding', which states that the complexity of a module's workings should be concealed from its user.

As well as being useful to define variations in user-visible behaviour, classes can be used to define variations in implementation. Because a method body is invisible to any program invoking an object's method, external routines can be prevented from becoming dependent upon implementation details.

9.4 **A class hierarchy**

The problem that object-oriented programming is trying to solve is how to produce programs which are variations on existing ones. Variations in programs are primarily introduced because a variation in what the data is about becomes important to the end-user (e.g. the *New* method below). But in production software, variations may be introduced to provide more efficient implementation mechanisms (e.g. the *Area* method in section 9.5).

The designer can represent variations on a theme using a class hierarchy, as introduced in chapter 4. A class hierarchy may be developed from the bottom-up by generalisation of similar sub-types as we propose in chapter 12, or from the top-down as in the following example.

<u>Illustration</u>

A user of the quadrilateral package who mostly creates squares may complain about having to specify all four corners (a,b,c,d), since it would be easier for a square to specify only the top left-hand corner (a) and the length of a side (l).

You can imagine a hierarchy of super-classes and sub-classes, which define more and more specific kinds of quadrilateral, for which you might want more and more specific variations of the *New* method.

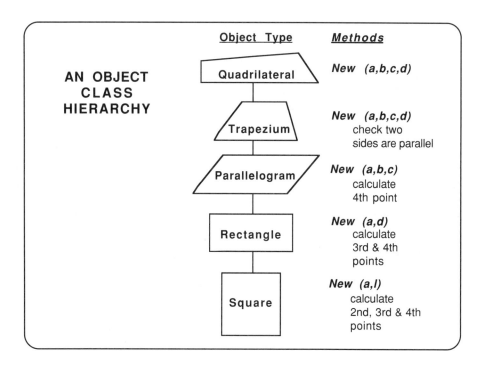

Apart from the *New* method, for other purposes, a square is just a variety of quadrilateral. Once a square has been created, all of the general quadrilateral methods outlined above can be used without variation. This notion of things being like other things, except for some more specific properties which have to be handled in a special way, is fundamental to the operation of object-oriented programming.

9.5 Inheritance as a modelling concept

Class hierarchy as inheritance tree
We could define a unique set of attributes and methods for each class in the class hierarchy. Since this would involve repetition of attributes and methods in several places, this would be rather clumsy. To save this repetition, a class hierarchy may be further defined as an 'inheritance tree' in which a sub-class automatically shares all the properties of its super-class.

Illustration
We don't have to define a *Move* or *Draw* method for a square, since it inherits the method defined for a Quadrilateral. All sub-classes of Quadrilateral act as if Quadrilateral's *Move* and *Draw* methods belong directly to them. Similarly we don't have to define any attributes.

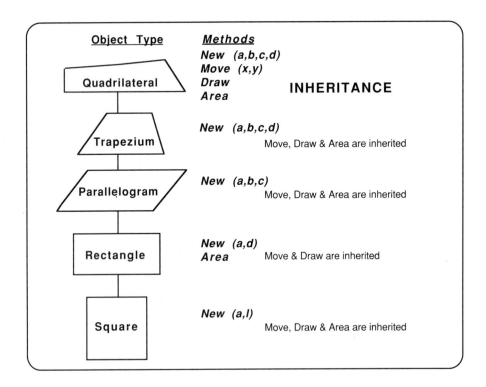

Notice that all Quadrilaterals have unique *New* methods, but there are only two *Area* methods (Rectangle has its own *Area* method, which is then inherited by Square). These are examples of 'overriding' and 'redefinition'.

9.6 **Equivalent and polymorphic methods**

A method may be redefined in two different ways: first, as an equivalent method which so does the same job; second, as a polymorphic method which does a different job. Equivalent and polymorphic methods are mainly of benefit in production software and at the programming level, and are usually of little interest to the information systems analyst.

Equivalent methods in different object types do exactly the same job in different ways; they are usually designed to give a performance benefit. Polymorphic methods in different object types do different jobs in response to the same message; they may be designed to save the programmer having to remember different function calls.

Overriding and redefinition are the devices used to create equivalent and polymorphic methods. An OO programmer may define properties of a sub-class object which **override** those the object inherits from its super-classes. **Redefinition** is the feature of object-oriented design by which a sub-class object may override any inherited property, replacing it by an equivalent or polymorphic property of its own.

Equivalent methods
Methods, operating on different classes in one inheritance tree, are equivalent if they produce identical results, given identical sets of input parameters and given object instances with equivalent attribute values.

Illustration
For example consider the Area method for calculating the area of a Quadrilateral. When operating on a rectangle, these two methods are equivalent:

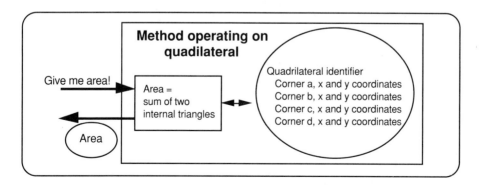

Since the method for calculating the area of a quadrilateral is a difficult and time-consuming task (note we have been superficial here, ignoring how the area of internal triangles is calculated from the attributes listed above), we would clearly prefer to use simpler and faster formula where possible, as shown below.

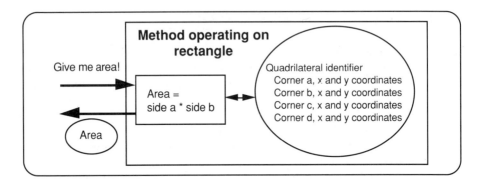

Here the method (give me area) is the same, but the method body is different. To summarise the example:

Object type	Method Body
Quadrilateral	Area = Sum of internal triangles
Rectangle	Area = Side a * Side b

Equivalent attributes

The object's attribute values must be equivalent, but need not be identical. Although redefinition is almost always discussed in terms of methods, attributes may also be redefined. Of course, where attributes are redefined, then most if not all methods will have to be redefined as well.

Attributes belonging to different classes in one inheritance tree are equivalent if all equivalent methods produce identical results, given identical sets of input parameters. For a square, you could reduce the list of attributes by defining only the coordinates of opposite corners:

Quadrilateral attributes
   Quadrilateral identifier
   Corner a, x and y coordinates
   Corner c, x and y coordinates

The dangers of redefinition

Even where restricted to equivalent methods and attributes, redefinition is a dangerous facility. It is tempting for an individual to define new sub-classes, and redefine methods, for their own arcane purposes, leading to a messy and cumbersome design. Some kind of data manager is needed to control the development of a class hierarchy.

Worse still, redefinition can be used to destroy the notion of a class hierarchy. One method can be overridden by a slightly or totally different method. Calling this 'polymorphism' does not make the idea any more controllable or systematic.

Polymorphic methods

Polymorphic methods are not strictly equivalent, but they ought to be equivalent at some higher level of abstraction. Polymorphic methods in different object types do different jobs in response to the same invocation message.

It can be argued that redefinition to create polymorphic methods undermines the notion of a class hierarchy. Meyer (1988) says 'Unrestrained polymorphism would be incompatible with the notion of type'. He suggests it should be limited to methods which can be inherited. The trouble is, it is always possible to invent an abstract super-type, simply for the purpose of providing an inheritance route for polymorphic methods.

Polymorphic methods may be designed to save the programmer having to remember different function calls. For example suppose discounts are calculated as different percentages in Customer Account and Supplier Account. What an OO programmer may do here is create a super-type called Account, then declare an 'empty method' in this super-type called Calculate Discount, then redefine this method in each of the sub-types to become the method appropriate for that object type.

While this may be useful to a programmer, it doesn't seem to give much benefit to the systems analyst. The systems analyst still has to specify various methods separately (e.g. Calculate Customer Discount and Calculate Supplier Discount). Useful examples in information systems design are rare.

However, there is an analogy to polymorphism in the methodology. Each effect correspondence diagram specifies those objects which receive the same message, that is, the same event. Actually this is not completely true. Some entities in an effect correspondence diagram may not require the whole event data, and a few entities may require additional data passed from another entity. However, it is true enough for this discussion of polymorphism to say that an effect correspondence diagram specifies the set of entity types which are polymorphic, that is, must respond with different methods to the same event message.

We do not recommend that a composite or super-type entity is created for each event type. For information systems, an effect correspondence diagram is a more appropriate form of specification for the entities affected by an event type.

9.7 **Multiple inheritance**

If two or more class hierarchies are combined together, the result is a network data structure in which an object may inherit from two different ancestors. This is called 'multiple inheritance'. While it is useful when the two ancestral paths contain *different properties* (methods and instance variables) which are inherited by the common sub-class, it causes complications where different definitions of *the same property* can be inherited by the sub-class.

<u>Illustration</u>
Does Square inherit its Area method from Rectangle or Rhombus (which inherits it from Quadrilateral)? The answer doesn't matter very much if the methods are equivalent.

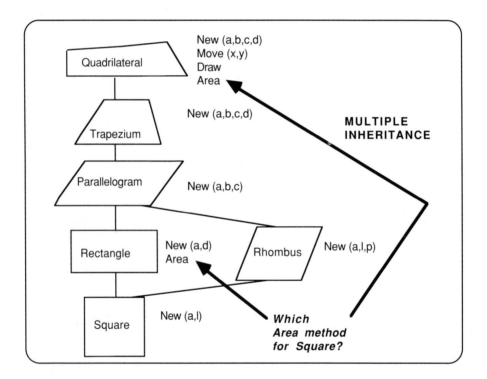

Jacobson (1991) says 'The use of multiple inheritance is controversial within the object-oriented community'. Objections seem to arise from four origins. First, some OO environments do not support multiple inheritance. We can reject this objection out of hand since it puts the cart before the horse.

Second, multiple inheritance makes a mess of any attempt to describe the world in a single hierarchical structure. This is to be so frightened of facing up to the complexity of the world that almost nothing of real interest can be done. Multiple inheritance is an inevitable consequence of any attempt to model the real-world. So if an information system is to model reality, its specification languages must handle the concept of multiple inheritance

Third, studying even small examples of multiple inheritance soon reveals that class hierarchies may be unstable, they may have to be revised to accommodate new classes. The evolution of class hierarchies is a real concern (see chapter 12), but it does not in itself suggest that multiple inheritance is a sign of bad practice in analysis or design.

Finally, there is the concern that the inheritance route may be corrupted if overriding by polymorphic methods is allowed in the class hierarchy, but this is a worry even where multiple inheritance does not occur.

9.8 **Physical data storage of object instances**

There are two kinds of information about objects in class hierarchy. There is information about the properties of the class and about the properties of object instances. Object instances have two kinds of property: methods which exist only at execution time and instance variables which persist between method executions. The variables must be stored somewhere, using some kind of a database management system.

A typical OO environment stores all objects' instance variables in main memory; object instances only exist while the program is running and disappear when it stops. A conventional database management system stores object instances which persist in a physical data structure for days,weeks or years.

A typical OO environment does not store object instances any way constrained by the data structure or inheritance tree. So changing the logical data structure, amending the way classes are related together, requires no amendment or relocation of the stored data. A conventional database management system usually stores object instances in a physical data structure which is derived from the logical data structure. For database efficiency, detail objects are clustered around the master object to which they are related. This gives a performance advantage, since related objects can be found on the same 'block' of disk storage, at the expense of costs on changing the logical data structure.

The table summarises how two storage and implementation mechanisms map onto two different modelling ideas.

| | | Modelling concept | |
		Class hierarchy (type-subtype)	Association (master-detail)
Implementation mechanism	Inheritance tree	OK (inheritance)	**Unreasonable**
	Key-based relationship	OK (delegation)	OK (foreign key)

It is easy to get confused here, because it is difficult to separate the thoughts and words to with modelling from the thoughts and words to with implementation mechanisms.

9.9 **Inheritance as an implementation mechanism**

Although 'inheritance' is often used loosely as another word for a class hierarchy, OO enthusiasts usually mean more than this; they mean to imply an OO environment implementation mechanism which does not store instances of an 'abstract super-class'.

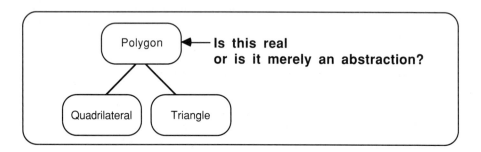

Abstract super-classes

It is impossible to create an instance of an abstract super-class. The super-class is merely an abstraction, a place to record properties which are common to the sub-classes. So given the above class hierarchy, polygon instances could not be created; only quadrilaterals and triangles could be realised as an object instances.

How the inheritance mechanism works

In our example, whenever the user draws a quadrilateral on the screen, at the same time the OO environment must create it as a class of quadrilateral object (typically somewhere in main memory), storing the values of its attribute instances, including its key and its class (discussed below):

Object data
  Object key   e.g. 99
  Class   e.g. rectangle
  Object attributes

Object key

To distinguish one instance of an object from another, OO environments store a unique identifying attribute or key within each instance of class. The key of an object cannot be altered, since it is the identity of the object.

An object's key must be allocated (by the user or more usually in an OO environment by the system) when the object is first created. The object's data is stored in a location which is addressable using this key. The key can be used to retrieve the object whenever it is to undergo some process.

Object base class

An OO environment must store the **base class** of the object instance, along with its key and other attributes. The base class is the lowest level class to which it has been defined as belonging, e.g. rhombus. In some OO environments the base class may be invisible, not accessible to the programmer. However, the base class must be used by the OO environment itself to cross-reference an instance of an object to the class of that object, as described in the inheritance tree.

Execution of a method on an object instance

Suppose a message is sent requiring invocation of a method 'M' upon an object whose identifying key is 99. The OO environment would:

- retrieve the object's instance variable values, using the key 99
- find the class in the inheritance tree, using the stored class
- identify the relevant method* for that class
- execute the method body on the instance variable values
- store the changed instance variables.

* That is, the method named M associated with that class of object, or if it has no method named M, the method named M in its nearest super-class.

Storing object instances independently of the data structure

A typical OO environment does not store object instances in any way constrained by the data structure, or inheritance tree. Each object is stored separately from any other, in a location determined by the operating system and addressable via its unique key.

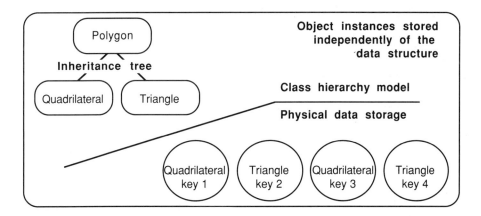

So an OO environment is insensitive to at least some kinds of change in a class hierarchy. For example, the inheritance tree can be modified by inserting a new class of object without any influence on the data stored about individual objects.

Using one key range

Another mechanism for increasing the flexibility of the data structure is to allocate each object a key drawn from a single range. So to locate an object you need know only the value of its key attribute, you do not need to know its class. The main benefit is that if the data structure is altered, there is no need to amend the key attribute (or foreign key attribute) of any object. For example, Smalltalk is an OO environment where there is only one kind of key, a single range of identifiers, for all the objects in a system.

Database management systems

Some more conventional database environments now provide something like the object-oriented mechanism for storing sub-class object instances. Using an inheritance tree, properties of ancestral class(es) are copied into the descendant object instance. For example, a car would be stored as a single object instance, inheriting all the properties of a vehicle (which is an abstract super-class).

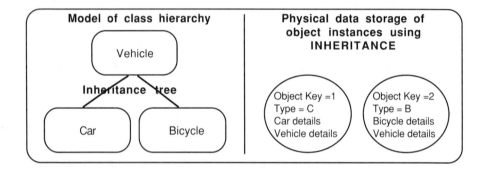

9.10 Delegation as an implementation mechanism

Real super-classes

It is possible to create an instance of a real super-class. So given the above class hierarchy, a polygon instance could be created either instead of, or as well as, a quadrilateral or triangle. There are three alternative explanations of this.

The real super-class is an *additional, unspecified sub-class.* An instance of a real super-class may be created because … it is an additional kind of sub-class to those shown in the class hierarchy as sub-classes. Thus a polygon instance would be a polygon with more than four sides. This is a poor explanation. To accommodate an additional kind of sub-class, the class hierarchy should be extended with a new sub-class.

The real super-class is a *parallel object to the sub-class.* An instance of a real super-class may be created because … it is the parallel realisation in a super-class instance, of the parts common to different sub-classes. Thus when a quadrilateral or triangle instance is created, a polygon instance will be created as well, carrying information common to a quadrilateral or triangle. This is the idea behind 'delegation', which can be used in place of the inheritance mechanism, an idea to which we shall return shortly.

The real super-class is an *unknown sub-class*. An instance of a real super-class may be created because ... the user does not know or care which sub-class it is. Thus a polygon may be created by a user unaware of whether it is a triangle or quadrilateral. This is a valuable idea because its effect is that the class hierarchy may be extended with new sub-classes, without any effect on objects which have already been stored. It cannot be made to work if the inheritance mechanism is used, but it can if 'delegation' is used (see later).

By the way, an OO-environment may permit real and abstract super-classes to be mixed in the same hierarchy.

Class hierarchy implementation mechanism: delegation

If a database environment does not provide automated inheritance mechanisms, it will certainly provide an equally valid implementation mechanism called delegation, where each level of the class hierarchy can be realised as a record in the database.

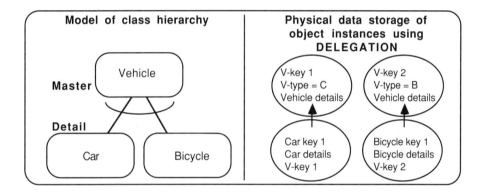

Delegation means, in the example, that a car would be stored at one and the same time as two record instances, a car and a vehicle (the latter is a therefore a 'real' super-class).

9.11 Implementation of an association

The reaction of an information systems designer to what has been described so far might be, 'This is all very well, but class hierarchies are not the main feature of the real world which I have to model. What concerns me far more is how to model and implement associations between objects, such as one department which employs many employees'.

Given an association, we shall use the convention of calling the one object the detail and the other object the master. Various other terms have been used elsewhere, for example:

master	= supplier	= owner	= parent
detail	= client	= member	= child

Association implementation mechanism: key-based relationship

An association between master and detail objects is usually implemented, in both OO environments and relational database management systems, via what we call a **key-based relationship**. Instances of the detail class will contain a foreign key, or pointer, referring to an instance of the master class to which it is linked by an association.

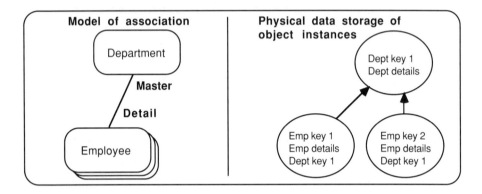

It is efficient and effective to use a key-based relationship to implement an association. We have heard it suggested that the inheritance mechanism might be used to implement an association, but this is not a very helpful suggestion. It means the department will become merely an abstract object, and all of the department data will be duplicated in each employee object; in other words the data will be unnormalised, resulting in all the consequent update anomalies which are avoided by normalising data in the first place.

All database management systems support this kind of mechanism. Actually, records in a database may be connected to each other by means of indexes, tables or chains of pointers, where these pointers may be physical database locations rather than logical keys. But these deeper levels of implementation need not concern us here; we shall concentrate on the use of logical keys, as a typical relational database management system does (at least on the surface).

Using multiple key ranges

In information systems, each class of object usually has its own kind of key, its own range of identifiers. So to identify an object one must know first its class, then the value of its key. Giving each class its own range of keys has practical advantages; to anticipate points taken up in chapter 10:

- there is no bottleneck in the key allocation process
- natural identifiers, understood by users, can be employed
- compound and hierarchical keys can be made from 'foreign' keys
- minimal extra space is needed for system-generated keys.

9.12 **Aggregate objects in data modelling**

Most OO authors draw an analogy between aggregation and some kind of entity data modelling concept. Rumbaugh *et al.* (1991) say that composition is a 'special form of association not an independent concept' in which the objects are 'tightly bound' together. Hughes (1992) says that the master object is an 'abstraction' from the detail objects. He defines three forms of data-oriented aggregation:

- aggregation of properties around an object   *
- aggregation of one-from-many types   †
- aggregation of one-from-many instances.   †

We find it convenient to define three different forms of composition and aggregation. Below we show the correspondences with the above list by means of annotations:

- aggregate object   *
- composite object   †
- composite method.

We define an **aggregate object** as a restricted type of composite object containing a set of parallel objects all dependent on the same primary key. So an aggregate object is fully normalised and may not include lists or repeating data. This corresponds with the first of Hughes' definitions. He quotes as an example the aggregation of 'attributes of an object to form an entire object'. Consider the data items in a record.

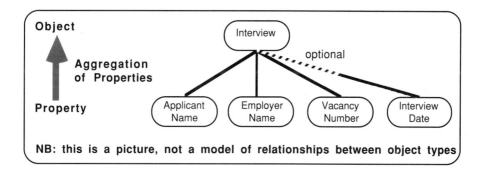

There are three ways such an aggregate might be implemented. You could turn the attributes into operational masters as described in chapter 11.

You could implement the aggregate object as one relational database record. In this case, physical database management operations like read, write and delete record will be propagated from the aggregate to all its components; but note that these operations are to do with database management, they are not part of the real world model. See 'what the methods are not' in chapter 13.

Third and most interestingly, you could pair off each attribute with the key of the main object, so each attribute becomes a **parallel aspect**. Chapter 12 suggests this can have practical uses in avoiding contention problems, in database distribution and application integration.

Aggregation of one-from-many types

People commonly say aggregate objects are composed from objects related by *part of* relationships. This kind of aggregate object is only weakly centred on the idea of identity and is therefore fragile. This diagram is Hughes' example, except we've added the Audio System to illustrate the possibility of an optional component part.

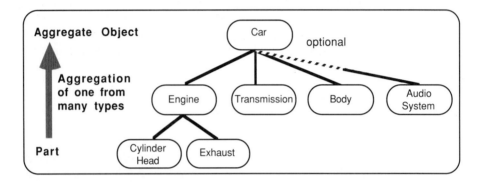

Treating Car as an aggregate object may be unsatisfactory. Each part may be labelled with a unique identifier. The audio system may be stolen (*will* be stolen more likely).The engine may be built before the car; later it may be fitted in another car.

If events like Move Car, Park Car and Sell Car trigger the propagation of methods from the aggregate to its components, this is better modelled in the conceptual process model than in the data model.

9.13 Composite objects in data modelling

We define a **composite object** as a set of parallel or nested objects sharing or inheriting the same identity. A composite object need not be second or third normal form, it may include lists or repeating data.

In the External Design there are composite objects such as windows and reference lists. A GUI software design theory needs to handle composite objects. But where is the idea useful in the Conceptual Model? It does not sit well in the entity data model.

Hughes suggests that in the following example, Reservation may be regarded as a composite object made of the object types Person and Flight.

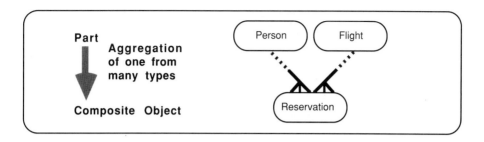

Treating Reservation as a composite object seems unsatisfactory. If Person and Flight are not modelled as distinct objects, then methods on a Reservation which affect the encompassed objects (say, changing a Person's address) would lead to update anomalies. If events such as Make Reservation and Cancel Reservation trigger the propagation of methods from the composite to its components, this is better modelled in the conceptual process model than in the data model.

Composition of one-from-many instances

This may be viewed as master with a set of details, where the whole shares the same identity. There is an analogous entity data modelling idea, that is the idea of a Dependent Master in a Sum of Relationship, shown in the top-left box in the four-way classification of relationships introduced in chapter 11.

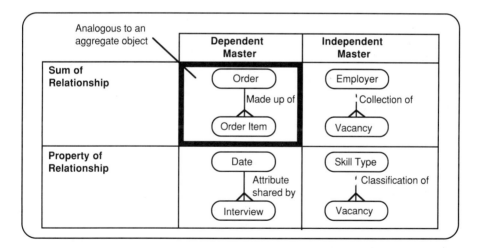

We don't find that thinking of Order as a composite object is useful. Usually Order Items need to be identified individually so they can be added, altered or cancelled one-by-one. It is true that the delete operation may be propagated from the composite object to its components, but this operation is to do with database management rather than the real-world model. See 'what the methods are not' in chapter 13.

If events in the Conceptual Model such as Delivery and Invoice trigger the propagation of methods from the Order to its Order Items, this is better modelled in the conceptual process model than in the data model.

9.14 **Composite methods in process modelling**

Remember the purpose of defining a composite object is to model a situation where a method on a composite object is propagated to its component objects. For example, if a Polygon is a composite object made up of several Point objects, then the operation Move Polygon must trigger several Move Point operations. In our own CASE tool, composite objects on the screen must behave in unison, so operations such as Move and Delete must be propagated from the object the user has selected to all the objects it contains or is connected to.

Does propagation occur in information systems?

Yes, but for most events in an information system, the method in the composite object would be different from the methods in the component objects. The method to cancel an Order must trigger a method in each Order Item to cancel it, but it will for example set the state variable to a different value, so simple propagation isn't enough.

What is the equivalent idea in information systems?

Composite objects do appear in our conceptual modelling techniques, but in the conceptual process model rather than the data model. We propose that every event is a transient composite object and fires a composite method. We define a **composite method** as a set of methods operating on one or more object types, all triggered by the same event or super-event. We record a composite method in the domain of process modelling rather than data modelling, in an effect correspondence diagram. See chapters 13, 17 and 18 for more detail.

Why not show composite methods in the data model?

There is a mismatch of composite method and object lifetimes. Composition features strongly in OO environments which have been developed in the context of graphical user interfaces, where all the objects on the screen live about the same length of time. It is not hard to imagine both the objects and their composite methods being specified in one data model. Unfortunately, in information systems, composition is usually very short-lived compared with the long life of the stored data. To show all the necessary short-lived compositions in the data model, it would be necessary to include each event in the data model, perhaps as a box surrounding the objects which it effects. A composite which is created to enable propagation of methods needs to last only for the duration of the event which triggers the methods. For information systems, it is better to model such composition in the specification of events.

Chapter 10

Using OO ideas in large information systems

For those who think that OO programming (because it delivers benefits at the programming level) will deliver the benefits that users of large information systems need, this chapter outlines the reasons for why OO programming is not enough, and concludes that what is needed is a synthesis of OO programming ideas with entity modelling ideas.

10.1 **What is different about information systems?**

We are primarily interested in the problems facing the designers of large multi-user information systems. There has always been an uncomfortable distance between production software engineers and computer scientists on the one hand and information systems analysts and designers on the other. They barely recognise each other's problems. This section highlights three fundamental features of information systems which set them apart from production software:

- the public rather than private nature of specification
- the large numbers of objects
- the multi-threading of processes.

Private levels of discourse

If you consider the class hierarchy shown in chapter 9, you will see that the objects are drawn from different levels of discourse, public and private. What the user wants to say is simply, 'give me the area of this quadrilateral'.

The fact there are many different kinds of quadrilateral is entirely irrelevant to the user. The only reason this data structure has been developed is for internal design performance, to speed up the programs which deliver the result of certain enquiry methods.

This is not a very good example because the differences between different kinds of quadrilateral are visible to the user. A better example would be if what the users perceive and talk about in public about as Polygons are actually made out of Points at the private implementation level. So a Polygon is a composite object, implemented in terms of a different kind of base object altogether.

This example·is more typical of OO programming. Composite objects and inheritance trees are used to represent deeper and deeper levels of implementation, more and more refined implementations of what is known to the user as a single concept.

Public level of discourse

Information system data structures are not like this. All the objects in the Conceptual Model are at the same level of discourse. In fact they are all at the public level (note that we are not talking about access rights based on authority or security here). The user may wish to ask questions directly about any of the objects in the data structure.

More than this, the user may require each class of object to exhibit substantially different behaviours. For example, we might introduce an update method which is applicable only to squares, having no equivalent method for any other quadrilateral:

Square reshape method
        'redraw top right corner of square at position x,y'.

Let us say this method is unique to squares. It is not inherited from above (from rectangle). In information systems, a method is usually unique to its class. This limits the value of inheritance trees as a means of increasing the reusability of system components.

Large numbers of objects

The very usefulness of a computerised information system is at least partly related to how often data objects of one type are repeated. The more objects there are, the greater the need for an information system to record and control them. One-to-many associations are not a strong element in the world of OO programming, but they are commonplace in large information systems. It is via one-to-many relationships that systems grow to be large, since at each level of the data structure the number of objects is multiplied. Large numbers of objects cause problems. They create the need for efficient data storage and retrieval devices and database management systems. They make difficulties for database designers.

Multi-threading of processes

Harking back to the 'primacy of data' principle, repetition of processes is caused by repetition of data objects. To create, update or display one instance of a data object, we need to repeat a process which is designed to handle any instance of that data object type.

Data object instances may be repeated serially, that is, iterated one after another. Serial repetition of a data object may be handled by repeatedly adding each new object as a detail of a one-to-many relationship in a data structure. But if only the current data object is of interest, then it may overwrite the previous one. Serial repetition of the associated process is naturally handled by iteration, either within a program or within the operating schedule.

Data object instances may be repeated in parallel, that is, alongside each other at the same time. Parallel repetition of data objects may be handled by storing them on separate processors (not our concern here) or else by storing them in a one-to-many relationship in a data structure under the management of one processor (very much our concern here). To handle parallel data objects, the associated process must be repeated in parallel. This **multi-threading** or 'interleaving clash' is at the heart of two difficulties in the design of large systems.

First, to implement multi-threaded processes using only one copy of the program, we must separate the program from the **state vector** (or set of local variables) it maintains. Each state vector must be stored on backing store and retrieved when an input message arrives which is relevant to it. The larger the number of multi-threaded processes, the more important it becomes to store and retrieve data objects efficiently. We pick up this theme in the next section.

Second, multiple users of the system may be in contention for the same data and may interfere with each other's work. Multi-user controls are considered in chapter 24.

10.2 **Five things to be provided by a DBMS**

Whilst OO programming delivers the benefits it claims at the programming level, the benefits that users of large administrative data processing systems need will not be provided by OO programming alone. Some reasons for this are to do with the need to manage large databases in an efficient manner. Others are to do with the need for a more sophisticated methodology.

There follows a summary of ways in which the OO approach, as it is revealed through programming languages, must be complemented by database management systems.

The database (or file-store) must be managed

To date, applications which have been implemented in an OO programming language tend to be at the operating system end of software development. They also tend to be concerned with objects close to the heart of the computer system, such as stacks, lists, shapes on screens, etc. OO programming languages are very much biased towards the kind of application where the objects are:

- few enough (up to thousands) to be stored in main memory
- temporary (alive only during the execution of a program)
- related in a simple structure of classes and sub-classes.

By way of contrast, the designer of an information system usually deals with objects which are:

- sufficient in number (millions or billions) to require backing store
- permanent (alive between executions of a program)
- related in a·complex data structure.

Since the population of objects in an information system will be too large for main store memory (this may be viewed as a side-effect of one-to-many relationships) and will need to be stored between executions of the system processes, a complete theory of OO database design must include how to manage the storage and retrieval of objects to/from backing store.

Database management must be efficient

Typically, an OO program stores all the required data about object classes and instances in main memory. Object instances only exist while the program is running; they disappear when it stops. There is almost no concern about speed of data retrieval.

Typically, an information system stores all the required data about object instances on backing store. Object instances must be stored while the program is not running. There is considerable concern about speed of data retrieval.

Whatever we do with OO ideas must capitalise on what modern database management systems can offer, rather than negate them.

Deadlock must be prevented

Given the notion of a commit unit (see next section), there is possibility that two commit units may be executed in parallel and compete for access to the same objects. The situation known as deadlock, where two commit units grind to a halt, each waiting for an object to be released by the other, must be prevented from happening or reversed when it does happen.

Allocation of user-friendly keys must be permitted

To distinguish one object instance from another, systems must assign a unique key to each object. To map each object instance onto its real-world counterpart, systems analysts must assign a user-friendly key to each object. Keys in information systems are not just an implementation mechanism; keys are seen and manipulated by end-users, so keys must be defined by systems analysts as visible properties of objects.

The typical OO mechanism is to allocate each object a key drawn from a single range of key values. To find an object you need know only the value of its key, you need not know its class. The main benefit is 'data independence'. If the data structure is altered there is no need to amend the key attribute or foreign key attribute of any object.

The typical business system mechanism is to allocate each object a key drawn from the range of key values for its class. To find an object you must know first its class and then the value of its key. This has some practical advantages:

- there is no bottleneck in the key allocation process
- natural identifiers, understood by users, can be employed
- compound and hierarchical keys can be made from 'foreign' keys
- minimal extra space is needed for system-generated keys.

In a complete OO methodology, it must be possible to accommodate both ways of identifying objects.

One-to-many relationships must be handled

A complete theory of OO database design must handle data structures which contain both class hierarchies and one-to-many relationships between objects. Should we use 'inheritance trees' or 'master-detail relationships' to connect these objects?

Class hierarchies are typical of OO applications. The data structure is composed of objects related as super-classes and sub-classes. This kind of relationship may be implemented using either inheritance trees or master-detail relationships.

One-to-many relationships are not a strong element in the world of OO programming, but they are commonplace in large information systems. Indeed they are an inescapable feature of large systems, because it is via one-to-many relationships that systems grow to be large in the first place. While it is clearly efficient and effective to implement one-to-many relationships using master-detail relationships, it is impractical to implement a one-to-many relationship using an inheritance tree, since the data will be unnormalised, resulting in all the update anomalies which are avoided by normalising data in the first place.

10.3 **Four things to be provided by modelling techniques**

We have seen that entity data modelling is not enough to get major reuse of system components. There follows a summary of ways in which the OO approach must be further extended to get the benefits we are hoping for during information system design.

Methods operating on different objects must be co-ordinated

It is typical of OO programming applications that in response to a user request, a program either operates on one object instance (a member of one class hierarchy) and invokes a single method, or else that it operates on a prime object, and all the other objects it operates on are somehow slave objects invoked from and controlled by the method body invoked in the prime object. Typically the slave objects are not directly manipulable at the end-user's level of discourse, because they belong to the realm of implementation, rather than to the end-user's universe of discourse.

It is typical of information systems, however, that a program cannot be executed without reference to many different object instances of several different classes, all significant in the end-user's world, and it is vital that the various methods involved are co-ordinated.

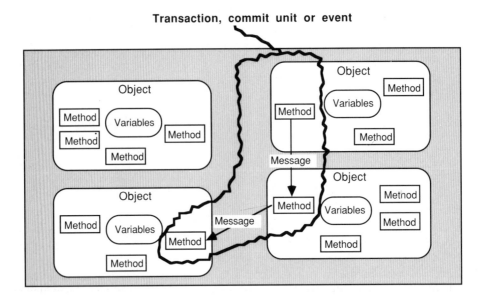

A group of methods which must be executed together is called a 'commit unit'. In a commit unit if one method fails, they all fail.

Events must be modelled

Whereas the missing design concept is a 'commit unit' which links several methods together, the missing analysis concept is an 'event', that is:

- a real-world happening, discrete and indivisible
- a group of input data items which must be entered together
- the trigger of a commit unit.

A complete OO systems development approach must able to recognise and model the events which affect entities.

Objects must all be at one (public) level of discourse

OO programmers tend to create class hierarchies of object types at different levels of discourse, public and private. An inheritance tree is used to represent deeper and deeper levels of implementation, more and more refined implementations of what is known to the user as a single concept. The main reason for lower levels of classification is efficiency: to speed up the programs which deliver the result of certain enquiry methods.

Information systems analysts do not build data structures like this. They define objects at one level of discourse, the public level. Users expect to able to ask questions directly about any of the objects in the data structure.

Also, users expect each class of object to exhibit substantially different behaviours, which means that a method is usually unique to its object class. This limits the value of inheritance as a means of increasing the reusability of system components. A complete theory of OO database design must allow the user to specify that each class of object has unique methods, independent of the object classes it is related to.

An analysis methodology must be developed

An OO programming language provides some tools to implement the idea of reusable objects; these concepts have been proven in limited kinds of application (using OO programming languages such as Smalltalk, and C++).

But an OO programming language does not itself help the analyst to define an object or the methods associated with it, or the programs which co-ordinate methods on different objects. What has been lacking to date is a practical systems analysis and design methodology, supported by CASE technology, which shows how these concepts can be applied to the design of large database systems.

What we are seeking to introduce here is a complete OO analysis and design methodology, to control the development of large-scale database systems, supported by CASE technology.

There is now evidence to suggest that entity event modelling techniques fit the bill. It is possible to achieve substantial reuse of processing components by using a CASE tool to take advantage of common processing (represented in entity behaviour models) and automatically specify invocation paths through common code (in the form of interlinked event procedures). This is the most promising path along which entity modelling techniques can be developed.

10.4 **The place of OO ideas in the 3-Schema Architecture**

It can be seen that OO environments are based on the assumption that there are object classes common to different programs, or even systems, which can be defined independently of those programs or systems, and reused over and over again. Where and how does this idea apply in information systems?

Taking up the diagram which introduced the methodology, to increase reuse we need different OO ideas in the Conceptual Model and External Design.

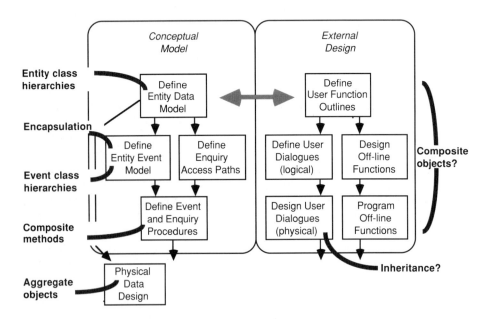

Note that the idea which seems most useful in increasing reuse in Conceptual Modelling is that of event class hierarchies rather than entity class hierarchies

The use of OO ideas in the Conceptual Model

Entity class hierarchies and reuse of object attributes

Whatever is needed in the way of a class hierarchy, or inheritance tree structure, can be captured in the entity data model, by introducing super-type entities. The designer can factor out behaviour common to various sub-types into their super-type entity.

However this idea is not as useful in practical systems analysis as might be hoped. In practice, we have found few data structures which are common to (reusable between) distinct information systems. Some reasons for this are discussed in chapter 12.

Encapsulation

SSADM has long encapsulated data and process specification by combining entity data modelling with entity event modelling. Entity event modelling is composed of two parts, entity-oriented behaviour modelling and event-oriented process modelling

Entity behaviour modelling is already an OO technique in so far as it encapsulates the data and process views of an entity. An entity behaviour model completely specifies all the effects of events on that entity. Each effect is composed of operations to update an attribute, relationship or state variable of the entity.

For each event in the entity behaviour models, the analyst can produce an effect correspondence diagram to show the co-ordination of event effects in different entities which are triggered by that event. The effect correspondence diagram may viewed as a program specification for a database update routine.

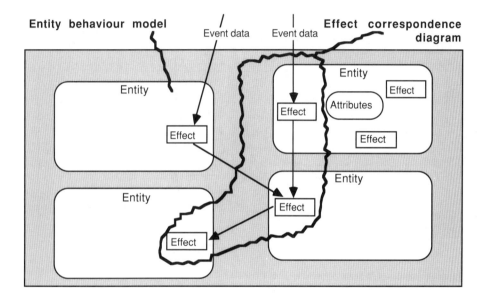

One event may be input in many different contexts; that is to say the process for an event may be reused in different parts of the External Design. But there has been no formal description yet of how to discover and capitalise on the further opportunities for reuse within an event.

We have been careful above to use the term 'event effect' rather than 'method'. Sometimes these are one and the same, but it turns out that methods are not fully documented using entity behaviour modelling as described in SSADM. Sometimes the same effect may be defined more than once, as triggered by two different events. In this case there is one method being invoked by two events.

Event class hierarchies and reuse of object methods

To identify reusable methods shared by different events, entity behaviour modelling techniques must be extended to incorporate the notion of **super-events**. Super-events have the benefit of simplifying entity behaviour models, effect correspondence diagrams and the event procedures produced from them.

Super-events create three new concepts in SSADM. First, the common effect on one entity triggered by more than one event, which is called a super-effect or a method. Second, the set of methods described in the effect correspondence diagram for an event or super event, which might well be called a **composite method**. Third the event class hierarchy, whereby an event may invoke super events, which may invoke further super-events and so on.

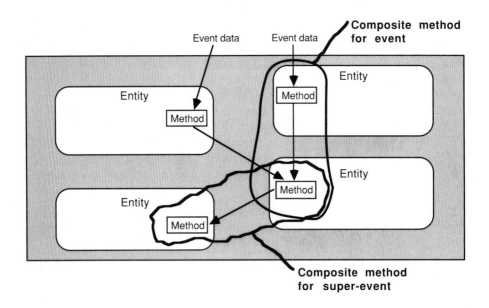

Super-events enable common code to be detected in the entity behaviour models and specified as composite methods invoked by several event procedures. These composite methods are specified in the form of effect correspondence diagrams. Whenever a new event is added under a super-event in an entity behaviour model, it can use the composite method already tested and implemented.

See part four for a demonstration of how reusable composite methods can be developed from entity behaviour models which incorporate super-events. We have further proven the ideas by automating much of the development work in a CASE tool.

The use of OO ideas in the External Design

Note that External Design objects, such as buttons and windows, are not a prerequisite for using the notion of objects in the Conceptual Model or Internal Design. The diagram below illustrates how the External Design may be linked to the Conceptual Model.

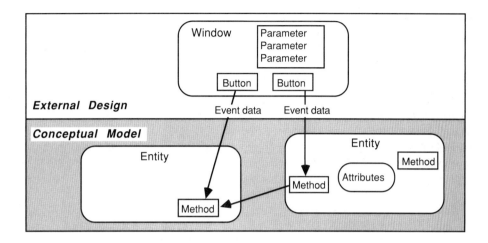

In the External Design it seems likely that OO ideas to do with composite objects and inheritance may be more useful

Composite objects? User interface objects such as windows and reference lists certainly look like composite objects. Using some GUI design tools, the ease of creating objects which inherit the properties of previously designed objects, enables designers to put together new user interface designs swiftly. This is especially attractive where the early presentation of a prototype design to users is expected or needed. See part five for further discussion.

Inheritance? User interface designers use inheritance in an informal way all the time. Modern user interface management systems enable them to copy an object from one window or dialogue to another (carrying forward the properties of the object as they do this) then they revise the new object. This is an intuitive, temporary, even playful, use of inheritance, however it can be formalised by developing standards and style guides to impose the reuse of design components. See chapters 22 to 24.

The use of OO ideas in the Internal Design

Chapters 12 and 18 discuss Internal Design, but we give it less attention than the other schemas. We usually expect that the Internal Design will be relatively simple, that each entity type can be mapped onto one database record type. The whole purpose of the 3-Schema Architecture is that more complex mappings should not affect the Conceptual Model or External Design.

Note that an OO database management system is not a prerequisite for using OO ideas in systems analysis and design. If it is to be useful for implementing large information systems, an OO database management system must have the notion of a success or commit unit, handle the back-out of updates to objects within a success unit, and have an efficient way of reading and writing the instance variables of objects (including sets of related objects).

Cross-schema communication

A major theme of this book is the need to simplify the jobs of system specification and maintenance by separating concerns. We promote the 3-Schema Architecture as a device for doing this. Of course, the three schemas cannot entirely be separated; they must be designed in harmony and there must be communication between them.

Cross-schema obligations

The notion of obligations was mentioned briefly in chapter 9. We have read a protest that obligations are not a proper OO idea, implying that each object should be responsible for the entirely validating the input messages it receives. Jackson (1975) exposed the foolishness of this argument, which leads ultimately to an infinite nesting of processes where each process checks the result of the previous one.

Within the scope of a system being designed, input data should be validated on entry to the system, and validation tests should not be repeated thereafter. In terms of the 3-Schema Architecture, each schema has an obligation to provide valid data to the others.

We find it difficult to define succinctly what 'valid' means here, but at the very least it means a message must be correct in terms of format and syntax. The External Design has an obligation to invoke the Conceptual Model with syntactically correct events. The Conceptual Model has an obligation to invoke the Internal Design with syntactically correct operations such as create, read, write and delete entity. In the same way, the responses to these invocations should be syntactically correct.

The designer of each schema should have faith in the designer of the other schemas. The alternative is anti-reuse; it means duplication in both the system specification and the implemented code, with all the attendant specification, performance, configuration management and maintenance problems.

Within-schema obligations

Likewise, within each schema, each process or object must be responsible for doing its job correctly and must output only valid data to the next.

Cross-schema objects

A single object may have properties in each of the schemas (say an Internal storage format, an External display format, and some Conceptual validation criteria). Suppose the user asks for an object which already exists in another system to be added to the Conceptual Model. We would like to reuse the object without defining new External and Internal views of it. We need a way of defining a Conceptual Model object and attaching to it the baggage of its External and Internal views, so that these can travel with the conceptual object.

More research into this may be useful. At the moment we are envisaging this working at the atomic level of system specification. It probably implies a central repository of data items which is relatively independent of the internal database schema or the user interface (most current implementation tools tie data item definition rather too closely to one or the other). However, larger objects might be included under the same scheme.

Part Four:

Conceptual Modelling

Chapter 11

Entity data modelling

For those new to the subject, this chapter reviews well-established entity data modelling techniques, both entity relationship modelling and entity attribute modelling, though there is a lot more to say about entity data modelling than can be said here.

For other readers, experienced in data modelling, it introduces the Hi-Ho case study used later to illustrate entity event modelling techniques, and highlights some differences between our methodology and others such as OMT.

11.1 **Resumé of the methodology**

Part one presented the 3-Schema Architecture as a way of viewing and designing information systems. According to this view, the users' processing requirements of a system can be divided into two parts, the Conceptual Model and External Design, and the processing of the physical database is defined in the Internal Design. It is proposed that each schema should be specified and implemented as separately as possible.

This extract from an earlier diagram shows the analysis and design techniques used in the Conceptual Model and the chapters they are discussed in.

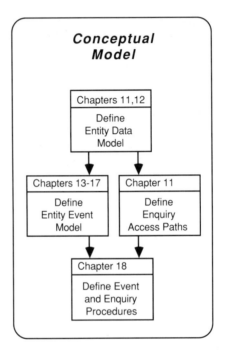

The main emphasis of part four, after the first two chapters, will be on entity event modelling, where we have more original contributions to make. This large chapter on entity data modelling is intended mainly to set the scene for the entity event modelling techniques which follow.

There is insufficient space in this book to give a complete description of either entity data modelling or entity event modelling techniques as we teach them, so further publications are planned.

11.2 **Methodological background**

Several methodologies have been developed for designing an information system which is based around a central database. Perhaps the most successful have been Information Engineering (in the USA) and SSADM (in the UK). Both of these grew out of ways of teaching principles of database design in a machine-independent way. At the heart of both methodologies lies the notion of an entity data model.

More recently OO methodologies have been developed which borrow entity data modelling ideas from information systems design methodologies. For example, data modelling in Rumbaugh's OMT methodology may be seen as following Information Engineering, or at least as coming out of the same school, which we believe to have been founded by Chen in the United States.

There are a few differences between our approach to entity data modelling and that of Chen, Rumbaugh and others. Some differences will be immediately apparent to readers arriving at this chapter from these different backgrounds; important differences are explained within this chapter.

For the time being we are going to assume that an object is the same as an entity, as defined in entity data modelling. We challenge this assumption in later chapters by suggesting that an entity should be divided into parallel aspects, each a finite state automaton. Having defined an object as being a finite state automaton, each parallel aspect of an entity ought be considered a distinct object.

For the time being we are going to assume that an entity has no more attributes than would be allowed a third normal form relation. In several places, notably chapter 5 and chapter 18, we challenge this assumption by suggesting that master entities ought to 'know about' their details, and therefore not be in first normal form. In chapter 24 we further challenge this assumption by suggesting a complete theory of multi-user interface design must include some ideas about how to maintain and refresh lists of objects, however this is a problem for the External Design not the Conceptual Model.

We take several ideas and principles from chapter 4 as the basis of our approach to entity data modelling. *Primacy of data:* for most large information systems, the analysis and design of the database has a higher priority than the analysis and design of processes. *Identity:* each entity instance must have a unique identity, both to differentiate it from other entities and to enable the user to map it onto a real-world entity or concept. *Association* between two entities is modelled by a relationship. A relationship always connects a master entity to a detail entity. *Generalisation* of sub-type entities into super-types is modelled using a class hierarchy.

Generalisation and *suppression of detail* are tools for reverse engineering an entity data model out of a physical database definition. An entity data model can be viewed as an archetype of the specification required by a relational or network database management system. An entity data model can be viewed as a rudimentary database design, suppressing details required by a given database management system; and not optimised from a performance point of view. How much has to be done to transform an entity data model into a physical database depends on the chosen database management system and the performance constraints.

11.3 **Preliminary remarks**

Notations

This chapter is not so much about the syntax of entity data models as about their semantics. We are mainly concerned with the meaning of entity data models. Having said this, of course we have to use a formal syntax. We introduce the notation in the body of the chapter and summarise it at the end. There are many other notations which support more or less the same semantics, for example, the E-R notation introduced by Chen and popular in the United States, and Rumbaugh's OMT notation which is shown at the end of this chapter for comparison purposes. Leaving aside the methodological differences discussed later, readers should not be too concerned about differences between entity data modelling notations, or even slight differences in the semantics supported by them.

Multiple versions of a data model

To paraphrase Jackson's observation on programming, the beginning of wisdom for the analyst is to recognise the difference between building a data model which works after a fashion (at the expense of many programmer hours) and getting the data model right. The next step is to master the different ways that the same real world may be modelled using a given data modelling notation. The final step is learn how the data model should be supplemented with other documentation, with parallel versions of the data model if necessary.

Stage of development

In SSADM the data model is developed through several levels of refinement:

  step 210: 1st cut data model for chosen business system option
  step 320: 2nd cut data model developed as entity relationship model
  step 340: 3rd cut data model refined by data and enquiry access path analysis
  step 360: 4th cut data model refined via entity event modelling
  step 620: physical data model, for database design.

And people say that SSADM is not a spiral or iterative method!

Adding details

You may find it helpful to make normally-hidden details visible on a data model. It is more than reasonable to attach a label to each end of a relationship, describing the *role* that an entity plays in a relationship. This can help the analyst to clarify the meaning of the relationship and the entities it relates. It may reveal some new entity or relationship is needed. However, we often omit relationship role names for the sake of simplicity of presentation. And we always omit them in the case of a class hierarchy, where the role names are always the same, that is, sub-type *is a* super-type.

You may find it helpful to expand an entity box to record or reveal list the names of *attributes* and/or the *methods* of that entity.

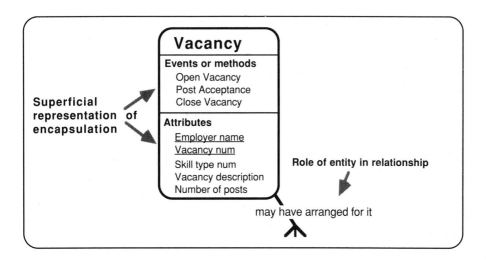

Suppressing details

People have been trying for twenty years to extend entity data model-like notations to more completely specify a system's business rules and processing requirements. We believe that extending the entity data model to cover several scores or hundred of pages is not the answer. There is a limit to what can be specified in one kind of diagram, so the entity data model (even the one shown above with attribute and event names on it) will require backing documentation.

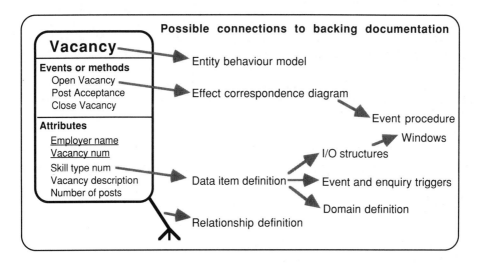

This backing documentation should be tightly integrated with the entity data model. A CASE tool could enable you to directly access the relevant backing documentation. You might be able to click on a method name to show the ECD which contained that method.

As the entity data model grows larger and more elaborate through various refinement activities, you will want to show less and less detail on it. A CASE tool should offer you the option of showing more or less detail on the entity data model. When dealing with the size of system we are interested in, with several hundreds of entities, you will probably wish to show the expanded picture of an entity only in parallel versions of small parts of the data model.

Encapsulation

Listing the names of events or methods for an entity is a step towards object-orientation, but only a very small step. What matters is not whether the methods are shown on the entity data model diagram, but how you:

- discover the 'right' set of events or methods
- name them
- specify their workings
- specify the message passing between methods
- maximise reuse of methods.

In other words, you need a systematic way of developing the backing documentation. The relevant technique is entity event modelling. Entity behaviour models are used to specify all the update processes of the entities in the entity data model. But where are the 'methods'? Does a method correspond to an event, an event effect, an operation, or something else?

Before embarking on entity event modelling (step 360 of SSADM), you should assume that as far as one entity is concerned, each event invokes one method and each method is invoked by one event. You should name methods after the events which trigger them. Begin by identifying the **method invocations** rather than the methods. There are a few situations where the same method will be invoked by more than one event. Recognising this reusable method as a **super-event** leads to some simplification of entity event model and the code generated from it. But we are straying from the point. This chapter is supposed to be about data modelling, not process modelling.

Choice or level of entity definition

What are entities? It turns out that there are three different views of what an entity is:

- identity-oriented
- identity and type-oriented
- identity and parallel aspect-oriented.

For simple case studies like the one in this chapter, there is little or no difference between the three views. This chapter takes the basic identity-oriented view. Chapter 12 illustrates the type and parallel aspect-oriented views.

11.4 **Discovering the entities**

Several approaches have been suggested for finding the entities to be modelled. Where there is an existing system, reverse engineering may reasonably be used. Some people start by listing objects which are physically tangible, but this is too limited an approach, and is rejected for reasons given in chapter 4. A common approach is to look for nouns in text descriptions of the existing business or the system to be designed, but this a very arbitrary and subjective technique, which might work on case studies (like the one below) but does not work so well outside of the classroom

It is impossible to invent a method which guarantees, at the very start of a project, the correct identification of the objects to be included in a system specification, but there is a property of an entity which helps in doing this. An entity, according to Webster's Collegiate Dictionary, is a thing which has: *'distinctness of being, either in fact or thought'*.

Identity-oriented view

The etymology of 'entity' and 'identity' is revealing. An entity is something we can distinguish from other entities of different types, and from other entities of the same type. This property of distinctness can help us to identify the important entities in a system. Where people need to distinguish one entity from another, where they care about identity, they will make this distinction by a name or 'key'.

For example, each football club in a league has a unique name. The league will not accept two clubs with the same name. Everyone (from the league management to the supporters) accepts that the club may sack their manager, transfer players, move from one ground to another, or even share a ground with another club, but something as small as a change of name will meet with fierce resistance. The history of the club is associated with its name.

With hosts of entities to keep track of, businesses usually find that names are not enough. To help people identify and reidentify things, businesses (not just computer systems) use keys, alpha-numeric identifiers.

In analysing a business scenario, the keys themselves are unimportant, but the fact that people have cared enough about the identity of entities to invent and use a key to distinguish one from another is important. It tells us that these entities are valuable to the users of the system.

So when you discover a key, in analysing a user's business, you have discovered a thing which the users think is important. At least, they care enough about things of this type to introduce a means of distinguishing between them. In other words you have discovered a very strong candidate for an 'entity' in your data model.

Case study

The following specification is deliberately incomplete, because we want to show how the later entity behaviour modelling techniques will make us ask questions about the system and hence find things out.

Hi-Ho is a recruitment agency who advertise vacancies in a limited range of defined skill types. Hi-Ho has many offices. Each office registers employers on its books, who are then able to advertise vacancies via Hi-Ho. Hi-Ho will only accept a vacancy which can be ascribed to one of its defined skill types. Each office registers applicants provided that they have at least one of the skills Hi-Ho is interested in.

The bulk of the day-to-day work is registering vacancies and applicants, matching them against each other by skill and setting up interviews for the applicants with employers. If an interview is successful (leads to a post acceptance) then Hi-Ho sends an invoice to the employer.

Look for keys in this picture of elements of our case study.

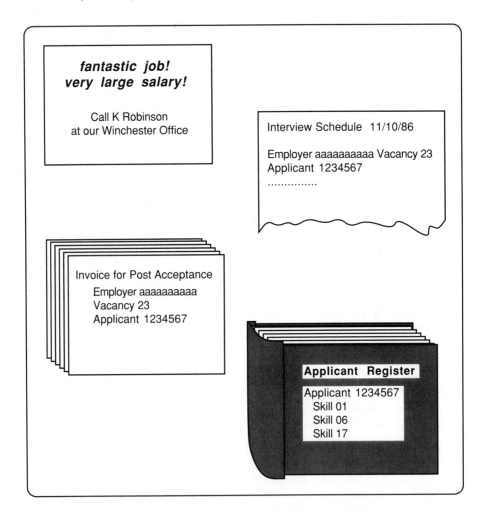

A search through the documents to be found in a Hi-Ho office readily reveals some important entities in the system, viz: Employer, Vacancy, Applicant, Skill Type, etc.

11.5 **Discovering relationships between entities**

Independence of and dependence on other objects

Many people suggest starting analysis with questions about the 'cardinality' of relationships between objects, but we think that cardinality is a mask for the more important question of whether an object can exist without a relationship to another object.

The most important question to ask about a relationship is: Is there a relationship at all? Then we should ask: Can one object exist without the other? To express the initial analysis questions in terms of zero, one or more on scale of cardinality is misleading. The question of whether there is any constraint on how many detail objects may allowed in the relationship is different from and secondary to questions about the existence and identity of the objects.

So to build an entity relationship model from the entities listed earlier, the analyst should study each pair of entities, looking for constraints on the relationships between them. The analyst may clarify this by asking the questions given below. Four questions are all that is needed to reveal the nature of relationship between two entities.

To discover a direct relationship
- for an entity A is there more than one entity B?
- for an entity B is there more than one entity A?

yes-yes	reveals no relationship (or a many-to-many, later to be resolved)
yes-no	reveals one-A-to-many-B
no-yes	reveals one-B-to-many-A
no-no	reveals one-A-to-one-B

The analyst now knows there is a relationship between the pair of entities, but not whether it may be optional at one or both ends. To constrain the relationship further, the analyst should ask the next two questions.

To discover if one or both ends of the relationship are mandatory
- can an entity A exist without an entity B?
- can an entity B exist without an entity A?

no-no	reveals A and B are both dependent on the relationship
no-yes	reveals A is dependent, B is independent
yes-no	reveals A is independent, B is dependent
yes-yes	reveals A and B are both independent

After asking these four questions, the analyst knows if there is a relationship between two object types, and whether the number at either end of the relationship is zero, one or many.

Example

For an Employer is there more than one Vacancy? Yes. For a Vacancy is there more than one Employer? No. So there must be a one-to-many relationship, one Employer to many Vacancies.

Can an Employer exist without a Vacancy? Yes. Can a Vacancy exist without an Employer? No. So the relationship must be mandatory from the Vacancy's point of view and optional from the Employer's point of view.

To define the master and the detail

In this order of precedence, the analyst should take the first reason which applies to define which is the master and which is the detail:

- if one A to many B, then A is the master
- if A can exist without B (but not vice versa), then A is the master
- if A is given identity before B (but not vice versa), then A is the master
- else revise the model, or pick one entity arbitrarily as the master.

Where the first three reasons do not apply (because the relationship is a symmetrical one, such as a many-to-many, or a one-to-one which is optional at both ends) some further analysis may reveal which entity is the natural master of the relationships, by causing a revision to the model in one of the ways shown later in this chapter.

Case study

By asking the above questions of the entities in the case study, we discover a number of relationships between entities, determine whether the number at either end of the relationship is zero, one or many, and assign the label 'master' or 'detail' to either end of the relationship.'

Independent master: dependent detail(s)

This is the most common kind of relationship. Examples in Hi-Ho are shown below:

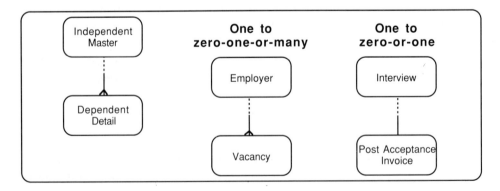

Note that by the time we have taken history into account, a one-to-zero-or-one relationship often becomes a one-to-zero-one-or-many. For example, if a replacement invoice must be issued if the Employer 'loses' the first, perhaps we will have to keep an audit trail of all the invoices issued following a successful Interview.

Dependent master: dependent detail(s)

This is a reasonably common kind of relationship, usually representing what might be called an Aggregation.

Inventing 'mobile telephone' as an entity type with its own unique identity, given to every Placement Consultant, examples in Hi-Ho are shown below:

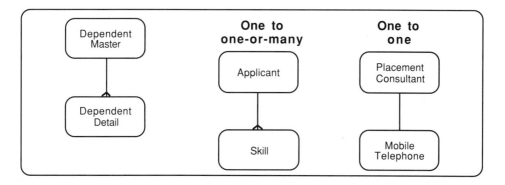

Dependent master: independent detail(s)

This is a less common kind of relationship, often representing an Aggregation made up of preexisting independent details, such as a team made up of employees, or an order which is made up by collecting together a group of already defined stock requirements.

Assuming a Date is not interesting unless it is made up of one or more Interviews, and an Office Manager cannot be identified without an Office to manage, examples in Hi-Ho are shown below:

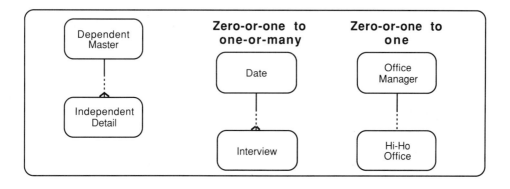

Independent master: independent detail(s)

This is a reasonably common kind of relationship, which represents a very loose association between independent entities. It is very common to find that on further investigation there is a missing entity type which should be introduced between the two entities (see section 11.6).

Suppose that each Applicant may or may not be assigned to a Placement Consultant within an office. And suppose that an Interview may be run in-house (in the interview room in an Hi-Ho office), in which case the Interview must be matched to an Interview Slot in some kind of office diary.

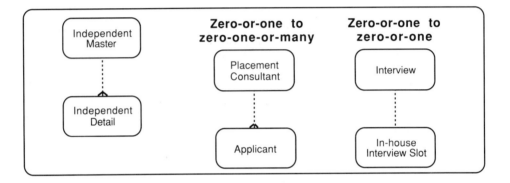

Classifying relationships

We have seen attempts to classify relationship types such as the matrix below:

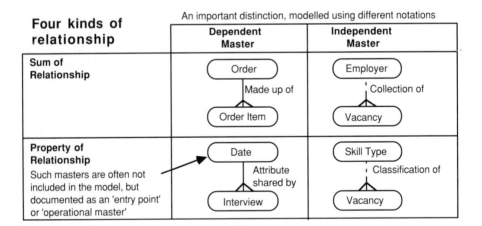

However, you cannot specify all the semantics of relationships in a data model by classifying them with words. To specify all the semantics, you have to model the specific behaviour of the two entity types at either end of the relationship.

11.6 **Constraining the entity relationship model**

Merging one-to-one entities

As a general rule we can merge entities which are in one-to-one correspondence, since they must have, or can be given, the same identity. One of the two entities then becomes a property of the other. We can also merge entities which are in one to zero-or-one correspondence, treating one as an optional property of the other.

So in the case study, four of the entities can be removed from the model, becoming properties of their related entities.

Entity type	becomes attribute(s) of	Entity type
Mobile Telephone		Placement Consultant
Office Manager		Hi-Ho Office
In-house Interview Slot		Interview
Post Acceptance Invoice		Interview

In fact we are going to drop all four entities on the left, even as attributes, in order to simplify the case study.

Reasons to retain one-to-one relationships

A one-to-one relationship may be shown in the entity data model, or appear in the database design, for one of five reasons:

- if it is crossed by an exclusion arc in a class hierarchy (actually, this makes the relationship optional at one end, not truly one-to-one)

- to connect two entities which are over time connected in a many-to-many relationship, but at any instant in time are constrained to no more than one in either direction (we normally resolve such a case in the data model by introducing a link entity with two monogamous relationships, as described in the next section)

- to resolve contention problems, or record an alternative key or access point to an entity (we normally do this in the physical database design, not the data model)

- to separate the parallel lives of an entity type, where a single entity type has more than one state variable (we usually do this only where supported by the next reason)

- to partition the **parallel aspects** of an aggregate entity, for distribution of a database between locations, to ease the integration of distinct application systems, or to reduce contention for data in a multi-user environment.

Constraining loose associations

The job of the analyst is not to build a many-to-many relationship between each and every pair of entities 'just in case', nor is it to make every relationship optional 'just in case'. The job of the analyst is to identify the business rules and constraints by which the users can make manageable sense of the real world.

Analysing many-to-many relationships

A many-to-many relationship can and should always be resolved by introducing a 'link entity' between the two entities in the many-to-many relationship, as shown below:

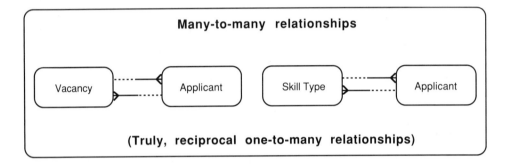

Analysing the first of these examples reveals a new and very important entity, Interview. Analysing the second reveals an entity we mentioned before, Applicant Skill.

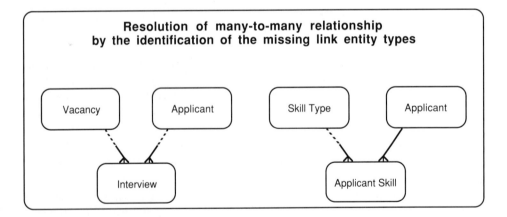

Notice that in both examples the new link entity is important in its own right, not merely an adjunct to its masters.

Analysing optional relationships

A similar kind of resolution may be applied wherever a relationship is optional at both ends. The examples given earlier may be resolved as shown below:

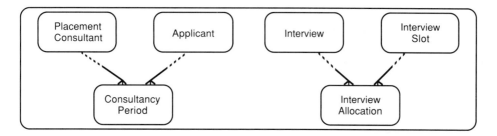

Such a resolution is always worth investigating; in many ways it is a fuller model of the real world, and it usually simplifies the entity behaviour modelling.

But if there is no conceivable requirement for historical information (say for audit purposes), then the entity data model (at least the one shown to users) should not be elaborated in this way.

Constraints missing from the entity relationship model

The evidence suggests that it is just not possible to show all business rules and constraints in an entity relationship model. At least, people have been trying to find a way to do this for more than a decade and they have yet to succeed. Chapters 14 to 18 show how all constraints can be modelled in entity behaviour modelling. However, there are two specific kinds of constraint which might easily be annotated on the entity data model, although we have seen no attempt to do it.

Fixed masters are not distinguished from changeable

Generally it is assumed that a detail may swap from one master to another. There is no notation to show a detail is permanently attached to the same master. This is always true if the key of the detail entity is hierarchical, but may be true in other cases as well. Here are two examples of fixed masters.

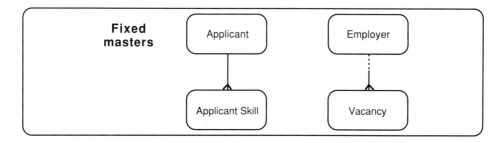

A changeable master means a detail can switch from one master to another. This is sometimes true of mandatory relationships, but more often of optional relationships. Every independent detail may potentially change from one master to another.

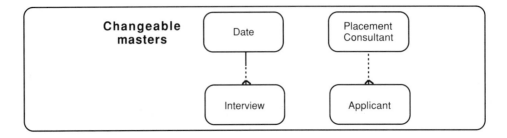

Wherever a master is changeable, the question may be asked - *over time*, is it really a many-to-many relationship? Introducing a new 'link entity', our examples appear as shown below:

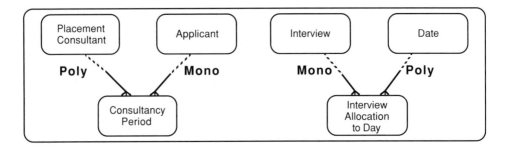

Such a resolution is always worth investigating; in many ways it is a fuller model of the real world, and it usually simplifies the entity behaviour modelling. But if there is no conceivable requirement for historical information (say for audit purposes), then the entity data model (at least the one shown to users) should not be elaborated in this way.

Monogamous and polygamous details

Removing a changeable master by resolving the many-to-many as shown above always introduces a monogamous detail. In adding history to the model we often introduce a 'monogamous' relationship from a master to a detail entity.

In a polygamous relationship, many details may be active at the same time. In a monogamous relationship, only the latest detail entity can be active, the rest are dead (or historical).

11.7 **Case study review**

Here is the sum of what we know about Hi-Ho so far.

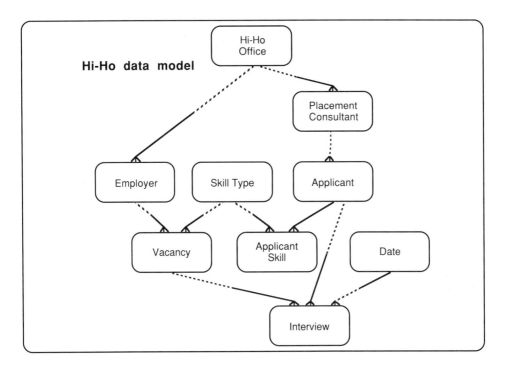

Note that there are no monogamous relationships in this model, but there are some changeable masters (Placement Consultant and Date) which would lead to monogamous relationships if they were resolved by the introduction of many-to-many link entities.

The entity behaviour model of an entity with a changeable master very closely resembles the entity behaviour model of an entity with a monogamous detail. This is significant because it shows that modifications of the entity data model which are visually significant, but conceptually trivial, have little effect on the entity event model.

11.8 **Refinements of the entity relationship model**

Refinement of a 'double V' relationship

A 'double V' relationship occurs where two details are owned by the same two masters. Below, Applicant Skill and Interview are both owned (directly or indirectly) by Skill Type and Applicant. In such a case you should look for a relationship between the two detail entities.

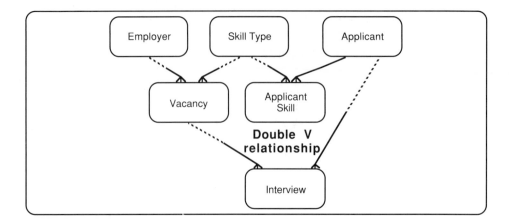

Is there a relationship between the two details? Let us ask the questions given earlier:

- For an Applicant Skill is there more than one Interview? Yes.
- For an Interview is there more than one Applicant Skill? No.

An Interview is only arranged after the automatic matching process has located an Applicant with the same Skill Type as the Vacancy. The Interview results from that one Applicant Skill, and should be related to it in the model.

Refinement of a 'triangular' relationship

After linking the Applicant Skill and Interview entities, we are left with a 'triangular' relationship.

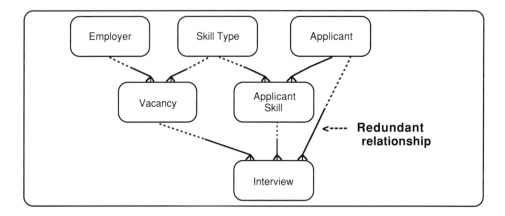

In a triangular relationship, if the same set of details is found coming down the long relationship as is found coming down the two short relationships, then the long one can be discarded.

Note that not all triangular relationships are resolvable in this way; sometimes it is not true that the same set of details is found coming down both routes, especially where there are independent details (optionally connected to one or both masters) at the bottom of the triangle.

11.9 **Mutually exclusive relationships**

Suppose some Applicants try to register with Hi-Ho without any of the Skills which Hi-Ho are interested in. Hi-Ho will permit these Applicants to register, provided that they have some other relevant qualifications to their name. Whereas Applicants and Vacancies are normally matched automatically by Skill Type, Placement Consultants must match these unskilled Applicants' qualifications by hand against the Vacancy descriptions.

There are two mutual exclusions. An Applicant has either formally defined Skills or informally recorded Qualifications. An Interview is arranged either as a result of the Applicant having a specific Skill Type, or as a result of an undefined or intuitive matching of Qualifications.

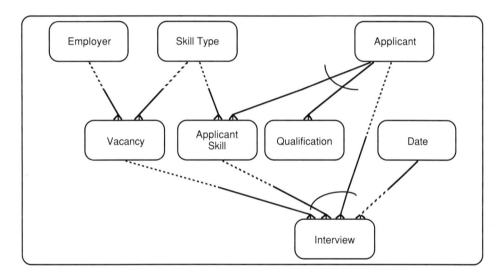

Mutual exclusion between relationships is explored further in chapter 12. For the remainder of this chapter we are going to undo this latest development of the case study.

11.10 **Entity attribute modelling**

At some stage the entity relationship model must be supplemented with further detail, by listing the attributes of each entity. Below we have symbolised three kinds of attribute by the use of underscoring, plain text and italics, thus:

- primary key   (the identity of this entity)
- foreign key   (the identity of a master entity)
- *non-key attribute.*

Office
>   Office Name, *Office-address*

Employer
>   Employer Name, Office Name, *Employer Telephone Number*

Vacancy
>   (Employer Name, Vacancy Num) Skill Type Num, *Vacancy Description*

Skill Type
>   Skill Type Num, *Skill Description*

Applicant
>   Applicant Num, Office Name, *Placement Consultant Name, Applicant Name, etc.*

Applicant Skill
>   Applicant Num, Skill Type Num

Interview
>   (Employer Name, Vacancy Num) Applicant Num, Skill Type Num, *Interview Date, etc.*

Date
>   Date

Implementing identity via a key

The identification of entity instances is fundamental to the successful operation and usefulness of any system. In both graphical user interfaces and information systems, it must be possible to distinguish one entity from another. Furthermore, in an information system, it must be possible to identify entities in the system with their counterparts in the real world. It is this second criterion which leads to some difficulties.

To implement an entity's identity, information system designers allocate a key to the entity type. To paraphrase Hughes' description of relational theory (1991), a key of an entity is a subset of the attributes which have the following time-independent properties:

- unique identification: the value of the key uniquely identifies each attribute of the entity
- non-redundancy: no attribute of the key can be discarded without destroying unique identification.

To Hughes's definition we add one more important property of a key:

• permanence of value: the value of the key must be fixed during the life of the entity.

Having assigned a value to the key of an entity instance it cannot be changed, since to do so would destroy the concept of identity. This simple and obvious rule is the counter to Hughes' objection to using keys as identifiers.

Problems may arise because of the conflict between the need to identify entities in the system with their counterparts in the real world, and the need for a key's value to be unique and fixed throughout the life of the entity.

Keys in the OO world

In a graphical user interface, the shapes on the screen *are* the entities which the user is interested in; that is to say they have no counterpart in the external or real world. So while the user has to be able to distinguish one entity from another, the user has no need to identify entities in the system with their counterparts in the real world.

Where the user can directly identify an entity of interest by pointing at it, or clicking on it with a mouse, or saying 'that one please', then the user does not need to know its key. Typically, the way that one entity is identified from another within an OO environment is by a meaningless key, drawn from a single range allocated to all entities of a system, a key which the user never sees (see chapters 9 and 10 for discussion).

Keys in the information systems world

The key of an entity in an information system is not just for the use of computer programmers; it must also be designed to be useful to users of the system who must identify entities in the system with their counterparts in the real world. This leads designers into a dilemma when allocating keys to entities: Should they use artificial or user-friendly keys?

Artificial keys

Artificial keys may have to be allocated for all kinds of implementation-oriented reasons. Typically OO environments require all objects to be identified by an artificial key. Otherwise, artificial keys may have to be allocated where an entity does not have a key in the real world, or has no reliable key. For example, since people's names are notoriously non-unique, the Applicant entity will require an artificial key:

Applicant
    Applicant Num, Office Name, *Placement Consultant Name, Applicant Name, etc.*

There are certainly strong arguments for employing artificial, system-generated keys, and we support the use of such keys where they are needed (for example, by an OO environment). But if an artificial system-generated key is not readily used by users in their day-to-day business, then another more user-friendly key may be needed as well.

User-friendly keys

While artificial keys may be introduced, it is normal and advisable to adopt the most user-friendly keys which are available, given the constraint that they must remain fixed.

Some, especially those who come from an OO programming background, may object to our emphasis on the importance of user-friendly keys. But such keys are necessary wherever a system is a model which is interpreted by users as tracking real-world objects, rather than being directly connected to those objects, as in a process control system or graphical user interface.

In designing an information system, it is vital that we help the users to identify entities in the system with their counterparts in the real world. Otherwise the system will become useless, as users ascribe data attributes and behavioural events to the wrong entities, and then cannot locate the entities they are interested in.

User-friendly keys are easily allocated where an entity type comes from the real world with a ready-made identifier. Master entities at the 'top' of the model are the most likely to be given user-friendly keys.

Some top-level master entities are directly and naturally identifiable as unique types or categories (for example, in the case study: Office, Skill Type and Date). It is natural to allocate the names of these entities as their keys:

Office

    <u>Office Name</u>, *Office-address*

Having said this, although a Skill Type description must be unique, if the user already employs a shorthand numbering system for skills (perhaps in another business system) then this shorthand key may be preferred, as in our example:

Skill Type

    <u>Skill Type Num</u>, *Skill Description*

Other top-level master entities may have names which are not naturally unique, but because they are less numerous than lower level entities, users may reasonably take the risk that two high-level master entities with the same name will not occur, or can be readily distinguished if they do occur. For example, you may reasonably assume that an Employer is uniquely identifiable by name, provided that users accept that two Employers with the same name must be distinguished by adding a modifier (perhaps a suffix such as a country name):

Employer

    <u>Employer Name</u>, Office Name, *Employer Telephone Number*

The downside of allocating a user-friendly key, such as Employer name, is that its value may change. Let us say that Company Law makes this so difficult as to be an exception not worth considering.

Hierarchical (or composite) keys

A hierarchical (or composite) key contains at least two levels, where the lower part is only unique within the higher part. The higher part may stand in its own right as the key of a master entity.

The key of a master entity cannot be sufficient to identify a detail entity. However, it can be combined with a unique identifier in a hierarchical key, for example:

Vacancy

<u>(Employer Name, Vacancy Num)</u> <u>Skill Type Num</u>, *Vacancy Description*

In this example, the key is hierarchical. That is, the entity requires its own key within the key of a master entity. Vacancy Num is not unique by itself, but only acts to distinguish between Vacancies for the same Employer.

Entities which have a hierarchical key must be dependent details of a fixed master entity. If the master could change, then the key could change, which by our rules it cannot.

Compound keys

A key of two or more independent parts, is a compound key. Each part of the compound key should stand in its own right as the key of a master entity. For example:

Applicant Skill

<u>Applicant Num, Skill Type Num</u>

Combining user-friendly keys

Rather than assign new artificial keys to entities at the bottom of the model, they are better identified by hierarchical keys and compound keys constructed from the keys of the higher level master entities. This usually gives a more user-friendly key for the lower level entity, though it may contain artificial elements.

For example, Interview has a compound key made up of one hierarchical key and two other keys:

Interview

<u>(Employer Name, Vacancy Num)</u> <u>Applicant Num</u>, <u>Skill Type Num</u>, *Interview Date, etc.*

The objection that this makes for lengthy keys, and tedious data entry, can now be overcome by the adoption of graphical user interfaces, where users can easily select desired entities by pointing at items within lists.

However, the objection that user-friendly keys are more likely to be volatile needs to be taken into account. A hierarchical key or compound key must be made from the keys of fixed masters, not changeable ones.

Should an entity type have two kinds of key?

To ensure an entity has a unique identity throughout its life, the designer may prefer to employ an artificial, system-generated key. To help the users to identify entities in the system with their counterparts in the real world, the designer will prefer to employ a user-friendly key.

Should the designer allocate a key which the users find meaningless? Should the designer allocate a user-friendly key to an entity, with the risk that its value may change? There is a case for saying that the two purposes of a key should be separated, and two keys allocated to an entity. In practice, designers usually expect one key to fulfil both purposes; it is this compromise which is the cause of some difficulties.

Non-key attributes

Most of our entities have at least one attribute which is not a key or foreign key. Non-key attributes may be divided into two types:

- replaceable: those which can be replaced with a new value
- calculable: those which can be initialised, incremented or decremented.

Some non-key attributes (especially text data) have an almost unlimited range of values. For example, Vacancy description. Other attributes may have a limited range of values. For example, Interview result is one of three values: Post Acceptance, Refusal of Post and Applicant Rejection.

Transforming non-key attributes into relationships

Inversion of attributes

Inverting the non-key attributes of an entity, may give rise to one or more master entities.

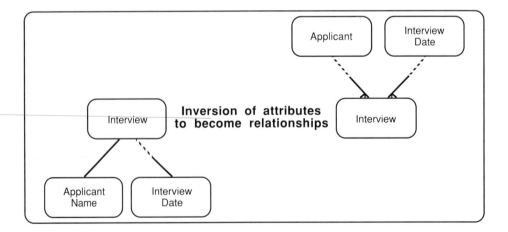

Addition of mutually exclusive attributes

An optional attribute can be extended into a class hierarchy. This happens when one or more mutually exclusive attributes are added alongside the optional attribute.

Suppose for example that only managers have a salary grade and operators receive a weekly wage based on productivity. This (along perhaps with other differences in their properties) may lead to the development of a class hierarchy.

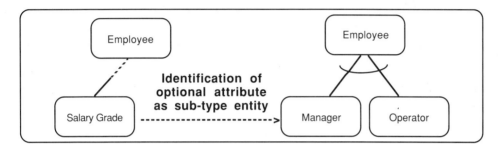

Addition of history

By adding a historical perspective, an attribute may become a detail entity.

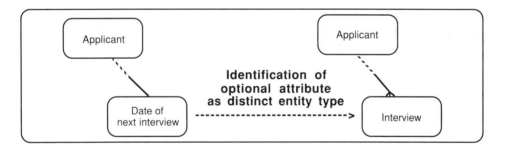

11.11 A binary data model

In this context, there are two reasons to introduce the concept of a binary data model. First, the binary data model shows that the distinction between attributes and relationships is not as clear as one might imagine. Both are properties or **aspects** of an entity. It turns out that in modelling the behaviour of an entity aspect, it doesn't make much difference whether the aspect is an attribute or a relationship. Second, the binary data model sheds light on the concept of an **operational master** entity.

A binary data model has no non-key attributes at all. To arrive at a binary data model we simply invert non-key attributes into master entities (so that the non-key attributes become foreign keys). For example we could raise the non-key attributes in the case study to become new entity types, as shown below.

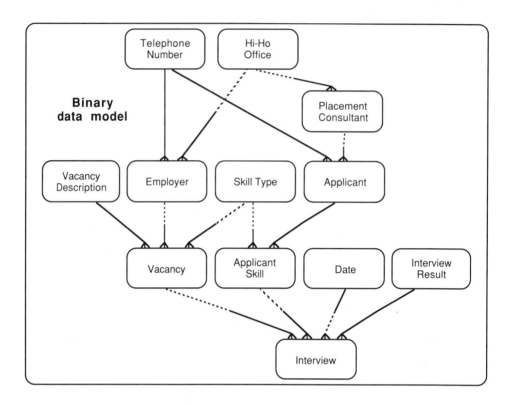

Why make a non-key attribute into an operational master? This is done to support the users' information requirements. A vital step in entity data modelling is to validate the model against the users' needs, by ensuring that the model provides access paths for known enquiries. To begin with, an enquiry access path can be drawn as a partial view of the data model, with an entry point.

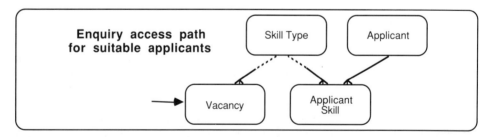

There is more to enquiry access path analysis than drawing such a picture, and it is a very important topic in our courses. The section which follows is only a brief overview, because we do not have enough space in this book to do the subject justice.

11.12 **Enquiry access paths**

There are two reasons for specifying enquiry access path. First, to validate and refine the entities and relationships in the data model. Second, after the data model has been validated and refined, to specify an enquiry process for coding in a suitable language such as SQL or COBOL (see chapter 30 for notes on automated transformation).

There are two ways the data model can be refined by enquiry access path analysis. First, the data model may be revised to provide a direct access route to the required data: that is a path which accesses *only the entities relevant to the enquiry* (this can be especially important in distributed systems, where the data model should be designed so that a local enquiry process does not needlessly access data in other locations). Second, the data model may have to be extended to contain data required for the enquiry.

There are two steps in validating and refining the data model to support an enquiry. First, find or create the entry point (the thing identified by the enquiry input parameters). Second, find or create entities to provide the data, and relationships to provide the access path. These steps may mean adding an **operational master** entity.

There are two features of an operational master entity which distinguish it from any other kind of entity. An operational master is:

- a key-only entity (has no non-key attributes)
- introduced only to provide an access path to the detail entities which it owns.

There are two outcomes for an operational master entity. It may acquire attributes or relationships of its own, and thus become an entity like any other. Or it may become an index, used to optimise database access. Either way, the operational master will figure in database design.

Logical and physical data models

For purposes to do with real-world modelling, simplification and presentation to users, it is right to *exclude* operational master entities from a data model. But for purposes to do with the physical design of the system, it is right to *include* operational master entities in a data model.

From now on we shall assume that two entity data models are maintained, a logical data model without operational masters shown on it, and a physical data model with them on. On the latter, it is helpful to distinguish operational masters from other entities, by using a different notation.

The logical data model (without operational masters) is the one we shall use for entity event modelling in chapters 14 to 18. This means that storage and retrieval of operational masters belongs in the Internal Design. Operational masters may in fact not be stored as records at all, but manufactured when they are needed by some kind of routine in the PDI.

Two mistaken beliefs about operational masters

First, it is untrue that SSADM4 shows no operational masters on the data model. Most operational masters can be recorded as an entry point arrow on an entity in the physical data model, typically annotated with a non-key attribute such as a state or date. Or, if the operational master is likely to acquire attributes or relationships of its own, it may be recorded as an entity like any other in the logical data model.

Second, it is untrue that an operational master can have no master entities above it. Where entry to the data model is required upon a compound key, the analyst may add a key-only link entity owned by the various entities whose keys it contains. If this means the creation of a three-part compound key, then advice on 4th and 5th normal forms becomes relevant, and the three-part key might be derived from various two-way link entities (see next section).

When to add operational masters

This table summarises some advice on adding operational master entities.

If the enquiry entry point is	then add to the data model
the primary key of an existing entity	nothing
a characteristic of an existing entity	an operational master entity
a characteristic repeated within an entity	an operational master entity, and a link entity
a compound of data from several entities	a compound entity linking several master entities

Case study

We have no space to construct enquiry access paths for the case study, but examples are given in Duschl & Hopkins (1992) and the following conversation reveals the need for at least one operational master.

Analyst: 'Are you interested in viewing Vacancies by Description? or Employers by Telephone Number? or Interview by Date?'

User: 'Only the last of these. We like to list all Interviews due on a given day.'

The result of this user interview is that Date will be an operational master of Interview in the physical data model.

11.13 **Relational data analysis**

Relational data analysis is a technique for simplifying relatively complex structures of data items, as they are presented on forms, screens or flat files. The end result is a set of 'relations' in Third Normal Form (sometimes called TNF). When a relation is in third normal form, then given a value for a key there is only one possible value for any given data item. From now on we shall use the word 'entity' rather than 'relation'.

Choosing a key for a document, relation or entity
Guidelines for choosing a key are, it should:

- uniquely identify one of the data groups represented in the unnormalised data
- not be repeated within the unnormalised data
- be unique for each occurrence of the unnormalised data group.

If there is a choice of key items, then, all other considerations being equal, choose:

- one item rather than several
- numeric rather than alpha
- fixed length and format rather than variable length or format
- short items rather than long ones.

Normalisation to third normal form (TNF)
Normalisation is a technique, not described here, by which data is reduced through first and second normal forms, to third normal form. Once normalisation has been carried out two tests can be applied to ensure that the entities are in third normal form. (It is unfortunate that these two tests are missing from the relevant SSADM4 chapter.)

The first TNF test
Is there only one value for each data item in the entity, given a single value for the key? If the answer is 'No', there is a mistake at either first or second normal form to be investigated and corrected.

The second TNF test
Does a data item in the entity depend only indirectly on the key, and more directly on another item uniquely identified by the key? If the answer is 'Yes', there is a third normal form case to be investigated and corrected. This third normal form problem may be not immediately visible, because the 'other item' is in another entity.

Normalisation to Boyce-Codd normal form
Boyce-Codd normal form is a variation of third normal form which eliminates possible anomalies where there are several candidate keys which share a common attribute.

Analysis of a compound key with more than two parts

Entities with keys of more than two parts may be analysed to reveal entities with keys made up of various permutations of the parts of the key.

Imagine that Surgical Operation has a three-way key, of Patient, Hospital and Surgeon (perhaps date and time ought to be included as well, but we shall gloss over this). In addition to the three obvious entity types, there may be others. Assuming all Surgeons in a Hospital are allowed to operate on all Patients in the Hospital, analysis may reveal the following entities.

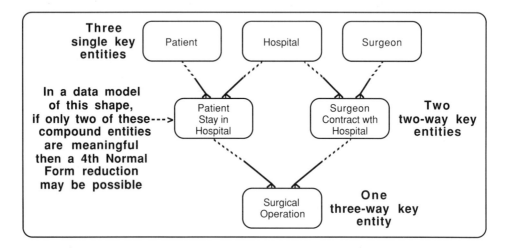

Now suppose Surgeons in a Hospital are only allowed to operate on a Patient in the Hospital after the Patient has signed a consent form specifying the Surgeon. This further constraint means an extra entity type should be modelled.

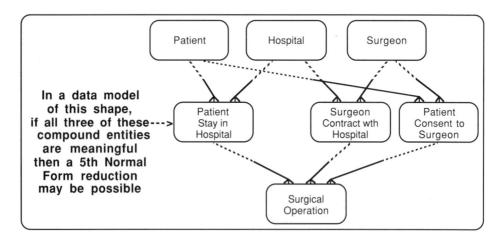

The three-way key entity in the above example is necessary. It models something in the real world and may have attributes of its own. But a three-way key may result from formal data analysis, perhaps of a poorly designed input or output document, where there ought instead to be two or three two-way compound keys.

Normalisation to fourth and fifth normal forms

Fourth and fifth normal forms are more easily illustrated via entity data modelling and enquiry access path analysis, than through normalisation. Given a three-way compound key, we recommend the analyst sets out to construct a data model showing all valid or meaningful combinations of keys.

Fourth normal form is to do with replacing an entity which has been allocated a three-way compound key, into two entities with two-way keys. If the constructed data model resembles the first one on the previous page, then if the entity at the bottom:

- has a three-way compound key
- is a key-only entity (has no non-key attributes)
- can be derived by joining the two sets of two-part key entities

then there is a fourth normal form problem, and the three-part key only entity can be discarded (provided that the two two-way link entities are retained).

Fifth normal form is to do with replacing an entity with a three-way compound key into *three* entities with two-way keys, because there is a 'join dependency' preventing all possible combinations of the key values from existing. If the constructed data model resembles the second one on the previous page, then if the entity at the bottom:

- has a three-way compound key
- is a key-only entity (has no non-key attributes)
- cannot be derived by joining any two sets of two-part key entities
- can only be derived by joining all three sets of two-part key entities

then there is a fifth normal form problem, and the three-part key only entity can be discarded (provided that the three two-way link entities are retained).

Note

For a key-only entity which is a candidate for removal under fourth or fifth normal form, but which is itself a master entity (owning a set of details) there are two options:

- discard it, and derive it when needed
- include it as an operational master entity in the physical data model.

A similar situation is discussed in chapter 18.

Consolidation

If the relational data analysis technique is applied to several different documents, screens, files, etc., then the result will be several distinct sets of third normal form entities. Where entities share the same key, they can be merged. This is called 'consolidation'.

Representation of relationships between entities

After consolidating entities, where the primary key of one entity is found in another entity as a 'foreign key', then the two entities may be connected together in a data structure as shown below.

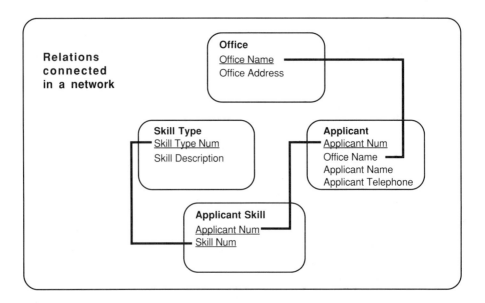

This is clearly equivalent to an entity data model. For a given system it is possible that different analysts may build the two kinds of model in parallel.

One established method of cross-validation is to draw an entity relationship model from general analysis and interviewing techniques, to construct an entity attribute model from relational data analysis of input and output reports, screens and files, then compare and merge the two models.

Relational data analysis of inputs and outputs has the benefit of encouraging analysts to study the input and output data thoroughly. The alternative is ongoing validation of the entity relationship model by relational data analysis of each entity in it, but this may mean that analysts do not pay enough attention to the user interface, by which the system will first be judged by users to be a success or not (c.f. the remarks in chapter 4 on output-driven system design).

11.14 **Comparison with OMT notation**

This is a diagram of notations used in OMT. Since there is no distinction between aggregates of Dependent details and Independent details, words must be added to the diagram to make this distinction.

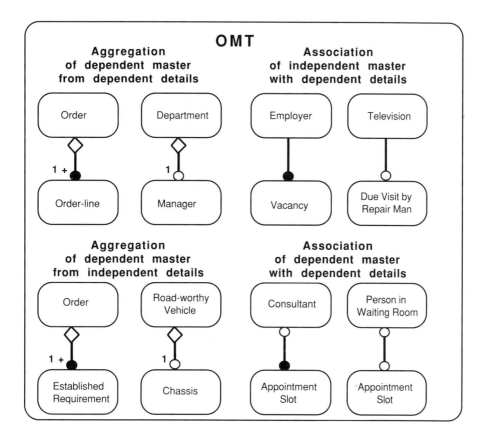

In our attempt to draw corresponding pictures of OMT and SSADM notation, we've used the word 'aggregation' as OMT does rather than as we do.

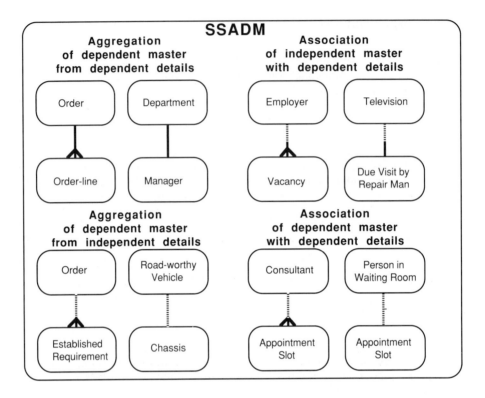

In our notation, two of the relationship notations (exemplified by Road-worthy Vehicle to Chassis and Television to Due Visit) look like an inversions of each other. As far as we can tell, it would make no difference if the two examples were swapped over.

For class hierarchies, which are discussed at length in chapter 12, the notations are more obviously equivalent.

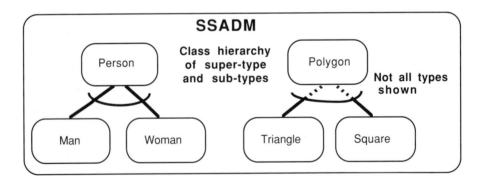

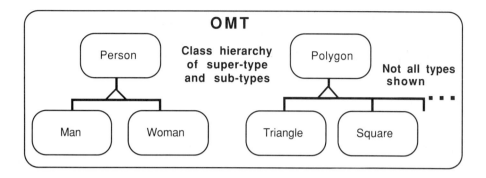

11.15 Comparison with OMT methodology

Turning to the methodology behind the notation, there are a few points where our methodology differs not only from OMT but from some other approaches based on Chen-style entity relationship modelling. The first two points might be viewed as the application of Occam's Razor to cut out redundant concepts.

No properties of relationships
We never attach any attributes or behaviour (or 'methods') to a relationship connecting two entities. Wherever it seems that we might be obliged to do so (to specify, for example, a many-to-many relationship), we always define a new entity type in the entity data model, which rightfully becomes the owner of these properties. Some prefer to suppress such 'link entities' from an entity model, but we suggest that analysing and naming the new entity type is an important step in systems analysis, and may reveal further analysis questions to be asked.

No three-way relationships
We never show a three-way relationship between entities. Wherever it seems we are obliged to introduce one, we always define a new entity type in the entity data model, linked to existing entities by two-way relationships. Rumbaugh at al. claim 'professor teaches course in room' as an example of a three-way relationship which cannot be resolved by introducing a three-way link entity, but it can. Probably they mean to say that this entity should be further resolved (as shown in section 11.13) into the two-way link entities 'professor teaches course' and 'course runs in room'. Without further specification of requirements, it is not clear whether adding these two-way link entities removes the need for the three-way link entity or not.

The next two points are to do with the dividing line between logical system modelling (not concerned with implementation environment or system performance) and physical system design.

No distinction between abstract and real super-types

We do not distinguish at the modelling stage between abstract and real super-types. We regard this as an issue for physical implementation, influenced as it is by the target programming language and database management system.

No relationship sort order

We do not specify at the modelling stage the sequence in which entities are sorted within a relationship. We regard this as a decision to be taken during physical design for optimisation of system performance, mainly because different events and enquiries may need to access a relationship in different sequences, and only by sizing and timing can the optimum sequence be chosen. However, a relationship which only exists to support one event or enquiry might reasonably be specified as being sorted in the sequence need by that event or enquiry.

The final two points are to do with differences in terminology and concepts.

Different meaning for aggregation

Whereas most OO writers define aggregation as being a 'made-up-of' relationship, we define aggregate objects, composite objects and composite methods more specifically, see chapters 9 and 12.

Different understanding of non-disjoint sub-types

OMT includes the notion of class hierarchies with non-disjoint sub-types, that is, sub-types which are not mutually exclusive. We view these as aggregations rather than class hierarchies.

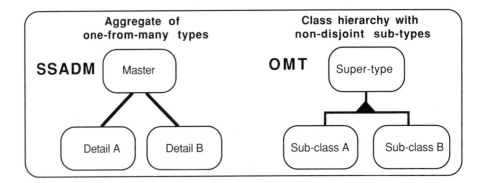

Chapter 12 explores the idea of class hierarchies and aggregations in entity data modelling.

Chapter 12

Reusable objects in entity data models

For systems analysts who want to build reusable components into entity data models, and apply object-oriented ideas, this chapter covers the use of mutually exclusive relationships, entity class hierarchies and generalised reusable entities in entity data models.

12.1 **Reuse in entity data modelling**

Systems analysts must know how to:

- model entity class hierarchies and aggregations in an entity data model
- ensure data attributes and processing routines are not defined more than once.

The idea of a class hierarchy as an inheritance tree is very important in this respect, but the idea of inheritance as an implementation mechanism is not. The analyst building a data model need not and should not know whether the database designer will employ inheritance or some other implementation mechanism such as delegation.

A more important issue is why the analyst may find it advisable *during analysis* to alter what at first seems to be a class hierarchy by rolling the super-type down into distinct sub-types, or rolling up the sub-types into their super-type, or converting class hierarchy into some kind of aggregation. This is quite apart from what the database designer may choose to do at implementation time.

Within the development of one information system, class hierarchies are clearly very useful. But entity class hierarchies do not seem as common in data modelling as might be hoped. Generalised entity super-types form only small percentage of a typical information system model. Generalised *event* super-types are usually more common.

What about the possibilities for reuse between information systems?

How shareable are entity class hierarchies?

To date object-oriented programming languages have been very much concerned with implementing production software such as compilers and screen handling systems, rather than information systems. Part of the reason for the success of object-oriented programming languages in the development of production software is that class hierarchies can be borrowed from one developer by another, then extended for the purposes of the latter.

The world modelled in developing production software is a very restricted one. Varied as operating systems may seem to be, they deal with a limited range of man-made objects *inside a computer.* It is clear that they must all handle similar objects (data item types, records, windows, buttons, devices, blocks, etc). It is easy to imagine that object class hierarchies will turn out to be reusable between such systems.

It is not so clear that business information systems share reusable components to the same degree. The world that is modelled by information systems is a much wider one, of *objects in the business world and in the natural world.* Because information systems deal with substantially different areas of concern, it is less common that a class hierarchy developed for one system will be useful in another.

At the end of this chapter we shall say more about why reuse of super-type entities between systems is so difficult to achieve in practice. Most of the chapter is concerned with reuse within a single system.

12.2 **Advanced entity data modelling**

We propose that three distinct views of the entity data model can and should be developed:

- identity-oriented data model
- identity and type-oriented data model (the type view)
- identity and parallel aspect-oriented data model (the object view).

Chapter 11 showed the development of the identity-oriented view. This chapter shows how this view may be extended to show sub-types and super-types, and parallel aspects.

Identity-oriented data model

To begin with (say at step 210 of SSADM), the analyst should develop a basic entity data model, showing the entity types which the user recognises must be identified one from another. We thank UBS for permission to use a variant of an order processing case study called Expo. There is no room here to specify or develop Expo in full, but here is a first attempt at the entity data model which we use as the basis of illustrations in this chapter.

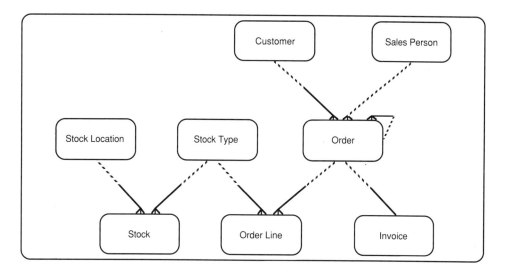

In following sections we analyse this entity data model looking for super-types and sub-types. Notice the recursive relationship; it is often revealing to analyse such a relationship in terms of entity sub-types.

12.3 **Representation of a class hierarchy**

Mandatory sub-types

To show an entity class hierarchy, you can draw an exclusion arc across one-to-one relationships. The arc makes the relationships optional at the super-type end. For example, an Order may be placed by a Customer **or** generated by the system. And when an Order's Processing Date comes around, an Invoice will be raised if the Order can dispatched in full, **or** if a Partial Order can be generated for the stock on hand and dispatched at once.

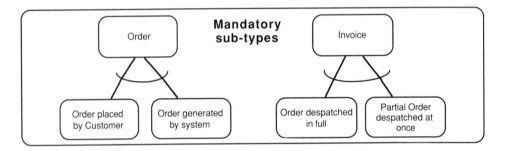

Optional sub-types

To show the super-type does not have to be one of the sub-types, you can draw the lines as optional at the super-type end. This can have two meanings. First, it can mean the sub-type is not known yet; for example an Order will eventually be dispatched in full, **or** else split into two partial orders, one for stock on hand dispatched at once and one for the remainder.

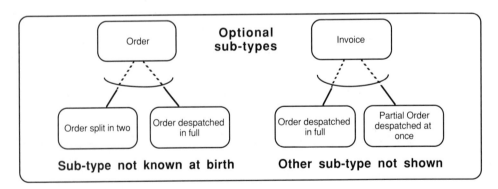

Second, it can mean there is another sub-type not shown, perhaps because it has no additional properties. For example, Invoices may be raised for reasons other than orders which have been dispatched in one way or another.

Parallel or orthogonal sub-types

Combining the above models reveals an example of orthogonal or parallel sub-types.

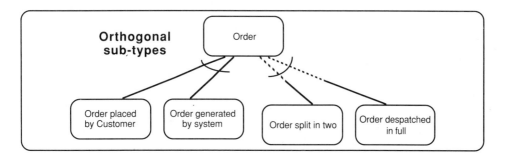

Aside: recursive relationships can usually be analysed in terms of parallel or orthogonal sub-types. Given that a recursive structure has a top and bottom, the orthogonal sub-types can generally be named:

- 'top' or 'not top' and
- 'bottom' or 'not bottom'.

Multiple inheritance

Combining the above models reveals an example of multiple inheritance.

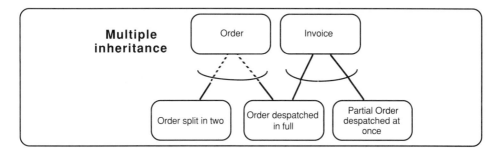

Process model sub-types

Remember, the data model is not the whole story. There are sub-types which you might think about during analysis, and which must be represented somewhere in the system specification, which cannot be shown in the data model.

In this particular example there is an important sub-typing of Order. When the Processing Date for an Order comes around, it will be either completeable and at least partly dispatchable or uncompleteable and not dispatchable at all. An Order cannot be completed if there is no stock on hand for any of its order lines, or if the Customer's credit limit is insufficient to pay for the Invoice raised.

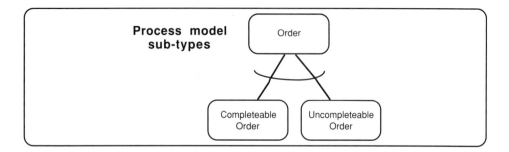

This binary choice is fundamental in the system's process model. It appears in the specification of the Processing Date event, but it is transitory and cannot be shown in the data model.

Not only is this a transitory selection, it is a backtracking problem. You cannot tell whether an Order is completeable until you have processed all the Order Lines, calculated the amount due and checked the Customer's credit limit. The effect correspondence diagram for the Order Processing Date is a challenging design problem, but not further discussed here.

Combining class hierarchies

It is no trivial exercise to combine the above models to give a fuller picture of the case study. There are several ways to do it. The best of the answers we have come up with is shown below. Note the two **recursive** relationships labelled with text.

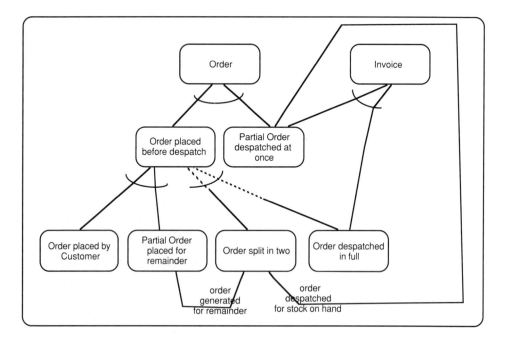

Let us sound three warnings about data models in general, and class hierarchy representation in particular. First, beware that the same real world may be represented by data models which look different. Second, do not be distracted by your preference for a different notation from concentrating on the ideas which follow. Third, beware that the same data model diagram may mean different things. These warnings are explained in detail below.

Same semantics - same syntax - variants of the picture

Beware that the same real world may be represented by data models which look different. You should learn to recognise where different diagrams are equivalent, that is express exactly the same set of business rules.

For example, you can show an entity class hierarchy using one-to-one relationships crossed by exclusion arcs, as shown below.

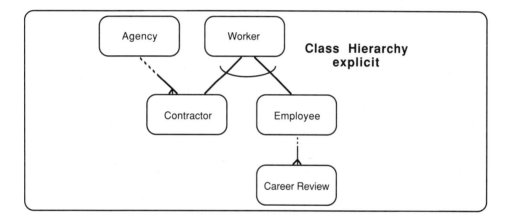

You can show the same thing in an identity-oriented data model by drawing exclusion arcs across one-to-many relationships, as shown in the next diagram below.

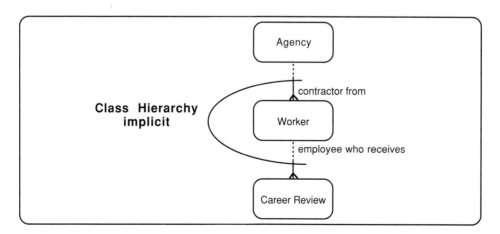

In the second diagram, one might say the sub-types have been 'rolled up' into their super-type. But although the sub-types are not shown explicitly in the picture, the exclusion arc shows they are still present. They will still appear elsewhere in the system specification, in the form of options in processing routines.

Analysts and designers need to recognise these two kinds of model can be exactly equivalent. To prevent the possibility of drawing two pictures of the same situation, some have suggested outlawing mutual exclusion between one-to-many relationships. But this modelling tool is needed, so any discussion of entity class hierarchies has to acknowledge the use of this alternative modelling tool.

Note that the entity event model is unaffected. The same entity event model underlies any variant of an entity data model drawn using the SSADM notation. For both the data models above, there must be an entity behaviour model for Worker with a high-level selection where the two options are Contractor and Employee.

Same semantics - other syntax

The data model syntax is secondary to its semantics. If you convey the exactly same meaning using a different data modelling notation, this is OK. If you prefer a different notation, try redrawing the diagrams in this chapter using your preferred notation. You should find little difficulty in doing this if your notation is well enough developed. The OMT notation shown at the end of chapter 11 would be a reasonable alternative.

Another popular notation uses nested boxes to show 'sub-type' boxes within a 'super-type' box. This is entirely reasonable for simple hierarchies, but it is not so clear when representing multiple inheritance or orthogonal sub-types. We prefer to reserve boxes which encompass entity types for representing the boundary of partial views, class hierarchies and aggregations, as illustrated later.

Note that the entity event model is unaffected. The same entity event model underlies an entity data model drawn in SSADM and OMT notations.

Same syntax - other semantics

Most unfortunately, beware that the same data model may mean different things, that is, be a front for different entity event models. You have to live with some ambiguity because it is not possible to express all semantics in a data model (at least, many have tried to extend data modelling notations to do this and failed). In general, a data model doesn't tell the whole story; for this you have to look at the data and processing detail suppressed behind the data model diagram.

In particular, any entity class hierarchy notation might be used to describe some relatively obscure situations other than class hierarchies. You can distinguish entity class hierarchies by the convention of labelling all lines between boxes with a relationship role name *except* within a class hierarchy, where the line must always be an 'is a' relationship.

Note that the entity event model is affected by ambiguity in a data model notation. The ambiguity will be resolved by means of different entity event models.

12.4 **Discovery of class hierarchies**

In building an entity relationship model (say at step 320 of SSADM) it is very valuable to analyse the basic entity types looking for sub-types and super-types. There are two possible directions the analysis may take, from the bottom up and from top down.

Bottom-up generalisation of sub-types into a class hierarchy

Two entity types in Expo benefit from bottom-up generalisation. Customer and Sales Person have common properties and can be viewed as sub-types of Person.

Top-down decomposition of an entity into sub-types

Two entity types in Expo benefit from top-down decomposition. One is Stock Location: it turns out that Stock is maintained in Warehouses and Sales Offices, which the user considers to be very different kinds of place. The other is Order, which you can analyse to reveal the various sub-types shown in the previous section.

The result of this bottom-up and top-down analysis may be recorded in the data model. It is possible to preserve the original picture of entity types by enclosing the class hierarchies in larger boxes, as shown below.

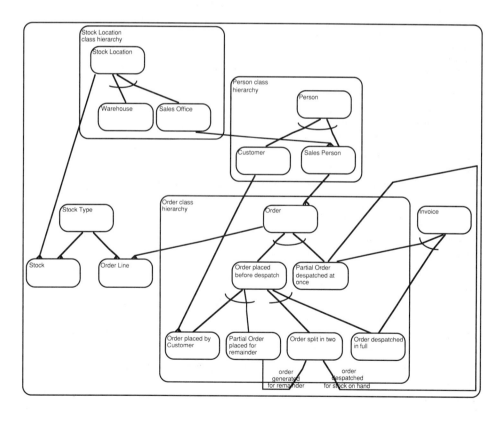

You could have drawn two intersecting class hierarchies under Order and Invoice. But a reasonable rule-of-thumb is to place a sub-type which belongs under two super-types in the class hierarchy of the type whose primary key it shares. We have chosen to place all sub-types of Order under Order, leaving Invoice as a stand-alone entity type.

This analysis has been useful. The meaning of some relationships has been clarified. First, not all Orders are placed by Customers. Second, the recursive one-to-many relationship can be divided into two recursive one-to-one relationships. Third, each Sales Person works for a Sales Office.

12.5 **Relational data analysis of class hierarchies**

During entity attribute modelling (say when carrying out relational data analysis in step 340 of SSADM), the analyst should look to map each class hierarchy onto normalised relations, not just to prepare the model for database design. The analyst has four choices: leave the class hierarchy alone, roll it down, roll it up, or convert it into an aggregation.

Rolling down
If a super-type has no attributes of its own, the analyst should discard it and separate the sub-types. In Expo, if Warehouses and Sales Offices have no attributes in common, then Stock Location will have no attributes and may be discarded.

What if a super-type has no attributes, but does have a method? Such a super-type might be created to hold a polymorphic method, but the situation is so rare in information systems as to be outside of our scope.

Rolling up and aggregation
If the answer to any of the questions below is 'yes' and the sub-types share the same user-friendly key, the analyst should roll up the sub-types into their super-type. If the answer is 'yes' and the sub-types have different user-friendly keys, the analyst may remove the exclusion arc and convert them into parallel aspects of an aggregation.

Do the sub-types share the same attributes?
In Expo, the various sub-types of Order share the same attributes and the same key, so they may be rolled up into a single entity type.

May sub-types attributes be added together?
The sub-types must be strictly mutually exclusive. Only sub-typing which applies to 100% of cases should be shown in the data model. In Expo, some people play Customer and Sales Person roles at the same time. Since Customers and Sales Persons have different keys, we convert the sub-types into parallel aspects of an aggregation.

Note that mutual exclusions which a true most of the time, but not all, may appear in the clustering of data items into boxes or windows at the user interface. Note also the distinction between 'business rules' and 'business policies' in chapter 29.

In Expo, the result is that all three of the class hierarchies apparently mutate into something else during analysis. One has been rolled down, one has been rolled up and one has been restructured into an aggregation of distinct entity types.

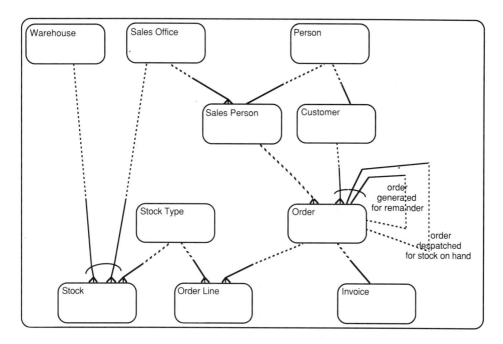

But note that two of the class hierarchies have been replaced by exclusion arcs over ordinary key-based relationships; this means they are still present and will still appear in the entity event model. Customer and Sales Person have enough properties of their own and enough properties in common to leave them and Person as distinct entity types. But Person is no longer a class hierarchy, it is now an aggregation of parallel roles.

Is the division into sub-types stable over time?

The world is full of taxonomies and systems of classification, but many are not stable enough to be embedded in the data model of an information system. Taxonomies are man-made creations, artificially imposed on the real world. The world has a nasty habit of throwing up examples which don't fit existing classifications, which cause them to be restructured or even abandoned. For a simpler and more robust data model, it is often advisable to roll up entity sub-types into their super-type.

For example, you might at first divide Investments into two sub-types, Stocks with a fixed interest and Shares with a profit-sharing dividend, but then discover 'preference shares' (a UK term, different from 'preferred shares' in the US) which earn both a fixed interest rate and a dividend. Given the loosely defined terminology and mobility of the investment market, it is probably safer to define Investment as an aggregation of interest and dividend paying elements.

12.6 **Restructuring class hierarchies to account for time**

The analyst should ask of a class hierarchy: Over time, may an object instance can change from being one sub-type to being another? In Expo, one Person can be a Customer several times and a Sales Person several times. Our first thought was to change the model as shown below, bringing back the class hierarchy under Person Role.

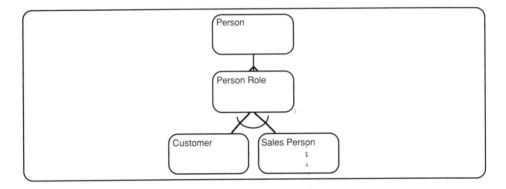

But this model doesn't allow us to express the one-at-a-time nature of Customer and Sales Person roles. We need two monogamous relationships from Person to what had been regarded as 'sub-types', as shown below.

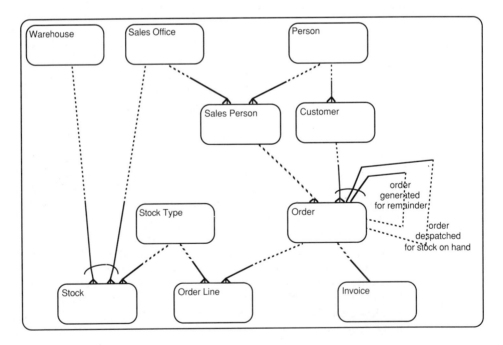

Of course there are many information systems which feature strictly defined entity class hierarchies. Even if these are a relatively small percentage of the whole data model, you must know how to model them and implement them. To make sure we have one class hierarchy for implementation, we are going to reinstate the Stock Location class hierarchy.

12.7 The behaviour of class hierarchies and aggregations

During entity event modelling (say at step 360 of SSADM) the analyst will take an 'object view' of the data model rather than a 'type view'. Rumbaugh *et al.* say that aggregation is not the same as generalisation and that confusion between them should be avoided. We agree and propose showing them in separate data models. In practice, we find it helpful to maintain several views of the entity data model, some of these are partial views, some are 'type' views' and some are 'object views'.

Readers may find the rest of this section only makes sense after chapters 13 to 18, however the diagram at least illustrates that the aggregation view of objects in an entity data model is potentially orthogonal to the class hierarchy view of the same objects

The entity behaviour view of class hierarchies

During entity behaviour modelling, the analyst should build an entity behaviour model for class hierarchy as a whole, as though it were a single entity. The class hierarchy entity behaviour model will always contain a high-level selection reflecting the structure of the class hierarchy, whether or not this is shown the picture presented in the data model. In Expo, this means there will be one entity behaviour model for Stock Location. The behaviour models of Warehouse and Sales Office will only appear within the main entity behaviour model for Stock Location, as options of a high-level selection.

Possible parallel super-type entity behaviours

It is often necessary to describe the behaviour of the super-type entity in two or more parallel lives. The first and most important is the 'general' entity behaviour model, with a high-level selection between sub-type lives. A potential parallel life is a 'super-event' entity behaviour model which expresses the behaviour common to all sub-types and provides a place to define super-events as low-level selections of events in the sub-types.

The event view of class hierarchies

In the effect correspondence diagrams, the analyst should include one box for the class hierarchy as a whole, as though it were a single entity. In the event procedures there will be operations to create, read, write and delete instances of the class hierarchy. These operations will make no distinction between the various sub-types.

If the class hierarchy is later implemented by delegation, some extra code must be written in the PDI, for example to stitch super and sub-type records together to satisfy a read operation. There is an analogy here with the OO idea of the inheritance mechanism.

The entity behaviour view of aggregations

During entity behaviour modelling, the analyst may decompose entity types into parallel aspects. These can be shown as distinct object types within boxes labelled 'aggregation'. You need not draw an entity behaviour model for the aggregation itself, only for the parallel aspects. One of the parallel aspects, the dominant one or aggregate object, can be given the job of handling any general properties of the aggregation.

In Expo, the various parallel aspects are shown below, together with a few other things we find out during further analysis of the case study.

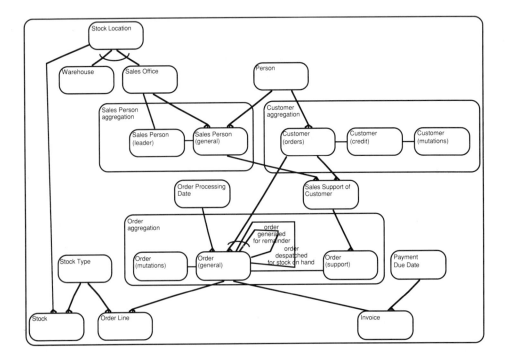

Notice how relationships can be assigned to each parallel aspect. In each aggregation one of the parallel aspects, the dominant one or aggregate object, can take responsibility for general properties such as the primary key.

Note also that this decomposition does not go as far as showing each attribute and relationship as a parallel aspect. Attributes and relationships which share the same state-transitions can be lumped together in one parallel aspect.

The event view of aggregation

In the effect correspondence diagrams, the analyst should include one box for each parallel aspect of the aggregation, as though they were distinct entities. One parallel aspect may act to filter events for another. The first may divide an event into two optional event effects and pass on only one of these event sub-types to the second.

12.8 **Looking for reusable objects**

We are now going to pursue a variant of the same case study in which Warehouses and Sales Office do share attributes and individual Stock Items are recorded. In looking for reuse, you should look for duplicate data and processes. This entity data model contains some entities which look like they might be duplicates of each other.

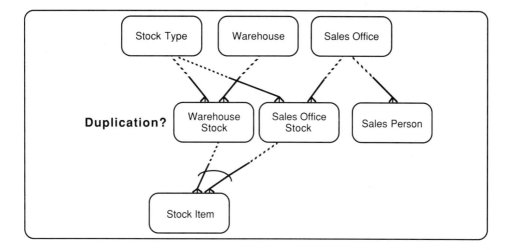

Looking at the data model isn't enough to confirm the duplication; you must examine the suppressed details, both data attributes and processing routines. Here are the data items which are recorded as attributes of the similar-looking entities.

Warehouse	Sales Office
Warehouse Name	Sales Office Number
Warehouse Address	Sales Office Address
	Sales Office Manager

Warehouse Stock	Sales Office Stock
Warehouse Name	Sales Office Number
Stock Type Code	Stock Type Code
Stock On Hand Amount	Stock On Hand Amount

Both Warehouse Stock and Sales Office Stock have compound keys, made up of two foreign keys. Apart from the first of their foreign key items, the two entities are exactly the same. What about the behaviours of these two entities and the processing routines defined to implement these behaviours? Let us assume they are virtually identical.

This duplication cause some unnecessary work for the system builder. For Warehouse Stock and Sales Office Stock, two parallel sets of input, update and output processes must be designed and constructed, differing only in the tiniest of ways. To get rid of the duplication, our first thought might be to pass the exclusion arc upwards, combining the two Stock entities as shown below.

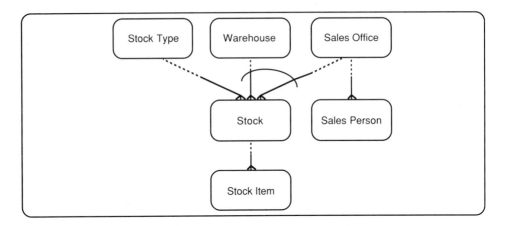

But this model hasn't solved the problem, since much of the processing will have to be repeated, with slight variations, to account for the two mutually exclusive cases. You want to reshape the model so that the two Stock entities are truly merged.

Creating a class hierarchy from the bottom up

It is possible to turn mutual exclusion between one-to-many relationships into a class hierarchy. For example, Warehouse Stock and Sales Office Stock might be regarded as sub-types of Stock.

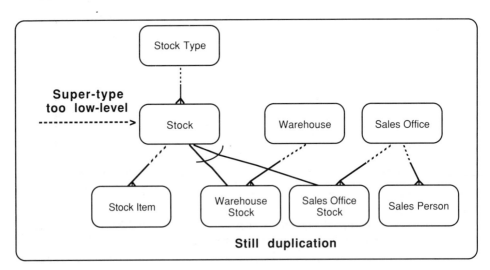

The above model looks different from the previous one, but it means the same thing. The super-type has been introduced at too low a level in the model. It is better to create a new entity super-type at a higher level, to make a home for attributes or relationships which are common to both Warehouse and Sales Office, that is Stock Location.

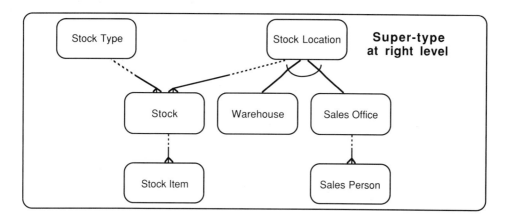

The analyst should move all attributes and relationships common to the sub-types to the super-type entity. For example, Stock Location grabs the attribute Stock Location Address and the relationship to the detail entity Stock.

Advantages? The main advantage of having one Stock entity instead of two becomes apparent when we introduce an amendment in the section after next. Also, the Stock entity is now shown as the thing it truly is, the resolution of the many-to-many relationship between Stock Type and Stock Location.

Disadvantages? There is now an extra entity type, Stock Location, and you must decide whether to make the key a selection between the keys of its sub-types, or create a new key for the super-type.

12.9 Allocating a primary key to a super-type

You may think that allocating a key is merely an implementation issue, but since keys appear in the user domain, they are an analysis issue. There are two design options.

Super-type key as selection of sub-type keys
You could allocate the primary key as selection of sub-type keys as shown below:

Stock Location
    Stock Location Key selection of
           either   <u>Warehouse Name</u>
           or   <u>Sales Office Number</u>
    Stock Location Address

Note that the optional keys have different data lengths and data types. Some database management systems cannot handle a key like this. While this may be a serious problem to a database designer, it is not really relevant to our methodology, which should not bend to suit any specific implementation environment. But worse, the mutually exclusive properties of the Stock Location entity mean that there will still be unnecessary duplication in the process model.

Super-type key as new key

Alternatively, you may allocate a new artificial key to the super-type. The attributes of the new super-type entity become:

> Stock Location
> > Stock Location Key
> > Stock Location Address

The new key may be allocated to other entity types. There are three design steps to consider.

Introduce the super-type key into the sub-types

The key of the super-type entity must appear in sub-type entities, at least as a foreign key if not the primary key.

Possibly use the super-type key as the primary key of sub-types

With super and sub-type entities we usually follow the object-oriented line that they all share the same primary key. Having created a new primary key in a sub-type, what to do with the former key? Warehouse Name and Sales Office Number are examples.

If the former sub-type key is artificial and not important to users (such as, let us say, Sales Office Number), it should be discarded.

If the former sub-type key is user-friendly (such as Warehouse Name), it should be preserved alongside the new key as an attribute of the sub-type. The former sub-type key may now be regarded as a 'candidate key' or 'alternative key', and may still be used as a foreign key elsewhere in the system.

Possibly introduce the super-type key as a foreign key in detail entities

The analyst should track down all the entities which held as foreign keys the former sub-type keys, then decide whether to replace them by the new super-type key.

In Sales Person, the new super-type key must replace Sales Office Number (the higher part of its hierarchical key). In the new Stock entity, the new super-type key may be used to replace the mutually exclusive choice between Warehouse Name and Sales Office Number. The end-result is shown below.

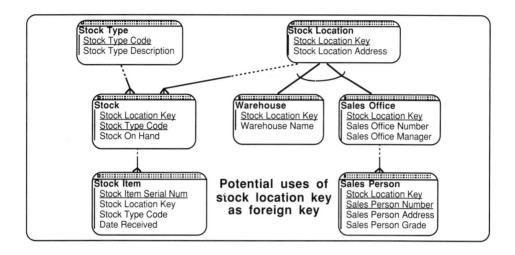

12.10 **Reuse of data and processing components**

A super-type entity saves a little duplication in data and process specification. A bigger benefit comes if you need to introduce a new entity which has all the same characteristics. Suppose you want to record the Service Depots which hold Stocks. For each Service Depot you wish to record its Address and the list of Stocks held at that Service Depot. Since a Service Depot has all the characteristics a Stock Location has, it is easy to plug the new entity into the data model, as shown below.

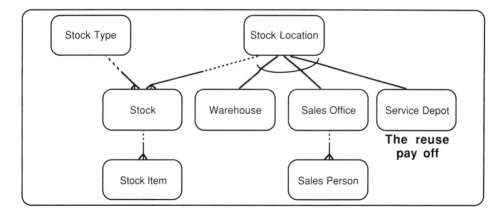

The main advantage is you do not have to add any data or processing for the Stocks at the Service Depot. The existing database structure and user interface for adding and updating Stocks will require no revision. This is the pay-off we have been hoping for from object-oriented ideas, but see the last section of this chapter.

12.11 **Internal design**

Database implementation mechanisms

The systems analyst may pass to the database designer a data model which contains both class hierarchies and aggregations. In database design, several possible implementation mechanisms have long been established.

Class hierarchy implementation	Aggregation implementation
Reverse inheritance	Relational aggregate *
Delegation	Distributed aggregate
Inheritance mechanism	

There is a strong correspondence between implementation mechanisms listed in the same row of this table. All but the one marked * are listed by Rumbaugh *et al.* (1992, page 386). Here we give them names, suggest preferred options and highlight the role of the PDI in hiding the implementation mechanism from the Conceptual Model.

Class hierarchy: database implementation mechanisms

Reverse inheritance

Reverse inheritance is a mechanism whereby the database designer (or possibly the database management system) elects to store an object instance as the highest super-type, perhaps completed with null properties for sub-types it does not match. This is analogous to the analysis step we called 'rolling' up sub-types.

We presented some questions to help the systems analyst decide whether to roll up entity sub-types into their super-type. The database designer has several implementation-oriented motivations to revisit these analysis questions. First, databases containing live data are not so readily restructured as data models on paper. Second, databases built using delegation can be inefficient in terms of data accessing. Third, the chosen database management system may not support the inheritance mechanism. For these three reasons, the designer should ask these questions:

- is the class hierarchy stable over time?
- does saving access path time matter enough to rule out delegation?
- does the implementation environment rule out the inheritance mechanism?

Any 'yes' answer is support for employing reverse inheritance as the implementation mechanism. We call it reverse inheritance because perversely, the super-type entity may be said to inherit the characteristics of its sub-types. The effect of this on the database design of the example is shown below, using the data model notation.

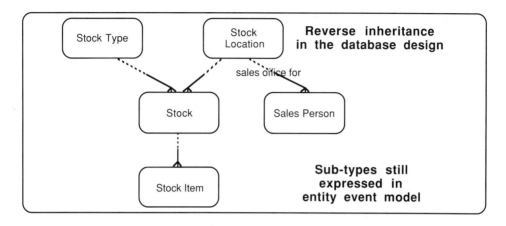

Delegation

Delegation is a mechanism whereby the database designer (or possibly the database management system) elects to store an object instance by means of distinct super and sub-type records related via key-based relationships. Advantages include:

- separation of entity types the user thinks are different (e.g. Order and Invoice)
- facilitation of database distribution and application integration
- reduction of multi-user contention for data.

The database designer (not the analyst) who chooses to implement a class hierarchy using delegation should add a type indicator into the super-type entity. This **discriminator** enables processes which navigate the data model to 'know' which of the two sub-type records exists without having to search for them. For example:

Stock Location
> Stock Location Key
>
> Stock Location Type   (indicates either Sales Office or Warehouse)
> Stock Location Address

The inheritance mechanism

Inheritance is a mechanism whereby the database designer or the database management system elects to store an object instance as the lowest sub-type it can be matched to, extended with properties inherited from its super-types. At its extreme this means implementing only the lowest level sub-types as database record types; this is analogous to the analysis step we call 'rolling down' the super-type.

We do not recommend the database designer chooses this path. We have always found it easier to employ reverse inheritance or delegation. These implementation mechanisms are sound, practical, efficient, and provide designers with sufficient options for balancing sizing and timing tradeoffs.

We dropped a list of reasons not to use the inheritance mechanism from this point in the book, when we noticed that in the case of delegation, the PDI acts much as though it were implementing the inheritance mechanism, assembling the instance variables of super and sub-types together whenever they are needed.

Class hierarchy: the process/data interface

The entity event model is not affected by the choice of implementation mechanism. Where the event procedures include create, read, write and delete operations, these operations must be translated by the PDI into physical database operations.

If delegation is chosen, a read entity operation will be implemented by assembling the data from distinct super and sub-type records. The discriminator attribute may prove very useful here, facilitating a top-down read path through the class hierarchy.

Alternatively, the logical entity event model can be transformed into a physical one. For delegation, the entity behaviour models of the various sub-types can be partly removed from the super-type and placed in distinct diagrams. They cannot be entirely removed, due to the need for events which create and delete sub-types to appear in the super-type's life as well. The result is that the super-type entity behaviour model will be a little smaller, but the total set of documentation will be larger, due to some overlap between diagrams.

Aggregation: database implementation mechanisms

We regard what some call class hierarchies with 'non-disjoint sub-types' as aggregations. The detail entities are not so much sub-types as **parallel aspects** of the aggregation. We are keen to distinguish class hierarchies from aggregations because although they may look similar on the data model, their process models are very different.

In our data model, suppose a Stock Location may be at once a Warehouse, Sales Office and Service Depot. These parallel aspects may be shown as below.

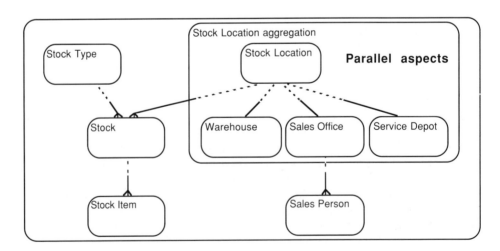

There are two implementation mechanisms for aggregations:

- relational aggregate (c.f. reverse inheritance)
- distributed aggregate (c.f. delegation).

The first is the conventional implementation path, whereby all the parallel aspects are rolled up into one record type. Rumbaugh *et al.* recommend the second, where parallel aspects are implemented as distinct record types connected by key-based relationships. This may help the database designer to partition a database for distribution or application integration, and to minimise contention for database records in a multi-user environment.

Aggregation: the process/data interface

The entity event model is not affected by the choice of implementation mechanism for an aggregation. Where the event procedures include create, read, write and delete operations for the parallel aspects, these operations must be translated by the PDI into physical database operations.

If 'relational aggregate' is chosen, the PDI will ignore any read operation for a parallel aspect after the first one, since this will collect the instance variables for all the parallel aspects at once.

12.12 Limits to reusability

We suggest five reasons why entity class hierarchies do not turn out to be as reusable between different information systems as we would like.

There aren't many useful super-types around

We model super-types wherever we find them within an information system, but in practice we find few super-types are shareable between distinct information systems. Those that are tend to be drawn from the very limited range listed here:

- Point in space, or location
- Point in time, or date
- Person or organisation.

Perhaps the manufacturers of database management systems should be providing these entities for us as standard record data types, rather than data item types.

To slot in, a new sub-type must match the old super-type

Reusability can clearly be achieved where the new entity is to be processed in exactly the same way as an existing super-type entity. But if it turns out that the data attributes or processing behaviour of the new sub-type (Service Depot) is significantly different from the other sub-types (Sales Office and Warehouse), then there is less to be gained. Often, looking for reusable super-types more trouble than it is worth.

To keep order, a data manager is needed

To achieve the benefits you must build some kind of corporate data model. This may have to cover several relatively discrete systems, with only small elements in common. Who is in charge of this model? Who changes it to accommodate a new system or user requirement? Who decides what super-types will be useful?

It is dangerous to allow anyone to add new super-types and sub-types into the model. Changes to the data model must be managed. Probably the responsibility for authorising changes will be given to one person, the data manager. The role of the data manager is vital. Done well, the job will provide opportunities for saving time in system development. Done badly, the job may actually handicap new systems development.

To get benefits, forethought is needed

To speed up future system development, and minimise the redesign which is necessary, some thought may be given now to defining the characteristics of data in the immediately required system, so that it will serve the purposes of future systems. For example, you might make sure that the Stock Location Address is long enough to accommodate foreign country names, in case your business grows to become international.

But such forethought can have harmful side-effects. It can make the immediately required system less user-friendly. It can slow down the development of the immediate system. The future requirements may never materialise.

To be useful, a super-type should have a user-friendly key

It is hard to make use of a super-type entity if it does not have a user-friendly identifying key. Locations can be identified by a map reference, and possibly height from sea level, and thus cross referenced to a Geographical Information System. Points in time can be identified by a date or a time within a date.

But keeping track of people and organisations by name only is a notoriously difficult problem. People present themselves with many variations of their name, even changing it altogether on marriage. How do you recognise that the same person appears in a medical records system as a doctor, a patient, a pharmacist, a mother, etc.? What if one company takes over another?

So what can you do?

It is a mistake to hope for too much from data modelling alone. What you need are further techniques for analysing and specifying the common processes which are shared between different database programs. It seems there is more reuse to be achieved by developing **event class hierarchies** than by developing entity class hierarchies. This is where object-oriented ideas pay a dividend in information systems development and this is what chapters 13 to 18 describe.

Chapter 13

Entity event modelling concepts and notations

This chapter defines the concepts ('event', 'event effect', 'method', etc.) at the heart of the methodology. It also introduces notations to be used in documenting an entity event model, and shows some stereotype components. It does not describe the methodology for building the model, which follows in later chapters.

13.1 **Events, effects and methods**

How to discover the events which affect an object is a topic for the next chapter. This section distinguishes the notions of event, event effect and method.

Two views of a system

At this point the reader may find it helpful to review chapter 7, where it is shown that entity event modelling is concerned with modelling the dynamics of a system. Two complementary views of a system are built, which may be summarised thus:

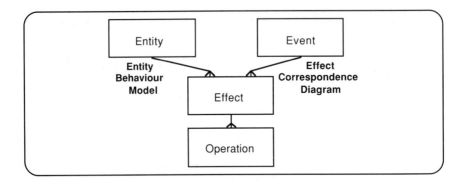

This meta-model is oversimplified. We could include the concept of a 'method' in it, but this would obscure the simple picture needed at this point. Instead, we define how methods fit into the picture through the development of examples.

What is an event?

What we mean by an event is three different things. First, we mean *an event in the real world*. An event is anything which happens in the real world, such as a physical movement, a decision, a date or time. But for a given system, we are only interested in those events which affect the entities of the system, and which the system can know about. So, we must select from all the possible events which happen in the real world:

- those events which affect entities in the system
- those events which can be detected
- those events which can be represented to the system as input data.

Second, we mean *an input data group*. An event is the representation to the system of a movement, decision, date, or other happening in the real world, as input data. Most events must be input by users, but date and time events may be internally generated by the system, from a calendar or clock.

Third, we mean *a database update process*. In the implemented system an event will trigger an elementary database update process, one which must succeed or fail as a whole. But to name an event, we use a noun which represents the thing which happens in the real world, or a moment in time, *not* the name of the operation or process triggered by the event.

Events as commit units

Some people confuse events with user functions, or what might be called 'business events'. Other people confuse events with the operations executed within or outputs produced by the process triggered by an event. Object-oriented enthusiasts sometimes confuse events with effects or with methods. To avoid these confusions, the main idea to keep in mind is that:

- an event is the real-world equivalent of a commit unit.

We shall specify (partly automatically from the set of entity behaviour models) an event procedure for each event, which may be thought of as a database update routine. An event procedure changes the entity data model, from one consistent state to another, updating one or more entities. It must succeed completely, or else fail.

It is meaningless to look at the states of any of the affected entities during the processing of an event; the system will be inconsistent. For example, half-way through processing a Stock Transfer event, when the total Stock Items at one Warehouse has been reduced, but the total at the other has not yet been incremented; an enquiry on the overall total of Stock Items will show less than it should. In the same way, it is meaningless to look at the state of an entity while an event effect is being dealt with. For example, the Amount Outstanding may have been reduced but the Number Of Payments made may not yet have been increased.

Events and enquiries

It is probable that a complete theory of entity event modelling would make no distinction between events and enquiries. Each enquiry can and probably should be regarded as an event, and included within entity behaviour models of the entities it accesses.

However, for practical reasons, because of the points of difference mentioned in chapter 6 and to prevent the entity behaviour models from becoming too complex, it is convenient to distinguish enquiries from events. We analyse and design the enquiry processes using a different set of techniques.

There is usually no difficulty distinguishing events from enquiries, because an event leaves the data model in a different state, while an enquiry leaves it in the same state. Some events have one or more 'enquiry effects', and these are discussed below.

Event effects

An effect is one effect of an event on an entity, that is an appearance of an event inside an entity behaviour model. Three kinds of event effect may be included in an entity behaviour model: an **update effect**, where an event changes an attribute, relationship, or state variable of an entity; a **validation effect**, where an event tests the state of an entity in order to be processed; an **enquiry effect**, where an event gathers data from an entity (without changing it) for the purpose of updating another entity.

To generalise, an entity behaviour model should include any event whose update effects are determined by the state of an entity. But if an event gathers data from an entity (without changing it) merely for the purpose of output, then this enquiry effect is usually not shown in the entity behaviour model.

One type of event may have several alternative effects within one entity behaviour model. For example, a Payment may simply reduce the Amount Outstanding on an Instalment, or be the one which is sufficient to pay it off completely.

Methods

A method represents the effects of an event on an entity. The reader may imagine that a method is the same as an event effect. This is true for simple examples, but later we shall see that a method may be somewhat larger. A method may encompass different effects which one event has upon one entity; it may even encompass the common effects of different events. A method will be one of:

- an event effect
- a selection of optional event effects (triggered by one event)
- a super-event (triggered by more than one event).

What the methods are not

We have seen attempts at object-oriented systems design which suggest that the methods required to manage objects represented in a database are physical operations like *Store*, *Modify* and *Delete*. This cannot be so. These are things which are done to the physical representation of a conceptual object rather than to the conceptual object. They belong to the universe of discourse of the implementation environment, not to the universe of discourse of the problem definition.

The methods need to be drawn from the same universe of discourse as the objects. For example, the methods for a stack object would include *Push* and *Pop*, which are meaningful manipulations of a stack; the methods are not *Decrement stack pointer and move parameter to location pointed to by stack pointer* or *Move value at location pointed to by stack pointer to return parameter and decrement stack pointer*, which belong to the universe of discourse of a particular implementation of the methods.

The records in a database implement conceptual objects which represent the actual objects in the real world. The database updating activities implement changes due to real-world events affecting those real-world objects. Therefore, the methods we are interested in must act on the conceptual objects in a way which directly models the way the events act on the real-world objects.

Entity behaviour modelling

The technique we use for analysing and specifying the effects of events on entities is called entity behaviour modelling. It leads an analyst to model the *dynamic* aspects of the system in entity behaviour models.

13.2 **Entity behaviour models**

In the methodology, entity behaviour models are built both to analyse the effects of events and to record the effects of events upon entities. Once the events have been identified, the analyst looks for sequential patterns between these events and models these in an entity behaviour model, recording only the *valid* sequences of events.

An entity behaviour model defines the behaviour of a single type of entity from the moment it becomes of interest to the system to the moment it ceases to be of interest. It defines what happens to the entity and what the entity does. It shows those events affecting (or affected by) an entity and the pattern of these events. The pattern is composed from sequences, selections and iterations of sub-patterns and of effects of events.

The purpose of building entity behaviour models is twofold. During *analysis* they help us understand the entities better; we often have to change the entity data model as a result of the analysis of some fairly trivial entity behaviour model. They also enable us to pin down how the user expects the system to work and how exceptions to the normal operation of the system arise. During *design* they give us a formal method for constructing event procedures.

In object-oriented terms, an entity behaviour model describes the behaviour of an object by showing the time sequence of method invocations and the constraints upon them. An entity behaviour model is a grammar defined over the method invocations for an object.

OO and control-structured paradigms

In any object-oriented approach there will be constraints on when methods can be successfully invoked for a particular object instance. For example, you cannot successfully Pop a Stack Entry unless you Push it first.

A strength of the Smalltalk paradigm is the way in which no control structure sits over the methods to enforce such constraints which instead have to be implemented by setting and testing state variables. At the same time, a weakness of the Smalltalk paradigm is the way in which no control structure sits over the methods, because this makes the context in which they are invoked obscure and impedes the analysis of what constraints, preconditions or rules need to be applied. What is a strength at execution time is a weakness at analysis and design time.

We need a way of enjoying the analysis-time benefits of control structure and context, and the execution-time benefits of state manipulation. The analysis-time benefits are gained in our methodology by building entity behaviour models as control structures sitting over the methods.

Even in the relatively trivial Hi-Ho case study there are some significant benefits from analysing the methods in the rich context of the control structures which surround them. In a more complex system, it is impossible to believe the analysis can be completed without such a context.

Stereotype behaviour for master entity of monogamous relationship

The full methodology contains detailed rules and several stereotype entity behaviour models, covering common circumstances in entity event modelling. It is not the purpose of this book to present all these rules and stereotypes. However one place for using a stereotypical entity behaviour model is to show the pattern of events handling a relationship to a 'changeable master' or a 'monogamous detail' as defined in chapter 11.

There are four stereotype models which show a repeated cycle of events using an iterated sequence; the four stereotypes terminate in different ways. One of these stereotypes is illustrated by example below.

Suppose an Applicant is related to Interviews by a monogamous relationship. In other words, we are allowed to arrange only one Interview at a time for each Applicant, having to wait for the Interview Result before arranging the next one. Then in the entity behaviour model of Applicant, we would show an iterated sequence of events.

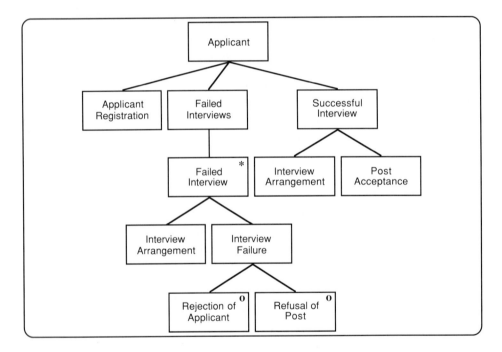

(The 'backtracking' technique needed to overcome the 'recognition problem' of deciding whether an Interview Arrangement is successful or not is outside the scope of this book.)

For the case study, this model over constrains events. It stops a second Interview being arranged until the result of the first is known. It prevents many Interviews being arranged in parallel for one Applicant.

Stereotype behaviour for master entity of polygamous relationship

Except where the detail occurs monogamously (one at a time) it is impossible to show the sequence of events which affect a detail entity within the entity behaviour model of its master. But the sequence of events affecting one detail will not be lost: it must and will appear in the entity behaviour model of the detail entity (see Interview later).

In the master's behaviour model, the most we can say about the pattern of events between the birth and the death of the Applicant is that there is a random mixture of Interview events. In an entity behaviour model, a random mixture of events is always shown as an iterated selection.

In fact, wherever entities are related by a polygamous relationship, the stereotype behaviour model for the master of the polygamous relationship contains an iterated selection (random mixture) of the birth and death events of its detail entity. So we'll now correct the entity behaviour model, and at the same time allocate some operations to it.

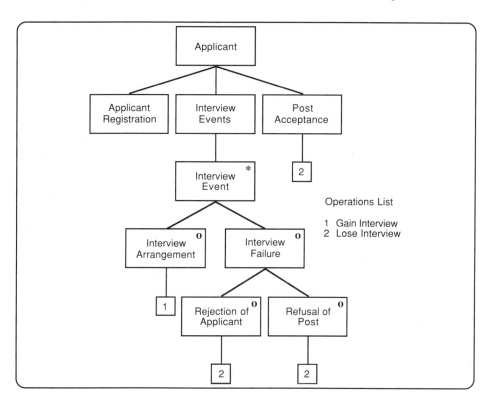

13.3 **Recording operations triggered by an event**

We extend the diagram by identifying the operations needed in the bodies of the required methods, then allocating them to the appropriate method invocations. An **operation** is an action done to an entity as part of the effect of an event on that entity; for example, 'Subtract Amount of Payment from Amount Outstanding'. Because entity behaviour models are hierarchical, they lend themselves to the addition of such processing detail; whereas some other notations leave no room for operations.

Listing operations

You can use a checklist of operations types, a conceptual data manipulation language, to help in listing the operations which update an entity. We have found it necessary to refine and extend the SSADM checklist for our CASE tool (Model Systems, 1993), but here we are content to use the following very informal operation types.

- tie, cut, swap master entities
- gain, lose detail entities
- initialise, replace, calculate, increment or decrement each non-key attribute.

You should list **tie** and **cut** operations for detail objects; these allow a detail object to store the identifier of any master object to which it needs to send a message; they will be implemented in both OO and relational database environments. You should list **gain** and **loss** operations for master objects; these allow master objects to store the identifiers any detail objects to which they need to send messages; they help you to analyse the effects of events on entities; they will be implemented in an OO environment but may be dropped in a relational database implementation.

The first event in a behaviour model must create an entity instance. You need not list a **create** operation because it can be automatically allocated to the relevant event procedure. You should list operations to update 'interesting' attributes, but you may omit operations which reveal nothing because they simply replace one attribute value with another and have no immediate effect on any other part of the system.

Allocating operations

After listing an operation, you should allocate it to the relevant event effect box(es) of the entity behaviour model. In doing this you record not only the behaviour of the entity, but also the life history of each attribute and relationship belonging to that entity. The above example records the behaviour of the relationship from Applicant to Interview. Later, you (or a CASE tool) should transfer the operations from the entity behaviour model into the specification of the relevant event procedures (see 15.3).

Case study

Before we show an example, note that the last diagram is wrong! The behaviour model must match the data model. In the data model, Interview is not connected to Applicant, but to Applicant Skill. So some of the structure we have drawn (with operations to gain and lose Interviews) really belongs in the entity behaviour model of Applicant Skill. Nothing happens to an Applicant entity in our case study after it is born (together with a set skills) until the Applicant accepts a post.

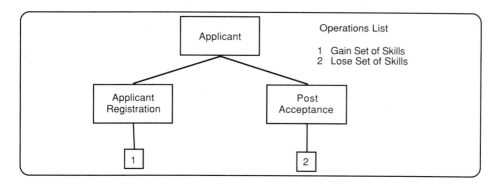

No skills are added to an Applicant or removed during the Applicant's short stay with Hi-Ho. Introducing the Applicant Skill entity behaviour model, notice it shares the same birth and death events as Applicant. The two entities are born and die together.

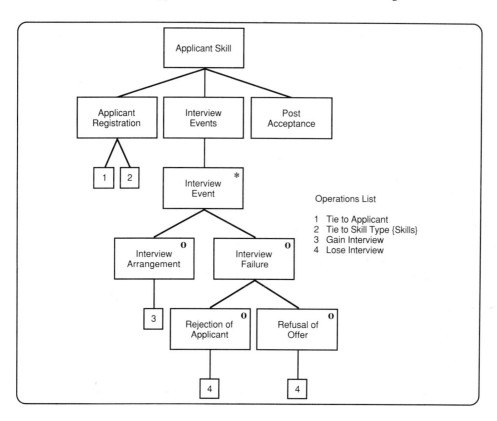

13.4 **Recording the state of an entity after each event effect**

Meyer (1988) says, 'by introducing a state and operations on this state, we make the type specification richer' and 'the view of objects as state machines reflects types which are more operational, but this no way makes them any less abstract.'

An entity's 'state' is the position of the entity within its life. Knowledge of the current state is needed to test whether an input event is valid or not. So in addition to the attributes identified through techniques like relational data analysis, each entity may include space for one or more state variables, and the analyst must specify the value of the entity's state variable which is set by each event effect.

Successor states

The successor state of an event effect may be shown to the right of an event effect box. In OO terms, we identify the object's successor states for each of the method invocations and annotate the bottom right-hand corner of the box representing the method invocation with the successor state variable value as shown below.

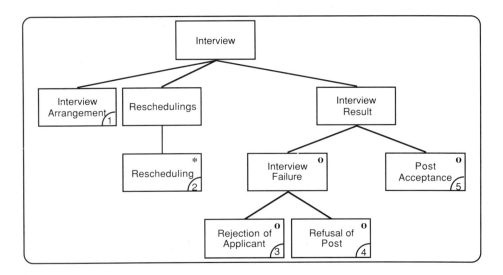

The numerical value which is given to a state variable at any point is unimportant. The birth event in entity behaviour model above sets the state variable to 1; it could equally well set it to 99, A or Z

The translation of a state variable value into meaningful text for display at the user interface (such as 'interview arranged and awaiting result') may be performed within the External Design, as discussed in chapter 29.

This diagram shows the approach described in SSADM4, that is, we have assigned a unique value of the state variable to each event effect. There are a number of reasons to suggest that 'optimisation' of state variable values is desirable.

Optimised states

You may reduce the number of states required by unifying the states of events, using a simple set of rules which enable us to identify equivalences between states. Briefly, the rules are to unify states which end options under a selection (unless an option ends with an iteration) and unify the state before an iteration with that after each iterated component.

So let us optimise the states, and show the operations which must be allocated to the entity behaviour model. All the states labelled '1' in the diagram below are equivalent to each other, and all the states labelled '2' are equivalent.

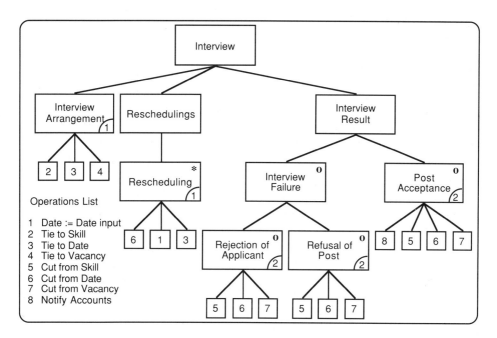

Advantages of optimised states

Optimising states eases maintenance. It reduces the need to alter valid prior state tests in event procedures when a new event is added to the entity behaviour model.

Optimising states enables further optimisation of the code. Where an event effect does not change the state, that is valid prior state = successor state, then the operation to set the successor state may be omitted. This is particularly likely where an event has an 'enquiry effect' on an entity.

Optimising states helps us to identify super-events and reuse common code in different event procedures.

Optimising states enables mechanical translation of entity behaviour models into state transition diagrams with states which correspond to the best that an intuitive design could achieve.

Where are the methods?

For the Interview object investigated so far, naively assuming each event effect is a method, there seem to be five methods:

- *Interview Arrangement*
- *Post Acceptance*
- *Refusal of Offer*
- *Rejection of Applicant*
- *Rescheduling*.

Their effects on an instance of Interview are constrained as follows:

- *Interview Arrangement* must come first and can only occur once
- *Post Acceptance* can only come at the end and can only occur once
- *Refusal of Offer* can only come at the end and can only occur once
- *Rejection of Applicant* can only come at the end and can only occur once
- only one of the three kinds of interview result can occur
        (that is *Post Acceptance*, *Refusal of Offer*, and *Rejection of Applicant*)
- *Rescheduling* can occur only after *Interview Arrangement*
- *Rescheduling* can occur only before one of the three kinds of interview result
- *Rescheduling* can occur zero, one or many times.

The relationship between the methods of Interview, and the operations needing to be performed in the method bodies, have been shown diagrammatically by building a control structure to sit over the method invocations showing what sequence method invocations occur in, which invocations can be iterated, and which ones are alternatives of each other.

However, there is a complication here. Two of the event effects trigger the same method.

A potential super-event or method

Any low-level selection between event effects may reveal two events having the same effect on the Applicant entity. In the case study, having now allocated operations and state information to the diagram, we can see that the effects of the two events Rejection of Applicant and Refusal of Post are sub-types of the same generalised effect - Interview Failure. What we have discovered here is a *super-event*, or in object-oriented terms a *method*, invoked by two different events. We'll come back to this point later.

Valid prior states

The entity behaviour model defines all of the *valid* sequences of events in the life of the entity. For each event effect in the entity behaviour model, it is possible to define all of the values of the state variable which may validly precede it.

The valid prior states of an event effect may be shown to the left of an event effect box.

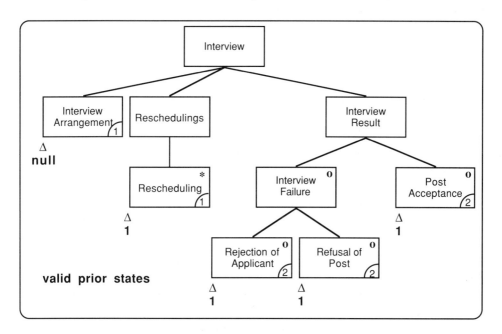

Although valid prior states are annotated something like this in SSADM4, we shall not record them for two reasons. First, because the shape of the diagram already expresses the states and we expect all successor states and valid prior states to be assigned and documented automatically. Second, because valid prior states will later be documented as preconditions in the event procedures.

Automatic documentation of successor states and valid prior states

An important feature of structured entity behaviour model diagrams is that the analyst need never think about states. A CASE tool can:

- allocate successor states after each event effect
- optimise successor states
- deduce the valid prior state(s) of an entity when each event arrives
- insert tests for valid prior states into the event procedure specifications.

13.5 **Recording multiple states of an entity**

A **parallel life** is usually specified to maintain a **parallel aspect** of an entity type where there is a structure clash between cycles in different entity behaviour models. This often happens where one aspect may flip between two states. For example, the relationship from the master Television to the monogamous detail Loan flips from 'available for loan' to 'on loan' and back again; but Repairs can happen at any time.

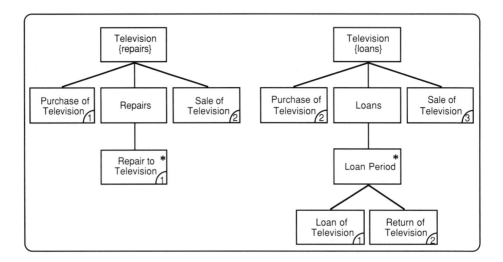

Each parallel entity behaviour maintains its own state variable. There is no need for either parallel entity to refer to or modify the state variable of the other. Note again that actual of value assigned to a state variable is unimportant. The birth event of the entity behaviour model to the right above sets the state variable to 2, which means 'available for loan'.

SSADM4 and a related methodology known as LSDM document parallel lives within one diagram. It is said there is a 'primary' life, and one or more 'secondary' lives. In a secondary life, an event may refer to the state variable of the primary life. However, there are three objections to this:

- it can be very difficult to express several parallel lives within one diagram
- truly there is no 'primary' or 'secondary' life, all lives are of equal status
- it fails the OO principles of 'encapsulation' and 'information hiding'.

To express the last of these objections in less academic words, it is harder to maintain a system where the rule is that one entity behaviour may inspect the state variable of another. It is theoretically more sound, and usually easier, to record parallel lives in separate diagrams. This enforces the principle that each state variable is maintained independently of any other.

13.6 **Recording multiple effects of an event**

Sometimes an event may have several different effects on an entity type, that is, appear more than once in its entity behaviour model. These effects are always distinguished by adding an **event effect name** in brackets after the event name.

Sometimes these different effects on the entity arise because quite distinct instances of the entity are affected by the same event. If the event knows, before examining an entity, what effect it is going to have, then an **entity role name** should be added as well.

Event effect names

One type of event may have several alternative effects within one entity behaviour model. For example, since it turns out there may be many Posts for one Vacancy, a Post Acceptance (not last) will leave one or more Posts to be filled, but a Post Acceptance (last) will reduce the number of Posts to zero, and so kill off the Vacancy completely.

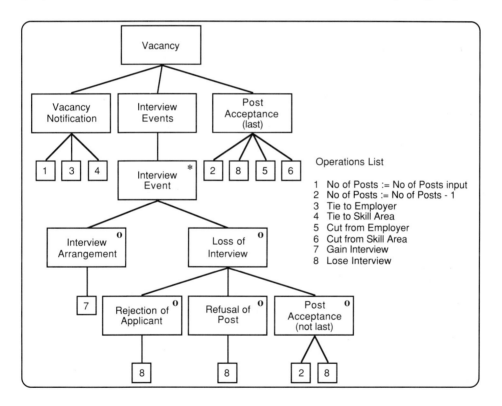

Entity role names

An entity role name describes the entity which is being affected by an event. It is needed where a choice between event effects depends on the identity of (or access route to) the entity. That is, the entity plays different *roles* with respect to the event.

For example, a Stock Transfer affects two Warehouses - reducing Stock in the old Warehouse and increasing Stock in the new Warehouse. The Stock Transfer event, before examining a Warehouse entity, knows which effect it is going to have, so an *entity role name* is added in a second set of brackets, thus:

Event name	Effect name	Entity role name
Stock Transfer	(reduce stock)	[old]
Stock Transfer	(increase stock)	[new]

13.7 Effect correspondence diagrams

An effect correspondence diagram is drawn for each event. It specifies the coordination of those event effects in different entities which are triggered by one event.

Given the entity behaviour models drawn earlier for Applicant, Applicant Skill, Interview and Vacancy (though they are far from finished), we can begin to specify the effect correspondence diagrams for the events in these entity behaviour models. For example the Applicant Registration event affects one Applicant and a set of Applicant Skills.

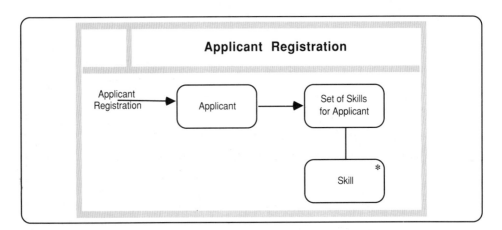

The Post Acceptance event kills off an Interview and an Applicant, causes the loss of an Interview from an Applicant Skill, and may or may not kill off a Vacancy, depending on whether it is the last post or not. Later we shall see there is a great deal more to the Post Acceptance than this.

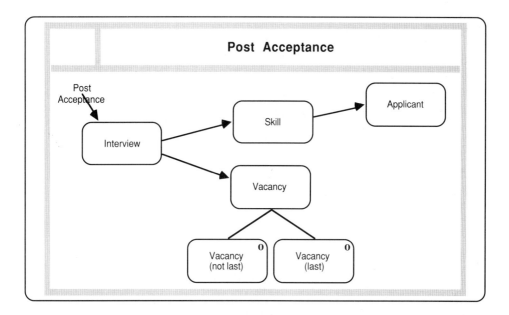

This technique of drawing effect correspondence diagrams has largely been automated. Given an entity data model and a set of entity behaviour models, we generate much of the effect correspondence diagrams automatically using a CASE tool (see chapter 30).

13.8 **Event procedures**

The effect correspondence diagram may be regarded as the implementation-independent end-product of systems analysis. They may be used to specify programs in both OO and conventional programming environments.

SSADM assumes a conventional database management system will be used to provide automatic roll-back in the event of failure, so the effect correspondence diagram can be mechanically transformed into an event procedure, a natural commit unit of database processing. But given an object-oriented database management system, or the wish to implement in an object-oriented style, designers can use the techniques outlined in chapter 18.

We use a CASE tool to generate the event procedure from the entity behaviour models and effect correspondence diagrams. The tool will show the procedure in the form of a Jackson structure, or pseudocode, or 'action diagram' (the Information Engineering term).

Below is what the event procedure for Post Acceptance looks like as an action diagram. Notice in particular the 'Fail' statements which make tests upon the states of the entities involved, and abort the procedure if any entity is in an invalid state.

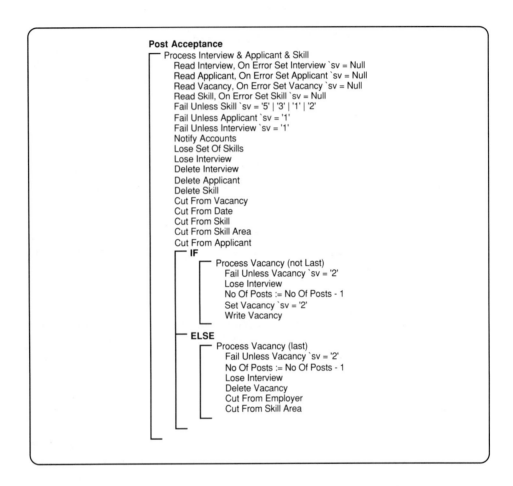

In fact there's some work to do yet on the entity behaviour models of the case study, so this is only a first draft of the event procedure.

13.9 Looking for reuse of events and their effects

Defining and documenting the distinct notions of events and their effects helps us to achieve reuse in two ways. We look out for reuse of each event, and reuse of each effect by different events.

Reuse of events

The separation of concerns between Conceptual Model and External Design leads to opportunities for reuse. Events may be input via many different External Designs, so different input functions may make reuse of the same database update routine.

Reuse of super-events

Within the Conceptual Model, entity event modelling, as it has been defined for example in SSADM, doesn't lead to a great deal of reusability. To identify reusable methods shared by different events, entity event modelling must be extended to incorporate the notion of super-events. A super-event can be identified in an entity behaviour model where two or more different events have the same effect on the entity (that is, they trigger the same operations and result in the same state). In our example, we have found Interview Failure.

Super-events alter the nature of entity behaviour models. Let us call the entity behaviour model which records the super-event, the 'home' entity behaviour model. The super-event may now be treated in other entity behaviour models as an elementary component, which saves duplicating within these other diagrams the sub-structure shown in the home entity behaviour model.

Super-events alter the nature of effect correspondence diagrams and event procedures, and may dramatically simplify each one. In addition to one effect correspondence diagram and event procedure per event, there is an effect correspondence diagram and event procedure for each super-event. The event procedure for the super-event is a kind of sub-routine, invoked from each of the events which appear underneath it in the home entity behaviour model.

Whereas we have previously created a flat list of independent event procedures, with code duplicated between them; by adding super-events, the end result is a network of reusable database routines.

Benefits of super-events

It takes significantly less effort to do entity behaviour model analysis with super-events. Super-events have the benefit of simplifying entity behaviour model, effect correspondence diagram and event procedure diagrams.

Super-events enable common code to be detected in the entity behaviour models, and specified as routines invoked by several event procedures, these routines being recorded as effect correspondence diagrams. Whenever a new event is added under a super-event in an entity behaviour model, it can use the common routine already tested and implemented.

In part four we shall prove these ideas by developing reusable effect correspondence diagrams and event procedures, from entity behaviour models which incorporate super-events. We have further tested these ideas by automating much of this development work in a CASE tool, as suggested in part six.

13.10 Entity event modelling in object-oriented terms

Knowledge elicitation

Knowledge is elicited during systems analysis by analysing the behaviour of entities. Entity behaviour modelling is a knowledge acquisition technique. It sometimes proves a surer mean of identifying objects than entity data modelling or relational data analysis, and certainly provides an important validation of these approaches. It provides a step-by-step means of finding out about events and their effects on entities, and documenting these effects. Entity behaviour models are:

- control-structured objects
- more basic and more understandable than database update procedures
- a prescriptive step-by-step way of analysing conceptual processes
- an incremental way of analysing the Conceptual Model
- a framework for knowledge acquisition.

To benefit from object-oriented ideas entity event modelling must be taught thoroughly, including methodical steps, the use of stereotype entity behaviour models, the use of disciplined quits and the optimisation of state variable values.

Specification of methods
Method invocations are documented in entity behaviour models, methods are documented in effect correspondence diagram. Entity behaviour modelling is extended to force out the recognition of methods shared by several events, by adding the notion of super-events. An entity behaviour model completely specifies all the methods for one object, including elementary database update operations and state changes, we suggest more clearly than the textual specification of methods employed in most object-oriented notations to date.

Specification of events and co-ordination of methods
The co-ordination of methods in different objects triggered by one event is specified in an effect correspondence diagram. The effect correspondence diagram may be regarded as the implementation-independent end-product of systems analysis. But assuming a database management system will be used to provide automatic roll-back in the event of failure, the effect correspondence diagram can be mechanically transformed into a event procedure, a natural commit unit of database processing.

Specification of preconditions and postconditions
Preconditions and postconditions are documented as state variable values. It isn't necessary to show both events and states. The states can be mechanically generated from a structured entity behaviour model, so the analyst need never be aware of states in Conceptual Modelling (their interpretation at the user interface is a separate concern).

Specification of integrity rules and constraints
Integrity rules and constraints are modelled and implemented as test on state variables. Given a complete entity event model (entity data model + entity behaviour models + effect correspondence diagrams), the generation of a pseudo-code specification for a database update routine which captures the integrity rules (in terms of tests on entities' state variables) is entirely mechanical and automatable.

13.11 **Other notations**

A variety of other notations have been proposed by OO authors for modelling the processing or behavioural view of entities. Some use more method-oriented notations.

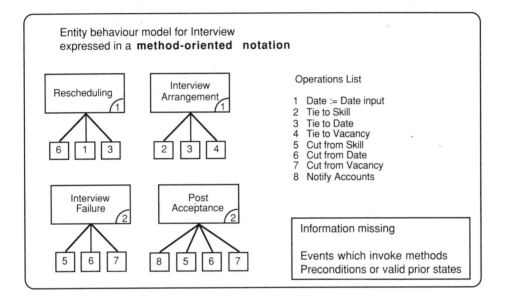

Other authors use more state-oriented notations.

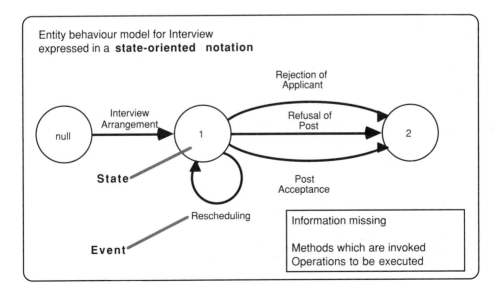

Tests for a notation modelling conceptual processes

There are a number of things an entity event modelling notation should do. Some of these are listed below.

Represent events

Events are important. This is a major theme of this book. We present notations which encourage the analyst to analyse events, then design processes to implement them. Entity behaviour models and effect correspondence diagrams are event-oriented. Other notations tend to present events as secondary or incidental. A state-oriented notation may discourage the analyst from thinking about events and documenting them; a method-oriented notation may provide no support at all for documenting events.

Separate events from the methods they invoke

Events and methods are quite distinct concepts. Some events trigger more than one method, and some methods are triggered by more than event. State-oriented and method-oriented notations tend to confuse events with methods; some assume they are one and the same.

Separate events from their effects

Events are quite distinct from effects. One event may trigger many effects in different objects, and trigger one of different optional effects in one object, depending on the state of that object. State-oriented and method-oriented notations tend to confuse events and their effects; some assume they are one and the same.

Show the valid sequence of effects and methods

A method is usually constrained to work only when the entity is in a specific state or range of states. This precondition needs to be understood, and an entity behaviour model greatly helps to make the context visible. Method-oriented notations fail to make visible the *context* in which a method is applied to an entity.

Separate the Conceptual Model from the External Design

Approaches which are helpful in the External Design are not necessarily helpful in building the Conceptual Model and vice versa. For example, data flow diagrams, which are useful in investigating the external input and output data flows, are little help in documenting the processes of the Conceptual Model. Some OO notations fail to keep the concerns of the External Design and Conceptual Model apart, because they are not backed by a methodology which does this.

Help the analyst apply analysis techniques

Most OO authors seem unaware of the developments in entity event modelling techniques which have taken place in recent years. Entity behaviour modelling is all about encapsulating the data and process views of an object; it has a proven track record and it may viewed as one of the best established object-oriented techniques.

Advantages of our notation

We prefer using regular expressions to model entity behaviour, not only because they do the things listed above, but mainly because:

- they encourage the detection and use of stereotype components
- they are supported by a well-defined methodology.

A big advantage of the structured notation is that standard shapes of entity behaviour model have been defined for representing familiar kinds of constraint or business rule, and these can be combined in various permutations. This advantage cannot be overemphasised and we shall emphasise it often. Stereotype entity behaviour models help us to meet the objectives set out in chapter 2.

Minimum development effort

The valid sequence of events is shown in the shape of entity behaviour models. So states can be deduced from the diagrams. The analyst need never document states, or even think about them. A CASE tool can automatically assign states to the diagrams, and insert the tests for valid prior states into the specification of database update processes.

By way of contrast, state transition diagrams emphasise states; events appear as the agents which move an entity from one state to another; events cannot be deduced from states, so both states and events must be recorded.

Understandability of design objects

Given a set of user requirements, two analysts should produce entity behaviour models of very similar shapes. By recognising stereotype components, one analyst can more immediately understand the work of another. By way of contrast, state transition diagrams are free format, their shape has no meaning.

Rapid response to end-users

Stereotype entity behaviour models help designers to more rapidly change entity behaviour models in response to a change in user requirements.

Minimum amendment effort

Stereotype entity behaviour models help the designer to locate the relevant components of the system.

Reusability of design components

Entity behaviour modelling has been extended with the notion of super-events to help in the identification or detection of reusable components.

Completeness of knowledge acquisition

Entity behaviour models have a greater capacity for carrying processing detail. Entity behaviour models provide more information than state transition diagrams, such as knowledge about behaviour cycles and expectations. State transition diagrams show only the 'leaf level'; they don't help with objective incremental knowledge acquisition.

Because entity behaviour models are hierarchical, processing detail (operations) may be appended to them, enabling process specifications to be derived directly from them. Because state transition diagrams are free format, there is no easy way to document processing detail on them.

Incremental path from design to implementation

Stereotype entity behaviour models help us to create a methodology which speeds up development. By asking a defined series of analysis questions, stereotype entity behaviour models can be added together in a methodical manner. The methodology comprises both analysis steps (helping the analyst to discover events, analyse their effects, construct entity behaviour models and refine the entity data model) and design steps (helping the analyst to complete the entity behaviour models with processing detail, transform the entity behaviour models into effect correspondence diagrams and transform the effect correspondence diagrams into event procedures).

We have automated much of these last two design transformations within a CASE tool. There are also some prospects for helping the analyst during the analysis steps, by giving the tool knowledge of the stereotype components.

Learnability of design process

Stereotype entity behaviour models help us to create a methodology which is teachable. Entity behaviour models can be constructed using objective criteria rather than subjective judgement.

Entity behaviour models are easy to learn where regular expressions are already in common use. Many organisations already use regular expressions to specify the structure and detailed content of any data flow (whether for input to relational data analysis, for program specification and design) and the structure and detailed content of any procedure (whether database enquiry and update processes or I/O processes).

Zero-defect implementation

Entity behaviour modelling is a correctness-assuring technique. Taking extra time to specify the entity behaviour models will reduce errors in the implementation, and reduce system testing time. Whether this trade-off is worth it, will depend on the cost and risk factors of a given system. The more important it is that a system should work correctly from the outset, the more important the role of methodical analysis becomes.

Automation of techniques is correctness-assuring. The mechanistic generation of effect correspondence diagrams and event procedures from entity behaviour models provides increased assurance of correctness.

Working backwards, we regard as entity behaviour modelling as a means of proving or improving the correctness of effect correspondence diagrams.

Chapter 14

Identification of objects, events and methods

This chapter describes the very first step of entity behaviour analysis, to identify the events by looking for the triggers of effects on entities in the entity data model.

14.1 **Introduction**

The previous chapter introduced entity event modelling concepts and documentation conventions, but did not describe a methodology by which entity behaviours can be analysed and an entity event model is built. This chapter and the following chapters show how entity behaviour modelling:

- is used to analyse the users' requirements for a database system
- is a relatively objective requirements capture technique
- can be enriched by the use of object-oriented programming ideas
- can be used to produce a object-oriented programming solution
- can be used to generate reusable code.

The case study is used to exemplify the methodical step-by-step nature of the approach we use to:

- apply the first steps of a control-structured analysis
- identify the methods implicit in the control-structured analysis
- use these methods to restructure the analysis
- apply this hybrid approach to complete the analysis.

The final step in the development is to show how the method invocations discovered during the analysis can be implemented in a conventional third or fourth generation programming environment and database management system.

Object-oriented or object-based?

There is a school of thought which distinguishes between object-oriented and object-based approaches. Readers who are convinced that the benefits they are seeking are to be gained from an approach will not be too concerned about distinction. However there are those who worry about it, and we should make our position clear.

We regard the methodology to be described hereafter as being fully object-oriented by any reasonable definition of the term. The term object-based is sometimes used by OO programmers as a way of dismissing analysis and design methods which follow the control-structured paradigm and do not obviously exhibit all the concepts used in object-oriented programming languages. We intend to demonstrate that a grand unified theory is possible, and that the distinction between object-oriented and object-based approaches is not at all useful in analysis and design above the level of the implementation environment. The only chapter where the distinction might matter is chapter 18.

14.2 **The case study**

Briefly, Hi-Ho Recruitment is a company which maintains registers of job Applicants and Vacancies. Applicants are matched to Vacancies on the basis of the Applicants' possessing the required Skills. Each Vacancy, which may have several available slots (or 'Posts'), is classified as belonging to a single Skill Type. An Applicant may have several Skills, each belonging to a different Skill Type. If no result has been received by one week after an Interview has been scheduled, the Employers are contacted to follow up the Interview and check its progress.

The top-level data flow diagram (see part five for notes on its development) for Hi-Ho is as shown below.

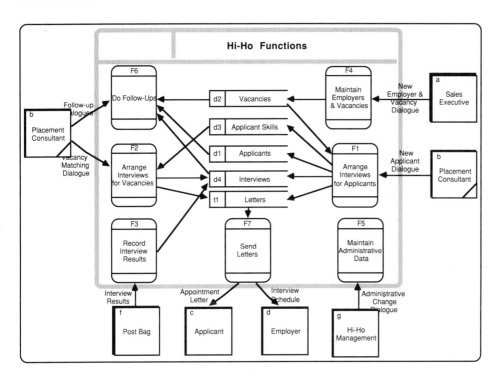

In part five we show this same diagram using the SSADM4 notation. Here, just for sake of illustrating a different methodology's notation, we have used the Gane and Sarsen notation.

14.3 **Finding the objects**

The objects in the system are taken to be the entities in the system's entity data model, as developed in chapter 11 and shown below. Note that the entity event modelling techniques described hereafter are not restricted to this kind of data model. Lying behind the boxes are attribute descriptions; these are not discussed directly in the rest of this case study.

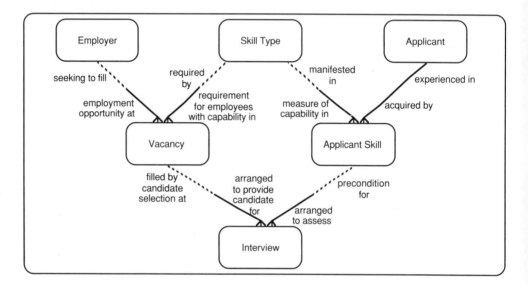

Most of the relationship types in the diagram have the same cardinality; for any relationship instance there may be one and only one master instance and zero, one or more detail instances. The only exception is the relationship which must have at least one detail, that is, an Applicant must have at least one Applicant Skill.

14.4 **Finding the methods triggered by events**

First of all, the analyst should understand what events and methods are. This was discussed at length in the previous chapter and should become clearer as we develop the case study. This section contains advice on identifying events and methods.

Name methods after events

As we shall see, in object-oriented systems design there are strong causal relationships between invocations of methods on different objects. When an event occurs, all of the objects it affects must be affected in a consistent way. For example, if an applicant accepts a post there will be one less post available for the vacancy.

In order to maintain control of the documentation, we normally assign names to the events and use those event names as method names consistently throughout our analysis. Thus there will be a *Post Acceptance* method for **Interview** to enable the system to forget it, and a corresponding *Post Acceptance* method for **Vacancy** to make it lose a post. These represent the effect that the Post Acceptance event has on two different objects in the system.

The relationship between methods invoked in different objects by the same event is a reflection of the relationships between those objects in the entity data model, so we use the entity data model to drive our analysis of the methods.

Do not name methods after implementation operations
Chapter 13 discussed why the methods required to manage objects represented in a database are not physical operations like Store, Modify and Delete.

Name events after the triggers of update effects on entities
An entity behaviour model should include the events which update the entity. Updating effects can be classified into five (not mutually exclusive) kinds:

- entity birth and death effects
- relationship and attribute change effects
- state change effects.

A single event can have one or more of these five effects upon an entity. We identify events by looking for the causes of these effects, by asking what events trigger operations upon the 'aspects' (relationships and attributes) of an entity.

Note that an entity behaviour model may include not only update effects, but also validation effects and enquiry effects. For a discussion of these, see chapter 13.

Omit trivial attribute change events to begin with
Many information systems store a large number of simple non-key attributes, which can be individually replaced without any knock-on effect elsewhere in the system. These attributes might lead us to identify numerous simple events, one for each attribute, where each event merely replaces the current value of an attribute with a new value.

Entity behaviour modelling is often more manageable if the simple attribute-changing events are postponed to a second pass. To begin with, we concentrate on the events that create and kill off entities, make and break relationships and change entity states.

Alternatively, it may be possible to simplify the entity event model by lumping together all the trivial attribute change events for one entity type, as a general 'Replace Entity Details' event. This works if it can be assumed that unchanged attributes can be reinput along with the changed ones without any side-effect on the system. This is an assumption behind some application generators.

Don't make an event too big or too small

An event is a small parcel of system behaviour. On entering the system, an event will trigger an update process which will move the system from one consistent state to another and *cannot* be partially executed.

An event is an atomic particle in the sense that it cannot be divided. By definition, if the process which applies the event to the system is only partially executed, then the system will be left in an inconsistent state.

Divide composite events into smaller distinct events

Beginners often define as events things much larger than events, which are really more like user functions. Do not define a series of things which could happen independently as a single event.

For example, consider an input document which notifies us of the birth of several entities of the same type. If the batching of the entities on a single input document is not significant to the updating of the data model, then it is better to regard the document as being composed of several distinct birth events, than to define an event for the whole document which will be the birth of an arbitrary number of entities.

On the other hand, do not split one event into distinct events

Whatever must succeed or fail as a whole cannot be split into two or more events. For example, if it is a rule that an applicant must belong to an office, then a transfer of an applicant between two offices should not be split into distinct 'dispatch' and 'receipt' events.

Give each entity its own birth event, usually

In general, each entity type has its own distinct type of birth event. But a dilemma often arises where the user wishes to create a set of detail entities at the same time as a master entity. Is this one event, or a series of distinct events? Here are two rules to help us.

- If a master entity *can* legitimately exist without detail entities, then the birth event of the master entity should not create detail entities and the detail entities *must* have their own birth event.

- If a master entity *cannot* legitimately exist without detail entities, then either the birth of the master entity will create detail entities as well and the detail entities *may* have their own distinct birth event, or the master has no birth event of its own and is created by the birth of the first detail.

Case study

The methods we are interested in must act on the conceptual objects in a way which directly models the way the events act on the real-world objects. In order to discover those methods, we look at our entity data model and ask what real-world events cause changes in the conceptual objects and in the relationships between them:

- Why does an object of a given type get born or come to the attention of the system?
- When does an object die or become no longer of interest to the system?
- What, if anything, causes an object to swap from one master to another?
- What causes an optional relationship to be established or disestablished?
- What causes change in an attribute?
- Does anything cause a significant state change?

The events that we discover by asking these questions about an object will form our first attempt at defining the methods required for that object. Applying these kinds of questions to the **Interview** object, for example, we find that we need at least these five methods:

Method	Purpose to
Interview Arrangement	create the **Interview**
Post Acceptance	enable us to forget a successful **Interview**
Refusal of Offer	record an unsuccessful outcome, instigated by the applicant
Rejection of Applicant	record an unsuccessful outcome, caused by the employer
Rescheduling	change the **Date** of an **Interview**

14.5 The analysis technique

We analyse the methods and the relationships between their invocations in two passes through the entity data model.

In the first pass (chapter 15), we are concerned with establishing the fundamental methods, the constraints that apply to them within an object, and the birth dependencies between objects, that is, under which circumstances master objects can acquire new detail objects.

The first pass is performed by starting with the objects at the bottom of the entity data model, that is, those objects which have no detail objects, analysing their methods, then looking at their masters and, in turn, looking at their masters' masters and so on.

In the second pass (chapter 16), we are concerned with establishing exceptions that can occur and with death dependencies between objects; e.g. whether the presence of a detail object prevents the death of a master object, or whether the death of a master object causes the death of a detail.

The second pass is performed by starting with the objects at the top of the entity data model (that is, those objects which have no master objects) and analysing their exceptions, then looking at the effect of (or constraints on) their deaths in their detail objects and, in turn, looking at their details' details and so on.

Chapter 15

Analysis and specification: first pass

In the first pass we are concerned with establishing the fundamental methods, the constraints that apply to them within an object, and the birth dependencies between objects, that is, under which circumstances master objects can acquire new detail objects. The first pass is performed by starting with the objects at the bottom of the entity data model.

15.1 **The first pass through the data model**

In the first pass of entity behaviour analysis, we only build the entity behaviour model of an object after we have already defined all its details' behaviours.

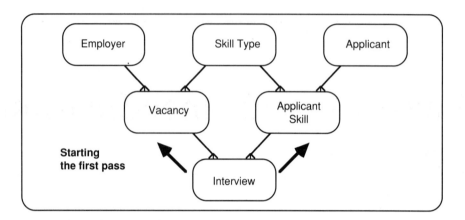

The first-cut Interview behaviour model (developed in chapter 13) is shown below.

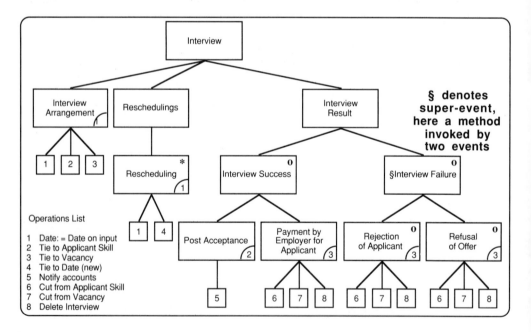

Next we next look at the masters of Interview, that is Vacancy and Applicant Skill. The behaviour model of a master entity is usually drawn to include an iterated selection of the birth and death events of its detail. Why? Primarily to show birth dependencies between master and detail entities.

Birth dependencies

A birth dependency is a check by a detail object that its master is alive and well, that is, in a fit state to give birth to the detail. The way we show a birth dependency is by identifying the event that causes the birth of a detail object, then including an iteration of method invocations which this event type makes on the master object in the middle of its life (that is, in the valid state between birth and death).

If we implement using a relational database management system, this kind of birth dependency might later be automated as a referential integrity check, but we have several good reasons not to rely on this.

First, we do not know yet, and deliberately choose to postpone deciding, what kind of implementation environment might be used. The model we are building is a conceptual one, independent of any implementation mechanism.

Second, the birth dependency might be more elaborate than can be captured by a relational database management system. It might depend upon some state change in the life of the master entity, more subtle than simply its own birth.

Third, the invocations of the master on the birth of details have another purpose. They allow the master to remember the identifiers of its detail objects. Such a list of identifiers would contravene first normal form, but this is merely a constraint applied by relational database management systems, and the list may be required in an truly object-oriented database management system.

Finally, we are proposing that rules or constraints such as birth dependencies *should* be specified in the entity event model rather than entity data model. We think that there are limits to what is possible in the way of developing the semantics of entity data models to cope with rules and constraints.

Death dependencies

In a similar way and for similar reasons, we identify the event causing the death of the detail and include an iteration of method invocations causing the master to forget its details. However, the full expression of death dependencies must wait until the second analysis pass.

NB: logical death is generally not the same as physical deletion

Should the logical death event of an entity delete it? In general the answer is no, the analysis and design of logical death events should be separated from and precede the analysis and design of physical deletion events. But we have no space in this book to complete and illustrate these separate analysis and design steps. So for the sake of keeping the case study small, we are going to fudge the issue by deleting most of the entities on their logical death, or on the next event after it. Extremely astute readers may notice this means the relationships from Skill Type to Vacancy and Applicant Skill must be made optional at the detail end of the relationship.

Vacancy

So, the Vacancy entity behaviour model will include an iterated selection of the birth and death events of Interview. What about the birth and death of the Vacancy itself? For its birth, an object type will commonly have a distinct birth event, creating an instance of the object and doing nothing else. In this example we have Notification of Vacancy.

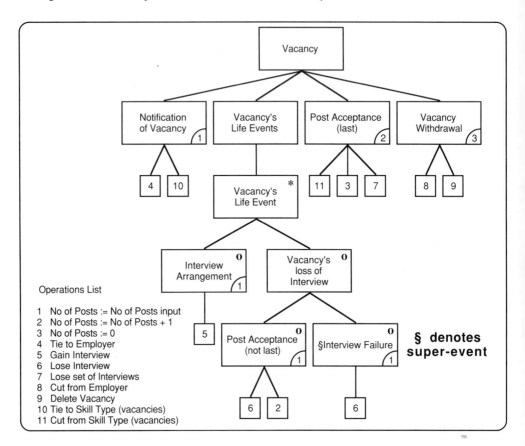

Operations List

1   No of Posts := No of Posts input
2   No of Posts := No of Posts + 1
3   No of Posts := 0
4   Tie to Employer
5   Gain Interview
6   Lose Interview
7   Lose set of Interviews
8   Cut from Employer
9   Delete Vacancy
10 Tie to Skill Type (vacancies)
11 Cut from Skill Type (vacancies)

Optional effects of an event

When we investigate the death of Vacancy we discover something interesting. The Vacancy represents a requirement by an employer to fill several posts of the same type; so the Vacancy remains open while posts are offered and accepted until the last post is filled, when Post Acceptance of the last post causes the Vacancy to die. So one instance of one of the events causing a Vacancy to lose an Interview causes the death of Vacancy; the other instances don't; which means the event type has optional effects.

Applicant Skill

Next we look at Applicant Skill, the other master of Interview. Here Post Acceptance is a death event because, when the Applicant gets a job, the system is no longer interested in the Applicant or any of his/her Applicant Skills. However if an Interview ends unsuccessfully Applicant Skill loses that Interview but doesn't itself die.

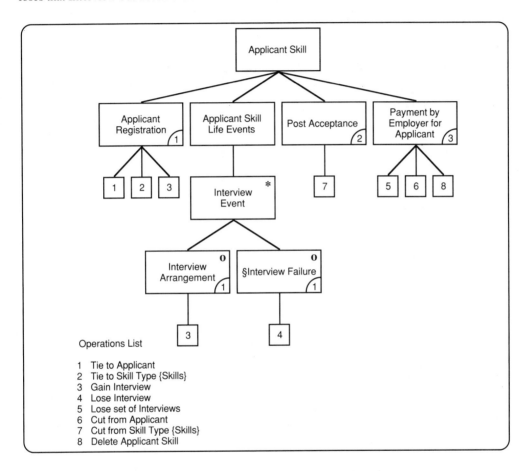

Notice the super-event makes an appearance in this behaviour model as well.

Continuing the first pass

Since we only start to build the entity behaviour model of any object after we have defined its details' behaviours, having defined Vacancy and Applicant Skill, we can now move on upwards in this fashion.

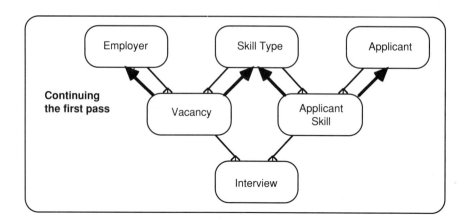

Assuming that an Applicant cannot gain any Skills while in the system, the Applicant behaviour model is very simple. To begin with we only consider a successful Applicant. Later we'll consider unsuccessful cases.

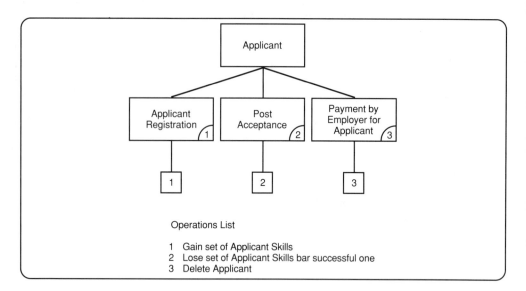

Employer

The Employer entity behaviour model is shown below.

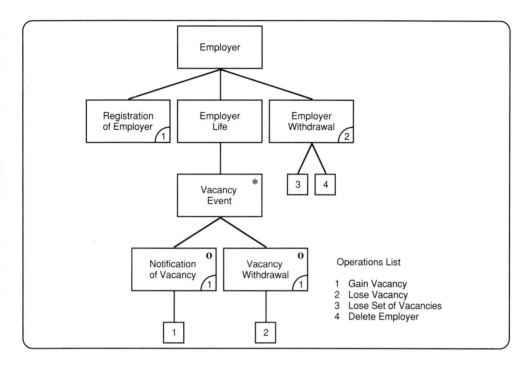

An entity with parallel aspects

Skill Type causes a small problem. It is the master of two different details, Vacancy and Applicant Skill. Later, when we look at how method invocations caused by the Post Acceptance event propagate round the system, we see that they can arrive at the same Skill Type object from these two different routes. Via one route, Post Acceptance always causes Skill Type to lose a whole set of Applicant Skills. Via the other route, Post Acceptance may (when it is the last post for a Vacancy) cause Skill Type to lose a Vacancy.

This is a kind of parallelism problem, which, like others, is best managed by splitting the affected object into two or more parallel aspects. Each of these parallel objects handles its own aspect of the data independently of the other.

The first of these parallel objects handles the Skill Type to Vacancy relationship, and we've arbitrarily chosen it to handle any general data about Skill Type itself.

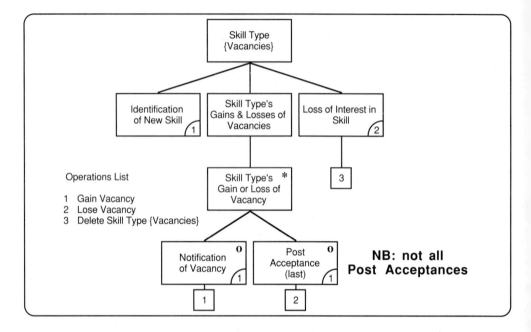

The other handles the Skill Type to Applicant Skill relationship:

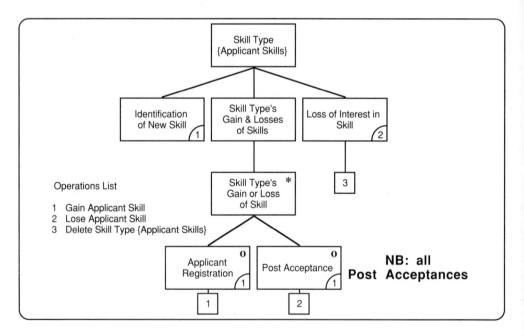

15.2 **The difference between methods and method invocations**

The methods, and the events which invoke them, are usually the 'leaf' nodes of the behaviour diagrams. The exceptions occur where there are super-events, or optional effects.

Method as common procedure invoked by different events

Consider the Interview behaviour model on the first page of this chapter. At first sight, it may seem like we need five methods:

- Interview Arrangement
- Rescheduling
- Refusal of Offer
- Rejection of Applicant
- Post Acceptance.

But look again. Two of these putative methods, Refusal of Offer and Rejection of Applicant, have exactly the same set of operations and exactly the same successor states. In general, where two or more leaf nodes have the same set of operations and successor states, we can abstract a single method, of which the leaf nodes are invocations.

So in our example, Interview Failure is the method; Rejection of Applicant and Refusal of Offer are invocations of the method.

Method as super-event passed on from another entity

During the two passes of analysis, we are constantly looking for situations where the invocation of a method on one object results in a corresponding invocation (or set of invocations) of methods on another object. The rule which says that a master object's behaviour diagram should normally include an iteration of method invocations corresponding to the method invocations causing the births of its details identifies such a situation.

But if two events invoke exactly the same method of an object in exactly the same way and that method needs to invoke methods of other objects there is no point in that second object's having to know exactly why the first object's method was invoked.

What this means is that instead of introducing iterations of Rejection of Applicant and Refusal of Offer into the masters of Interview, we can achieve exactly the effect we require by introducing iterations of Interview Failure. After it has hit Interview, an event of either type behaves in exactly the same way in its journey through the objects to which Interview is connected. Interview Failure is a kind of 'event super-type' which from Interview onwards subsumes the effects of its two sub-types Rejection of Applicant and Refusal of Offer.

So in our example, the Applicant Skill entity behaviour model is slightly simpler than it would otherwise be, because we can include the super-event Interview Failure, rather than the two events which invoke it separately in Interview.

Method as optional effects of an event

In a similar way, the behaviour of Vacancy can be simplified by replacing Rejection of Applicant and Refusal of Offer by Interview Failure. But here we hit a different complication.

There are two different invocations of the Post Acceptance method in the Vacancy's entity behaviour model. One just causes Vacancy to lose an Interview and reduces the number of posts by one. The other kills off the Vacancy. The affected Vacancy is the only object which knows how many posts it has unfilled; it is the only one that can decide whether it should die.

The method body for the Post Acceptance method needs to be a selection between the two different outcomes of the method. The leaves of the diagram, in the most general case, define *a type of method invocation yielding a particular successor state*. The method itself is not directly represented in the entity behaviour model but represents a kind of orthogonal cut across the entity behaviour model:

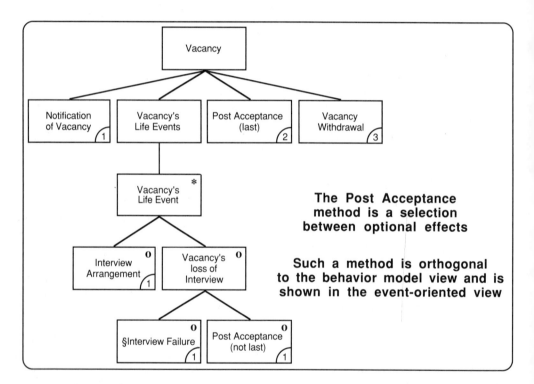

15.3 **What a method body looks like**

Having defined the entity behaviour model of an object, we are in a position to say what its methods are and what the bodies of those methods are. For example, the Post Acceptance method of Vacancy must make a choice between the two successor states it can lead to; this choice is based on the value of the instance variable No of Posts. It must set the appropriate successor state. If the last post is not being filled Vacancy can forget the identifier of the Interview resulting in Post Acceptance. Before any of this is done however, the method needs to check that the Vacancy object is in a valid state.

If the implementation environment is not one which can automatically and transparently save (or delete) and restore the object's instance variables (probably the normal case in object-oriented systems design), the instance variables need to be read before the method proper is executed and written or deleted afterwards. The following diagram shows the different outcomes for the Vacancy's Post Acceptance method and the required operations.

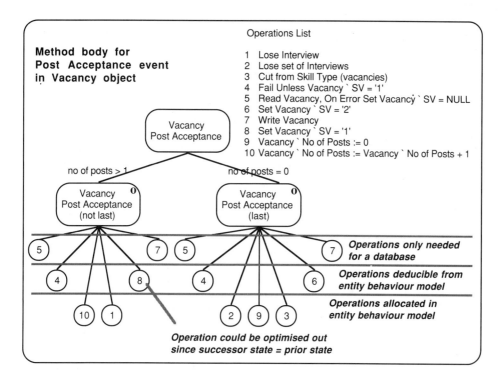

This approach allows us to gain the analytic benefit of the rich contexts provided by the entity behaviour models, yet still end up with a set of method bodies loosely coupled through state variable setting and testing.

Notice that the method has a two-part name (Vacancy and Post Acceptance). We follow a convention where, if a method can only be invoked by a single event the event name plus the object name is used to name the same method. This helps us keep track of methods invoked by an event. In practice, we can and do shorten the name in two different ways; when looking at the system from the perspective of a particular object, we can omit the object name component from each method name, and when looking at the system from the viewpoint of a particular event we can omit the event name component from each method name.

15.4 Co-ordination of object method invocations

In the system being constructed, which is typical of most information systems, several objects may be hit by any given event. Some examples follow.

Applicant Registration event
The Applicant Registration event causes the Applicant Registration methods to be invoked in Applicant, Applicant Skill and Skill Type.

We show the pattern of invocations caused by a given event in a diagram we call an 'effect correspondence diagram'. As applied in object-oriented systems design, an effect correspondence diagram can be read from left to right, the leftmost box representing an invocation of the appropriate method of the 'home' object. Sets of arrows from right to left show subsidiary method invocations. The invocation of a set of methods on each detail object of a master is shown by an iteration component similar to that used in the entity behaviour model diagrams.

The name of the event causing the method invocations is shown in bold. Unless otherwise documented, the names of the invoked methods are identical to the event name. Thus the method invocations caused by the Applicant Registration event (an invocation of the birth method of Applicant, followed by several invocations of the birth methods of each of the applicant's Skills, each of which invokes a detail gain method in an appropriate Skill Type) can be shown as follows.

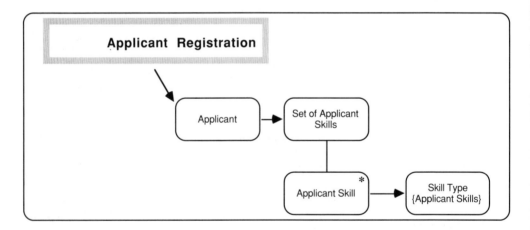

Usually when an event hits several objects there is an easily identifiable one (which we call the 'home' object) which has its appropriate method invoked. The method body in the home object will invoke methods in other objects, and so on through the network of objects. Sometimes a subsidiary invocation will be of a corresponding method in a single object of another type; sometimes it will be of the corresponding methods in a set of objects of another type. Well-defined rules exist for determining whether the invocation is of an instance or a set.

One of these rules says that if a master and detail object share a birth event, then an invocation of the master's birth method causes a set of invocations of the details' birth methods, one for each detail being born at the same time as its master. Thus the Applicant Registration event, which registers an Applicant together with all his/her Skills, invokes the Applicant Registration method of the appropriate Applicant which, in turn, invokes the Applicant Registration methods of each of his Skills.

Another rule says that if an event invokes the birth method of a detail object and a gain detail method of a master object then an invocation of the birth method of the detail causes a single subsidiary invocation of the gain detail method of the master. Thus the invocation of the Applicant Registration method of Applicant Skill causes a single invocation of the Applicant Registration method of Skill Type.

Post Acceptance

Where a method body includes a selection, as for example Vacancy's Post Acceptance method does, the selection is shown in the effect correspondence diagram. Each part of the selection may give rise to different subsidiary method calls.

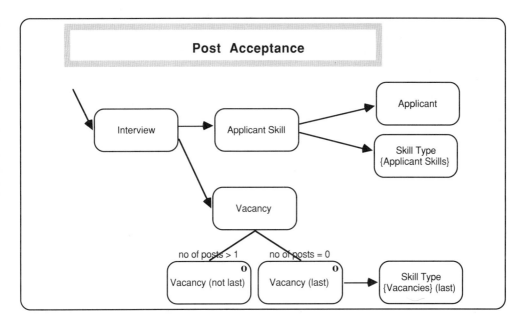

Note that Skill Type objects are invoked through two quite separate invocation paths; this is a justification for splitting Skill Type into two different object types.

Note also that this is only the first pass version of Post Acceptance, the final version is a good deal more complicated.

Invoking a super-event

When the same method is invoked by any one of several events and then, irrespective of what event invoked it, makes several subsidiary invocations acting as an event super-type, effect correspondence diagrams are drawn for the basic events up to the points where they invoke the common method.

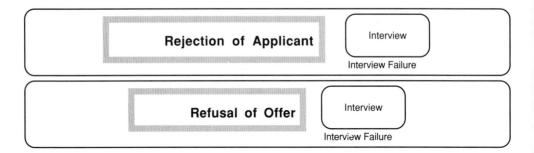

The super-event thereby invoked

A separate effect correspondence diagram then shows the propagation of the event super-type through the appropriate objects in the system.

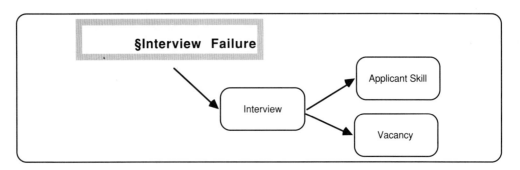

15.5 **The remaining effect correspondence diagrams**

The remaining effect correspondence diagrams for the first pass analysis through the data model of our case study are shown below. First, there are four birth events.

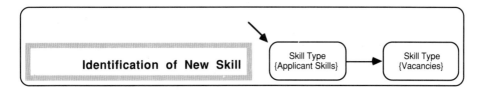

Notice the separation of parallel aspects above. See the discussion in 12.7 and 12.11.

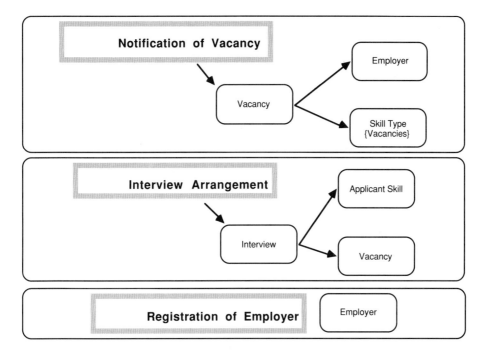

Then there are two update events.

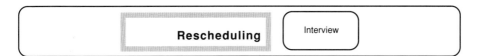

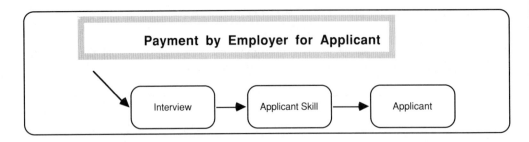

The final two death events, Employer Withdrawal and Loss of Interest in Skill, are trivial at this stage. They will be documented after the second pass, when more has been discovered.

Chapter 16

Analysis and specification: second pass

In the second pass we are concerned with establishing exceptions that can occur and with death dependencies between objects; for example, whether the presence of a detail object prevents the death of a master object, or whether the death of a master object causes the death of a detail. The second pass is performed by starting with the objects at the top of the entity data model.

16.1 **Starting the second pass of the analysis**

In the second pass, we work down the data model as shown below. For each entity type, we ask whether there are any exceptions to their behaviour which we have not yet captured, such as whether there are any exceptional ways in which they can die.

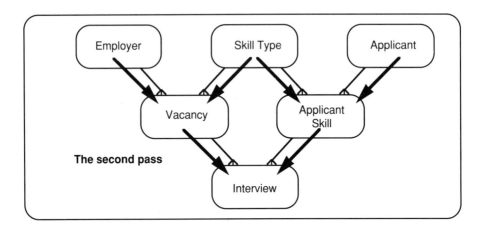

Strictly, deletion should be considered in a third and distinct pass. However, to keep down the size of the book we are going to combine the analysis of logical deaths with the design of a physical deletion strategy. This topic merits more attention than we have space to give it and the deletion strategy below is by no means the 'best'.

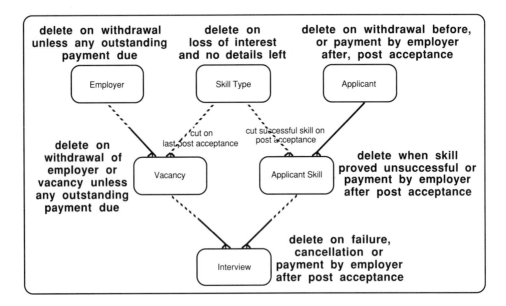

Starting with objects that have no masters, we don't discover any exceptions in the lives of Skill Type or Employer. But looking at Applicant we should discover that we need to allow for the fact that not all Applicants get jobs. This can be shown using one of two stereotype models, known as **alternative death** and **early death**.

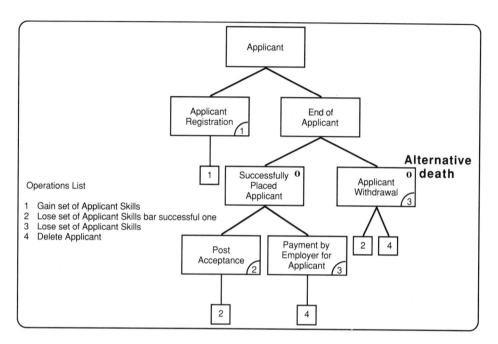

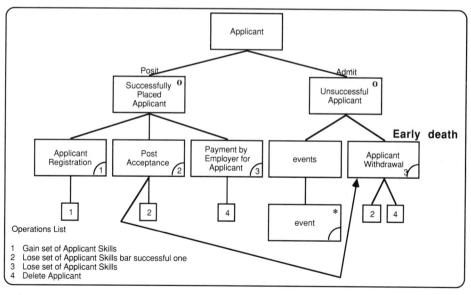

We are keen to illustrate one example of **backtracking** in the book, since this is needed in other examples. In the above diagram we have used Posit, Admit and Quit constructs to specify the switch from the Successfully Placed Applicant context to the Unsuccessful Applicant context. However, the backtracking mechanism is not described in this book and it is not needed in the case study, since the above diagram can be redrawn using the 'alternative death' stereotype.

16.2 Subsidiary method invocations of death methods

Having looked at entities with no masters, the next step is to work down the entity data model asking about how the deaths of masters affect, or are constrained by, the deaths of their details.

An alternative death

At its simplest, death of a master may just be an alternative death of its details. What happens to the set of Applicant Skills when an Applicant dies? We need to think not only about the successful skill, the one which got the applicant the job, but the unsuccessful skills, for which other interviews may have been arranged.

The Applicant Skill behaviour model, modified to take account of this thought (and two thoughts not yet discussed), is now as follows.

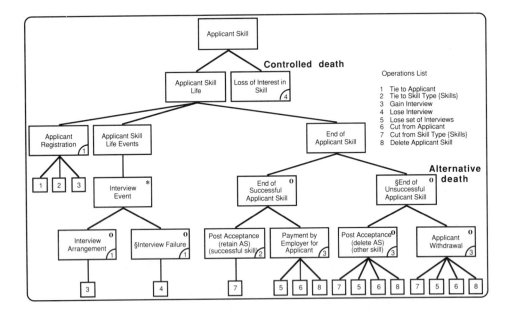

A restricted death (use controlled death stereotype)

Another possibility is that we may wish to prevent a master from dying while it has details. For example, we may want to prevent a Skill Type from dying while it still has live Applicant Skills. We do this by defining a method in Applicant Skill which can detect that Loss of Interest in Applicant Skill (the death method of Skill Type) occurs only at the very end of an Applicant Skill's life.

By providing a similar Loss of Interest in Applicant Skill method in Vacancy (shown above), we can prevent Skill Type from dying while it still has an outstanding Vacancy.

A cascade death (use alternative or early death stereotype)

In analysing exceptions we are likely to encounter the need to allow an entity to die early. For example, if the Employer Withdrawal method of Employer is invoked, what happens to each unfilled Vacancy the employer has? Vacancy will need a method which allows it to die early. The alternative death stereotype is used below.

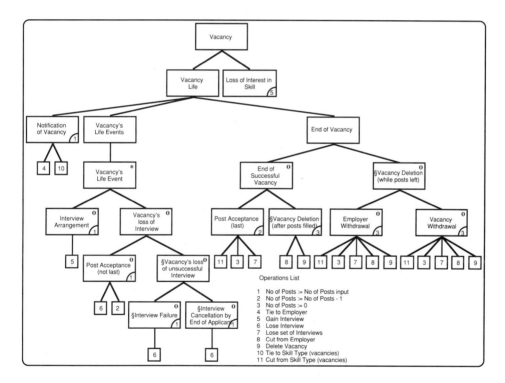

The early death stereotype, which is necessary in other examples, always involves 'backtracking'. The model would become a high-level selection between filled Vacancy (the posit) and unfilled Vacancy (the admit). Unfilled Vacancy would be drawn as a sequence of a collapsed structure, an iteration of 'event', followed by a selection of the 'early death' events which cause it to finish early. Quit arrows would be drawn to this from the posit, using rules and stereotypes not described in this book.

16.3 **Bouncing back up the data model**

When we introduce a master's death method or method invocation into a detail object, we need to introduce corresponding new death methods or invocations into all the other masters of that detail.

Employer needs no modification, but the entity behaviour models of the two Skill Type object types have to be modified to show the new ways in which they can lose the detail entities they own.

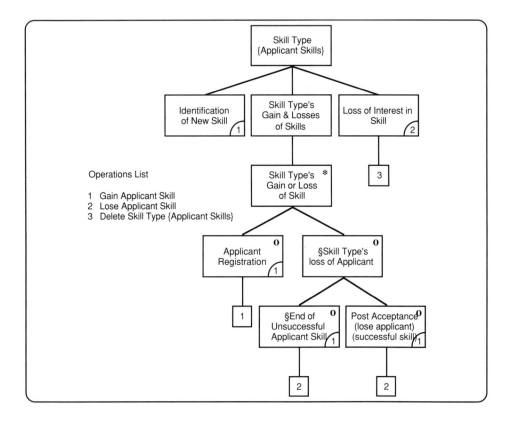

In this and the next diagram we have anticipated the fact that some events bounce back up the model from the extended Interview behaviour model, shown in the next section

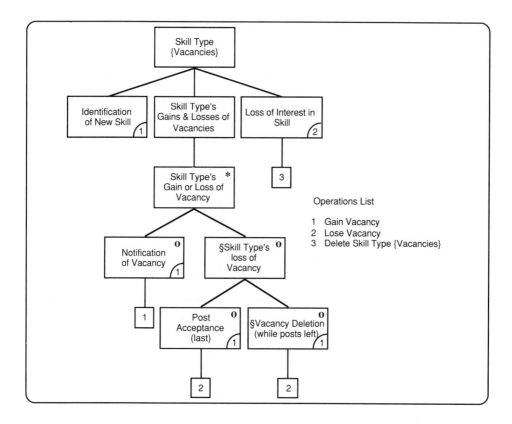

16.4 **The end of the second pass**

Arriving at the bottom of the model, we have to ask if the death methods of Vacancy and Applicant Skill need to have an effect on Interview.

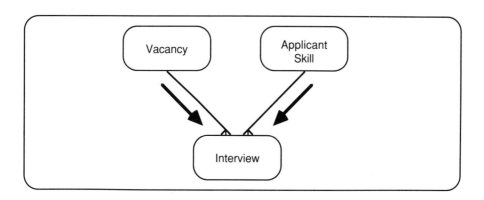

We thus discover a need to terminate interview arrangements if the applicant withdraws, the employer withdraws totally from Hi-Ho or just withdraws a vacancy, if the applicant accepts a different post before attending all of his/her interviews, or if the last post on a vacancy is offered to and accepted by an applicant before all applicants for that vacancy have been seen.

So Interview needs some appropriate early death methods and method invocations.

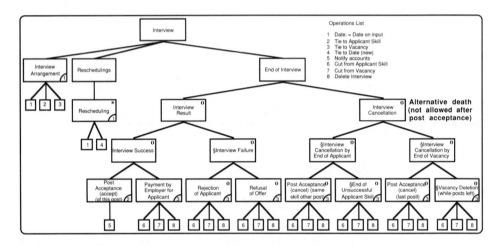

Finally, the early death methods of Interview have a bounce-up effect on its masters. These effects have already been shown for Applicant Skill and Vacancy.

Chapter 17

The completed set of method invocations for the case study

This chapter revises and extends the effect correspondence diagrams to accommodate the discoveries made during the second pas of analysis.

17.1 The event class hierarchy

This chapter revises and extends the effect correspondence diagrams, principally to allow for:

- a death method in a master object invoking an iteration of death methods
- a loss method in a master bouncing up from an early death of a detail
- a combination of the above two reasons.

After this, we can draw an event class hierarchy (or rather network) to show where the super-events or common methods are invoked from. We present the resulting diagram first, because it gives an overview of the documentation in this chapter.

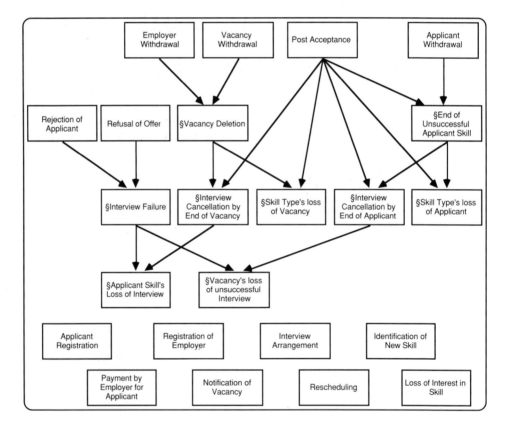

We used a CASE tool to generate the structure of this diagram from the effect correspondence diagrams of the case study. See chapter 30 for discussion of other ways in which a CASE tool may help in systems analysis and design.

17.2 **A master object invoking an iteration of death methods**

A death method in a master object invoking an iteration of death methods, one in each of its details, is shown below.

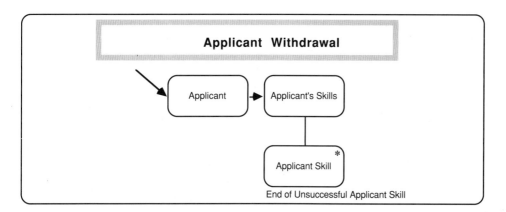

A second example is shown below.

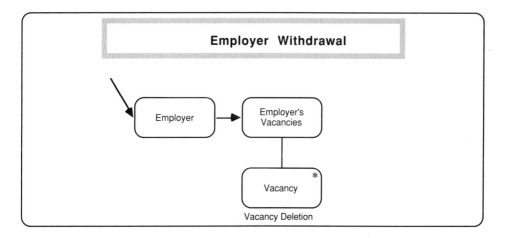

Through a super-event, Employer Withdrawal cascades down through another level of iteration, as shown below.

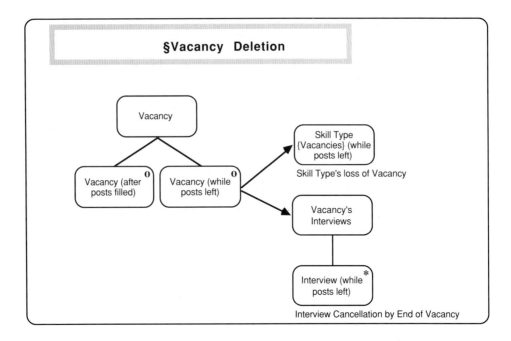

Two other death methods, both of which cascade down through iterations at the same level, are shown below.

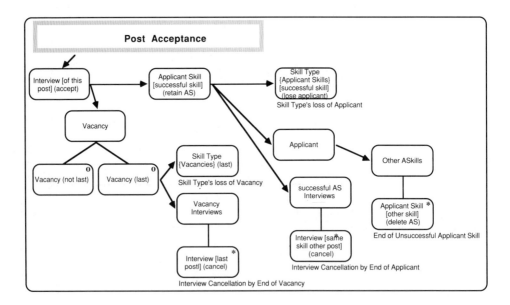

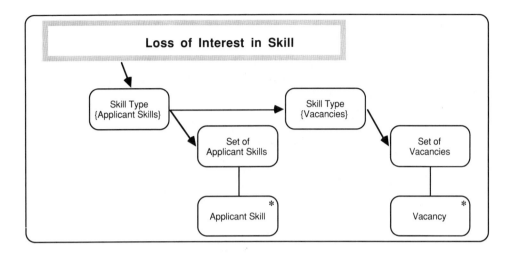

17.3 **An early death method bouncing back upwards**

A loss method in a master object, triggering the early death of a detail 'link' object, can bounce back up the other side of the many-to-many link, as shown in these two examples.

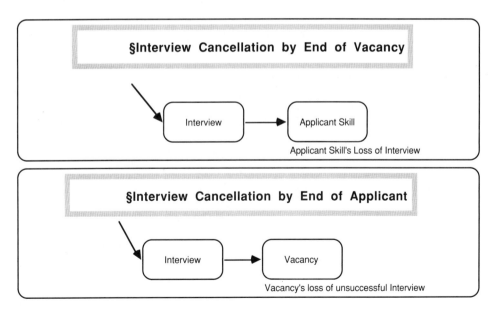

Coincidentally, these two diagrams have also introduced new super-events and described their patterns of invocation.

17.4 **A combination of the above two reasons**

A death method in a master object invoking an iteration of early death methods, combined with the early death of the detail 'link' object bouncing back up the other side of the many-to-many link, is shown by this example.

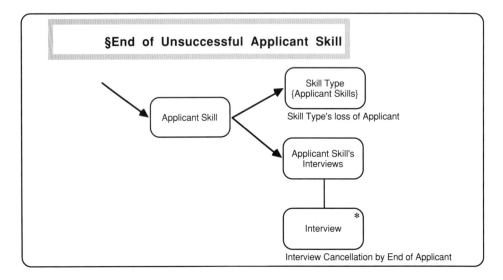

Two of the effect correspondence diagrams which are now changed to invoke renamed methods are shown below.

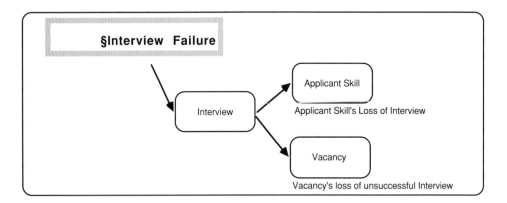

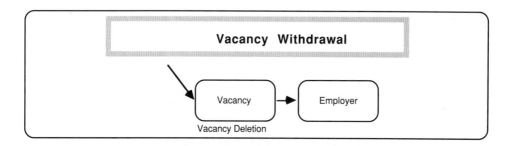

The remaining effect correspondence diagrams from the first pass are totally unchanged. The following events remain as documented in chapter 15:

Applicant Registration
Identification of New Skill
Interview Arrangement
Notification of Vacancy
Refusal of Offer
Registration of Employer
Rejection of Applicant
Rescheduling.

There is one more event which remains unchanged from the first pass, for the reason given in the diagram below

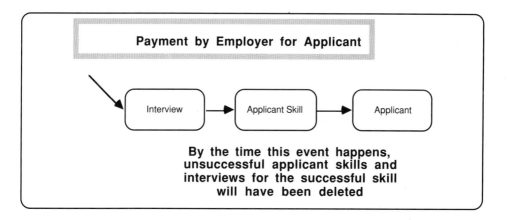

Finally, there are simple methods which can be invoked by more than one event or super-event.

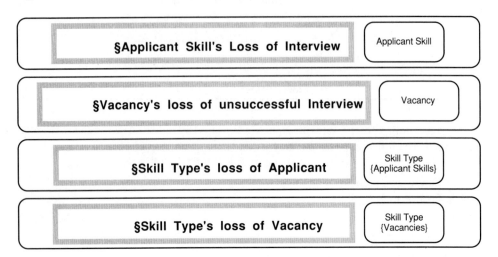

Chapter 18

Implementation of events

This chapter illustrates various ways in which the effect correspondence diagrams of an entity event model may be transformed into working programs.

18.1 **Object-oriented implementation**

It turns out that an event procedure may be viewed as a highly optimised form of object-oriented specification, where the communication between objects takes place via the common 'working-storage' of the process. However, people are looking towards more object-oriented styles of implementation, where each object is coded separately, and the event process is implemented by objects passing messages between themselves.

One reason for this is robustness. The idea is that new objects can be added to a system, without requiring amendment to or retesting of the old objects. This is more difficult to achieve than might be hoped, but there are prospects of increasing robustness in this way.

Given a set of effect correspondence diagrams like this one:

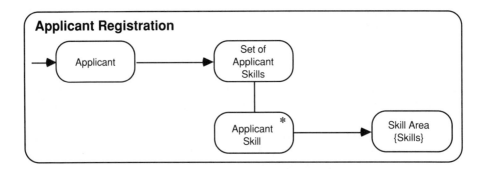

Several implementation solutions are possible, depending on variations in the specification to be implemented and the implementation mechanisms which are available.

The first big question is: Should events be transmitted **round-robin** from one entity to the next, or to each object from a single **event manager**? Either approach is possible. Curiously, it turns out that the latter approach may be optimised to become an event procedure, much as in standard SSADM.

The second big question is: Must the message passing in each effect correspondence diagram be designed by hand, or is it possible to prescribe a standard message passing protocol for an effect correspondence diagram? This guide suggests a standard message passing protocol is possible, but it may be too clumsy for efficient implementation.

The discussion which follows moves from a simple round-robin approach to message passing, to an event-manager approach, by an examination of the problems which may prevent the simple approach working

To begin with, in simple cases, a method specified in an entity behaviour model can be extended to include the method invocation(s) required to invoke any related entities shown in the relevant effect correspondence diagram. Given a suitable OO environment, they can then be implemented directly.

Handling iterations

The first question which arises is to how an iteration in an effect correspondence diagram should be handled.

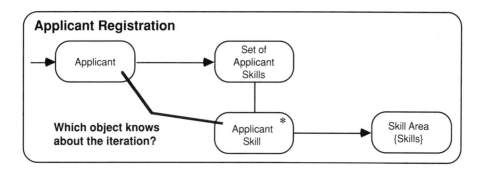

There are at least three approaches. The iteration of detail method invocations may be placed in one of the following places.

As a loop in the relevant method of the master entity

This means extending the method in the master entity with an iteration of invocations of related methods in its detail entities. This may be viewed as the most natural approach. It is in accord with the view that a master entity should somehow 'know about' its details. It keeps the model close to its implementation where for implementation reasons a master entity holds a list of its details.

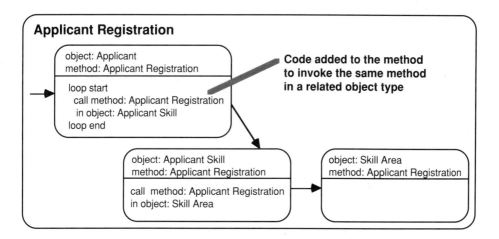

As a method in a 'class-level' object owning all the details

This means inventing a class-level object, either for all detail entities, or for all details attached to the given master. A method of this object will be the iteration of detail invocations, specified as either as an iterated selection, or as some kind of 'select' statement which returns a list of details matching given criteria.

However, rather than create a new object type, people find it convenient to specify class-level methods as extra methods alongside instance-level methods, which leads us to a third solution.

As a 'class-level' method in the detail object

This might be viewed as an optimisation of the second approach. The main practical problem is how to connect the class-level method for selecting detail entities, and the instance-level method which is to be invoked in each detail entity.

Where the two methods may be combined in a single operation, there is no problem. But if the two can only be combined as steps within a sequential procedure, then it turns out that some kind of loop must be coded in the method of the detail, which works through the list provided by the 'select' operation.

The placement of an iteration in the method of a detail object may be convenient, but it looks rather strange from a modelling point of view.

Handling roll-back

Not all OO environments support roll-back of commit units. If the database management system does not do this, then something like a two-phase commit must be coded on top of the basic event message passing.

In our example, what if the method in Applicant Skill fails for some reason? What if the method in the first Skill Area succeeds, but the one in the next Skill Area fails? We have to extend the communication protocol, with something like a two-phase commit.

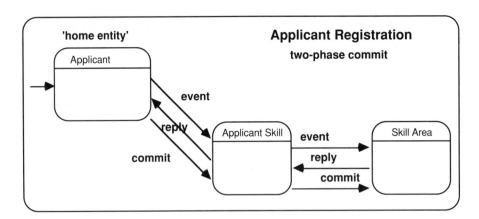

Handling non-straightforward communication

What if objects need to exchange information before they can process an event? Examples of this in practical information systems are few and far between, but wherever communication between entities is needed, there are two possible solutions:

- design a message-passing protocol by hand to suit the event
- use a two-phase commit, and get the home entity to collate all replies

Given the second approach, in the first phase, the event is fanned out through all the objects and these objects return local data with their replies. In the second phase, the 'home entity' collates all the replies, decides whether the event succeeds or fails, and initiates the commit phase by sending out the results of its computation. In this case the 'home' entity starts to take on the role of 'event manager'.

Handling multiple hits on an entity instance

A problem which does not seem to be recognised in OO literature to date is that one event instance may hit the same entity instance more than once. The event may thus lock an entity from receiving further messages from itself!

There are two reasonably obvious situations where multiple hits may occur, related to stereotype shapes in the data model: the **V shape** or multiple many-to-many link and the **diamond shape** or boundary clash.

V shape, multiple many-to-many link

In the above many-to-many relationship, an Applicant can only have one Skill of each Skill Type, but in other many-to-many relationships this restriction does not apply and there may be a multiple many-to-many link. For example, an Employee may have several Tasks within the same Workstep. Assuming each Task has its own serial number (not a compound key of Employee and Workstep) then the two models below both allow an Employee to perform several Tasks within the same Workstep.

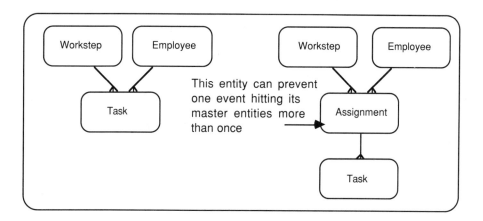

The model on the left may lead to an effect correspondence diagram which resembles the one shown above, but with the possibility that an event travelling from Workstep via Task to Employee may hit the same Employee more than once.

The model on the right avoids the multiple hit problem by the addition of a key-only or operational master record into the physical database. This record, called Assignment, represents all combinations of keys, and owns a set of the detail or link entities.

It should be noted that this is a change to the physical data model, not the logical one. The storage and retrieval of the extra record type should be handled in the process/data interface (PDI), not in the entity event modelling. This means some extra design work later on.

In practice, it is usually inconvenient to add such an operational master record type. It is easier to code extra PDI processes, such as one which is invoked just before the event, and derives the relevant list of detail link entities. And it is easier still to adopt one of the process-oriented solutions outlined below.

The diamond shape, boundary clash

Where a detail entity has two masters, and these two masters share (perhaps much higher in the data model) the same master, then there is the possibility that an event travelling down the model from the top to the bottom will arrive at the same detail entity via two different routes. This may happen for example in copying down a death event down two sides of a 'diamond shaped' data model.

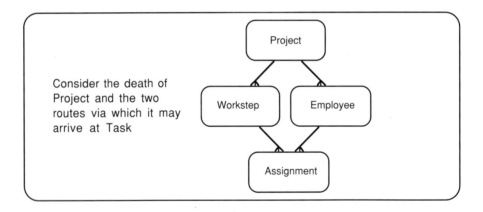

This is very much akin to a 'boundary clash' in JSP, since the same detail entity is being grouped for a single process into two incompatible sets. Unfortunately it is not susceptible to a simple data modelling solution (like the V shape was), and so we need to look at processing modelling solutions.

Even though the manipulation of the data model may resolve some 'multiple hit' problems, these three process modelling solutions provide more general solutions.

1   Sort out messages when they get to the object

Assuming the locking provided by the database management system is not sufficient, you must add code to lock the entity on the first invocation of the first phase of an event, and unlock the entity on the last invocation of the second phase of the same event.

In the first phase, the necessary code must ask the question, Has this entity already been accessed by this event? To do this it must store not only the lock on the entity, but remember the identity of the event which locked it.

In the second phase, the necessary code must ask the question, Is this the last time this event will hit the entity? To do this it must remember the number of hits in the first phase, and countdown during the second phase until all have been committed.

This extra code should be shielded from the entity event model, which should know nothing about locking, or other multi-user issues. In terms of the 3-Schema Architecture the code belongs in the Internal Design, and in terms of SSADM it is a module of the PDI.

2   Add an event manager to sort out and pass different messages

You can introduce some kind of event manager program which keeps a track of which entities have already been invoked with an event in the first phase, and when each is invoked for the last time with a commit message in the second phase.

3   Move the database processing into the event manager program

This is really the conventional programming solution. We have arrived by a circuitous route at what SSADM calls the 'Update Process Model'. This is a highly optimised form of OO implementation in which objects communicate via the working storage of a single procedure, rather than by sending messages to each other. The next section expands on this idea.

18.2 Conventional programming implementation

In the absence of an OO environment, or where it is more convenient to implement in a conventional programming or application generation environment, the method invocation groups defined by the effect correspondence diagrams can be turned into database update sub-routines. These can be called by a scheduler such as a TP monitor, or by each other.

For example, consider the Applicant Registration effect correspondence diagram shown earlier in this chapter. If we convert the one-way directional arrows into one-to-one correspondence arrows, we get the following version of the diagram, in which the arrows now show one-to-one correspondence between method invocations.

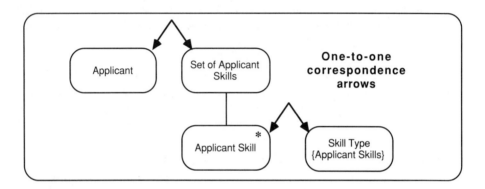

In a conventional programming environment, we can now merge method bodies which are invoked in one-to-one correspondence with each other, so that they are combined within one process component box of the program structure.

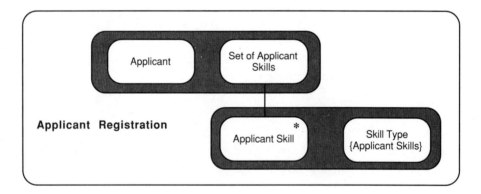

After introducing an extra level of sequence, which enables us to preserve the well-formed structure of the diagram when we allocate operations to the top component, we get the following program structure.

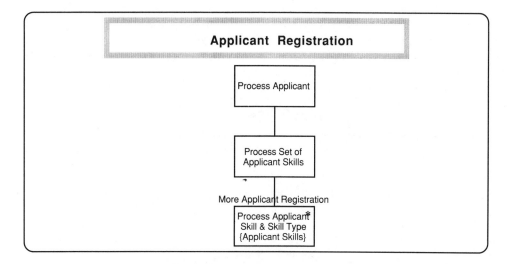

We transform this into an 'executable' program by:

- transferring the operations from the original method bodies
- adding database manipulation operations
- adding invocations of groups of methods being implemented as other sub-routines
- adding iteration conditions.

Redundant operations

The reader may notice that some of the operations in the following examples are redundant. For example:

- 'gain' and 'lose' operations (which we allocated to event-effects in the entity behaviour models) are redundant in a typical database environment
- state variable setting operations which do not change the state-variable value from its prior state are redundant
- where a delete operation is allocated to an event-effect in the entity behaviour model, then all other operations under the effect are redundant.

Since we are using a CASE tool to perform mechanical transformations, it costs us no effort to carry these operations from the entity behaviour models through the effect correspondence diagrams to the event procedures. Of course, most programmers would optimise them away.

The diagram below was generated automatically from the effect correspondence diagram. It is executable in the sense that it would be possible to construct some interpreter which could execute diagrams of this type.

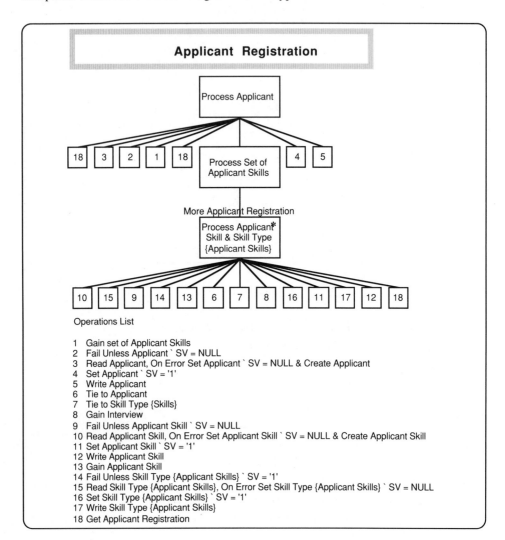

Applicant Registration

Process Applicant

18 3 2 1 18   Process Set of Applicant Skills   4 5

More Applicant Registration

Process Applicant*
Skill & Skill Type
{Applicant Skills}

10 15 9 14 13 6 7 8 16 11 17 12 18

Operations List

1   Gain set of Applicant Skills
2   Fail Unless Applicant ` SV = NULL
3   Read Applicant, On Error Set Applicant ` SV = NULL & Create Applicant
4   Set Applicant ` SV = '1'
5   Write Applicant
6   Tie to Applicant
7   Tie to Skill Type {Skills}
8   Gain Interview
9   Fail Unless Applicant Skill ` SV = NULL
10 Read Applicant Skill, On Error Set Applicant Skill ` SV = NULL & Create Applicant Skill
11 Set Applicant Skill ` SV = '1'
12 Write Applicant Skill
13 Gain Applicant Skill
14 Fail Unless Skill Type {Applicant Skills} ` SV = '1'
15 Read Skill Type {Applicant Skills}, On Error Set Skill Type {Applicant Skills} ` SV = NULL
16 Set Skill Type {Applicant Skills} ` SV = '1'
17 Write Skill Type {Applicant Skills}
18 Get Applicant Registration

It is also executable in the sense that it can easily be transformed to a conventional programming language or into pseudocode:

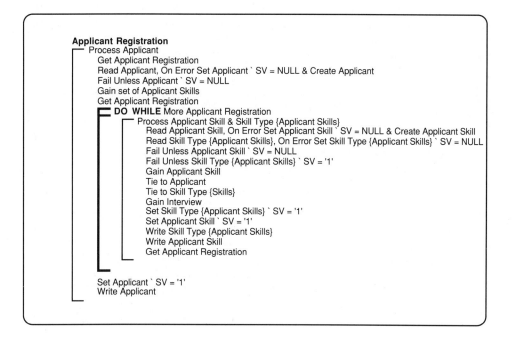

```
Applicant Registration
  Process Applicant
      Get Applicant Registration
      Read Applicant, On Error Set Applicant ` SV = NULL & Create Applicant
      Fail Unless Applicant ` SV = NULL
      Gain set of Applicant Skills
      Get Applicant Registration
      DO WHILE More Applicant Registration
          Process Applicant Skill & Skill Type {Applicant Skills}
              Read Applicant Skill, On Error Set Applicant Skill ` SV = NULL & Create Applicant Skill
              Read Skill Type {Applicant Skills}, On Error Set Skill Type {Applicant Skills} ` SV = NULL
              Fail Unless Applicant Skill ` SV = NULL
              Fail Unless Skill Type {Applicant Skills} ` SV = '1'
              Gain Applicant Skill
              Tie to Applicant
              Tie to Skill Type {Skills}
              Gain Interview
              Set Skill Type {Applicant Skills} ` SV = '1'
              Set Applicant Skill ` SV = '1'
              Write Skill Type {Applicant Skills}
              Write Applicant Skill
              Get Applicant Registration

      Set Applicant ` SV = '1'
      Write Applicant
```

Jackson (1975) shows how this pseudocode or 'schematic logic', as he calls it, can be easily translated into COBOL.

18.3 A few more modules/methods for the case study

The sub-routine which implements the Post Acceptance method invocation group is the largest and most complex of all in the case study. It can be developed by following the same path as for Applicant Registration. First, we enclose the components of the effect correspondence diagram which are in one-to-one correspondence.

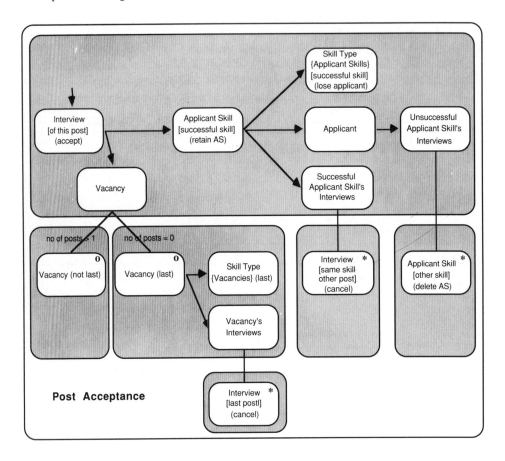

Then we can transform this diagram into a program structure and allocate operations to it.

After introducing two extra levels of sequence, which enable us to preserve the well-formed structure of the diagram when we allocate operations to its components, we get the following program structure.

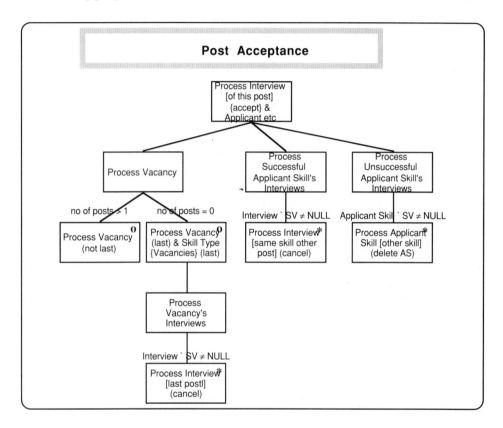

Again, we transform this into an 'executable' program by:

- transferring the operations from the original method bodies
- adding database manipulation operations
- adding invocations of groups of methods being implemented as other sub-routines
- adding iteration conditions.

The program structure after operations have been allocated to it is too large for inclusion in this book, but we can show the transformation of it into the format of an action diagram, or pseudocode.

```
Post Acceptance
 ┌─ Process Interview [of this post] (accept) & Applicant etc
 │     Get Post Acceptance
 │     Read Interview (of this post), On Error Set Interview (of this post) ` SV = NULL
 │     Read Vacancy, On Error Set Vacancy ` SV = NULL
 │     Read Applicant Skill (successful skill), On Error Set Applicant Skill (successful skill) ` SV = NULL
 │     Read Applicant, On Error Set Applicant ` SV = NULL
 │     Read Skill Type {Applicant Skills} (successful skill), On Error Set Skill Type {Applicant Skills} (successful skill) ` SV = NULL
 │     Fail Unless Applicant Skill (successful skill) ` SV = '1'
 │     Fail Unless Applicant ` SV = '1'
 │     Fail Unless Interview (of this post) ` SV = '1'
 │     Interview (of this post) ` Notify accounts
 │     Lose set of Applicant Skills bar successful one
 │     Cut from Skill Type {Skills}
 │     Invoke §Skill Type's loss of Applicant, and Fail If §Skill Type's loss of Applicant Fails
 │     Read Applicant Skill (other skill), On Error Set Applicant Skill (other skill) ` SV = NULL
 │     Read Interview (same skill other post), On Error Set Interview (same skill other post) ` SV = NULL
 │   ┌─ IF no of posts > 1
 │   │    ┌─ Process Vacancy (not last)
 │   │    │    Fail Unless Vacancy ` SV = '1'
 │   │    │    Vacancy ` No of Posts := Vacancy ` No of Posts + 1
 │   │    │    Lose Interview
 │   │    │    Set Vacancy ` SV = '1'
 │   │    └─   Write Vacancy
 │   │
 │   ├─ ELSE no of posts = 0
 │   │    ┌─ Process Vacancy (last) & Skill Type {Vacancies} (last)
 │   │    │    Read Skill Type {Vacancies}, On Error Set Skill Type {Vacancies} ` SV = NULL
 │   │    │    Fail Unless Vacancy ` SV = '1'
 │   │    │    Lose set of Interviews
 │   │    │    Vacancy ` No of Posts := 0
 │   │    │    Cut from Skill Type (vacancies)
 │   │    │    Invoke §Skill Type's loss of Vacancy, and Fail If §Skill Type's loss of Vacancy Fails
 │   │    │    Read Interview (last postl), On Error Set Interview (last postl) ` SV = NULL
 │   │    │  ┌═ DO WHILE Interview (last postl) ` SV ≠ NULL
 │   │    │  │   ┌─ Process Interview [last postl] (cancel)
 │   │    │  │   │    Invoke §Interview Cancellation by End of Vacancy, and Fail If §Interview Cancellation by End of Vacancy Fails
 │   │    │  │   └─   Read Interview (last postl), On Error Set Interview (last postl) ` SV = NULL
 │   │    │  └─
 │   │    │     Set Vacancy ` SV = '2'
 │   │    └─   Write Vacancy
 │   │
 │   │  ┌═ DO WHILE Interview (same skill other post) ` SV ≠ NULL
 │   │  │   ┌─ Process Interview [same skill other post] (cancel)
 │   │  │   │    Invoke §Interview Cancellation by End of Applicant, and Fail If §Interview Cancellation by End of Applicant Fails
 │   │  │   └─   Read Interview (same skill other post), On Error Set Interview (same skill other post) ` SV = NULL
 │   │  └─
 │   │  ┌═ DO WHILE Applicant Skill (other skill) ` SV ≠ NULL
 │   │  │   ┌─ Process Applicant Skill [other skill] (delete AS)
 │   │  │   │    Invoke §End of Unsuccessful Applicant Skill, and Fail If §End of Unsuccessful Applicant Skill Fails
 │   │  │   └─   Read Applicant Skill (other skill), On Error Set Applicant Skill (other skill) ` SV = NULL
 │   │  └─
 │        Set Interview (of this post) ` SV = '2'
 │        Set Applicant ` SV = '2'
 │        Set Applicant Skill (successful skill) ` SV = '2'
 │        Write Interview (of this post)
 │        Write Applicant
 └─       Write Applicant Skill (successful skill)
```

The remaining examples are shown in the form of structure diagrams.

An example of a sub-routine which implements a method invocation group invoked by the Post Acceptance event (and also by other events) is shown below.

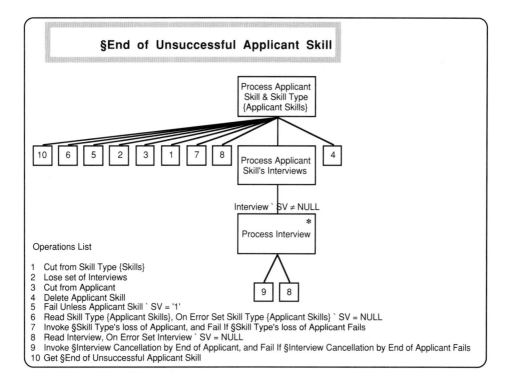

§End of Unsuccessful Applicant Skill

Operations List

1 Cut from Skill Type {Skills}
2 Lose set of Interviews
3 Cut from Applicant
4 Delete Applicant Skill
5 Fail Unless Applicant Skill ` SV = '1'
6 Read Skill Type {Applicant Skills}, On Error Set Skill Type {Applicant Skills} ` SV = NULL
7 Invoke §Skill Type's loss of Applicant, and Fail If §Skill Type's loss of Applicant Fails
8 Read Interview, On Error Set Interview ` SV = NULL
9 Invoke §Interview Cancellation by End of Applicant, and Fail If §Interview Cancellation by End of Applicant Fails
10 Get §End of Unsuccessful Applicant Skill

And some simpler examples are shown below.

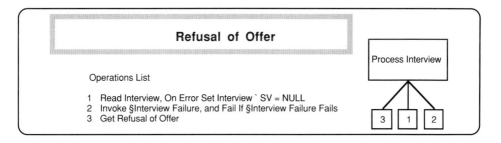

Refusal of Offer

Operations List

1 Read Interview, On Error Set Interview ` SV = NULL
2 Invoke §Interview Failure, and Fail If §Interview Failure Fails
3 Get Refusal of Offer

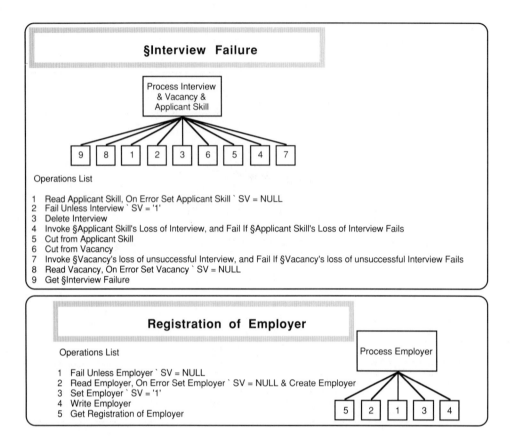

§Interview Failure

Process Interview
& Vacancy &
Applicant Skill

9 8 1 2 3 6 5 4 7

Operations List

1   Read Applicant Skill, On Error Set Applicant Skill ` SV = NULL
2   Fail Unless Interview ` SV = '1'
3   Delete Interview
4   Invoke §Applicant Skill's Loss of Interview, and Fail If §Applicant Skill's Loss of Interview Fails
5   Cut from Applicant Skill
6   Cut from Vacancy
7   Invoke §Vacancy's loss of unsuccessful Interview, and Fail If §Vacancy's loss of unsuccessful Interview Fails
8   Read Vacancy, On Error Set Vacancy ` SV = NULL
9   Get §Interview Failure

Registration of Employer

Process Employer

Operations List

1   Fail Unless Employer ` SV = NULL
2   Read Employer, On Error Set Employer ` SV = NULL & Create Employer
3   Set Employer ` SV = '1'
4   Write Employer
5   Get Registration of Employer

5 2 1 3 4

18.4 **Reuse of code in the event class hierarchy**

The approach described in chapters 14 to 18 constructs systems with significant levels of
reusability of program code. This can be seen from the potential invocations of the
constructed sub-routines in the event class hierarchy at the start of chapter 17.

Chapter 19

Conclusions and remarks about entity event modelling

The conclusions in this chapter are supported either by the work done on the case study and shown in earlier chapters, or by background work done but not shown.

19.1 **Limits to what has been presented in part four**

The need for training

If you wish to try out entity event modelling techniques without any formal training, we recommend you should omit the entity behaviour modelling step on the first system and build effect correspondence diagrams directly and intuitively. On the second and third systems, we recommend you build entity behaviour models and effect correspondence diagrams more or less in parallel with each other, using one to validate the other.

To develop a large system using entity behaviour modelling techniques you will need to do more than read the preceding chapters. We find that people need four or five days of training. This seems to us a very short time to learn a trade; systems analysts and designers are ludicrously under-educated compared with graduates of other engineering disciplines. We teach a methodical approach, including guidance on:

- when to use stereotype entity behaviour models
- standard models for logical death and physical deletion
- when and why parallel entity behaviour models are needed
- how to solve recognition problems (using posit, admit and quit concepts).

The key to our training material is a dozen 'stereotype entity behaviour models'. Once these are understood, the supposedly difficult concepts of 'parallelism' and 'quits' are much easier to learn.

We have not presented all the theory you need for all cases. There are various design problems which the full methodology must solve.

The multiple hit problem

Occasionally an event type is found which may travel via two or more routes and arrive at the same entity, on which it has in theory only one effect. See the discussion in chapter 18 of V-shape and diamond-shape models.

Non-behavioural rules

Some rules cannot be captured in entity behaviour modelling (or can only be captured with great difficulty). For these, other rules definition approaches may be simpler. We are considering a 'knowledge-based system' approach for recording what chapter 29 calls 'business policies' rather than 'business rules'.

Strategies for logical deaths and physical deletes

In the preface we put this up as an important problem in systems design. It can turn out to be a very complex design problem, and we have only scratched the surface of it in our case study.

Logical and physical entity modelling

Our methodology allows for there to be a difference between the logical data model and the physical data model. The logical data model is the one we have used for entity event modelling. Rather than construct two entity event models, logical and physical, we normally construct a PDI to handle the mapping of the logical data model onto the physical database. One of the things which might be dealt with in the PDI is the behaviour of operational master entities; however, these are usually trivial and may be added into the entity event model instead.

Finally, there are a few cases where entity behaviour models do not show the full set of effects which must be shown in effect correspondence diagrams. There is insufficient space here to explore all these issues, but we have tackled most of them, and intend to publish further in this area. To wrap up part four of the book, there are other points to be made.

19.2 **Each paradigm has something to offer the other**

In chapter 8 we wrote of two paradigms, the control-structured paradigm and the OO programming paradigm. In concluding part four, we should consider what they have to offer in developing the Conceptual Model of a system.

The **control-structured** paradigm makes the behaviour of the objects more visible. The behaviour is laid out explicitly in the entity behaviour models and does not have to be deduced by the examination of state variables.

The intermediate components in an entity behaviour model (those which appear above the 'leaf' level in a diagram) represent important descriptions of cycles of behaviour which cannot be represented in state transition diagrams. A large amount of the analysis and design required in systems development can be driven by the examination of a number of stereotypical behaviour patterns.

The case study developed in this book is too small to show many examples of stereotype behaviours, but it does show a very significant, though trivial-seeming, one. In a behaviour model, wherever an iteration of events or patterns of events is followed by another 'terminating' event and the iterated events appear in other behaviour models, then we need to identify where the terminating event appears in other behaviour models.

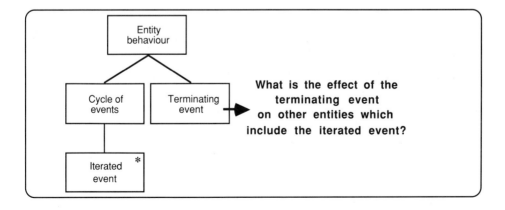

In the Hi-Ho case study this leads us to ask what happens, for example, to interviews currently scheduled, but which the applicant has not yet attended, if he/she accepts a job before attending them.

Variations of this case study have been attempted by thousands of students over the last eight or nine years. In none of this time, to our knowledge, has any student discovered the need to do something about this (for example, when performing a data flow diagram analysis) except when examining the applicability of the stereotype just described. A large number of other examples from case studies and real systems could also have been described here if space permitted.

The particular analysis approach outlined here has some pretensions to completeness in its attack on its problem domain, which is the time-varying aspects of object behaviour in discrete event systems. We believe, with some inductive evidence, that if the analysis approach is applied correctly (admittedly a very big if!), it should yield all the information needed; it does not depend on chance observations made by the users or serendipitous discoveries by the analysts.

Although this approach is highly successful in capturing systems behaviour and is highly successful in the information-hiding aspects of encapsulation, it has in the past been used without much attention to reusability of analysis or of program code.

The **OO programming** paradigm is highly successful at attaining *encapsulation* and reusability but less successful at making object behaviour explicit and visible. It also currently provides no general framework for discovering what the methods ought to be. Obviously you can ask questions but, we believe, there is no way to be sure you will manage to ask all the right questions. And of course you cannot be sure the user will think to answer the questions that you didn't think to ask.

We believe the required questions are provided by the examination of the object control structure, and of the relationships between the control structures of different objects, especially in terms of stereotype behaviour patterns.

19.3 A synthesis between the two paradigms

In part four we have attempted to develop a system's behaviour description following the entity behaviour modelling paradigm, but with the constraint on doing so of apparently aiming for a OO programming implementation.

In standard SSADM4, entity behaviour models and effect correspondence diagrams are developed without a conscious effort to identify the methods contained in them. In our version, identifying the methods makes explicit which of the leaf nodes represent a method invoked by an event or super-event.

Both authors independently developed versions of the Hi-Ho case study. Both expected that super-events would give a small (but still significant amount) of reusability. Both were surprised to find there was actually a very large amount of reusability, as shown in the event class hierarchy at the start of chapter 17. This reusability was mostly not an accidental property of a particular set of design decisions. It was fundamental to the nature of the system itself.

Of course, other systems may present less opportunities for reuse, but they will surely present some opportunities. Thus reuse can be achieved even where there is no class hierarchy in the data model (which has been the direction people have been looking in for increasing reuse).

Subsequent examination of real systems being developed using the standard SSADM4 approach revealed improvements that could be made using our new variant of the approach. These benefits are there even when the implementation is not a OO programming environment. A conscious attempt to identify methods while performing entity behaviour modelling would combine the power of the analysis and design approach with the relative economy of the reusable-method solution.

Entity behaviour modelling provides a reliable and powerful mechanism for discovering the valid predecessor states for method invocations and discovering the successor states those invocations should yield.

This means that entity behaviour modelling is not equally useful for all kinds of system. It is more useful where the system takes an active role and permits only a valid sequence of real-world events. It is less useful for 'record keeping systems' which can be built using the simple rules for the behaviour of entities which are assumed by an application generator (see chapter 21 for further discussion).

19.4 Information systems in an OO environment

Chapters 12 and 18 discussed OO-style analysis leading to implementation in a database environment. This section reviews and summarises some of the points already made about information systems implementation in an OO environment.

The need to control interactions between objects

An OO program in an OO environment usually has two characteristics not usually shared by an OO database system: there are relatively few objects (tens, hundreds, thousands) and the objects are drawn from different domains of discourse (some objects implement other objects).

We could of course implement the objects in a database system by having lower-level objects, but this is not relevant to the present discussion. We are trying to point out is that there are fewer objects in an OO program, and, to the extent that objects interact, much of the interaction is between levels of discourse; that is, between an object at a conceptual level and between objects which implement its representation. In such an interaction between levels the objects at the implementation level are frequently private to the object at the conceptual level.

By contrast, in a database system we are concerned with perhaps millions of objects, and we are concerned much more with interactions between objects at the same conceptual level. These objects are public. Subject to organisations' security policies, any user may potentially interact with any object. The interactions need to be controlled and co-ordinated in some way.

Events and commit units

There are parcels of method invocations which must be made together, in such a way that the user can't get information from the objects until the whole parcel of invocations is complete. Among other things, this means that failure of a method invocation on one object may need to condemn to failure what would have been an otherwise successful method invocation on another object. Even worse, in a multi-tasking system (and every data processing system is multi-tasking in this sense), two parcels of methods may be invoked 'simultaneously' covering overlapping sets of objects, and they mustn't be allowed to interfere with each other.

We need two things: an ability to identify at a conceptual level what the appropriate parcels of invocations are; and an implementation mechanism which enforces the success or failure of the parcel together and prevents one parcel from interfering with another.

At the conceptual level, the appropriate concept is that of the **event** used in the analysis approach described in this book. We define an event as being a single, atomic, consistent change in reality at the level of granularity being modelled in the system.

In a database system, the appropriate implementation mechanism is that of a **commit unit**, together with the record locking and logging and rollback mechanisms that support it.

In an OO implementation something similar is needed. The best mechanism involves objects which control access to other objects; such a controller object is equivalent to an event manager, as discussed in chapter 18. A deadlock and starvation-free protocol for implementing such control is described in Robinson (1979).

Efficient storage

In dealing with very large numbers of objects, their instance variables must be stored on backing store. But when an event occurs, a more or less predictable set of instance variables needs to be brought into memory together to process that event. Some kind of ability to tell the OO environment how to cluster its instance variables for efficient loading and unloading is needed, for example something similar to a DB2 clustering index. Efficient OO environments may be several years away, but chapter 18 has shown how OO designs can be implemented on top of today's efficient database systems.

19.5 Is the method applicable to process control systems?

Related methodologies (JSD from Jackson and OOA from Schlaer and Mellor) have been employed on real-time and process control systems. We propose that our entity event modelling techniques may provide a better methodology, that is, a better means to model each finite state machine, a better means to analyse co-operation between these machines, and better means for co-ordinating co-operating machines. We are experimenting with a case study in this area, to see how much benefit may be obtained from using super-events and effect correspondence diagrams. It seems that the notion of parallel entity behaviour models, barely featured in this book, will be important.

Part Five:

External Design

Chapter 20

Techniques for External Design

This chapter outlines several different approaches to External Design, including prototyping and rapid application development, and introduces the role played by application generators and graphical user interfaces in system development.

20.1 **Tools and techniques introduced in this chapter**

Part one of the book presented the 3-Schema Architecture as a way of viewing and designing information systems. According to this view, the requirements of a system can be divided into two parts or schemas: the Conceptual Model and External Design. The structure and processing of the physical database is defined in a third schema called the Internal Design. It is proposed that each schema should be specified and implemented as separately as is possible. Part four concentrated mostly on the Conceptual Model, including techniques for discovering and designing reusable components. Part five will concentrate on ideas, tools and techniques used in the External Design.

The use of OO ideas in External Design

The main OO idea we use in Conceptual Modelling is 'encapsulation'. The OO ideas we use, though less formally, in External Design, are 'composite objects' and 'inheritance'.

General approaches to External Design

This chapter introduces various approaches to External Design (some of them overlapping, some of them apparently antagonistic), draws distinctions between them, and incorporates them within a coherent framework. To begin with let us distinguish between prototyping and rapid application development techniques.

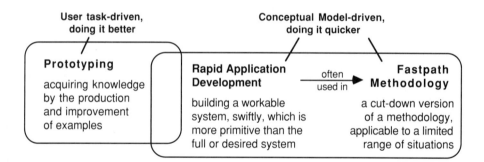

Prototyping techniques are used to improve the quality of a system's specification by developing examples and validating them. External Design prototyping is a user task-driven approach. It usually involves showing a draft user interface to users. It is about investigation and discovery of requirements. It is not necessarily backed by any software engineering at all.

Rapid application development techniques are used to foreshorten the full system development process, so that a system which is workable but more primitive than the full or desired system can be delivered sooner rather than later. Rapid application development is a Conceptual Model-driven approach. It means taking short-cuts and making pragmatic design decisions. It must be backed by software engineering (that is, it involves buying or writing code).

A *fastpath methodology* is a cut-down version of a larger methodology, tailored to specific circumstances. A fastpath methodology may be designed for a particular kind of business, application system, person, or implementation environment. For example we have developed a fastpath version of SSADM which is suitable for Microsoft Windows implementation environments; this uses rapid application development techniques from this book, but is not described here.

Specific External Design techniques

Given that both Conceptual Model-driven and user task-driven approaches are possible, this diagram names the user interface design techniques which are described in later chapters.

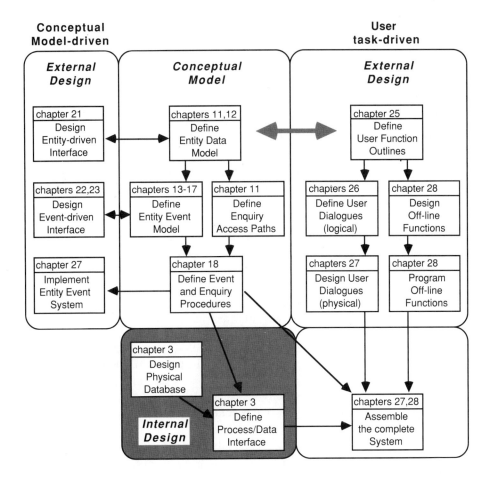

The diagram also shows the chapters in which each technique is described.

The use of different life-cycle models

Various life-cycle models have been offered for systems development, including:

- the waterfall model (see chapter 3)
- the spiral model (see chapter 3)
- incremental delivery (after Gilb and discussed in this chapter).

The latter two life-cycle models have been criticised as relatively vacuous, because they lack sufficient teachable steps and techniques. What is needed is a rationale which integrates the different life-cycle models. This chapter provides one, using the 3-Schema Architecture.

The use of different implementation tools

This chapter introduces the role of application generators and 4GLs (we shall use the term *application generator* only from now on) and of *graphical user interfaces* within the methodology. These implementation tools are discussed further in later chapters.

20.2 The use of OO ideas in External Design

OO ideas can be placed in External Design, though much less firmly than we have placed them in Conceptual Modelling. It seems likely that ideas to do with composite objects and inheritance may be useful.

Should we include external objects in the Conceptual Model?

In discussing the 3-Schema Architecture, Rumbaugh et al. say 'you should construct one object model for each external schema and another object model for the conceptual schema'.

We agree that the External Design and the Conceptual Model should be kept apart. External Design concepts such as user roles and user functions do not belong in the Conceptual Model. The names of user functions and user roles will appear at the user interface in the form of menu entries and window titles; they might also appear as the titles of partial data model views; but they should not appear in the entity data model or the database structure developed from it.

Chapters 22 to 27 show how to specify the data which flows between the two schemas in terms of event and enquiry triggers, and event and enquiry responses.

Should we use object models for External Design?

We are not yet convinced by the idea of building object models for the External Design. One suggestion is to draw a user view of the entity data model for each user role (perhaps adding composite objects and rolling up details) then drive External Design from this.

In part five we propose what we believe are better techniques. The fact that a specific

UIMS may use something which resembles an entity data model in documenting the structure of 'windows' or 'widgets' in a GUI is more a matter of physical design than systems analysis. Chapter 26 shows how the user interface can be specified using I/O structures, then simplified in the form of a dialogue structure.

Inheritance in the External Design

User interface designers use inheritance in an informal way all the time. Designers can put together new user interface designs by creating user interface objects which inherit the properties of previously designed objects. Modern development environments help them to copy an object from one window or dialogue to another (carrying forward the properties of the object as they do this), and then revise the new object. This is especially attractive where the early presentation of a prototype design to users is expected or needed.

This is an intuitive, temporary, even playful use of inheritance, unlike the formal and static kind of inheritance which occurs when a class hierarchy is defined in an entity data model. However, chapter 22 to 24 indicate how this kind of inheritance can be formalised by the development of standards which encourage the reuse of design components. There is a class hierarchy here, even if there is no data model.

Composite objects in the External Design

User interface objects such as windows and reference lists are certainly composite objects of a kind. Chapter 24 points out that the maintenance and refreshment of reference lists in multi-user environment requires a better theory of how to handle composite objects. We haven't done much research in this area.

There are looser notions of what a composite object is. You could suggest that External Design is all about the composition of Conceptual Model entities, events and enquiries into composites for the convenience of the user.

You could say that **user functions** are composites of distinct events and enquiries, organised to support the user in carrying out some task or business procedure. You could say that **user roles** are composites of user functions, at a higher level still. A production software engineer who uses an OO environment to build a UIMS will probably treat a **window** as a composite of all the symbols displayed in it, for the purpose of designing operating system functions like 'move window' or 'close window'. You might take the view that a window is a composite of entities and bits of entities extracted from the database, and/or a composite of events and enquiries collected for input.

It is not clear whether viewing user functions, user roles or windows as composites of Conceptual Model objects is helpful to the application designer. It is certainly a different view of composite objects from that taken by OO programmers. And to be strictly accurate, a window does not contain entities or events of the Conceptual Model at all; it contains only transient copies of entity and event data; it contains data streams which flow to and from the Conceptual Model. However, a new theory of composite objects might be built on such ideas.

20.3 **Prototyping**

Prototyping may usefully be defined as *'acquiring knowledge by the production and improvement of examples'*.

Prototyping is more appropriate to some areas of knowledge than others. It may have a small role to play in discovering features of the Conceptual Model, in helping to confirm the attributes or events of an entity with users. But it is much more appropriate in External Design (arriving at the ergonomically optimum design for windows and dialogues) and Internal Design (selecting an optimum file design). Prototyping helps here because what 'optimum' means is subjective rather than objective; the best trade-off between competing requirements cannot be defined in an algorithmic way.

Prototyping is usually concerned with External Design.

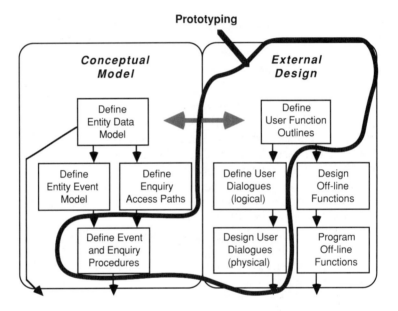

Prototyping defines systems by concentrating on the components inside the boundary above. Note that these components are dependent for their correctness on the correctness of the entity data model (for enquiry processing) and the entity event model (for event processing). Neither of these can be defined in a reliable way from a study of screen designs, unless the system is very simple.

There are three reasons why prototyping alone may be inefficient and unreliable in eliciting business knowledge in a system of any complexity, why it needs to be backed up by Conceptual Modelling techniques.

User views may be inconsistent: different users will be interested in the same areas of knowledge and will have screens covering similar areas of knowledge. But different users tend to see the same information in different contexts and at differing levels of granularity and detail. So if knowledge is elicited solely through screen designs, then there is a real danger that the screens will be inconsistent with each other. This means that designs produced later in the development process are likely to cause reworking of designs produced earlier in the process. The result is that development can be slower, not more rapid.

Analyst and user views may be inconsistent: what you see isn't always what you get. If the knowledge implicit in information displayed on a screen isn't subjected to analysis, then it can be interpreted inconsistently by analyst and user. For example, data typed on a prototype screen as an example of help text might be interpreted by a user as part of the functionality of the system (this really happened on a project where we had a consultancy role).

An External Design does not reveal the Conceptual Model: the screens give no hint of the processing which may be triggered 'behind the scenes' by a complex event. For example, if the system is only specified using screens, would you be sure to notice if a single button press on the last screen examined triggered deletion of the whole data base?

Having said this, prototyping is an excellent technology for developing and improving user interfaces. And provided that we can be sure that products produced early in the development process aren't changed as a result of knowledge gained later in the process, prototyping can be important in facilitating incremental delivery.

Things which are not prototyping

Functional prototyping is not prototyping in the sense we have defined it: it is not about developing a user-friendly interface. Functional prototyping is about rapid implementation of the Conceptual Model, using a naive user interface. Since functional prototyping is neither about 'prototyping', nor about what we call 'user functions', we include it under the heading 'rapid application development'.

It turns out that many so-called prototyping processes and techniques are really more to do with *rapid application development.* People who talk about 'functional prototyping' are probably talking about rapid application development, with limited External and Internal Design. People who say that prototyping necessarily involves the use of an application generator are probably talking about rapid application development of a Conceptual Model which is either small or simple.

In most disciplines, a prototype is not the real thing, but a model built to test a specification or discover how the real thing should be built. In building information systems, some people speak of prototyping as a rapid way to build the real thing. In practice, the rapidity of development probably comes from the tools used to implement the prototype (typically an application generator).

The division between prototyping and rapid application development may be reflected in implementation products. UIMS and GUI design tools are used for user interface prototyping. Database management systems and application generators are used for rapid application development.

20.4 **Rapid application development**

Rapid application development may usefully be defined as *'producing a workable system, swiftly, which is more primitive than the full or desired system'*.

RAD means more primitive Internal or External Design

In terms of the 3-Schema Architecture, the phrase 'more primitive' means more primitive Internal or External Design. One way to speed up systems development, so obvious it barely needs explanation, is to cut out Internal Design. This means implementing the entity data model as the database structure, and coding event and enquiry procedures as database routines, without giving any attention to the performance of the system.

Another way to speed up systems development is to implement the full Conceptual Model using a crude External Design, without working too long on the user-friendliness of the system. We introduce suitable RAD techniques in chapters 21 to 23.

RAD might mean using an application generator

Some people associate rapid application development with the use of an application generator. This will naturally speed up systems development in so far as the tool supports the implementation of a simple Internal or External Design. On the other hand, an application generator may slow down systems development if more sophisticated design options which it does not readily support must be developed and implemented.

RAD doesn't mean cutting back the Conceptual Model

Obviously a systems development project may be speeded up by reducing the scope of the Conceptual Model delivered in the first version of the system, but this approach is not truly rapid application development. Two approaches which do limit the scope of the Conceptual Model are time-box development and incremental programme.

Time-box development

Time-box development reduces the scope of the Conceptual Model by limiting time for systems development (to say, 60 days). This is an anti-methodical approach. It might be used in prototyping, it might help to motivate the project team, and it might help to focus their attention on what matters, but it cuts across any attempt to be systematic.

Typically the first system delivered has a Conceptual Model which is reduced in the sense that is *simpler.* While this means an application generator may be used in place of the more advanced methodology techniques (see chapter 21), and this may greatly speed up initial system delivery, this will give a short-lived system, one which cannot be incrementally developed. It is unlikely the resultant system can be readily integrated with other systems, either current or future.

Incremental programme

Under an incremental programme the first system delivered has a Conceptual Model which is reduced in the sense that is *smaller.* This has little or no effect on the methodology life-cycle, however it implies some kind of overall plan for delivery of the rest of the Conceptual Model in later stages. This plan should enable designers to migrate smoothly from the small system to the larger one.

How to plan the staged implementation of a single Conceptual Model and how to integrate successive system deliveries is outside the scope of this book. Chapters 24 and 32 offer a little advice, but we are currently developing 'software componentry' techniques to help with such incremental programmes.

Note that we draw a distinction between incremental programme and incremental delivery. In an incremental programme, the Conceptual Model is partitioned for delivery in stages. In incremental delivery, the Conceptual Model is built all at once and the user functionality is delivered in stages.

20.5 **Incremental delivery**

Given a stable Conceptual Model, it is relatively straightforward to deliver the External Design, or the Internal Design, in stages. This is a way of speeding up the first delivery of functionality to the users.

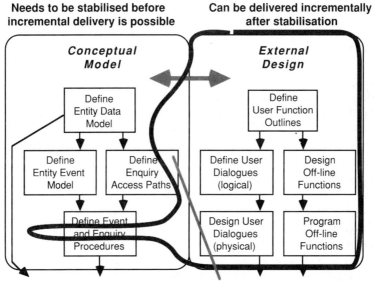

Significant Enquiry Access Paths must be defined in validating the entity data model, but others may be developed later.

To outline two of the user task-driven techniques shown here, logical dialogue design defines a dialogue as a sequence of events and enquiries, and physical dialogue design defines a dialogue in terms of windows and commands.

20.6 **Integrating the External Design and Conceptual Model**

Development by trial and error, prototyping and rapid application development can be more fun than fully systematic development. Those working at the implementation end of systems development are naturally inclined to use these approaches. But it is still necessary to know how a Conceptual Model can be methodically embedded within an External Design. Even if the theory is not followed to the letter, knowing it should help to minimise the 'error' in trial and error.

So how far should designers prototyping the External Design be concerned with the Conceptual Model? How can they ensure a smooth integration between the two design schemas? There are three possible levels of integration during system development.

Carry out systematic External Design after Conceptual Modelling

Making sure that the Conceptual Model (data and processing views) is stable and correct before developing the bulk of the External Design, gives two advantages. First, it enables External Design to be done systematically and so minimises the waste of effort in developing a throw-away prototype and reworking design products. Second, it facilitates incremental delivery of the system to users.

There is also a disadvantage. The approach may mean that users have to wait an unacceptably long time before they have any user interface to look at, and discuss with the designers. Feedback from the users to the designers is essential, and some early user interface prototyping is usually helpful.

Throw-away External Design, before Conceptual Modelling

This means trying out an External Design before defining the database, the database processing, or the error handling. Such user interface prototyping is helpful in defining user procedures and dialogues. It may be done outside the disciplines of the methodology. But managers and designers must realise that the prototype is unlikely to be the basis of the implemented system; they must plan to throw it away.

External Design and Conceptual Modelling in parallel

Analysts working on the External Design should be able to use design techniques and products which are quite distinct from those used in the Conceptual Model. But of course the design of the two schemas must be synchronised via a specification of the interface between them. This interface should be specified in terms of the messages they interchange: event and enquiry triggers, event and enquiry responses.

If the Conceptual Model is built in parallel with the External Design, then the Conceptual Model will be changing while External Design is proceeding. To minimise the risk of wasted effort, the interface between the External Design and Conceptual Model should be defined at an early stage and refreshed throughout the design.

One way to keep the Conceptual Model and the External Design in step is to use rapid application development techniques to support Conceptual Modelling. Showing the users a primitive user interface of the kind discussed in chapters 21 and 22 can help to validate both strands of systems development.

20.7 **External Design techniques**

The subsequent chapters in part five propose several new or revised SSADM techniques for External Design, some with uses in prototyping, others with uses in rapid application development.

Entity-driven interface design (see chapter 21) implements a primitive user interface to the entity data model, taking advantage of what application generators can do. While the resultant system may not implement all the business rules, it may have several practical uses, notably as a 'data fixing system'.

Event-driven interface design (see chapters 22 and 23) implements a primitive user interface to an entity event model, using GUI design principles. Applied after step 530 of SSADM4, it gives a fully workable system, which implements all the business rules. It generates mini-dialogues which provide all the basic functionality required, and are reusable in a variety of contexts to support users' tasks.

User-driven window design (see chapter 23) covers window design, including ways in which the user-friendliness of a user interface may be developed in a reasonably systematic way. It has three roles to play in the methodology. First, it is part of the event-driven interface design technique. Second, it can be used to support the investigation by prototyping of how users want a GUI to be presented. Third, it should be used to support the window design step in physical dialogue design.

Style guide definition (see chapters 22 and 24) gives standardisation of application style, including not only the more obvious 'look and feel' issues, but also the handling of multi-user problems to do with contention, locking and refreshment. It also identifies the scope for reuse of External Design components.

User function definition (see chapter 25) is a user task-driven approach to system specification. User functions are outlined as system processes designed to help users carry out their business tasks. Functions may be on-line or off-line. Off-line function design is covered in chapter 28.

Logical dialogue design (see chapter 26) is a systematic way to define a user-friendly interface to an on-line function, resulting in a machine-independent specification. The systematic approach ensures that the database procedures of the Conceptual Model can later be embedded within the dialogue. The user-friendliness comes from designing the dialogue so that users move from one stage to the next, carrying forward context data. A five-step design technique is introduced, the main product of which is a basic dialogue structure, drawn as a sequential structure of events and enquiries.

Physical dialogue design (see chapter 27) addresses design problems such as: elaboration of the dialogue to include errors, aborts and reversions, guidance of users between windows in one dialogue, and the storage of dialogue context data. A seven-step design technique is introduced, perhaps useful in step 650 of SSADM4, which leans in places on earlier techniques for support.

Techniques with multiple purposes

Recall the earlier distinction that rapid application development techniques are intended to foreshorten the full system development process, while prototyping techniques are intended to improve the quality of a system's specification. It is important for the designer to keep these different *purposes* in mind. However, some design techniques enable the designer to pursue both purposes at once, as well as making a contribution to full systematic development. This table is an attempt to illustrate the point.

has a role to play in / Technique	RAD — rapid implementation of:	Prototyping — validating the specification of:	Full Study — systematic development of:
Entity-driven interface design chapter 21	Entity data model Data fixing system Test database system	Entities' attributes Database designs	a platform for below
Event-driven interface design chapters 22 and 23	Entity Event Model (maintaining all the business rules and integrity of stored data)	Entities' events	a platform for below
Window design chapter 23		User-friendly windows for events and enquiries	a platform for below
Logical dialogue design chapter 26			User dialogues (machine-independent)
Physical dialogue design chapter 27		User-friendly navigation between windows	User dialogues (machine-dependent)

Conceptual Model spans the RAD and Prototyping columns across the first two technique rows.

External Design appears below the Window design row.

20.8 **Making use of the spiral model**

Various life-cycle models have been offered for systems development, including:

- the waterfall model
- the spiral model (after Boehm)
- incremental delivery (after Gilb).

This section provides a rationale which integrates the different life-cycle models, using the 3-Schema Architecture.

A prototyping/rapid application development methodology

It is possible to link various prototyping and rapid application development approaches in a methodology structure.

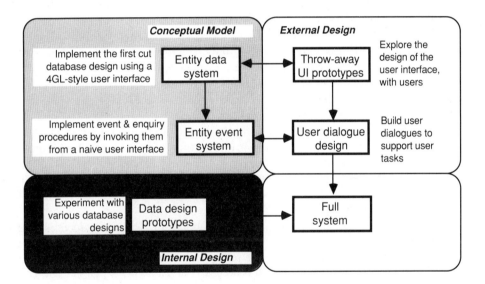

Most methodologies have a life-cycle which can be described as a 'waterfall model'. Prototyping and rapid application development do not fit nicely into a waterfall model. They need not be forced to fit. Another way to view what is going on is via Boehm's 'spiral model'.

The spiral model may be superimposed in many different ways upon a methodology. For one example, see chapter 3. Another variety of spiral model may be used to describe the effect of prototyping and rapid application development techniques on the methodology.

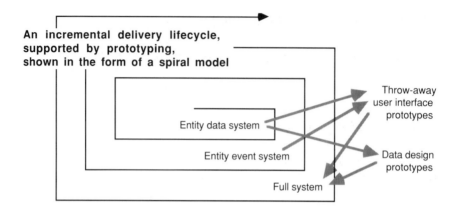

An incremental delivery lifecycle,
supported by prototyping,
shown in the form of a spiral model

Entity data system

Entity event system

Full system

Throw-away
user interface
prototypes

Data design
prototypes

This spiral view shows how a crude system can evolve into a refined one. Each time around the spiral involves a more or less complete pass through the methodology life-cycle, but each time the analysts and designers will place their emphasis on different stages and steps, and deliver a more complete system.

Prototypes sit outside this evolutionary process, but they may inform it, and be informed by it. Database design prototyping may be done at any point after the entity data system has been implemented and before the full system is delivered.

Whether each successive version of the system can or should be delivered to the users (following a kind of incremental delivery) depends on the specific system and the needs of its users.

Readers are not directed to follow this, or any other, spiral model. It is included here primarily as an explanation of how various prototyping and rapid application development approaches cut across the waterfall model of the methodology, and of how they might be organised in a systematic way. The waterfall model remains valid as a description of a traditional, less iterative approach and a tailored version of it might be used each time around the spiral.

We have more to say about rapid application development. Chapter 21 focuses on the use of application generators, for entity-driven interface design, and for database design prototyping. The next section introduces a role for event-driven interface design using GUI design principles, a technique which is described at length in chapters 22 and 23.

20.9 **Graphical User Interface (GUI) design**

What does it mean to design a GUI? There are at least three different interpretations:

- Adding a GUI to a database system
- Designing a GUI for a database system to interact with other systems
- Designing the software which implements a GUI.

Adding a GUI to a database system

The following chapters outline both Conceptual Model-driven and user task-driven techniques for adding a GUI to a database system. Designers may use both approaches in different areas of one system. The techniques have a big impact on External Design, but not on Conceptual Modelling.

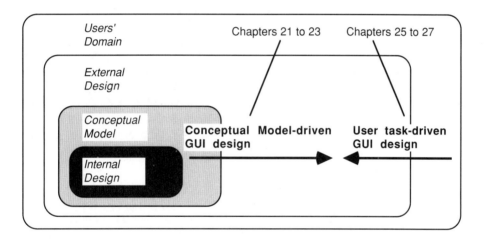

There is a lot to say about GUI design and about application style issues, including the handling of problems to do with contention, locking and refreshment.

Designing a GUI for a database system to interact with other systems

A very important role for a graphical user interface system is to provide a common interface via which users can control the interface between a database system and other office systems. This is outside our scope.

Designing the software which implements a GUI

It is unclear whether the methodology can make any contribution to GUI software design. Note that GUI and OO are distinct ideas; the one does not necessarily imply the other. A specific UIMS may employ OO programming concepts in its tools for building a user interface, but this has no direct impact on systems analysis at the level described in this book.

20.10 **More about event-driven interface design**

Event-driven interface design means implementing the Conceptual Model by developing a naive user interface to do the job of invoking the event and enquiry procedures and processing the replies (see chapters 22 and 23). The assumption is that more complex user functions and dialogues, which link several events and enquiries, can be developed later (see chapters 25 to 27).

Despite being an optional technique, event-driven interface design is a cornerstone of the methodology. It bridges the gap between the Conceptual Model and External Design. It provides a foundation on top of which more sophisticated dialogue design techniques can be developed. It provides a simple way to introduce some GUI design principles into the methodology, since it is now natural to use some kind of UIMS to implement a user interface as swiftly as possible. It suggests some simple standards for maximising reuse. And it has some potential for automation within CASE tools and application generators.

In order to build a working system (rather than a user interface prototype), the GUI designers must be given some kind of specification of the conceptual model and business rules. What usually happens is that given an entity data model, and perhaps a specification of the most important enquiry functions, GUI designers deduce more or less intuitively what the input events and database commit units will be. Often, little attention is given to linking these events in user-friendly dialogues.

Given the methodology's emphasis on entity event modelling, we expect that the GUI designer can be given a much more precise specification. We expect that *all the input events* can be specified by the conceptual modeller and handed over to the GUI designer for implementation.

The independence of design schemas
A GUI designer need not think about where the specification of events comes from, or be aware of whether the techniques of part four have been used or not. In the absence of a complete entity event model, the GUI designer might begin by assuming there are three events for each entity, that is create, amend and delete, though some backtracking from this will be necessary as a better model is developed.

Chapter 21

Entity-driven interface design

This chapter discusses the implementation of a primitive user interface to the entity data model, taking advantage of what application generators can do. While the resultant system may not implement all the business rules, it may have several practical uses, notably as a 'data fixing system'.

21.1 **Purposes of entity data implementation**

One very popular systems development strategy is to develop an entity data model and then use an application generator to produce what might be called an entity data system. Despite the limits imposed by the stereotypes of an application generator (some are mentioned below), there are seven good reasons to include in your systems development plan the building of an entity data system. The first four are rapid implementation reasons, the next two are prototyping reasons and the last is a systematic development reason.

Entity data implementation gives rapid implementation of:

A data fixing system

Despite the best endeavours of the systems development team a database may get out of step with reality in ways which cannot be corrected by normal update routines. An entity data system, unconstrained by integrity rules, will be needed to put things right. This data fixing system should be kept separate from the main information system, and used with caution (see also chapter 29).

A very simple system for users

If the Conceptual Model is so simple that all the business rules which the system requires can be specified as referential integrity rules, then an application generator may provide something close to the system which the users require, though some attention must then be given to dialogue design.

An interim system for users

Users may find an entity data system helpful while a full system is being developed. There is a political difficulty here; user expectations are raised by what can be done swiftly using an application generator. To lower expectations, you may deliberately limit the first implementation to a simple and crude system (for example, using only the 'restrict' delete rule). Also, you may explain by reference to the Pareto principle that the last 20% of the functionality will take 80% of the effort.

Entity data system	**Full system**
with crude user interface	with user-friendly interface
➤	➤
80% of the functionality	20% of the functionality
20% of the development effort	80% of the development effort

Note that the extra effort required to build a truly user-friendly system does not lie mainly in the development of the user interface; it is more a function of the need to program around the stereotype components provided by the application generator when given more sophisticated user requirements.

A test database
An entity data system may be useful for creating test data.

Entity data implementation helps with prototyping of:

The entity data model
Making the entity data model visible to the user on a computer screen can be a way to stimulate the discovery of user requirements, especially in defining the attributes stored for each entity. This is not the trivial exercise it sounds. There is often much debate about how far data should be typed and stored as data items, or left hidden in free text descriptions. Seeing how the data looks when presented on a screen may turn the debate one way or the other.

The physical database design
It is possible that no Internal Design will be necessary, because the entity data model can be implemented as the database design, without any modification or optimisation. But although this is the hope which underlies many application generators, it remains a vain hope for most large systems. An application generator may be used to develop different physical database designs, tuned in various ways (say with indexes or sorted sets), so that the performance of the most important or frequent transactions may be compared

What can be done to enhance system performance will vary depending on the database management system employed, but some general principles have been established and a 'universal first-cut database design' method is described in SSADM4. This is not the place to consider designing and testing various optimisations of the data design in any more detail. However it should be noted that an application generator may not provide the tools needed to optimise the database sufficiently.

Entity data implementation gives a platform for systematic development
The methodology is for developing the full system, meeting 100% of the system requirements, and designing the most user-friendly interface. In this context, the data model prototype should provide a platform for further systems development, especially for data design prototyping, user interface prototyping and entity event implementation.

But it should be noted that in making this progression, it may be necessary to turn off some of the automated functionality provided by an application generator. It is likely that the designer will have to turn off the 'binding' of windows/screens to database records (at least for data entry windows) and automatic referential integrity checking. These things are discussed further below.

21.2 **Application Generators and 4GLs**

When Jackson first published his program design method (1975), it was immediately attractive to those who had been looking for a program design methodology. It was convincingly successful in the design of simple programs. The limitations of the method were only revealed when applied to a large and complex program (as one may view a system).

The reverse is true of the methodology. It is designed to provide a theory of design for large and complex information systems. One of the difficulties in 'selling' it to application generator vendors, is that they already have simpler stereotypes for system design, which work adequately for small and simple systems, with few users.

Given an entity data model, there are stereotypes for how the system and its user interface may be implemented which have been successfully embodied in many application generators. These stereotypes include:

- the entity data model is implemented as a relational database
- each entity instance can be displayed in an 'entity window'
- each entity type can be displayed as an 'entity list' of entity instances
- data entry is done by overtyping the data displayed on an entity window or list
- most external errors can be specified declaratively using data types or domains
- most integrity errors can be specified using relational integrity rules
- most entities are deleted on their logical death.

There are good reasons to expect and plan to build an 'entity data system', using an application generator. Within the limits imposed by these stereotypes, there is no doubt that application generators can greatly speed up the implementation of a database. However, not all of these stereotypes are universally applicable to all systems. There are also areas in which a methodology cannot possibly follow the application generator model, because they offer very different stereotypes, for example in handling:

- repeating data groups within records (entities not in first normal form)
- enquiry and update processes for which SQL is inadequate
- update processes which affect several entities
- inter data item errors and more elaborate control errors
- inputs which may fail more than one business rule
- complex business rules, not definable in an entity data model.

One of the reasons why application generators do not offer the universal models we are looking for is that they compress into one view the separate concerns of Conceptual Model and External Design. The screens are seen as little more than a visual representation of the database structure. There is no recognition that inputs represent events in the real world, that an event must be processed as a commit unit, distinct from other events.

It appears that application generators, at least those which are based on the relational model, do not yet provide a good enough performance for very large systems. A major UK bank recently rejected a very well-known relational database management system for this reason. For large and complex information systems, it is still true that for efficient performance, some kind of network database must be employed.

But there is no doubt that application generators (such as ORACLE, INGRES and countless newer ones) can greatly speed up the implementation of a database; they have a very important role to play in the development of most information systems.

We expect designers to use application generators, at least for prototyping, if not for the final system. Designers might use both an application generator and a UIMS, or a tool which combines features of both (such as Microsoft Access).

After working within one implementation environment, it is easy for designers to fall into the trap of thinking that this tool defines the best or only way to do things. The core of the methodology is, and must remain, generic. It does not follow any specific implementation environment. It does not dictate the choice of tool. It permits the use of several tools, perhaps a network database management system (such as IDMS) for the Conceptual Model and a UIMS (such as TeleUSE) for the External Design. But if one overall piece of guidance may be offered, it is to select implementation tool(s) which enable the Conceptual Model and the External Design to be separated.

21.3 Things to watch out for in an application generator

Having said we expect designers to make use of application generators, it is important to say where an application generator may overlap with the methodology.

Readers may find it helpful at this point to read the more general discussion in chapter 29 on error testing and handling, where kinds of error are classified. Briefly, an application generator will provide declarative ways of specifying most **domain rules** and **external rules**, and some **integrity rules**. It can automatically test for these errors and generate an error message if one is detected. But there are limitations to look out for, such as those which follow.

How are domain rules specified?
A domain rule is a rule which defines the valid range of values for a data item. A domain rule can be tested at the user interface without reference to the database, but it may instead be treated as an integrity rule, as discussed in chapter 29.

Application generators usually expect a domain rule to be attached to a data item in a database record or in a window, and triggered by an attempt to enter a data item on a screen. An application generator may offer various ways to specify a domain rule for a data item, exemplified on the next page.

A **predefined data type** is a domain provided by the implementation environment, such as text, number and date. The domain of many data items can be specified this way. A **user-defined data type** is a domain defined by the analyst.

An application generator should provide you with ways to declare the domain for each data item, then provide automatic testing of this domain whenever the data item appears on entry to the system. There are many different ways to specify domains, and different places they might be recorded. For the data item Promition Grade or Country of Birth, an application generator may require or allow you to specify its domain as:

- a statement, expression or rule (e.g. Promotion Grade = >1 and <6)
- a named user-defined data type (e.g. Country of Birth = Country Name)
- a user-defined data type instead of or as well as a predefined one
- a property of an attribute in the data model or database
- a property of a data entry field in a screen or window
- a property of a data item in a central repository or data dictionary.

Some data items might be arranged to inherit from two or more levels of user-defined data type. This may be viewed as optimising the domain specification, if not the testing.

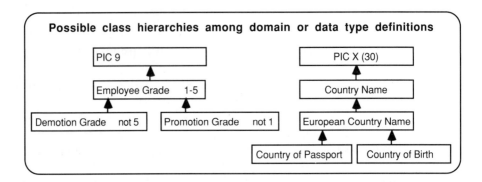

Possible class hierarchies among domain or data type definitions

The application generator may allow you to declare a class hierarchy of data types. Or it may provide one level of user-defined data type in the database and a second level as a validation rule in a data entry field. Or it may required you to declare each domain as a distinct data item, though their ranges may overlap thus:

- Employee Grade   must be in range 1 and 5
- Promotion Grade   must be in range 2 and 5
- Demotion Grade   must be in range 1 and 4.

Finally, note that all data types could be specified as entity types in the data model! See chapters 11 and 29 for advice on this.

Is there a central repository for data item definition?

Ideally the application generator will provide a central repository or data dictionary, so that the domain of a data item can be specified independently of the screen and entity or record definitions which contain it. It should enable a domain rule to be specified in one place, and inherited by all uses of the data item, whether on screens or in database records.

If your application generator does not recognise the fact that a data item can exist independent of screens or entities, then any data item domain may have to be specified in several places. This makes changes to the definition of any data item (which really should be made globally) very difficult to control.

Minimising redundancy - maximising reuse
A proper data item specification mechanism is needed to maximise reuse. There are many data items in a system, and managing their definitions occupies a great deal of design effort (perhaps more time than the more obvious task of managing the entity relationship model).

Are the error messages user-specifiable?

First, an application generator may offer only standard the error messages such as 'the value of the data item is prohibited by the rule declared for this data item', rather than user-specified such as 'Promotion-grade is not in the range B to E'.

Second, an application generator may offer only one validation rule and error message for each input data item. So although for 'Promotion Grade' we might declare a rule such as 'in the range B to E **and** > Employee Grade' the error message could not distinguish between these two reasons for error.

Can you untie the external data from database data?

Some application generators expect the designer to 'tie' or 'bind' the data items on display to attributes of entities. This will make it harder to separate the concerns of the External Design and the Conceptual Model. It will probably make it impossible to take an event-by-event view of data entry. It may make it harder to specify:

- 'domains' beyond the scope of one entity's attributes
- 'control item errors' for data items which are not attributes of any entity
- 'non-referential integrity errors'.

Can you turn off the binding of external data to database data?

To build an entity event prototype processing one event at time, or to build a full system handling non-referential integrity errors, it may be necessary to turn off the binding, at least in data entry windows, and code the error processing by hand.

When to turn on the binding of external data to database data?
Binding data items appearing in the External Design to data items in Conceptual Model is usually helpful in defining:

- an entity data model prototype
- reference windows in more sophisticated prototypes and full systems.

There is another kind of binding which can be useful:. All the appearances of a data item (in both External Design and Conceptual Model) may be bound to a global data item definition, held in some kind of data dictionary.

Can you turn off automatic referential integrity error handling?

Application generators usually provide a way to specify referential integrity error handling. The problem here is threefold: first, referential integrity errors are only a sub-set of all the rules which may have to be specified. Second, rules may be imposed in a way which actually runs counter to what is needed. Third, as chapter 4 suggested, integrity rules should be attached to events, not to entities or record types. The recommendation is therefore to turn off the referential integrity error handling.

*When to turn **on** automatic referential integrity error handling?*
We must temper the theoretical stance taken in this book with pragmatism. Given the estimate below (these are guesses, not backed up by research), it is likely that an application generator provides handy mechanisms for specifying most of the error-handling which can occur in a straightforward system.

the proportion of different kinds of error in a typical information system
which can be handled by an application generator

Domain rule	most of this kind of error
External rule	most of this kind of error
Integrity rule	50 - 95% of this kind of error

Crudely, we might estimate that if the percentage of integrity rules which are implementable as referential integrity rules is above 95%, then turning on automatic referential integrity error handling is probably a good idea. What to do about the 5%? The designers might agree with the users to provide a less user-friendly system, at significantly less cost.

If the percentage is lower than 85%, the designers will (we suggest) find the effort of handling these errors so great that they would be better advised to turn off automated referential integrity error handling. It is often harder to mix automated functionality with manually-designed functionality than to design the whole thing by hand.

Chapter 22

Event-driven
interface design

This chapter and chapter 23 introduce a new technique which builds a primitive graphical user interface for implementing an entity event model. The technique gives a fully workable system which implements all the business rules: it generates mini-dialogues which provide all the basic functionality which users need, and are reusable in a variety of contexts to support users tasks; it provides a way to introduce the basic features of GUI design which underlie the discussion in later chapters.

22.1 **Purposes of event-driven interface design**

GUI design experts! Read the last sections of this chapter and chapter 23 before the main body of the chapters, and note that our use of the word 'dialogue' may not match yours.

Event-driven interface design is a Conceptual Model-driven approach to user dialogue design, which develops a primitive but reasonable user interface to the system, one which will do the job of invoking the event and enquiry procedures and processing the responses. It is has two quite different purposes, as part of a prototyping technique and as part of a rapid application development technique.

Prototyping of the entity event model

Entity event prototyping (which may done in parallel with step 360 of SSADM4) is about testing some 'look and feel' issues. It gives the users a chance to see and modify the events and enquiries, and the responses to them. For the purpose of prototyping, it is not necessary to implement the event and enquiry procedures. The system might be run with 'stub' modules in place of the event and enquiry procedures. Some mock-up of the event and enquiry responses may be created manually.

Given an entity data model, it is not too hard for the designer to specify a more or less satisfactory list of input events, but is much harder to specify the system's response to each event until the user has seen some physical presentation of examples. Showing an entity event system to users may help to stimulate discussion of what event responses are needed. Having said this, event responses are standardised in the rapid event-driven interface design technique described in this chapter.

Implementation of the entity event model

Entity event implementation (which may be done after step 530 of SSADM4) produces a workable system. As a rapid application development technique, it has many useful characteristics. These are listed below.

Simplicity: it is a mechanical, easily teachable and partly automatable technique. Completeness: it generates mini-dialogues which cover all the functionality needed to maintain an entity data model (top down and user-driven approaches cannot guarantee this). Lack of redundancy: there is no duplication of effort; it does not generate components which are redundant (top down and user-driven approaches cannot guarantee this). Reusability: it generates mini-dialogues which are readily reusable. Usefulness: it generates those mini-dialogues which are in any case needed as the building blocks of longer user dialogues. Discovery: it prompts the specification of enquiries which may have been overlooked; a surprisingly large percentage of enquiries are predictable from the structure of the entity relationship model. User-friendliness: it generates mini-dialogues which are reasonably user-friendly, and some longer dialogues as well; at best it generates most of the dialogues the users are likely to ask for. Machine-independence: it assumes some kind of GUI or windows-based implementation environment, but is not otherwise machine-specific.

22.2 **Summary of event-driven interface design**

RAD style guide first, design technique second

Event-driven interface design is composed of two parts: the creation of a style guide and a design technique. Standardisation of the user interface style in a style guide is important because it gives the user a consistent 'look and feel', it gives the designer greater opportunities for reuse of components, and it enables suppression of detail from any individual system specification.

The first step of event-driven interface design is to adopt or create what we call a 'RAD style guide'. This style guide defines what it means to be an 'entity event system'. Other kinds of style guide, and further issues to be standardised, are discussed in chapter 24.

Please remember that this chapter suggests and exemplifies rather than dictates a style. It points to where standards should be set by people who want to speed up user interface implementation. Some of the proposed standards, those which are overly restrictive, will have to be relaxed in later chapters, where more user-friendly design styles are discussed.

Products of event-driven interface design

The entity event system is composed of a system entry menu, and mini-dialogues which string together entity, event and enquiry windows.

Inputs to event-driven interface design

To build an entity event system, the designer needs a specification of events and enquiries, and the entity data model they refer to. The designer need not be concerned with the internal workings of the Conceptual Model and Internal Design, but should be concerned with objects passing between the External Design and the Conceptual Model.

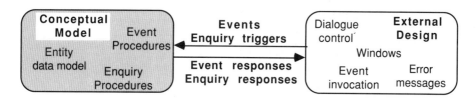

It is assumed that **events** and **enquiry triggers** and **enquiry responses** will have been defined during Conceptual Modelling, perhaps in the form of input and output data structures. But for the purposes of rapid application development, we shall make some simplifying assumptions about what the standard **event responses** will be.

Note that in the full system, the appearance of an event response at the user interface may vary according to the user function within which the event is invoked, being different, say, on a screen and a report.

Even more rapid application development

The technique does not depend upon the entity event model being complete. The minimum starting point is an entity data model, with a specification of only three events for each entity:

- birth
- death
- change of attribute values (other than fixed key values).

A system built from such minimal input will be little more sophisticated than one generated by an application generator. Clearly, the more complete the entity event model, the closer the entity event system will be to the final system. However, such a primitive entity event system might be used in a prototyping role.

Steps of event-driven interface design

The partly automatable steps, described at length hereafter, are:

Step 1: set standard style for reuse of interface design components
         set standards for reuse of reference components
         set standards for reuse of data entry components
         set standards for reuse of message windows

Step 2: provide user access to events and enquiries

Step 3: design entity reference windows and lists

Step 4: design event and enquiry windows
         map events and enquiries onto windows
         make input and output windows more user-friendly
         design multi-event windows
         merge data entry windows into reference windows
         add commands to link dialogues
         add commands for more specific entity reference lists

Steps 1 to 3 and the first activity in step 4 are relatively mechanical. They take a lot of the donkey work out of building an interface which will meet users' requirements. The windows and mini-dialogues developed thereby are workable, and in practice surprisingly user-friendly. It turns out that it is not too hard to join standard mini-dialogues together to support user tasks. Some of the user tasks can even be predicted.

Step 4 involves some less mechanical, more intuitive, design activities for making the entity event system more user-friendly. These activities partly anticipate the more user-oriented dialogue design techniques in chapters 26 and 27.

After step 4, an entity event system may be implemented using the techniques at the end of chapter 27.

22.3 **Basic assumptions behind an event-driven interface**

Reference and data entry windows will be distinguished

To develop a robust and user-friendly entity event system, quickly yet systematically, it is necessary to distinguish between reference and data entry windows. The distinction need not be maintained forever, as we shall see in chapter 23 when merging a data entry window into a reference window. But to begin with we shall make the distinction and highlight it using devices such as background colour, position on screen and 'shadowing' data entry fields.

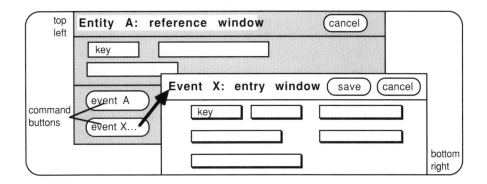

An idea which is important to the way an entity event system works is that context data (usually keys, or expanded descriptions thereof) can be carried from the entity reference window into the event data entry window.

There are several standard kinds of window

As well as the system entry menu (SEM), there are eight other kinds of window:

> for each entity
> > entity reference list (ERL)
> > entity reference window (ERW)
> for each event or enquiry
> > data entry window (DEW) or confirmation message box (CMB)
> > error message box (EMB)
> > success message box (SMB).

There are two more kinds of window. An event or enquiry response window (Eresp) will have to be designed for each enquiry, and for those relatively few events with complex effects. A list constraint window (LCW) may be designed, probably based upon the entity reference window, for the user to shorten or sort an entity reference list which is too long for user-friendly manipulation.

The standard kinds of window will contain standard commands

Some standard commands are mentioned here (© = 'Cancel'), but more explanation of how commands get to be placed in windows will be given later.

Window type	Commands in the window
entity reference list	birth event of a new entity instance & ©
entity reference window	other events in the entity behaviour & ©
event data entry window	'Save' & ©
event confirmation message box	'Yes' & ©
event error or success message box	'OK'

There are four standard kinds of mini-dialogue

Suppressing some details such as error message boxes, there are four basic kinds of mini-dialogue. There is no right answer here; these dialogues have evolved out of trial and error during our research; readers may adapt them. First, the mini-dialogue for an enquiry.

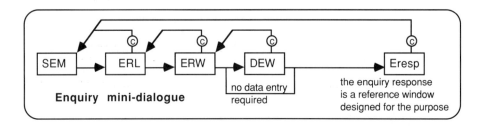

Enquiry mini-dialogue

Notice that if the data for the enquiry trigger is already shown in the entity reference window, then no data entry is required and the enquiry command will lead directly to the enquiry response, a specifically designed window.

Second, the mini-dialogue for a birth event, fired from an entity reference list. The default event response here is to show the entity reference window for the new entity, from which point the user has a range of options open.

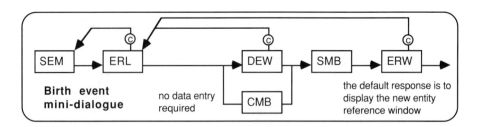

Birth event mini-dialogue

Third, the mini-dialogue for an event other than birth or death, fired from an entity reference window. The event response here is to refresh the entity reference window for the 'home' entity, after the event has been applied. However, the designer may find it necessary to design a specific event response window for events with a complex set of effects.

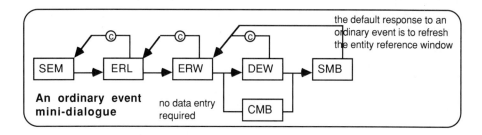

Fourth, the mini-dialogue for a death event. The default event response here is to refresh the entity reference list, omitting the entity which has just died. However, the designer may find it necessary to design a specific event response window for events with a complex set of effects.

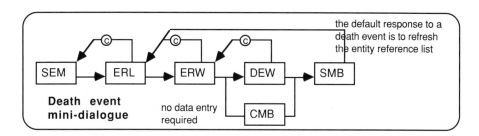

Entity reference lists may be shortened or sorted

One more standard kind of window mentioned above is the list constraint window, which might be invoked as a nested dialogue whenever the user finds an entity reference list is too long to manage and presses the command 'shorten list'.

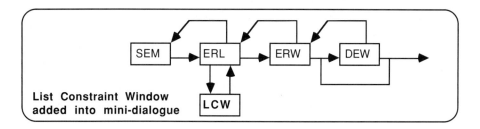

A list constraint window will probably look like the entity reference window. It may allow the user to enter specific values, or even ranges of values, into any data field. The list constraint window may be extended with a means to dictate the sorting sequence (perhaps placing numbers against data fields).

Command buttons will be placed in a standard way

A robust and reasonably user-friendly entity event system can be generated swiftly by placing the event command buttons in entity reference windows and entity reference lists as follows.

Place the event command button for any event except a birth event in the entity reference window of the 'home' entity (the 'lowest' entity whose complete key it carries)

Place the event command button for a birth event of an entity in the 'home' entity reference list.

Extra command buttons may be placed for user-friendliness

Further design decisions may be made. The birth event of an entity which is dependent on a master entity may be placed in the entity reference window of any (or all) of the masters it depends on. So the Interview Arrangement event may be placed in either or both the entity reference windows of Vacancy and Applicant Skill.

If an entity type depends on a master entity which depends on a master entity, should every master entity in the hierarchy hold the birth event command button? Perhaps Interview Arrangement should appear in Applicant as well as Applicant Skill.

It turns out that user dialogue design is partly about placing event command buttons in reference lists as well as entity reference windows. For example, a birth event command button (such as Interview Arrangement) might be placed in the entity reference list of any master it depends on (such as a Vacancy List).

Pressing cancel will have a defined effect

It is reasonably obvious that a cancel button should have the effect of closing the window which contains it. It is not so obvious where the user should be directed next. In an entity event system, we recommend that the result of pressing the cancel button will have the effects illustrated above and specified here:

Window type	Effect of 'Cancel'
entity reference list	display system entry menu
entity reference window	display entity reference list
event data entry window	display entity reference window or list
event confirmation message box	display entity reference window or list
event or enquiry response window	display system entry menu

This means that, on closing a window, return will normally pass to the previous window. This is convenient for a number of reasons, not least that the effect of an event on its home entity can be shown. What if the window from which a window was opened has itself been closed? For the time being we can rule this out by *making each data entry window modal* (see chapter 24 for what this means).

Current context commands should be visible, if there is room

Commands relevant to the current context should be immediately visible, assuming there is room for these commands to be shown. Pressing a button is the obvious means by which the user may issue a command. However, we use the expression 'command button' rather more loosely than most, as discussed below.

A command which is not context-dependent, or at least is common to many dialogues (such as the 'Quit' command) may appear only in a Pulldown menu. A function key is often allocated to such a command.

Many forms of command button are possible

By 'command button' we don't necessarily mean a button shaped object. In the examples it is easy to show command buttons as round-cornered boxes containing the name of the event or enquiry. But command buttons the user may press to send an event or enquiry could include buttons, menu entries, data item fields and icons. Icons are discussed towards the end of this chapter, but note here that it usually quicker and cheaper to design textual command buttons.

Command scripts will be written

We assume that on pressing a command button, some kind of script or macro is invoked, which itself invokes the relevant event or enquiry procedure. This script is the place to interpret any error-code which is returned from the Conceptual Model. See the end of chapter 23 for more details.

All commit units will be sent by user commands

The database procedure triggered by an event or enquiry is a commit unit. Some systems automatically save data from time to time, but users are likely to find this disconcerting. There should be a way for the system to recognise when the user has completed the input for any single event. In a first-cut entity event system the user consciously triggers the commit of each event or enquiry trigger by pressing a command button ('Save' or 'Yes' above) to commit the data. More subtle mechanisms, used for multi-event windows, are shown later.

The Conceptual Model will be kept in step with the External Design

Design decisions made in External Design may have to be reflected back in the Conceptual Model. For example, the Conceptual Model says an Applicant Skill is created only on Applicant Registration, but on seeing the External Design, the user might now request event command buttons for the addition and removal of Applicant Skills, independent of the birth or death of an Applicant.

22.4 **Set standards for reuse of reference components**

The previous section outlined the generic standards which define what it means to be an entity event system. The following three sections outline the areas where more specific standards should be set by the designers, illustrated by examples. To begin with two stereotype reference window designs are needed: entity reference lists and entity reference windows. These will be tailored for each entity type.

Use the functionality given by an application generator
Given that an application generator is used to develop an entity data prototype, many components of the kind shown below, especially entity lists, can be generated swiftly and automatically.

It is perfectly reasonable to carry forward these components into an entity event system, and into the full system, *as long as the user can be prevented from entering input data via an enquiry display.* Data entry in an entity event system works in a different way; users should be prevented from typing over anything they can see on a screen. This may mean turning off the 'binding' of windows to database records.

Standardise entity reference lists
An entity reference list is a scrollable list showing entity instances in rows, entity attributes in columns. The illustration shows standard commands which might be offered beside such a list, or else in some kind of menu.

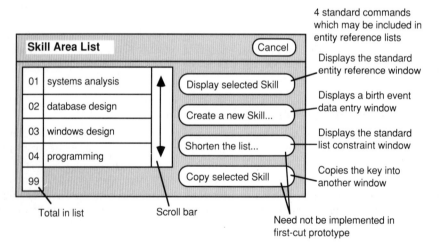

Entity reference lists will be used later, especially to find the entry point entity for an event or enquiry, and to select an instance of a master entity or user-defined data type for entry as a foreign key.

Standardise the enquiry triggers for an entity reference list

The standard trigger for an entity reference list is the selection of an entry on the system entry menu. Other triggers are possible, and some are illustrated in the examples which follow.

Standardise entity reference windows

An entity reference window is a more or less user-friendly display of the attributes of one entity instance. One should be designed for each entity type, showing the entity name as the title.

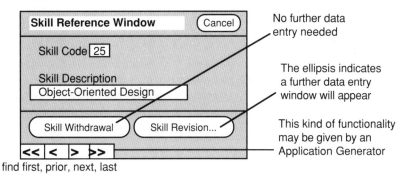

find first, prior, next, last

Standardise data contents

A simple standard is to display in an entity reference window only the attributes of that entity. Standards might include guidance such as:

- present data at top of the window
- present 'key' details at the top left.

The standard should be modified for specific entity types. For example, you may include a scrollable list of detail entities, or replace meaningless foreign keys of master entities by meaningful text descriptions.

Standardise search commands

Treating the entity reference window as one item in an entity reference list, one may design standard command buttons for moving to another entity instance of the same type. These commands may be iconised (as shown by the symbols <<, <, >, >> in the example). It would also be possible to display a scrollable window of entity instances, showing the current instance highlighted in the centre.

Standardise the style of event command buttons

Event and enquiry commands may be presented as buttons at the bottom of the window (or if too many, as Popup menus). An ellipsis (...) may be tagged onto any event or enquiry command which requires further data entry via another window.

Standardise the enquiry triggers for an entity reference window
Three standard places to trigger the display of an entity reference window:

- in an entity reference list - command to show the selected instance
- in an entity reference window - command to show first, previous, next, or last
- in a data entry window - the entry of valid enquiry parameters.

The last of these is illustrated in the next section.

22.5 Set standards for reuse of data entry components

Standardise event and enquiry data entry windows
Most events and enquiries, even when context data has been passed forward from an entity reference window, require further data entry. For these, possible standards for the data entry window include:

- use the event or enquiry name as the title
- present save/commit and cancel buttons in a standard position.

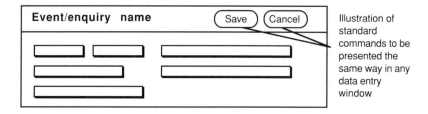

A more reusable design for enquiry triggers is shown below:

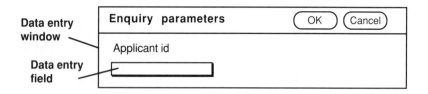

For enquiry triggers requiring a multiple item key to be entered, items may be input and validated one at a time through a succession of such simple windows (Microsoft Access uses this mechanism).

22.6 Set standards for reuse of message windows

Standardise event and enquiry confirmation boxes

For events and enquiries which can be invoked from an entity reference window without any further data entry, a standard confirmation message box may be designed. In this case 'Yes' has the same effect as 'Save' above.

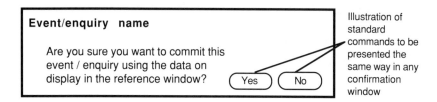

Standardise error responses

See chapter 29 for discussion of error testing. For the purpose of building an entity event system the simplest design for an event or enquiry error response is a standard message box containing an OK button.

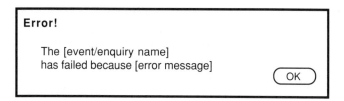

Standardise successful event responses

The user interface designer will seek to standardise the response to a successful event. The response can be divided into three parts, the success message, the report showing the effects of the event, and the next step.

The success message box

A reasonable convention is to begin by displaying a standard message box to be dismissed by an OK button.

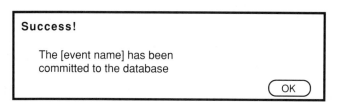

The report showing the effects of the event
It is possible in a first-cut entity event system to limit the event responses to those shown in the four standard flowcharts given earlier. Chapter 23 discusses the development of less standardised responses, updating lists on display and so on.

Moving on to the end or next stage of the dialogue
The earlier section on 'Closing a window' explained the general principle for where to go after completing a mini-dialogue. Other possible actions include:

- return to the system entry menu
- return to the prior state in the current user function
- move to the next state in the current user function.

The last two imply some kind of function and dialogue design, as discussed in chapters 25 to 27, beyond the scope of event-driven interface design.

22.7 Using icons for objects and commands

There is a body of ideas to do with 'mental modelling' (see for example, Kieras and Bovair, 1984 and Smith, 1982) which have little or nothing to do with modelling in the sense of entity modelling. Mental modelling is about metaphors or similes, and pictorial analogues or icons. The main conclusions we draw for GUI design from mental modelling literature are that an icon should be:

a) pictorial
b) already familiar to users
c) a model of the thing being controlled.

If icons are necessary for building a GUI, then we should say what kind of GUI needs them, and we should be clear whether these pictorial analogues are related to the Conceptual Model.

What kind of GUI needs them?
There seem to be two specific kinds of situation where there is value in presenting pictorial analogues to help people carry out their business. First, where users already use pictures to control their business operations, of which the main example is the use of maps by businesses such as gas, electricity, water, army and police. Second, where the desktop metaphor can be extended, say in linking a database system to an electronic mail system.

But outside of these two examples, there seems only a little to be gained by designing pictorial analogues to represent the things controlled by an information system. Most of the information about these things is conveniently presented to, and manipulated by, the users in text form. Imagine iconising the objects in the case study system as shown below.

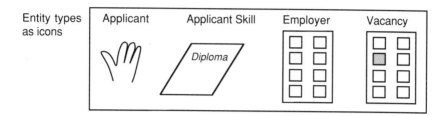

It might be possible to go further, to represent commands as icons, composed of object icons. The diagram here shows a command button composed of other icons:

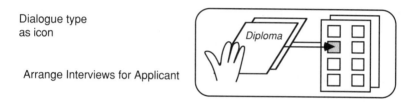

Or perhaps a command could be issued by dragging icons for the relevant entity instances over each other?

Three difficulties

In general, iconising objects and commands in the development of a GUI for a database system needs to be treated with caution. There are three difficulties:

- unfamiliarity
- instance representation rather than type
- syntax and grammar clashes.

First, are these icons, as mental modelling theory suggests they should be, already familiar to users? It might be fun to invent icons and grammars for combining them, but if these icons fail the familiarity test, they may confuse users rather than help them

Second, it is easy to represent entity *types* as icons on the screen, but harder to represent entity *instances*. Database systems often contain very large numbers of entity instances, and plastering long keys across the icons rather defeats the object.

Third, and crucially, it is very difficult to avoid clashes and conflicts with the icons (and possibly the grammar) invented by someone else.

Certainly it is simpler and quicker to present textual command buttons. We recommend that where iconising can prove valuable, say, when linking objects in a database system to objects on the desktop (say, a word processor, or electronic mail system) or on a map, then it should be carried out as a parallel design activity, by specialists. However, our personal experience suggest there are limits to the extendibility of the desktop metaphor, partly because of the potential for clashes noted above.

Mental modelling and Conceptual Modelling

In some cases the objects represented as icons may also be represented or stored as entities in the entity data model. But in terms of their design, the pictorial model of the things controlled by the information system has little to do with the entity model.

22.8 Concluding remarks

Things GUI experts don't like about this chapter

The event-driven interface design technique introduced in this chapter is aimed mainly at rapid application development and functional prototyping. The diagrams are the crudest illustrations we can get away with. To a GUI designer, the approach is rather too crude. Criticisms which may fairly be levelled at the chapter include:

- it is not a full GUI style guide
- there are too many windows
- there are too many buttons on display

Yes, this chapter is a very long way from being a full GUI style guide. It barely scratches the surface of 'look and feel' issues. Yes, there are too many windows. The next chapter introduces the design of windows which combine the functions of reference and data entry, but to do this topic justice is beyond our ambition. Yes, there may be many buttons on display at once; some of could be hidden in menus and Pop-up lists; it is only our laziness and diagram drawing tools which prevent us from illustrating this. Readers should look elsewhere for further GUI 'look and feel' guidance.

The division between this chapter and chapter 23.

The steps of the event-driven interface design technique introduced in this chapter are.

Step 1: set standard style for reuse of interface design components
Step 2: provide user access to events and enquiries
Step 3: design entity reference windows and lists
Step 4: design event and enquiry windows.

Steps 1 and 3 are discussed in this chapter. At least, the first step has been discussed and the third step needs no description beyond what has already been shown in the course of illustrating the case study. Steps 2 and 4 are discussed in chapter 23.

Chapter 23

User-driven window design

This chapter discusses window design, including ways in which the user-friendliness of a user interface may be developed in a reasonably systematic way. The technique assumes an event-driven interface design style guide is in place. The word 'windows' is used in the general sense, not implying any target implementation environment.

23.1 **The technique and the case study**

The steps of event-driven interface design listed in chapter 22 are:

Step 1: set standard style for reuse of interface design components
Step 2: provide user access to events and enquiries
Step 3: design entity reference windows and lists
Step 4: design event and enquiry windows.

This chapter covers steps 2 and 4. Step 4 includes ways in which the user-friendliness of a user interface may be developed in a reasonably systematic way. The GUI designer may use these ideas outside the narrow confines of the event-driven interface design technique, in prototyping a user interface, or developing a physical dialogue design as described in chapter 27. After step 4, an entity event system may be implemented using the techniques at the end of chapter 27.

The case study inputs to the event-driven interface design technique are as follows.

Entity data model: this is the data model shown in chapter 14.

Events: specific events to be considered from Hi-Ho case study include:

- Entry of a New Skill Type
- Skill Type Revision
- Applicant Registration
- Interview Arrangement.

Each event triggers an event procedure, which (for the purposes of External Design) is best viewed as a self-contained database update routine whose internal workings may be ignored. Note that each event and enquiry has a 'home entity' in the entity data model, so the key of this entity must be part of the input parameters.

Event responses: each event will return a message from the Conceptual Model to the External Design, indicating either failure or success. Failure will be expressed as a value of an error code, reflected at the user interface by an error message. Success will be an updated database, and will be reflected at the user interface in the standard ways discussed in chapter 22.

Enquiry triggers: each being analogous to event parameters, except that it triggers a commit unit's worth of database enquiry processing. Each enquiry trigger fires up an enquiry procedure, which (for the purposes of External Design) is best viewed as a self-contained database enquiry routine whose internal workings may be ignored.

Note that many standard enquiries (such as those for an 'entity reference list' or 'entity reference window') may be predicted and assumed rather than explicitly specified.

Specific enquiries to be considered from Hi-Ho case study include:

- Show List of Skill Areas (standard entity reference list)
- Show Applicant Details (standard entity reference window)
- Show Suitable Vacancies for Applicant.

Enquiry responses: each being the outcome of an enquiry returned from the Conceptual Model to the External Design, which will indicate either success or failure. Success will be a data stream, perhaps specified in the form of regular expression, destined for presentation at the user interface. Failure will be expressed as a value of an error code, reflected at the user interface by an error message.

23.2 Provide user access to enquiries and events

How will the user select or arrive at the data entry window for the event or enquiry they wish to run? The designer may provide many ways to access events and enquiries, but to generate a reasonably user-friendly entity event system it is sufficient to provide for event commands by placing buttons in menus and entity reference windows.

Entry to the system
A simple approach is to list all the various ways to enter the system, including events and enquiries, in a top-level system entry window.

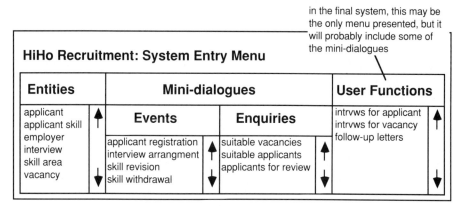

The user function menu results from the techniques in chapter 25. The user function menu is not fully developed in an entity event system. However the need for some user functions may be predicted from the entity event model, some user functions may be simply mini-dialogues, and other user functions may be manufactured by combining mini-dialogues.

Some ways to partition overlong system entry menus

Too many function or dialogue types? Functions not applicable to a given user role can be suppressed from the menus, as long as the user's role can be derived from the terminal identity, password or other data entered by the user.

Too many entity types? The entity data model may be divided into partial data models, and these sub-models listed in a higher level menu. These sub-models might correspond to business areas, user roles, or to distributed processing locations.

Too many events and enquiries? Events and enquiries might be partitioned by user role, or placed on Popup menus triggered from the entity menu.

What happens when a menu entry is selected?

There are many different ways to design the entry into an information system. The standard for a first-cut entity event system is that *all* menu selections take the user directly to some kind of entity reference list. The user then selects the correct entry point entity for the event or enquiry they wish to enter. A possible exception to this scheme is date or time triggered events.

Date or time triggered events

All events require the user to input the key of an entity which is an entry point for that event into the database. Notionally at least, events and enquiries triggered by a date or time have, as their entry point to the database, an operational master entity representing the date or time to which all affected entities are related. If there are no such operational master entities in the data model, extra entity reference windows for entering dates and times may have to be created, with commands for events and enquiries at the bottom.

In an entity event system, it should be assumed that some kind of system administrator or operator will be responsible for entering the date and triggering any specific event or enquiry dependent on that date.

Later, if the date or time can be collected by the system from 'today's date', then selecting the command button in the enquiry menu may lead directly to an event confirmation window of the kind shown earlier.

How to get to the right entity reference window?

Having selected an event, enquiry or user function, some kind of entry dialogue is required to arrive at the right entity reference window. It doesn't matter how this works. The standard way is to present an entity reference list, from which the user can select the entity of interest. Otherwise, the user might employ any kind of browsing mechanism provided by an application generator, or enter enquiry parameters in a data entry window.

Which commands will appear in an entity reference window?

Each event and enquiry may be presented as a command button in one or more entity reference windows. The result of the standard suggested in chapter 22 is that command buttons appearing in an entity reference window are events for which this entity is the home entity (other than birth events) and birth events for detail entities dependent on this entity. This standard is useful because context data can be carried from the reference window into the data entry window.

What happens when the event command is pressed?

Either display the event data entry window, with entry point key parameters already completed, or if no further data is required display an event confirmation window (see above). The event itself does not run until the save, or yes, button is pressed.

23.3 Map enquiries onto windows

A standard entity reference window enquiry

One way to trigger an entity reference window enquiry is via a data entry window designed with data fields to accept the data items required for the enquiry trigger.

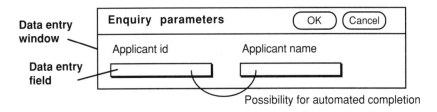

The enquiry is committed by pressing the OK button. If it is successful, the enquiry response appears in a distinct reference window, containing one or more text fields, scrollable where necessary. Usually, the data from the enquiry trigger (here just the Applicant id) will reappear in the enquiry response window.

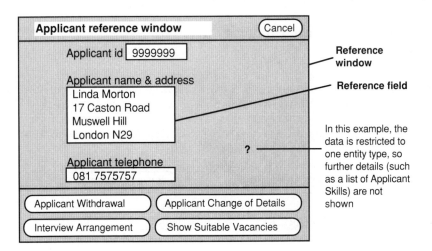

A more complex enquiry: Show Suitable Vacancies

Enquiry Trigger: this second enquiry requires the same input data as the first, that is the identity of an applicant. As long as the system is able to remember which of the two enquiries was originally invoked by the user, the two enquiries can reuse exactly the same window design for entering the applicant identity.

Enquiry Response: the successful response here is a variant of the Vacancy entity reference list, sorted by Skill Type and nested so that each Vacancy occupies two lines.

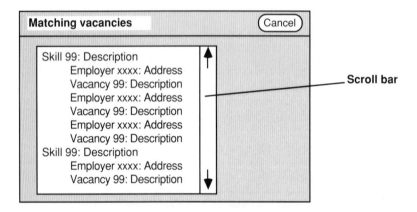

It is not always possible to display such a complex structured list using an application generator or UIMS. It may be easier to display each entry in the list one at a time in distinct windows.

It turns out that user dialogue design is partly about placing event command buttons in non-standard places, such as in the window displaying the result of a complex enquiry like this one. It is possible to invoke one or more Interview Arrangement events directly from this enquiry, as we shall see later in this chapter.

23.4 Map events onto windows

A birth event

The birth event of an entity without any master does not naturally belong in an entity reference window. Instead, it may be invoked from an entity reference list. Once a birth event has been invoked, the next step is for a window to appear within which the user can enter details of the new entity instance into blank data item fields, as shown below.

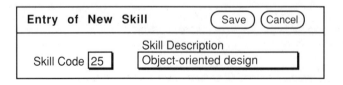

The event is committed by pressing the Save button. If it is successful, the system will close the event data entry window, then immediately display the entity reference window for the home entity, complete with the new data.

A non-key-attribute replacement event

For most events, since the event parameters will include the key of the home entity for the event, some kind of pre-event enquiry to check the existence and details of the home entity, or one of its masters, is likely to be helpful. The example shown below is a Skill Type Revision event, which may be entered as shown below.

Notice that the Skill Type Code can be automatically carried forward from the enquiry window into the data entry window. Perhaps the old Skill Type Description should be carried across as well; this is a matter of judgement.

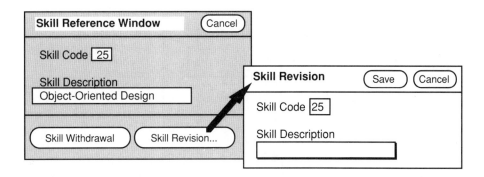

Again, the event is committed by pressing the Save button and if it is successful, the system will close the event data entry window and immediately display the entity reference window for the home entity, complete with the new data.

A change in the entity event model?

The Skill Type Revision event was not included in the case study during entity event modelling. The view was taken that a Skill description should never be altered, because the user cannot be sure that all the details which have been attached to the old description also belong to the new one. To change a Skill meant deleting the old and creating a new one (or perhaps more than one new one) to replace it.

In this chapter we assume the user has complained so much about this constraint that we are forced to include a Skill Revision event, as above. Should this event now be incorporated in the entity event model? Probably not, for one of two reasons. We might reasonably take the view that what the user has asked for here is really part of a **data fixing system** rather than part of the entity event model (see chapter 29), or that non-key attribute replacement events allowable at any time during the life of an entity are so trivial that they may be omitted from the entity event model.

23.5 **Make input windows more user-friendly**

Ultimately, the distinction drawn in chapter 22 between data entry and reference windows may disappear. At this point in the case study development, the distinction still holds. The example of a data entry window below illustrates several points not covered in chapter 22.

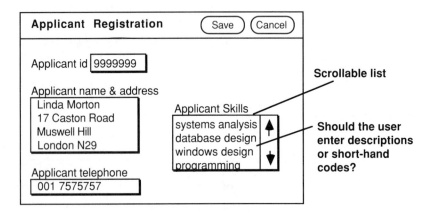

One event's data spans several entities

First, this is a relatively rare example where the data to be input for one event spans several entities. The Applicant Registration event creates an Applicant and several Applicant Skills (a master entity and a set of detail entities). So the window is 'unnormalised' and there is a list of data items to be input.

The event data is derived from more user-friendly data

Second, the event data entry window does not quite match the event data. In a first-cut entity event system, a data entry window is always constructed to provide a means of directly inputting the events and enquiry triggers. However, the scrollable list for Applicant Skills (which looks like a distinct window, but is not here regarded as one) shows Skill descriptions rather than Skill codes.

Translating input descriptions into codes

If skill descriptions are entered manually, the system must translate these into skill codes, before processing the Applicant Registration event. Of course the event may fail because an invalid description has been entered.

Using a GUI design, it is possible to prevent such a failure, by gathering skill descriptions from a nested or parallel dialogue (see next section); the skill codes might then be stored as 'hidden' properties of the windows on display.

Scrapping shorthand codes altogether

In non-GUI environments, shorthand codes were sometimes introduced just to save data entry effort. But using a GUI, assuming an entity instance (or data type instance) must have a meaningful candidate key, there is no need to store a shorthand code just to save data entry. The user can short-cut input by copying the required name from a nested or parallel dialogue (see next section). So should we scrap shorthand codes altogether?

There are two reasons to retain the shorthand code. First, though more meaningful to the user, full names or descriptions take longer to input than shorthand codes. So some users, in some situations, prefer to retain shorthand codes, at least as an alternative data entry mechanism. Second, the code provides a permanent key which need not be changed if the skill name has to be revised or retitled (as pointed out in chapter 11).

Conceptual Model rules should not be tested in the External Design

Given the classification of errors in chapter 29, the entry of an invalid skill code or description would be an integrity rule, and will not be reported until the event is saved. If the user insists on validation being done after the typing of each data item, then data entry fields must be completed in a defined sequence, and the event procedure must be run as a co-routine with the dialogue. Chapter 29 explains why the alternative of duplicating some of the validation rules in the External Design is not recommended.

But some business rules may applied in the External Design

We are concentrating on data entry windows in which the correspondence between the External Design and the Conceptual Model is fairly obvious. It is clear which events are to be input, and how they are derived from the input data. But there are cases where it is not so easy to spot the events in the input data stream, where the user wishes to manipulate the data on the screen, perhaps applying some informal business rules to it, before entering data into the database.

Typically this happens when the user has to break up some kind of 'Aggregate event' into discrete events. For example, a user might have to break up a single customer payment into sums which can be assigned to pay off different invoices, or break up a total amount of man-days into numbers which can be allocated to individual tasks. The user may perform this task by playing with data on the screen, using a spreadsheet-like format.

This book does not cover the design of a user interface to support the user in the manual implementation of business rules or procedures. However, this book does cover what should be done if the users elect to move these same business rules into the Conceptual Model. For example, if users wish to input a 'lump sum payment' and let the system decide how to allocate this payment across several invoices, then the rules for doing this will be specified within what we call an event.

23.6 **Make output windows more user-friendly**

In chapter 22, some simplifying assumptions were made about the response to an event. In practice, the appearance of an event response at the user interface may vary according to the user function within which the event or enquiry is invoked (being different say, on a screen and a report). The designer must generalise the event or enquiry response produced from the Conceptual Model so that it can be *reused* as the basis of the response needed in any specific user function.

While the error response can be generalised to simply an error code (see chapter 29 for how this can be reflected at the user interface by an error message), the successful response needs more thought. Some throw-away user interface prototyping is probably needed before the entity event model can be completed with reusable event and enquiry responses. So, let us move beyond the standard event responses suggested earlier.

The design of an on-line event response
The most complete response imaginable would be composed of three parts:

- a snapshot of all the entities to be affected by the event, before processing
- an animated movie showing each entity as it is updated
- a snapshot of all the entities affected by the event, after processing.

Event animation is an attractive idea, but difficult to implement. And for all but trivial events, a full report of the before and after pictures may be difficult to handle. We normally compromise by designing a limited report.

For a *trivial event* which affects only its home entity (Interview Rescheduling) it is easy to display the entity reference window (the Interview) as it appears after the event has been applied. If this entity reference window is already on display, then it should be refreshed (at least the one on this user's screen, if not on other screens) with the new data. One possible way to implement the refreshment of the entity reference window, available in some application generators, is to 'bind' the data on display to the data in the database. We recommend this feature is restricted to reference windows, and not used on data entry windows. It may in any case have to be turned off, for reasons of performance if no other. Binding is further discussed in chapter 21.

For an *event which affects little more than its home entity*, it may be possible to animate the effects, or at least display them to the user. For example, an Interview Arrangement, when done in the context of a window showing suitable Vacancies, has the effect of removing one of these Vacancies from the list.

For *an event with a complex and distributed effect*, the best we can usually do is print out some kind of report, perhaps in off-line mode. Typical of these are death events (which require only the key of their home entity to be entered) such as Post Acceptance. If each of the employers and applicants whose interviews must now be cancelled were connected to the system via a terminal, then on-line messages could be sent to them all. But a business rarely connect its system on-line to all the various and distributed entities it deals with. The best the system can do is print a report for the business user to act on.

23.7 **Design multi-event windows**

There are two reasons to design multi-event windows. First, the amount of data entered on each event is so small that the effort of opening and closing windows becomes burdensome. Second, to save the re-entry of data items which are common to each of several event instances (for example, arranging several Interviews for the same Applicant, as shown below).

Before we look at multi-event windows, what are the general design principles here? How do windows generally correspond to input events? We can attempt a classification of the possible combinations and permutations. This is complicated by the potential for confusion between event types and instances, and window types and instances.

Mapping events onto windows

Designing one window type to accommodate one instance of one event type is fine. This is the simplest and most robust approach.

Designing many window types to accommodate one event type is plausible. It is possible that an event *type* may be input in different ways through different window types, as long as one event *instance* is input via only one of these window types.

Designing many window instances to accommodate one event type is not reasonable. Avoid any design by which one event must be input through several data entry windows. If it appears that an event (the parameters for a commit unit) is to be input through more than one window, then either the event has been defined as larger than it needs to be, or one main window should be designed so that it suppresses details from initial display, using scrolling lists and Popup components.

Designing one window type to accommodate many event instances of one type is reasonable, and designing one window type to accommodate many event types is also reasonable. See below for examples.

A single event window

Interview Arrangement is a birth event. Given that some of the Interview Arrangement data can be carried forward from reference windows earlier in a dialogue, the window might appear as shown below.

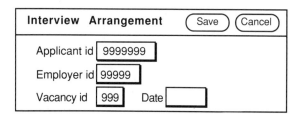

This single event window is fine for our case study, but what about cases where the user wishes to enter several events via one window, one after another, or side by side?

Unfriendly window design?

The window we have shown is rather unfriendly. It is too database-oriented, showing keys rather than text descriptions, but it keeps the illustrations small, and serves the purposes for which we introduce them. We are interested in the interface between the External Design and the Conceptual Model, which is composed of the data items shown.

Standards for an iterated event window

Suppose the user wishes to enter several Interview Arrangements one after another. Where an event may be iterated, one way of progressing to the next event is to clear out the data items from the data entry window after each successful 'Save', to show it is ready for a new event. But beware the danger that the disappearance of input data items from the Interview Arrangement after the commit of an event may confuse the user.

Standards for a multi-event window

We are going to stay with the Interview Arrangement example. However, the points in this section apply not only to windows containing many events of one type, but also to windows containing events of different types.

Suppose the user wishes to enter several Interview Arrangements side by side, within a single data entry window. The trouble with multi-event windows is: How can the user recognise and process each event separately? How is the system to know when the user has completed any one event and wishes to commit it?

Data entry is not about inputting data items, but about inputting events composed of one or more data items. To make this clear to a user, you might adopt the principle of shadowing of data entry fields on an event by event basis. This principle is not always tenable, as can be seen from four possible approaches for committing events.

1   Make the user step through one event at time

The first approach is to highlight only one event's worth of data items for data entry at a time. The user must press 'save' before moving on.

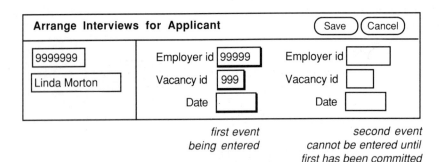

2   Design a distinct send button for each event

In the second approach, the user types at will over the data in the window, without any effect on the underlying data. Whenever any one event within that window is to be committed, the user selects the relevant command button. This command will commit only that event, and invoke the database update procedure.

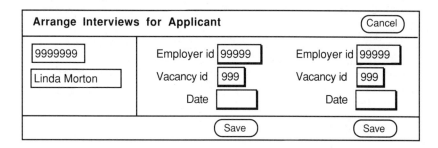

This is generally considered to be a poor style for GUI design. It means that to commit a windowful of trivial events, many buttons must be shown on the screen and the user has to press each of them.

3   Use the movement of the (text or focus) cursor

The movement of the cursor from one data item field to the next may be taken to indicate the input of an event. In the slickest of implementations, all data item fields for an event can be shadowed as the user places the cursor in the first of them, and as soon as the cursor leaves the last data item field for an event, the database update procedure can be fired.

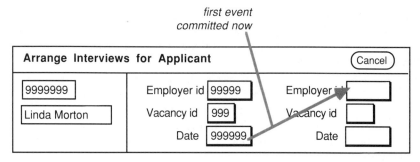

This is a reasonably intuitive approach where each of a series of events requires only one data item to be input. It is less intuitive for more complex events (like the one above) comprising several data items. Understanding of the event data group must be built into the system, so that all the data item fields for the event are shadowed during data entry, and no database update is committed until the user leaves that group of data items.

4   Send a batch of events with one send button

This way the user can type at will over the data on the screen, without any effect on the underlying data. Shadowing the data here is irrelevant. Whenever *all* the events within the window are to be committed, the user presses the command button.

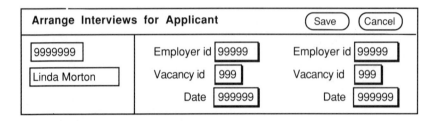

We can recommend this, with two reservations. First, an extra level of understanding must be built into the system about which events are contained in which window, and how to process a batch of them at once. Error handling is more complex than we have shown previously. What to do if some events succeed and some fail? We assume that each event which succeeds is committed (and perhaps reported as such) and each event which fails is reported somehow at the user interface.

Second, some application generators roll up the logical commit units into one physical commit unit. Though in a simple system (see below) this may involve as little as over-writing one database record, this makes it impossible to process the events one by one, as they really ought to be.

Aside on simple systems

Suppose, as is typical in systems built by application generators, a user can obtain any database record in a window on the screen, then update it by simply typing over data items on display. In the terms of our methodology, there are several trivial events being input in one window, one event for each attribute of an entity, where each event simply overwrites one attribute with a new value.

While this kind of simple system has a rather uninteresting entity event model (probably capturing no more Integrity Rules than those which may be expressed as referential integrity rules), the user still needs to understand the scope of an individual event, and the fact that each event is committed in its own right. This awareness is naturally encouraged by processing one event at a time, and giving a distinct response (OK or error) to each event which is input.

Relaxing the entity event modelling theory

There is a way to relax the theory so that it more closely corresponds with the application generator- entity data prototype - simple system - view of the world. That is to allow any or all of an entity's attributes (other than foreign keys perhaps) to be amended by a general 'update all attributes' event. This event may have to pick up unchanged attributes from the screen display, or somehow detect attributes which have been altered.

23.8 **Merge data entry windows into reference windows**

The enquiry for a list of vacancies matching an applicant may be shown as follows. Compare this with the general purpose response to the same enquiry in chapter 22. Note how the user is provided with **radio buttons** to choose one of the vacancies, and a command button for Interview Arrangement.

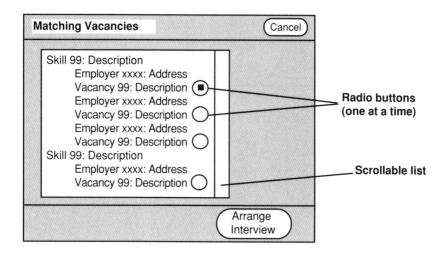

Since the applicant identity is already stored as context data, once a vacancy has been chosen and the button pressed, most of the required data can be carried into the Interview Arrangement window, leaving the user to enter only the interview date.

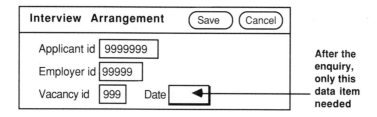

Now, though it breaks the rules of the RAD style guide set out in chapter 22, it is easy to go a step further and merge the data entry window into reference window which naturally precedes it in the dialogue.

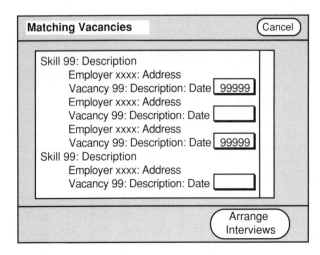

23.9 Add commands to link dialogues

A big advantage of a GUI is the opportunity it gives for both simplification and reuse of dialogues. In refining a GUI to be more user-friendly, the designer should be looking to reuse the mini-dialogues, entity reference windows and lists previously defined in a first-cut entity event system. There are three ways to join mini-dialogues together:

- nest one dialogue within another
- run two dialogues in parallel
- run two mini-dialogues in sequence.

Before we look at these, what do we mean by nested and parallel dialogues?

Nested and parallel dialogues
In a first-cut entity event system, a data entry window is always constructed so as to provide a means of directly inputting the events and enquiry triggers. But where some of the input data can be collected by enquiry from the system, then instead of elaborating the window with extra enquiry components, input data can be collected from a nested or parallel dialogue.

A nested dialogue is **modal**; the user must complete it before anything else. A parallel dialogue is **modeless**; the user can do something else and leave it incomplete.

Nested and parallel dialogues should be designed as independently as possible, not as an integral part of the dialogue which uses them. So:

- the basic dialogue design is not further complicated
- the nested and parallel dialogues can be reused elsewhere.

One side-effect of introducing a nested or parallel dialogue is that the data entry window design may be extended with extra command buttons. Often a special kind of button is used, called a Popup action box. Alternatively a list may be invoked by simply pressing in the relevant data item field.

Nest one dialogue within another

This strategy is suitable when entering a foreign key or data type, into a data entry window. The designer may use some kind of nested dialogue to show the instances of the type. We could add a Popup action box into the Interview Arrangement window, to help the user select the correct Applicant.

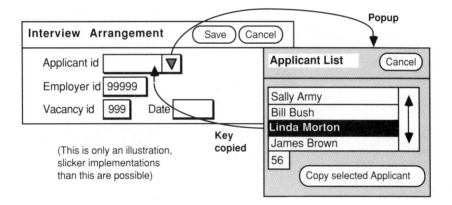

The idea is that the user highlights one entry in the list, and on pressing the copy button, the chosen applicant's key will automatically appear in the Interview Arrangement window. Both copy and cancel buttons will have the effect of dismissing the list. The Popup dialogue may be modal, meaning the user must respond to it.

Note however, the need for such Popup lists can be reduced by creating detail entities via the entity reference window of their master. Also, if the list is very long, users will want to be able to enter a value directly, or shorten the list as discussed earlier.

How far can entity reference lists be reused in nested dialogues?

In these examples we have shown something like the standard 'entity reference list' window shown earlier. However, the degree of reusability is limited because a variant of the standard list may be needed. Design effort may be directed towards, for example:

- suppressing details from the list (above, only applicant name is shown)
- constraining the data which may be copied from the list (often, only the key)
- translating user-friendly descriptions into codes or vice versa (see above)
- adding check boxes for batch entry (see below).

Run two dialogues in parallel

This is suitable when creating a set of detail link entities *together with* their master entity (type A). The designer may use a reference list to show instances of the other master entity (type B).

In the case study, consider entering the Applicant Skills into an Applicant Registration window. Instead of a nested dialogue, which automatically disappears after it has been used, a parallel entity reference list may be displayed. As the user moves around the screen, the reference list may switch between the foreground and the background, but it will remain on the screen until explicitly closed by the user.

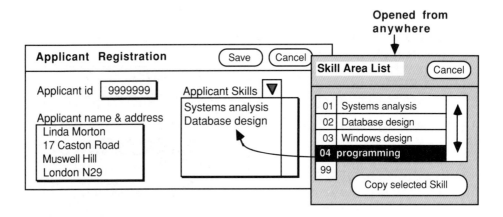

Run two mini-dialogues in sequence

Most of the mini-dialogues for inputting an event will end up at an entity reference window. The user may find it convenient to issue another event or enquiry command from the entity reference window, rather than return to the system entry menu.

Extending this idea, the user may wish to combine mini-dialogues to support some task or function. For example, when creating a set of detail entities linking master A to master B, the designer may join previously defined mini-dialogues like this:

- create or select master entity (type A)
- show reference list of other master entities (type B)
- place command buttons for creating link entities in the reference list.

NB: in the case study, the Arrange Interviews for Applicant dialogue, which is discussed at length from chapter 25 onwards, might be automatically generated from such principles!

23.10 **Add commands for more specific entity reference lists**

Apart from the list constraint window discussed in chapter 22, shorter entity reference lists may be displayed by giving users specific entry points and access routes. Three standard ways in which entity reference lists may be constrained by entering upon a related entity type are:

- show detail entities
- show related sister entities
- show matching sister entities.

The are shown more graphically below, as three ways the list of entity instances of type D may be shortened.

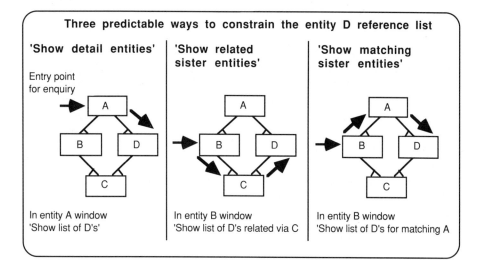

All these enquiries give different lists of instances of an entity type (type D in this illustration). The enquiry command buttons which trigger these enquiries will be placed in the entity reference window of other entity types (type A or B in this illustration).

23.11 **Concluding remarks**

Are user task-driven approaches still needed?

An implication which might be drawn from the chapters 22 and 23 is that event-driven interface design removes the need for any user task-driven approach to dialogue design. This is incorrect, for two very different reasons.

First, the technique relies on there being an entity data model, which must itself have been developed from a user-oriented view of the system requirements. Techniques for the analysis of enquiry access paths, and relational data analysis of input and output data flows, provide important validations of the entity data model. These techniques should be preceded by some kind of user task analysis.

Second, user task-driven approaches are needed, they do contribute to user interface design. Having two ways to tackle the same design problem is helpful. One approach will help to validate the other.

Not in the techniques so far presented: see chapter 24

Missing from event-driven interface design as currently specified is the idea that outputs might be produced at terminals other than the one where an event is input, as might be a requirement in a distributed system. Another omission is the idea of event animation, though the event response may be designed to substitute for this. Also, advice on multi-user problems to do with locking, refreshment and handling concurrent dialogues for one user is needed.

Not in the techniques so far presented: see chapters 26 and 27

Dialogue design has so far been given minimal attention. By 'dialogue' we mean something longer and more substantial than most GUI designers mean by the term. We mean a series of steps designed to help the user carry out some kind of user task.

For many purposes, users require little more than the kind of mini-dialogue generated, but some user functions require a more elaborate dialogue design, so more advice is needed on how events and enquiries (or mini-dialogues) are connected to support the users' tasks.

Dialogue state management may be needed to prevent the user from doing something which is impossible or inappropriate. The mini-dialogues of an entity event system impose a primitive level of dialogue state management. Further, commands in an entity reference window can be deactivated by a script which interprets the state variable of an entity if:

- the entity has passed the state where the event can be entered
- the entity has not reached the state where the event can be entered.

But the next level of dialogue state management, to support specific user functions, is beyond the scope of event-driven interface design, that is:

- hiding commands for those events not in the current user function or dialogue
- adding commands peculiar to a user function or dialogue.

Not in the techniques so far presented: see chapter 29

Error testing and handling has so far been taken for granted.

Chapter 24

More GUI style issues

This chapter discusses standardisation of application style. The emphasis is not so much 'look and feel' issues as on more software-oriented issues, such as handling multi-user problems to do with contention, locking and refreshment. The chapter also identifies some scope for reuse of External Design components.

24.1 **The need for standards**

This chapter is not a GUI style guide, it concentrates on specific issues which we feel are important, some of which are neglected in current GUI style guidance.

Problems for IT departments and users

Graphical User Interfaces (GUIs) and User Interface Management Systems (UIMS) are providing people with new opportunities and new problems. They are impressed by the new style of user interface and the speed of interface 'painting', but they aren't sure how to manage the work, integrate it with their existing systems, or relate it to existing methodologies. Database managers are nervous at the potential for database lock outs, performance degradation and corruption of database integrity.

Users too can find there are operational problems behind the attractive facade of the GUI they are given. They may feel they at the mercy of the system, rather than in control of it. They may be unable to skip from one dialogue to another and back again, be forced to complete the first dialogue or abandon it, become frustrated with messages like 'update not possible at this time' or 'selected record has been deleted by someone else'.

Some people expect that a GUI will solve all these problems. It may help, but only if it is managed properly. It opens up a Pandora's box of new design options. It creates new ways for designer to cause users to scratch their heads, which need to be controlled. The range of design options is enormous. It is important that two designers working on the same system design in the same way, otherwise the users will find the interface they are presented with confusing. One action may have different effects in different dialogues; different actions in different dialogues may have the same effect.

In short, organisations which expect to use windows-based technology for large database systems in an interactive, multi-user environment, need standards limiting the use of a GUI; first, so that users have consistent, intuitively reasonable views of what they are doing, second, so that acceptable performance is delivered.

Style guides

The standards which are needed can be documented in a 'style guide', and at least some of the elements in a style guide can be implemented as reusable system components.

It is misleading to place too much emphasis on the development of an 'application style guide' for one application. Most of its contents should be drawn from more generic guides. Outside the scope of any single application or development project, an organisation should acquire, develop and co-ordinate style guides to suit its purposes. There are several kinds of guide which are more generic than an application style guide, roughly from most generic down to least generic, these are:

- universal style guide
- RAD (methodology-specific) style guide
- machine-specific style guide
- corporate style guide
- application style guide.

A **universal style guide** should state those principles and standards of GUI design which are universally applicable across all installations and machines. The nearest thing we can find to a universal authority is a world-wide hardware manufacturer. Current publications such as IBM's *CUA*, and Apple's *Human Interface Guidelines* go some way towards what is needed, but leave room for considerable variance in application styles.

A **RAD style guide** (or methodology-specific style guide) should state principles and standards of GUI design for Rapid Application Development, that is for simplifying and speeding up the development of working prototype. Though more constraining than an Installation style guide, a RAD style guide may be more widely applicable; it may become part of the methodology used across many organisations and machines.

For example, chapter 22 contains a RAD guide to support the event-driven interface design technique. As more is learnt about how the users want the system to support their business tasks, these rules should and will be broken.

A **machine-specific style guide** should state the principles and standards of GUI design as constrained by the mechanisms of a specific implementation environment (say, Powerbuilder, Microsoft Access or TeleUSE). If an organisation chooses to go with one implementation environment, this guide may be embodied within the Installation style guide.

A **corporate style guide** should state those principles and standards GUI design best suited to the users of a specific organisation. It should be prefaced by some strategic study of the business areas in which systems are to be implemented. In practice, it is unlikely that different organisations will require very different corporate style guides, but in the absence of any higher authority, organisations will have to develop their own, or buy and adapt one developed by a specialist consultancy.

An **application style guide** adds the guidance on top of the guidance in the other style guides, which is original or unique to an application. After the first application style guide has been developed by an organisation, it may be incorporated in the corporate style guide. The next time round there may be little to write in the application style guide.

In the absence of any other input, an organisation might adopt the style guidance suggested in these chapters, but our intention is more to point to and illustrate the topics which should be covered in a style guide, rather than impose a set of rules on everyone.

What does the GUI part of a style guide contain?

The aim of the GUI part of a style guide is to ensure that applications have a consistent 'look and feel'. It should guide and constrain the design of:

- screen layout: the appearance and behaviour of displayed components
  system entry screens and menus
  data fields and lists
  commands (buttons, menus, etc.)
  universal commands (save, copy, delete, quit, undo, scroll bars, etc.)
  success, error, instruction, alert and help messages.
  pictorial analogues and icons

- dialogue navigation
    - navigation within and between windows
    - 'what happens next' (e.g. after a universal command or error message)

We are not trying to write a GUI style guide, but some examples of standards in the above areas were discussed in chapters 22 and 23 and this chapter concentrates on:

- modality: the balance between modal and modeless styles
- minimising contention between multiple users
- communication between parallel dialogues
    - automated data transfer between windows or dialogues
    - mechanisms for seeing and pointing (rather than remembering and typing)
- designing for reuse.

24.2 **Modality**

A modal dialogue is one which forces the user to reply to its request for information or instructions. Too much modality makes for an unfriendly user interface, so 'dialogues should be modeless' is a well-established principle of interface design. However there are many exceptions to this rule, circumstances where a modal style is appropriate.

Dialogue design is all about introducing modality into a system's user interface, exactly the right amount of modality, the amount that is desirable to support the user's work. This section looks in more detail at the role of modality in dialogue design.

Freedom to move modelessly between dialogues
The general principle 'dialogues should be modeless' means that designers should begin by assuming that users are free to make any reasonable jump between dialogues.

Note the word 'reasonable' here. There are cases where a modeless style is unreasonable, where a user's freedom should be constrained. For a trivial example, imagine a user must enter two data items, Style and Size, into a product description window. There is a business rule that not all combinations of Style and Size are allowed (say baby socks only go up to size 10). This is not just a matter of syntax validation after data input. The user should be prevented from modelessly switching into an enquiry dialogue to collect any Size from a Popup list of the values allowed for that data item, but should be forced to use a more limited Style/Size list.

Given a user may jump out of one dialogue into a second dialogue, leaving windows in the first dialogue open on the screen, a number of design questions must be answered in a standard way across related applications.

Is the user obliged to return to the first dialogue?
No, control passes completely to the second dialogue. The user may or may not return to look at the windows which have been left open.

Will database updates committed so far in the first dialogue remain committed?
Yes, even if the user never returns to complete the dialogue. Database updating is done on an event by event basis. Each event is committed separately. The database will not be locked to any window or dialogue.

When will any database locks made by the first dialogue be released?
It is not the normal practice to lock data to a window or dialogue, but just in case it is required, let us be clear that the dialogue would have to be 'timed out' in some fashion, to release any locks it had placed.

Modality within a dialogue

Designing a dialogue to support an end-user's task is all about introducing modality into the system's user interface. Some of the effort in dialogue design must be directed at limiting the possible commands available to the end user. This is true not only of GUIs. Some popular 4GLs allow far too much unconstrained navigation around an application, which means the application builder spends as much time removing the navigation options as coding the application in the first place.

The example in chapter 26 is intended to show what it means in practice to design modality into a dialogue. There is one particular form of modality which is worth discussing up front before getting into the detail of our case study example, that is the modal message box.

Modal message boxes

A message box consists of a single window which pops up over the active window. It is used to inform the user and/or request information or instructions from the user. Some call a message box a **dialogue box**, but we tend to use using the word 'dialogue' for a more elaborate sequence of events involved in carrying out a user's job function.

A message box usually contains buttons such as OK and Cancel. It may include help buttons which when pressed provide the user with a more detailed explanation of the message. Any or all of the buttons may dismiss the message box from the screen.

A modeless message box allows the user to interact with other windows on the screen: it may be used to implement help facilities. A **modal message box** forces the user to reply to its request for information or instructions. The user must dismiss the box before doing anything else. Modal message boxes have several uses.

For an **alert message**, it is normal to use a modal message box where the only possible response is to dismiss the box from the screen by pressing an OK button. It might say for example, 'another user has opened a window on this data'.

For an **error message**, it is common to use modal message box where the possible responses may be 'try again' or 'carry on regardless'. The error message might say for example, 'input failed because data is inconsistent with database'.

For a **busy message**, informing the user that some processing is taking place, it is normal to use a modal message box without any buttons. The message should tell the user what processing is actually taking place. Some implementations also change to a different cursor to demonstrate that the workstation is working (a moving watch or egg timer is often used).

The above is an attempt to make a generic statement about kinds of message box. To give a more specific example, in Motif 1.1 the XmMessage Box has the following six types: message, warning, question, information, error and working.

Modality and Popup lists

A modal style may also be used to implement the most simple kind of enquiry, the selection of a data type from a Popup list, where the only course of action is either to select one value from a short list of values and thereby dismiss the window, or else dismiss the window without selecting a value.

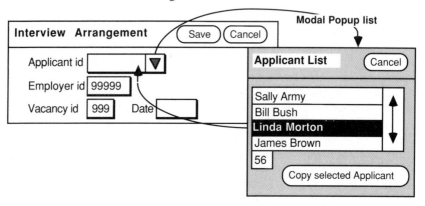

There are two potential problems to bear in mind. First, even this limited amount of modality may be undesirable if it prevents the user from doing anything else (perhaps seeking further information) before making a decision as to what to do next. Second, if another enquiry dialogue is required to display exactly the same information, but within a modeless reference window, then the modal Popup list may be regarded as redundant and therefore (at least slightly) anti-reuse.

However, varieties on the theme of a Popup list are useful in designing the most user-friendly interface. The designer may eliminate the above concerns by configuring the modality. For example, in Motif there exist several levels of so called 'dialogue styles' such as:

- modeless   no modal restrictions
- primary application modal   'parent' window blocked until confirmation
- full application modal   this window blocked until confirmation
- system modal   all windows blocked until confirmation.

24.3 **Minimising contention between multiple users**

Private views of data

For many software applications, a GUI seems a very natural way to work. As an end-user you can do all the things which seem sensible. You can keep lots of data views on the screen. You can shuffle them in front of and behind each other. You can cut and paste text (and perhaps diagrams) between data views in different tools (word processors, spreadsheets, drawing tools and CASE tools) without fear of unexpected side-effects.

This works well where each window is a view of a private file or data structure, which can cannot be seen or updated by any other user.

Shared views of data

Adding a windows interface to a large information system is another matter. Each window provides a view of one shared underlying data structure. This makes each screen into a multi-user system.

In a traditional multi-user system, different users may have different views of the underlying data on their screens. These discrepancies are obvious to any single user; they only become evident when objects behave in unexpected ways, or unexpected messages are received. This is perhaps most common in the handling of composite objects such as lists, where one user may be creating or deleting objects which are visible in a list currently displayed on another user's screen.

GUIs have created a potential for confusion in the user's mind which did not exist before. Using a GUI, each screen is like a multi-user system. One user can have many windows open at once, many views of the same underlying data on one screen. So the problems inherent in multi-user systems become obvious to a single user; any discrepancy between the views in different windows is immediately visible.

So if we are to prevent a user from becoming confused, if we are to design user-friendly interfaces, we need to think about how to control multi-user access to an information system, so that two independent user dialogues do not interfere with each other's work by accessing and updating the same underlying data. These issues are not entirely new, but they have a new importance, because of our desire to present the user with an interface in which they can be in control of what is going on.

Some easy answers

GUI designers are fond of inventing and quoting 'principles' like these:

'Avoid locking a database for a window'
This principle minimises the probability that users will prevent each other from accessing data. On the other hand, it maximises the likelihood that one user will change reference data currently on display to another user, which leads us to the next principle.

'Select before update'
This principle, meaning that users wishing to use reference data for data entry should

select it immediately before using it, minimises the risks of updates being rejected because the reference data is out of date. On the other hand, it may unnecessarily increase the user's workload.

'Always design modal Popup lists rather than modeless reference lists'
This principle minimises the likelihood that one user will change reference data currently on display to another user. The reference data doesn't hang around very long, it is dismissed by the next user action.

'Never refresh data'
This principle avoids a lot of hard design work, perhaps with the idea that this work may in the end degrade system performance to an unacceptable level.

But it should be pointed out that these are all principles for the *designer's* convenience, they are the easy ways to reduce potential problems of system performance and contention between users. The opposite and more difficult design options may in fact be better for users, depending on the direction in which design trade-offs lead.

Locking data to a dialogue (not to a window)
One way to tackle the problem of contention is to lock all the data currently being accessed by one user, so that another user cannot see it. This is quite apart from, and in addition to, the locking which takes place when processing a single event or commit unit.

In GUI design, a further level of multi-threading arises because there may be many windows on one terminal. It would be a mistake to lock data to a single window because it is not really the windows which are multi-threaded, but the dialogues. Where there are many windows in one dialogue, then these windows are co-operating in the performance of a single function and the data on one should not be locked from another. Where there are many dialogues on one terminal, then if locking is to be applied, each dialogue should lock its data from other dialogues. Where a dialogue contains only one window, this will appear to be the same as locking data to one window.

Ways to avoid the clumsiness of locks on all windows
Suppose the user is part of the way through an Applicant Registration, using the reference window of skills. Should the Skill Area reference list be locked?

If we lock the skill list, then this may be prohibitively inefficient. If this user leaves the dialogue unfinished while he/she goes to lunch, no-one else will be able to carry out any function using the skills during this time. A more efficient solution is required, as discussed in the next sections.

Lock data entry windows only
The system can distinguish reference windows from data entry windows, locking only the latter. This is a reasonable solution, but it leads to two problems.

First, if reference windows are not locked then the data in them may be updated, so we have to consider refreshing reference windows (see below).

Second, when the user comes to update the system with the new applicant, then he/she may be surprised to find that the update is rejected because a manager has deleted one of the applicant's skills (that is the skill category itself) via some other terminal, so we have to consider controlling updates to reference data (see below).

Refreshing reference windows

Suppose the office manager user creates a new skill, or deletes one. Should the reference window on the placement consultant's machine be **refreshed** with updates?

Ideally, the answer must be yes. But there are significant performance implications here, and design choices to make. Should we refresh:

- automatically on any change to the reference data?
- automatically for only the front window on all machines?
- automatically when a user brings the reference window to the front?
- not automatically, on a manual request only?

To implement refreshment of a reference list is tricky even in a single-user windows-based environment. Where refreshment of reference windows is impossibly resource consuming, there is an alternative approach, that is to **broadcast** a Popup alert message to all terminals, saying something like 'warning: the xxx reference window is now out of date'.

Both approaches are unusual in practice. It seems we need better design techniques for handling **composite objects**. Refreshment and broadcast both imply a message server process which knows about all active terminals and what windows are open on them. We need the ability to keep track of which objects are contained in which composite objects, and which composite objects are on display. Without techniques for doing this, a system with many users could produce a lot of distracting and unwanted updates or broadcast messages.

Controlling updates to reference data

When the user comes to update the system with the new applicant, then he/she may be surprised to find that the update is rejected because a manager has deleted one of the applicant's skills (that is, the skill category itself) via some other terminal. There are three possible solutions here.

'Select before update'

The user might be prepared to live with this kind of problem, especially if it is infrequent. The problem can be minimised by always selecting a reference list immediately before update. And the user can be reminded to do so in any error message. Otherwise we need an alternative way of protecting the user from interference by other users.

Lock reference windows up to a time-limit

The system could monitor a time-limit for a lock, at the end of which it returns to the user with a message of the kind 'confirm within 5 seconds if you wish to continue to hold the lock on the data in this reference window'. This confirmation might be automated if the system can detect activity at the user keyboard.

Time stamp records instead of locking them

The system could set a time-stamp on all records when it reads them, then record this time stamp along with the window in which the record is displayed. Later when the user wishes to update, the system could abort the update if the time stamp has been updated by anyone else in the meantime.

There are two problems with this, both of which lead to slower processing. First, every enquiry becomes an update as well. Second, users may find it difficult to complete any update due to the frequency with which common data is being updated by others.

Constraining users to behave modally

GUI designers often quote the principle that users should be free to operate in a modeless style. But it turns out that the more modeless the style, the harder it is for the user and the designer to control what is going on.

Faced with practical difficulties, some designers and some application generators swing to the opposite extreme. They impose the constraint that no user (or rather terminal) is allowed to engage at once in two dialogues (either of the same type or of different types). But this is a clumsy and unsatisfactory standard. In general we *ought* to be able to support users who want to do this kind of thing; we should learn how to do it.

Distinguishing between reference and data entry modes

A consequence of allowing several views of shared data is that users may be confused about which of these views are also available to, and updatable by, other users. Users will be less confused if they are made aware of what mode the displayed data is operating in, reference or data entry.

It should be said that this and the rest of this section is a proposal we are making, not a universally agreed set of principles. We have already seen in chapter 23 an example of why the user may want a window to act in both reference and data entry modes.

Two modes of data item field

Any data item field on a screen might be intended only to contain reference information retrieved from the database, or it might be intended for data entry (in which case it may or may not contain reference information). The two modes might be distinguished, for example by colour, or by shadowing a data entry field to give a 3D effect. We have adopted the latter convention.

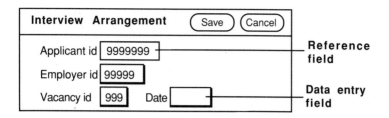

The methodology makes a contribution here. Data entry is not about inputting individual data items, but about inputting events composed of one or more data items, so the shadowing of data entry fields may be on an event by event basis.

Not all of the data items for an event need be input by the user. In the example given, the event is made up of three data items input by the user and one (Applicant id) taken from reference data already on display.

Two modes of window

It is helpful to distinguish between reference windows and data entry windows, perhaps by using a different background colour. A **reference window** contains no data entry fields, so no data entry may take place through it. A **data entry window** contains one or more data entry fields in which the user may enter data (that is, events and enquiry triggers). It is common to mix reference data and data entry data within a data entry window.

Each user should be aware that a window in reference mode is public property, possibly shared by other users, so data in it may be changed by someone else while the window is on view (whether or not this change is notified or broadcast to the user in question). A user should be confident that a data item field in a data entry window is private, not available to others, so cannot be altered by any broadcast.

Assigning a data entry window to one dialogue

Before we say any more, please note that in our methodology, **windows** and **dialogues** are distinct concepts. In a specific example they may be in one-to-one correspondence, but in the general case one dialogue may contain several windows and one window may appear in several dialogues.

A consequence of allowing the user to engage in several dialogues at once is that there is a potential for confusion as to which dialogue a data entry window belongs.

This confusion will obviously arise when two different dialogues of the same type are conducted in parallel. Say the user is dealing at once with two applicants, the user may open Interview Arrangement windows in two dialogues of the same type 'Arrange Interviews for Applicant'.

The same kind of confusion will arise when the same kind of data entry window appears in dialogues of different types. For example, the user may open Interview Arrangement windows in dialogues of two different types:

- Arrange Interviews for Applicant
- Arrange Interviews for Vacancy.

One way to avoid such confusion is to prevent the user from ever carrying out two data entry dialogues (of the same type or of different types) in parallel. But this is a clumsy and unsatisfactory standard. In general we *ought* to be able to support users who want to do this kind of thing, and we must learn how to do it.

Such confusion must be resolved by ensuring that everyone (users and programmers) knows which dialogue a data entry window belongs to. To ensure the *programmer* knows, the designer should specify the dialogue identity as a property of the data entry window. In a specific UIMS, it may be possible to identify the dialogue by the unique reference number of the first data entry window in the dialogue, by the device of creating each subsequent window in the dialogue as a 'child' of this first window. We assume here that either each child carries the 'parent' reference number, or there is a function to find the 'parent' of any window.

It is not so clear how to ensure the *user* knows. We make two very tentative suggestions. The dialogue identity might be displayed in each of its data entry windows. The designer might join the windows in dialogue together, so that if one moves they all move and if one is brought to the front then they all are.

Allowing a reference window to be used in many dialogues

The obvious use for a reference window is to display a list of entities or data types, but note that we do not mean to include Popup lists or Selection boxes under the term reference window. A reference window is left on display while other things are done. It is public property, possibly shared between several parallel dialogues under the control of one user, or even by several users (see example in chapter 27). The alternative, to open a new copy of the reference window for each dialogue or each user, leads to obvious and unnecessary confusion.

Should the reference window disappear when the last user/dialogue to reference it disappears? We recommend that on opening and/or closing a data entry dialogue, the user is offered the option of closing all reference windows as well, or leaving them open for use by other dialogues. The important thing is that a standard is defined (within an application, or better within an organisation) which prevents users and designers from having to work out a new mechanism each time.

Changing the mode of a window

In the context of a specific dialogue, once a data entry window has been completed with data, and the update has been committed to the database, the data entry window may turn into a reference window. Some signal should be given (e.g. change of background colour) to indicate this.

Changing mode in the opposite direction should be more difficult. If the user wishes to enter data through a reference window, they should first have to take some positive step (such as pressing a command button) to change the mode of the window. This should be made visible by a change in the background colour, shadowing of the relevant data entry fields, or whatever. We have already seen in chapter 23 an example of the user changing a window from reference to data entry mode.

24.4 **Communication between parallel dialogues**

Ideally the system will automatically carry forward values between successive windows involved in a single dialogue. But in copying data between parallel dialogues, the user must be responsible for transferring values between windows. There are several mechanisms for seeing and pointing (rather than remembering and typing). The use of them should be standardised in a style guide.

Parallel look-up dialogues

Manual copy and paste
Each Applicant Skill may be selected and transferred into the data entry window manually by a copy and paste operation. This is a straightforward feature which allows the user to copy the contents of a text field to temporary storage area often called a 'clipboard', then paste the contents in any other text field.

If this feature is made available on all text fields throughout an application, this means that any enquiry dialogue can be used to assist with data entry, without being specifically programmed to do so.

Automatic copy and paste
On frequently used enquiries, the copy and paste operation may be automated. This may be implemented by placing some kind of 'apply button' in the reference window, which when pressed will transfer the selected items.

But is it obvious which window will receive the items? What if two data entry windows are open, which will act as the recipient for the selected data values? Or if the Apply button is placed in the data entry window, then what if two reference windows are open, which will act as the sender of selected data values?

One solution is to remember which windows were the latest to be accessed. Another (safer) approach is to separate the copy and paste operations, by implementing an export button in the reference window and an import button in the recipient data entry window.

Drag and drop
Another way to transfer data between windows is to drag and drop. That is to select the desired data, drag it across the screen until it is over the recipient window, then drop it into that window. This mechanism is visible to the user, and leaves no doubt about where the data should be transferred to, however it doesn't prevent the user from attempting to drag and drop entirely inappropriate data.

Point and grab

Perhaps the best way to transfer data is to point first at where the data is to be entered, then point at the data to be entered. The 'grab' operation should only work on data items of the correct type for entry in the field which has been pointed to.

Batch transfer of multiple items

Should automatic transfer of data values be one at a time or many at once? Transferring one value at a time may be clumsy. The user does not want to keep swapping between the data entry window and the reference window, pasting in each skill one at a time, unless this can be done so that the movement back and forth between windows is seemlessly smooth.

Transferring several values at once may be more user-friendly. We might help the user to selected multiple skills by extending the reference window with **check boxes** as shown below. There are other devices, but this one is easy to illustrate.

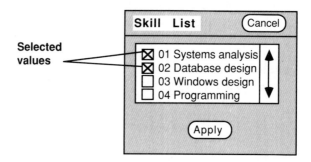

The user can highlight one or more skills in the reference window, then on pressing the Apply button (or by dragging and dropping, or simply by closing the window) copy them into the scrollable list within the Applicant Registration window.

Consequent design questions requiring standards answers

Should the batch of values overwrite or extend any existing list? We suggest it should extend rather than replace. The user will have to delete existing entries by hand if this is required.

Should the batch be added at the end of the list, or merged by sorting into it? This depends on whether the list is or can be ordered.

Should duplicates be allowed in the recipient window? Probably not.

What if there is no room for the whole batch? We suggest the recipient field must be scrollable; on receipt of a batch it will be automatically scrolled to its start or end point.

Parallel update dialogues

So far we have assumed that the data the user wants to enter can be found in the relevant reference list. But what if the data cannot be found? A parallel update may be required as well. This may be given a command button in the dialogue.

In the case study as described so far, the Entry of a New Skill dialogue is not a task for the placement consultant, so it is not given a command button in the Applicant Registration dialogue. If the placement consultant is in the middle of registering an applicant and finds that the applicant has a skill which is not in yet recorded in the system, then he/she may ask the office manager to enter the new skill at a separate terminal. If the officer manager agrees, he/she can call up the relevant function from the main menu to enter the new skill.

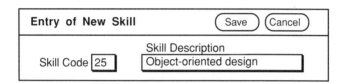

But the fact that Entry of a New Skill must be done by a different user is merely an accident of this example. What if the two update dialogues could be carried out on the same terminal by one placement consultant?

Consequent design question requiring a standard answer
Should the placement consultant create a new skill by entering an update event through the reference window designed for displaying a list of skills? No. The placement consultant should be made to enter the event through a distinct data entry window designed for creating a new skill. The user should be aware that reference windows are public property, shared with other users, so updates should not be done through them.

Refreshment of parallel and subordinate dialogues
Once the placement consultant has created a new skill through the data entry window, the next task is to enter this skill into the Applicant's skill list. But will the skill reference lists currently on display be refreshed with the new skill? To get around the difficulties of implementing locks and refreshment, it is common to impose the 'select before update' principle, to make the placement consultant redisplay the reference list before collecting data for entry into the Applicant's skill list.

On not testing integrity rules in the External Design
However newly displayed the Skill reference list is, it should not be used to validate the Applicant's Skills (see the footnotes at the end of this chapter.)

24.5 **Designing for reuse**

Factoring out dialogue components for true reuse

Identification of reusable objects and routines in the Conceptual Model can be made into a reasonably objective activity. Identification of reusable objects and routines in the External Design is a more intuitive activity, but there are several areas to look for reuse. It is easiest to start from the six window types described in chapter 22:

- Entity reference list
- Entity reference window
- Event data entry window
- Event confirmation message box
- Event error message box
- Event success message box.

It is possible to create six stereotype components here, which can be copied and tailored for use. Stereotype components provide a layer of reusability, but they do not give 'true reuse' of the kind talked about in object-oriented design circles. There are several areas to look for true reuse, as listed below.

Reuse of one window in different dialogues

Where the same event or enquiry trigger may be input via different dialogues, the same data entry window (or component of it) may be reused in these different dialogues. The window for entering an Interview Arrangement event is an interesting example. Suppose the Interview Arrangement command button is made available on the entity reference windows of both Applicant and Vacancy. The context data which may be carried forward is different, as shown below.

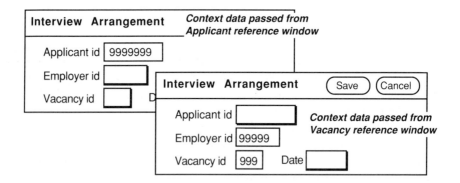

Depending on the implementation environment, the designer may be able to reuse the same window in both contexts, or the designer may have to design two different windows.

Reuse of one window design for different events and enquiries

Chapter 22 suggested that a *standard data entry window* might be designed for entering enquiry parameters. It may be possible to go further and design a *standard entity reference list* and *standard entity reference window*, where standard data items (say, the first two text data items) are displayed in a standard window. This may require standardisation of entities' attributes' data item types and lengths.

One kind of window received only little attention in chapter 23, that is, the list constraint window, used for shortening the entity reference list returned by an enquiry. Common input parameters include an alphabetic or numeric range, the key of master entity, or the key of a master of a master entity. It may be possible to write a *standard list constraint window* common to all entity types. Obviously this depends on standardisation of entities' attributes, where the key is stored, what kind of data item it is and so on.

Reuse of a data item field in different windows

Where the same *data item type or domain* may be input via different windows, the same data entry field may be reused in these different dialogues. For example, the data item types 'name', 'address' and 'telephone number' may appear as attributes of many entities and in many data entry windows.

Reuse of a nested dialogue

Where the same *data item type or domain* may be input via different windows, the same nested dialogue (e.g. a Popup list) may be reused to help the user select the value for input. This happens wherever several detail entities are linked to the same master entity (say, country of origin), because all the data entry windows via which the different detail entities are created will contain the same foreign key.

The nested dialogue should be designed independently of the data entry dialogues, so all the designer has to do is to incorporate the command button (perhaps the data item field itself) for invoking the nested dialogue in the relevant data entry window.

Reuse of parallel dialogues

Given a universal copy and paste function, any dialogue may be used by the user to help in the data entry task, for example, wherever a batch of data from entities of one type is needed for data entry, such as the collection of Skills for entry into an Applicant Registration window shown earlier.

Reuse through standard application style

Standardising the way a GUI should be designed (perhaps in a style guide) enables stereotype components to be developed to implement various design features; these components will be reusable by many designers.

24.6 **Footnotes**

We conclude with a ragbag of observations left out of the discussion in this and the previous two chapters.

Not testing business rules in the External Design

However newly displayed a reference list is, it should not be used to validate the data entry. Not only is it generally impossible to do all the validation (test all the business rules and the state of all stored data) without calling a database procedure, but it is anti-reuse and anti-amendability to specify and code the validation twice. To anticipate the advice from chapter 29, we recommend against duplicating validation which must and will be specified in the Conceptual Model (and coded in the event procedures) in the External Design. Where the user is concerned to reduce the amount of data entry before an error is detected, the event procedure may be implemented as a co-routine, first invoked before all the event parameters have been input.

The distinction between a data type and the key of a master entity

The distinction between a data type and the key of a master entity is fuzzy. In the case study, the list of Skill Areas might be viewed in either light. Data types are made into entity types if the user expects to be allowed to update them while other users are actively using the system. See also chapter 29.

A Popup list is similar to a Pulldown menu

A Popup list is similar to a Pulldown menu except that the Popup list appears when a click is made in the area (commonly a Popup action box) configured to trigger the display of that Popup list. A Popup list usually appears at the point at which the Popup action box is clicked. Popup lists may be context sensitive, that is to say unique to the window they appear in.

Where commands appear

Whether command buttons are included in a window or not is a matter for local standards. They might be included in menus, in a distinct 'log window', or in a panel permanently displayed across the bottom of the screen.

Chapter 25

User function definition

Having so far taken a Conceptual Model-driven approach to dialogue design, this chapter does an about-face, taking a user task-driven approach. User functions are outlined as a collection of system processes, designed to help users carry out their business tasks.

25.1 Users and user procedure design

For the least critical user functions, designers may employ the rapid application development techniques shown in the previous chapters. But for the most critical functions (say the 20% which are exercised 80% of the time and require 80% of the design effort), designers should spend time getting to know the end-users, their user procedures and the way they want to use the system. For these functions, more user-oriented design techniques are needed.

(Alternatively the RAD techniques in chapters 21 to 23 may be used for all the functions of the first delivered system, and user-friendliness can be the focus of the second delivery.)

End-users

SSADM proposes the documentation of several end-user concepts, before and during the design of a system, especially those which may be embodied as components of the implemented system. To begin with there are these concepts:

Concept	Hi-Ho example	SSADM documents
User job title	Senior Consultant	User Catalogue
User individual	Joe Soap	User Catalogue
User role	Placement Consultant	User Roles catalogue
User function	Applicant Registration	Function Definition
Authority to access function		User role/function matrix

In SSADM, the entitlement to play a specific **user role** with respect to the system may to be assigned any **user job title**, and to any **user individual**.

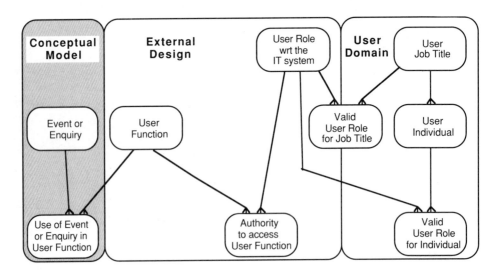

The user domain may not have to be formally documented. Finding out about user job titles and user individuals is valuable; formally documenting them may not be. Note the 'double v' structure. It is possible that the user role played by an individual is constrained by the valid user roles for their job title. If so, the model may be refined as described in chapter 11, and as follows.

Another user-oriented concept in SSADM is that several different dialogues may be designed for one function. We shall call each of these a **function variety**. Normally, only a small number of functions, the most critical ones, need more than one function variety to be designed.

The difference between a function and a function variety may be expressed in terms of the 3-Schema Architecture. A function is composed of several events and enquiries; and so gives the user access to a defined subset of the Conceptual Model. A function variety is a specific presentation of the function, designed to suit users with a specific level of experience and skills. So one function variety differs from another only in its External Design aspects.

The choice of a function variety may be made by the end-user, or constrained to those with the required **skill** (such as word processor experience, foreign language or university degree). In SSADM, it seems a skill level must be recorded as a kind of user role. But this confuses function with function variety and the *authority* to use a function with the *qualification* to use a function variety. Adding function variety, and skill needed to use a function variety, the revised meta-model is shown below.

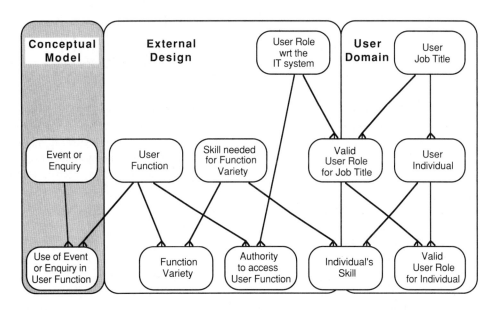

See the end of chapter 7 for some remarks on meta-models like this one.

User procedure design

'Perhaps because of the irresistible rise of relational database management systems... the typical system specification concentrates on the IT system itself - for example a diagram shows the users stuck around the edge of the system, putting data in and out.... Insufficient attention is given to the things that people actually *do* that the system is meant to support: the order in which they do things, the way they depend on each other to do something first...' (IOPENER magazine, November 1992).

What the users do and the way they want to do it are vital inputs to External Design, so we shall present several techniques for External Design, starting with data flow analysis and user function definition and continuing through logical dialogue design into physical dialogue design.

However, we have not set out in this book to address all the human factors involved. User procedure design is not fully within the scope of the methodology. Adding user task analysis and job design into the methodology would mean adding a 4th schema.

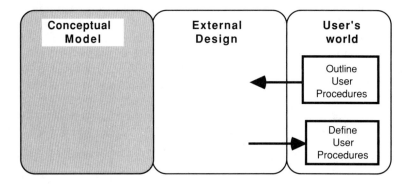

The techniques in this '4th schema' are outside the scope of the methodology defined in this book, but they may be related to the techniques in it. We have not so far been impressed by attempts to import OO ideas (or at least OO words) into the user domain. Some relevant work has been done in the field of HCI; this can be related to the External Design. More recently, our work on Euromethod modelling languages has focussed on using a 'soft systems' approach (based on Checkland, 1984) to define the users' business; this can be related to the Conceptual Model.

25.2 Uses for DFDs

Having pointed out that user procedure design is not fully within the scope of the methodology, the methodology does employ top-down, user-oriented techniques for External Design, starting with data flow analysis and user function definition and continuing through logical dialogue design into physical dialogue design.

This chapter concentrates on the first two techniques - data flow analysis and user function definition. As well as leading to the design of a user-friendly interface design, these techniques must also ensure that the External Design and the Conceptual Model are properly tied together, and should be compatible with the event-driven interface design techniques in chapters 22 and 23.

The general experience of people trying to specify a methodology based on DFDs, specify a CASE tool or a meta-model for such a methodology, or specify DFDs using 'formal methods', is that they have been unable to formally define the semantics of the DFD objects and the relationships between them (this point is amplified in the final section of this chapter).

For many years the construction of DFD hierarchies has been over-emphasised in system modelling methodologies. We hear that even Yourdon has been quoted as saying 'the DFD is dead'. Nevertheless, despite their weaknesses, we are content in our methodology to use DFDs, for several purposes.

Using DFDs in system investigation and scoping

DFDs are a good tool for defining the boundary of the system, and specifying the user interface in a machine-independent form (in terms of cross-boundary data flows). This makes building DFDs a useful step in systems investigation, in the early definition of requirements, and in starting the specification of the External Design.

So, we expect that analysts starting to specify a system will use something like DFDs to record the processing of data flows input by users and sent to users, even though we expect this specification to be supplanted later by the specification of individual user functions.

Using DFDs in system presentation

A high-level specification which suppresses low-level detail is sometimes useful as an overview of an existing system (or family of systems), without necessarily being decomposed hierarchically to any lower level.

In this way, a high-level DFD can be useful in helping people to get to grips with a system; it provides a framework on which to build their understanding. Note that DFDs do not have to be developed from the top down. A high-level DFD is more sensibly built by abstraction from the bottom up.

Using one DFD to specify a user function

Quite independently of a DFD hierarchy, a single bottom-level DFD (or something very like it) has a role to play in specifying the organisation of processes in a distinct system user function, at least at the highest level of a user function specification. Later to specify each user function we shall use something akin to a standalone DFD, but call it a 'specific function model'.

25.3 Data flow analysis of the case study

It is easy to criticise the use of DFDs as a formal specification tool (see the end of this chapter). Nevertheless we have managed to specify a hierarchical set of diagrams for our case study, such that each lower level DFD may be viewed as a decomposition of one process in the higher level DFD. Note that there are two artifices in the way we have built these DFDs.

First, we have managed to specify each 'user function' of the system in one bottom-level DFD, then build the DFD hierarchy from the bottom up. It is not always possible or desirable to do this, but it simplifies the presentation of the case study in this chapter. One reason it can be done for our case study is that there is little overlap between the components of distinct user functions. In other words, at the level of specification shown here there is no reuse of user function components. Having said this, there is considerable reuse of components at lower levels of system specification.

Second, the input data flows in the bottom-level DFDs have been defined such that each contains only one event or enquiry trigger. It is not always possible or desirable to define the DFDs in this way, but again it simplifies the presentation of the case study in this chapter.

Case study illustration of DFDs

For our recruitment agency, Hi-Ho, here is the top-level DFD for the required system, showing the scope of the system, the principal cross-boundary data flows, and the division of the system into 'user functions'.

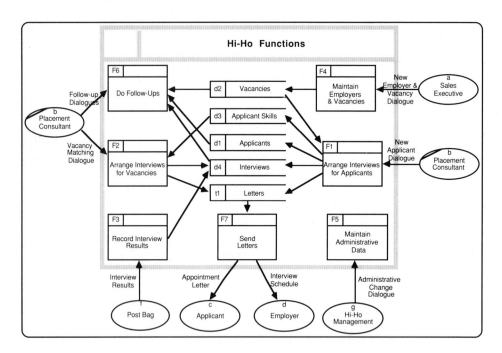

Only parts of this system are relevant to us in this chapter. We are interested in three of the 'user functions' defined in the top-level DFD: F1, F5 and F6.

Function 6 - Record Interviews Results

This function is specified in chapter 28. It is worth noting how different the DFD and the specific function model are.

Function 1 - Arrange Interviews for Applicants

The placement consultants want a user function to be designed to help in arranging interviews for applicants. The placement consultant will first register the new applicant together with his skills, then trigger an enquiry for all the suitable vacancies (those matching the applicant's skills), and finally arrange zero, one or more interviews for the applicant, by selecting vacancies from the list of suitable vacancies.

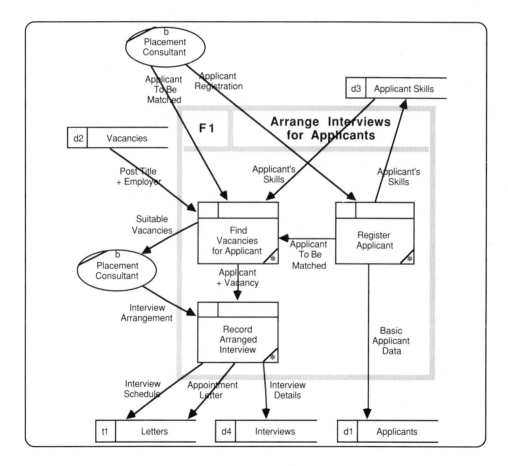

Again, it is worth noting how different this DFD is from the specific function model shown later in this chapter.

Function 1 - contents of input data flows

In general an input data flow on a DFD may contain several events and enquiry triggers. But in this case study we have defined the data flows such that each of the three data flows input by the Placement Consultant corresponds to just one event or enquiry trigger. It may not always be possible or desirable to do this, but it simplifies the presentation of the case study in this chapter.

Input data flow	Data items
Applicant Registration	Applicant Num
	Applicant Name And Address
	Applicant Telephone Number
	Skill Type (repeating item)
Applicant to be Matched	Applicant Num
Interview Arrangement	Applicant Num
	Employer Name
	Vacancy Number
	Interview Date

Function 5 - Maintain Administrative Data

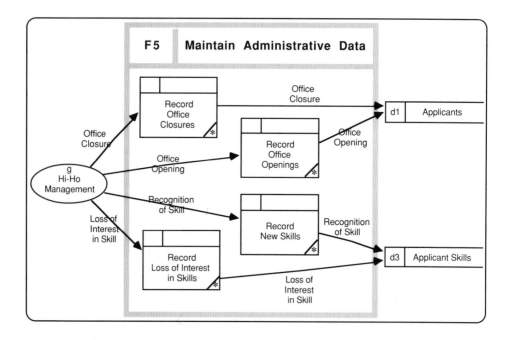

25.4 **User function definition**

Data flow analysis is not a necessary precursor to user function definition, but it usually helps. In defining the input data flows, the analysts and/or the users make early judgements about how the input data is best organised for input. It can be seen that these early judgements will constrain the technique of user function definition. This is no bad thing, since the number of ways to define user functions and dialogues would otherwise be too large. The early judgements may be more or less intuitive, but they should at least have some backing from the user with whom the DFDs were discussed.

Having drawn DFDs, the definitions of input and output data flows must be taken forward into a more formal specification of the External Design. The technique of user function definition is used to repackage the DFDs in the form of distinct 'user functions', each documentable using what we call a 'specific function model'. This repackaging is important for two reasons. First, while the semantics of DFDs are debatable, the semantics of a specific function model can be formally defined. Second, reuse between user functions is encouraged rather than inhibited.

A user function is like a DFD in that:
- it communicates with the outside world by input and output data flows
- it is composed of processes connected by intermediate data flows.

A user function is unlike a DFD in that:
- a user function is not decomposed from a higher level specification
- user functions may *reuse* common components (both processes and data flows).

The principal components of a user function can be documented using a kind of standalone DFD, but to avoid confusion with DFD concepts, from now on we shall use the following words in defining a user function:

- specific function model (rather than standalone DFD)
- procedure (rather than process)
- data stream (rather than data flow).

What is a user function?
To put it simply, a user function is a collection of system procedures which the user wishes to carry out together, to complete a business operation or meet some business objective. The trouble with this definition is that it doesn't tell the designer what to do. To get more specific advice, more specific question are needed.

How to decide the scope of a user function?
Determining the size and scope of a user function is a highly subjective process. A user function may be designed to be large enough to support a single business operation (whatever the user considers a distinct business operation to be). It may be designed to

be small enough to be reused within several business operations. The design choices lie in the hands of users and system designers.

It is often natural and convenient to define a user function around the processing of a single major input data flow and/or one major output data flow, as defined on a DFD. Modelling each data flow as a data-flow-structure, composed of data items, naturally defines the scope of the user function to handle it.

How does a user function help the user?

As far as any user sees from the outside, all a user function does is consume input data, and produce output data in response. How the input and output data is best presented on screens and reports is a matter for design, to be agreed by users and system designers. And in the case of on-line user functions, considerable design work will be involved in plotting the user's course through dialogue with the system (see chapters 26 and 27).

How does a user function work?

Apart from trivial user functions (displaying menus and so on) most user functions require access to the system's database. On the inside, a user function works by extracting events and enquiry triggers from the input data, triggering the relevant database procedures and collecting the data returned from the database.

How to record the components of a user function?

A user function is composed of processes communicating via data flows. We assume that a user function (on-line or off-line) can always be defined using a specific function model, even if the designer chooses not to document the user function this way. This assumption is important because it defines what a user function is, in terms of components we know how to specify formally: data streams and procedures.

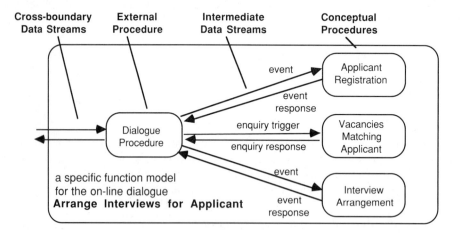

It is not mandatory to draw a specific function model for each function. For any function (typically an on-line function) which is composed of a single external procedure and many conceptual procedures (because the input data flow carries many events or enquiry triggers), it is reasonable to list the event and enquiry procedures which are invoked, rather than show them in the diagram.

Where a specific function model is drawn, we should be able to divide procedures (according to the 3-Schema Architecture) into external, conceptual and internal, as in the example above.

In the diagram below we have superimposed the same division of procedures upon SSADM4's standard template for user function definition called the 'Universal Function Model' which is especially useful in the definition of off-line functions (see chapter 28).

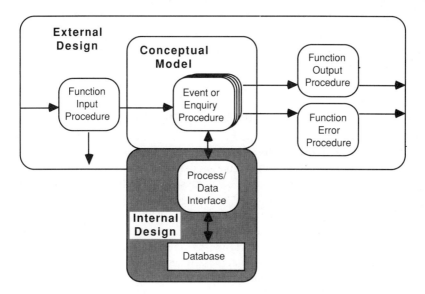

25.5 Products of user function definition

The main products of user function definition (these are comparable with but a little different from the products of function definition in SSADM4) are as follows.

User function definition: a textual description of the user function. This may include error handling narrative, but we recommend reserving this for dialogue dependent error conditions, since the documentation of syntax errors and integrity errors will be done elsewhere.

Specific function model: a kind of standalone DFD defining the function as a set of processes communicating via data streams. This is not a mandatory product. It may be ignored for those on-line functions which have the standard shape comprising a single external procedure which invokes a conceptual procedure for each event and enquiry trigger.

I/O data-flow-structure: a model of an input or output data stream in the form of a regular expression or Jackson structure. We recommend not merging the input and output structures of an on-line user function before dialogue design (see chapter 26).

In specifying I/O data-flow-structures, the designers will not directly be concerned with the Conceptual Model, but they should be concerned with objects which pass between the External Design and the Conceptual Model. It is vital to make clear how the events and enquiry triggers correspond to data groups in the I/O structure.

List of events and enquiries: initially it may be sufficient to list the events and enquiries involved in a function, but later we recommend identifying these directly in the data-flow-structure of the input data stream (see chapter 26).

User role/user function matrix: a matrix identifying which user functions a particular user role can use. We recommend not making a distinction between external entities and user roles. User role is probably what people mean when they place an external entity in the DFD in the first place.

25.6 Further specification of user functions

To begin with, the analyst is not forced to specify how the input data stream is related to events and enquiry triggers, or how the output data stream is composed of the responses to events and enquiry triggers. In fact the analyst may be distracted from defining the essential input and output data by physical design decisions, such as the batching of data for control purposes, or how much data can be presented on a screen.

But if it is desired to develop a prototype of the External Design which can be extended into system implementation, then prototype user functions must be designed to anticipate the communication between the External Design and the Conceptual Model. This means that the analyst must understand and document how the input structure is composed of events and enquiry triggers, and how the output structure is composed of the expected responses to events and enquiry triggers. Eventually the designers must identify where in the input structure the events and enquiry triggers are to be found. How to do this is shown in the next chapter.

To take a user function further toward physical implementation, we have to distinguish between on-line and off-line user functions. For **on-line** user functions, user function definition leads into dialogue design, a technique which produces a number of products specifying various aspects of a dialogue. Chapters 26 and 27 deal with the specification of on-line user functions, the design of dialogues using windows, the implementation of dialogues in a GUI environment, and the development of an approach to prototyping.

For **off-line** user functions, the universal function model should be developed into a specific function model during physical design. Chapter 28 shows how JSP techniques can be used to complete the specification and implementation of off-line user functions.

25.7 **The semantics of DFDs**

We use DFDs in our methodology, and we presented a set of these for our case study, but DFDs are not a mandatory or formal part of the system model. There are too many difficulties in defining what DFDs mean for them to be used in a formal specification. Some of the problems with DFDs are outlined in this section, which goes some way to explain why methodologies which rely on DFDs have not proved satisfactory. There are many awkward questions facing the DFD enthusiast.

What is a DFD process?

A process is a procedure for transforming the data flows it receives into the data flows it sends. The main purpose of drawing DFDs is to decompose a system into readily definable processes. While it is clear what it means to be process, it is not so clear what the data flows (which are shown entering or leaving the process) mean. When a DFD process executes, does it always consume all of its input data flows and produce all of its output data flows? Might these data flows be optional or mutually exclusive?

What is an external entity?

An external entity is something outside the system boundary which sends a data flow into the system or receives a data flow from it. An external entity is rather like a process, except that its internal workings remain undefined, only its products and consumables are visible.

To begin with many of the external entities may be identified with job titles in the user's domain. But since several people, possibly in different locations, may be expected to input the same data, or carry out the same user function, what tends to happen is that analysts are led to invent more abstract user roles, then name the external entities after these, rather than use job titles the user understands.

This is one reason why DFDs are not ideal for defining or presenting a user's job specification. It is normally better to define a user role by listing the several 'user functions' it entails. Some techniques connect the user functions for one user type in a kind of 'job stream chart' using a similar notation to DFDs.

What is a data store?

There are two kinds of data store. A **transient data store** is used to represent a data flow at rest between processes. It may be used to define what is later called a data-flow-structure. The distinction between transient data stores and data flows is a fuzzy one, as we shall see. A permanent or **system data store** is used to document where a process makes access to the entity data model. The general practice in drawing DFDs is to divide the entity data model so that distinct parts of it appear in distinct system data stores. There is no obvious reason why the stored data of a system should be partitioned in this way. Some have proposed recording only a single system data store, others propose leaving system data stores off the diagrams altogether. Neither proposal seems to make much difference to the effectiveness of DFDs in practice, since DFDs are usually used for the purpose of defining the External Design rather than the Conceptual Model.

What is a data flow?

It turns out that the concept of a data flow masks at least three distinct concepts. For a process-to-process data flow as many as three data structures might have to be documented.

Data-flow-structure: this is a physical container for data items, with a defined structure. It may be identified by a data flow name (and eventually in physical design, by some kind of file type). It can be formally specified by showing its data items arranged in a regular expression.

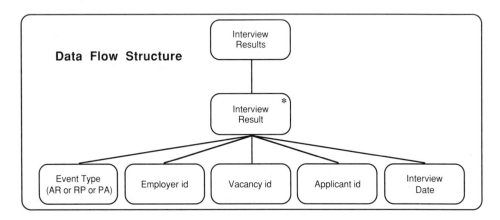

Data flow: this is one *use* of a data-flow-structure, being its passage from one place to another. It is identified by its data flow name, source name and destination name.

In a DFD, each data flow arrow (except those to or from a transient data store) represents a data flow. It is unclear how in DFDs the designer is supposed to represent the reuse of a data-flow-structure by different data flows, but one way to define a data-flow-structure, independently of any of the processes which use it, is to show it as a transient data store.

In the case of an off-line data flow (say, a serial file on magnetic tape), it is easy to envisage the data flow as a transient data store, but strictly every process-to-process data flow uses a data-flow-structure of this kind. The parameters passed between on-line routines are transmitted via a physical data flow. In a complete and formal system specification, someone will have to define the set of parameters which are used to invoke a routine, and the reply it produces. Some kind of data-flow-structure is being recorded here, quite independently of when or where it is used to connect any two processes. We'll come back to this point in a moment.

Process-view-of-a-data-flow: this is the structure imposed on a data flow, by the process which reads it or writes it. It is identified by its data flow name, source or destination process name, and input or output indicator.

If the designers apply JSP to define the process at one end of a process-to-process data flow, then the first step of program design is to draw a process-view-of-a-data-flow for view of the data flow seen by that process. A data flow with a process at only one end, requires only one process-view-of-a-data-flow. But a process-to-process data flow may be given two process-views-of-a-data-flow, both read and write views of the data flow. The general practice in drawing DFDs is to ignore this, to assume that a single data-flow-structure is sufficient for the purposes of specifying both read and write views of a data flow.

One way to specify all three data flow concepts

In general practice, the data flow arrows drawn on a DFD are truly data flows. Data-flow-structures and process-views-of-a-data-flow are not directly recorded. The documentation does not represent the possible reuse of data-flow-structures, and does not represent the case where a process-to-process data flow requires two process-views-of-a-data-flow (read and write views).

But a more formal practice is possible. To construct a complete and formal system model using something like the DFD notation, there would have to be three data structures for each process-to-process data flow:

- the data-flow-structure it instantiates
- input process-view-of-the-data-flow (reading the flow)
- output process-view-of-the-data-flow (writing the flow).

There is a way to do this using DFDs. The trick is to place a 'transient data store' on the middle of each process-to-process data flow.

Using this device, the DFD contains all three of the system specification objects implied by the concept of a process-to-process data flow. We can document each data-flow-structure as a transient data store, document each data flow as a pair of data flows into and out of the transient data store, and document the process-view-of-a-data-flow for each one.

Can DFDs be used to design a distributed system?

In specifying a system with a central database, it is assumed that all processes are executed in one place. What about a distributed system? You may think it will be helpful to annotate each process in a DFD with the name of a location. But it turns out that there are many difficulties with what it means to do this.

Given a process which takes data from an external entity and uses it to update a data store, which location should the process be labelled with? The external entity which enters the data may be in a different location from the data store which is updated. There may be several input data flows entered from different locations, several data stores stored in different locations, and several process components executed in different locations. There may be optional locations for data entry, the data storage or processing.

These complications, and others defined in further research we have done elsewhere, show that DFDs are not sophisticated enough to record the necessary information about location types and instances which must be documented in designing a distributed system.

Can DFDs be built into a hierarchical system description?

Yes, but with great difficulty. If you look at any substantial implemented system you will find it is a complex network of connected processes. Leaving aside the question of whether a hierarchical set of DFDs is constructed from the top down or from the bottom up, it is an unnatural way to model a network of processes. If a hierarchical specification is produced, then it must eventually be converted into a network form. A hierarchical view makes it needlessly difficult to discover, visualise or design this network. Graham (1991) points out that hierarchical decomposition actually makes it harder to discover or design reusable components at the bottom-level, and suspects that its original proponents (De Marco and Yourdon) never really intended it as a device to guide design.

There are in any case doubts about the semantics of DFDs above the bottom level of a hierarchy. Because detail is suppressed, the semantics of the higher level DFDs are hard to define. The following questions are about data flows, but the same questions may be asked of external entities and data stores.

Must every data flow in a bottom-level DFD be shown in the next higher level DFD? If so, then the higher level DFDs will become hopelessly complex. It is certain that details must be suppressed in some way. There are only two possibilities. Either a data flow in a bottom-level DFD can be omitted from the next higher level DFD, in which case the higher level DFDs can play no part in a formal system specification. Or several data flows in a bottom-level DFD must be somehow be aggregated into one data flow in the next higher level DFD.

How is this aggregation done? Concatenation? Collation? Surely not. The only plausible way we can think of to merge bottom-level data flows so that the aggregate data flow can still be described as a regular expression is as options of a single selection component in the higher-level data flow (not repeating the detail beneath each option of course). If you try doing this in practice, even with the best of CASE tool support, you will find it is enormously difficult to maintain the necessary cross-references between levels of the DFD hierarchy.

Having said all this, see the case study above. We have managed to build a hierarchical set of DFDs for the case study. Much of the business of information systems development is about force fitting what is truly a network into a hierarchical structure. For efficient system performance, what is truly a network database must be clustered into hierarchically structured blocks. For user convenience, what is truly a network of dialogues is presented via a hierarchy of menus. For programming convenience what is truly a set of co-routines is converted into a hierarchy of modules. If it is considered worth the effort, a hierarchical and formally consistent set of DFDs can be built.

Can a DFD be used to specify a single procedure?

A DFD is notoriously poor at specifying a single procedure because it does not represent sequences, selections and iterations as well as an action diagram (used in Information Engineering) or a Jackson structure. Attempts to extend the DFD notation with sequence, selection and iteration concepts have not been very appealing.

Chapter 26

User dialogue design (logical)

This chapter shows, given an on-line function, how to develop a logical dialogue which is user-friendly in that it helps users move from one stage of the dialogue to the next, carrying forward context data. ('Logical' means independent of any UIMS, TP system or other implementation mechanism.) The chapter also shows how to ensure that the database procedures of the Conceptual Model can later be embedded within this dialogue. A five step design technique is introduced, the main product of which is a basic dialogue structure drawn as a sequential structure of events and enquiries.

26.1 **Introduction to user dialogue design**

For an on-line user function, the next step after user function definition is user dialogue design. The diagram at the beginning of the chapter 20 showed the place of the technique within the methodology as a whole. User dialogue design has two faces. One specifies the sequence of input and output exchanges via which the user carries out a user function, making this as user-friendly as possible. The other specifies the things which a programmer must code using the implementation tool or language.

Why design dialogues at all?

The use of a GUI, where users apparently skip between windows at will, may seem to remove the need for dialogue design, but this is untrue.

It may be argued that if we design a distinct window for the input of each update event and each enquiry trigger (as in chapter 22), then the users can do whatever they like, jumping out of one window to another, inputting events in any sequence. Yes, we can get an 'entity event system' to work this way, but this design strategy is very clumsy as far the user is concerned (as we began to see in chapter 23). It leads to an unfriendly user-system interface, since to carry out what users regard as a single function they may have to input the same data items many times over.

What is needed is a technique for analysing things such as:

- how each exchange in a dialogue proceeds to the next
- what context data has to be carried forward
- how the user move between dialogues.

The difference between dialogues and windows

The arrangement of data items within a screen or window is important to the user, who wishes to make immediate sense of the data presented. It occupies a fair amount of design effort, as may be seen from other chapters. However, a common mistake is to assume that dialogue design is largely about screen or window design. In fact it is about designing the relationships between screens or windows.

In our methodology, windows and dialogues are distinct concepts. In the general case, one dialogue may contain several windows, and one window may appear in several dialogues, though in a specific case they may be in one-to-one correspondence.

26.2 **Introduction to logical dialogue design**

We divide user dialogue design into two parts. First, a machine-independent logical dialogue design technique (comparable with that in SSADM4) in which the user function's input and output data structures are analysed and combined to become the basic dialogue structure. Logical dialogue design is not at all concerned with screen or window design.

Second, a physical dialogue design technique, which elaborates the basic dialogue structure to include errors, aborts and reversions, and designs the physical screens or windows. The physical dialogue design technique may be defined at various levels of specificity. It might be defined for a generic UIMS or for a specific implementation tool like Microsoft Access.

Trial and error or methodical approach?

A new breed of designers is growing up, empowered by the latest User Interface Management Systems (UIMS), application generators and OO programming languages, but set apart by their different knowledge and expertise from more experienced analysts and database designers. They are happily generating code (lots of it) to implement the new generation of information systems, often uncontrolled by standards, conventions or methods.

These designers often emphasise prototyping, or trial and error. While trial and error has an important role to play within a methodology for External Design (as opposed to Conceptual Modelling), it is better to have a theory for how a Conceptual Model can be methodically embedded within an External Design. It turns out that given a completed entity event model and the input and output data flow structures for a specific user function, it is possible to be reasonably prescriptive about how to design the GUI for that function.

The approach to be described is very much more methodical than any other we have seen, so it must involve less trial and error. Whether being more methodical is always better and quicker, time and experience will tell. Our role here is to advance the most methodical approach we can, based on the best theory we have of how the External Design relates to the Conceptual Model.

A different starting point for GUI dialogue design

It is commonly accepted that in order to build a working system (rather than an interface prototype), the designer/programmer of GUI must be given some kind of specification of the conceptual model and business rules. What usually happens is that the GUI designers are given an entity data model, along with a specification of the most important enquiry functions. They then deduce more or less intuitively what the input events and database commit units will be. They may or may not give attention to linking these events together into user-friendly dialogues.

Because of its emphasis on entity event modelling, in our methodology the GUI designer can be given a much more precise specification. It is expected that all the input events can be specified by the conceptual modeller, then handed over to the GUI designer for implementation. Better still, an entity event system might be built, as described in chapters 22 and 23. It is also expected that the analysis of user functions will have provided some specification of input data required by the user in order to carry out their work.

26.3 **Summary of logical dialogue design**

The purpose is to produce a machine-independent specification of a user dialogue, which shows how the External Design corresponds to the Conceptual Model. The inputs are a user function outline, input and output data flows, and events and enquiries. The principal outputs are input and output data flow structures, a logical dialogue structure, and supporting documentation described later.

The steps of logical dialogue design are:

Step 1: Draw distinct input and output structures
Step 2: Find events and enquiries in the input structure
Step 3: Find event and enquiry responses in the output structure
Step 4: Create the dialogue structure
Step 5: Confirm the specification of events and enquiries

This technique develops only the basic dialogue structure. Later physical dialogue design techniques elaborate it to include errors, aborts, reversions and so on.

It is to be hoped that the input and output data structures of a dialogue will be at least roughly documented before dialogue design begins, in documenting the cross-boundary data flows on the data flow diagrams, or in documenting a user function. However, logical dialogue design starts with building the input and output data structures, as though from scratch.

Is it worth teaching the technique?

Users rarely decide exactly what the inputs and outputs will be until they have seen a physical user interface. So we recommend some throw-away user interface prototyping is done before specifying the input and output data flows for a user function.

Designers may in practice be reluctant to apply the systematic logical design techniques in this chapter. Given that a prototype has been developed, designers may prefer to use this as the user interface specification, rather than complete a machine-independent specification of input and output data flows.

The argument for *applying* the technique in this chapter is that where a machine-independent specification is required, then something like data flow structures will be needed.

Even if a machine-independent specification is not required, the argument for *teaching* the approach in this chapter is that we want to educate as well as train. We believe that teaching people to see systems development as a rational, ordered process will help them to improve their intuitive designs.

26.4 Case study: Arrange-Interviews-For-Applicant

For the on-line function Arrange-Interviews-For-Applicant, the inputs to logical dialogue design are shown below.

The function outline

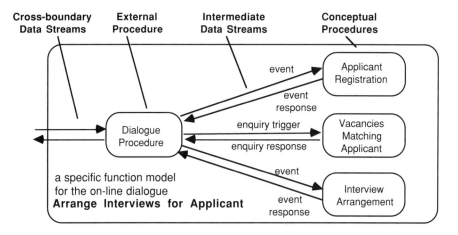

In the terms of this diagram, logical dialogue design is all about designing the External Design or **dialogue procedure**.

Entity event model

We assume that the Conceptual Model (the various event and enquiry procedures) will be specified as distinct products and implemented as distinct routines. To ensure integration can be achieved, the key point of correspondence will be the specification of events and enquiry triggers, and the specification of the response to each event and enquiry trigger.

In this user function the events and enquiry triggers are:

- event   Applicant Registration
- enquiry trigger   Applicant to be Matched
- event   Interview Arrangement.

A more detailed specification is given at the end of this chapter, where the difficulty is noted of working out from entity event modelling alone what the event and enquiry responses are.

26.5 **Step 1: Draw distinct input and output structures**

To begin with the data structures are drawn to represent the 'no error' case. The handling of errors is postponed. So the input structure for our user function will be composed of data items as shown below.

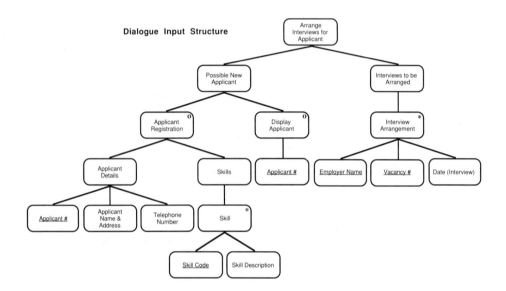

Note 1: We have shown the Applicant Num as a data item input within an Applicant Registration. If this is a system generated key, then it would in fact not be input at this point; this is what we shall assume from now on.

Note 2: There is no enquiry trigger (to find matching vacancies for an applicant) in the above diagram, because no data is input at this point, the Applicant Num can be read automatically from the data already on display. An event or enquiry trigger which requires no fresh data input may be called a **control trigger**. If the analyst does not recognise the need for a control trigger or represent it in the input data structure, then it should be discovered later, when looking for the input which corresponds with the output reply.

The first attempt at an output structure might look like this.

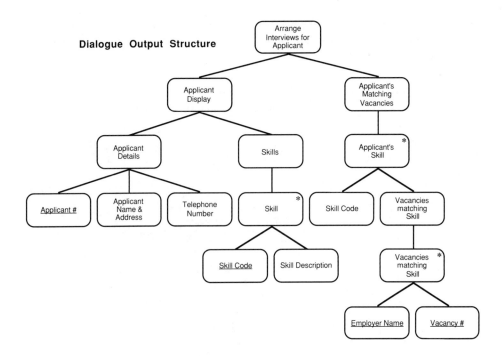

Dialogue Output Structure

A first attempt at an output structure should be composed largely if not entirely of enquiry responses. It does not include error messages or any 'OK' response to valid input events. As noted previously, the full output data flow structure will probably need to be developed through some kind of user interface prototyping.

Notice that the matching Vacancies for an Applicant are sorted by the Skill which they match.

26.6 **Step 2: Find events and enquiries in the input structure**

The analyst should create boxes in the input structure for the events and enquiry triggers, or rather the nodes in the structure which correspond to event and enquiry invocations. The rules are:

- one event must map onto one box in the input structure
- an elementary box in the structure cannot contain more than one event.

If the nodes are not obvious, examination of the output structure may reveal the need for additional boxes to represent events and enquiry triggers in the input data flow.

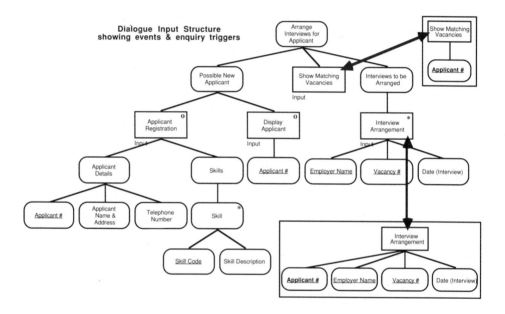

On this diagram we have shown two of the corresponding events and enquiry triggers. Notice that the input data structure does not require the Applicant Num to be input by the user, since it is carried forward in the dialogue as **context data**.

An aside on more complex input structures

We have so far looked at an input structure in which the correspondence between the External Design and the Conceptual Model is fairly obvious. It is reasonably clear which events are to be input, and how they are derived from the input data.

There are cases where it is not so easy to spot the events within the input data structure, where the user wishes to do a certain amount of manipulation of data on the screen, or in a transient data store, before entering data into the database.

Typically this happens when some kind of **aggregate event** (an informal notion, not part of the Conceptual Model) has to be broken up into discrete events by the user. Perhaps a single customer payment has to be broken up and assigned to several individual invoices. Or a number of man-days has to be broken up and allocated to individual tasks. The user may perform this task by playing with data on the screen using a spreadsheet-like format. We do not cover this part of External Design.

26.7 **Step 3: Find event and enquiry responses in the output structure**

The analyst should make sure the output structure is composed of the responses to each input event and enquiry trigger.

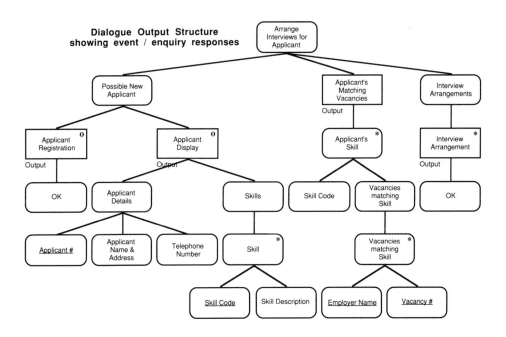

Notice the expected response to an event is simply 'OK'. The expected response to an enquiry trigger is more elaborate. As noted previously, the event and enquiry responses will probably need to be developed through some kind of prototyping. Error responses should not be added until physical dialogue design.

26.8 **Step 4: Create the dialogue structure**

The next step should be to merge the input and output data flow structures into a single I/O structure or dialogue structure. Each event or enquiry trigger is joined with its response under a single logical exchange (which could be labelled LGDE for the sake of conformance with SSADM4).

If we showed all the data items for each event, enquiry trigger and expected response, then the structure would be very large. The full structure is shown below.

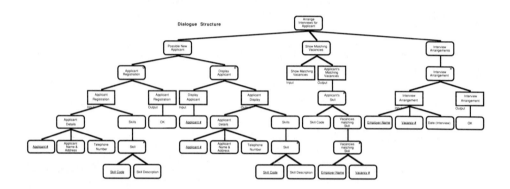

However, we recommend that the dialogue structure is not developed at all beneath the level of the logical exchange, since the analyst should document the details beneath a logical exchange box separately, in documenting the procedure for the event or enquiry trigger. The result will be a simple basic dialogue structure like the one shown below.

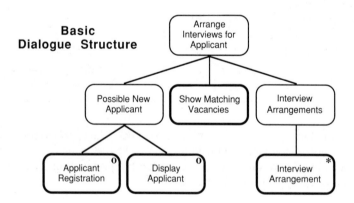

26.9 **Step 5: Complete the External/Conceptual interface**

This step will be redundant if the aim is to produce a prototype as swiftly as possible, or an entity event system has already been built as described in chapter 22, otherwise this step is needed to ensure that it will be possible later to integrate the External Design (user interface code) with the Conceptual Model (database or application code).

Since the dialogue has to invoke each event and enquiry procedure with the relevant event or enquiry trigger, and has to process the response, the designer should specify for each event and enquiry trigger:

- the data items required
- the Conceptual Model process to be called
- the data returned with an OK response
- the data returned with a Fail response.

While the error response can be generalised to simply an error-code (see chapter 29 for how this can be reflected at the user interface by an error message), the successful response needs more thought. Some throw-away user interface prototyping is probably needed before the entity event model can be completed with reusable event and enquiry responses. In the meantime, the standard event responses suggested in mini-dialogue of chapter 22 will do.

For example, part of the interface specification for our dialogue is:

Event or Enquiry Trigger	Event or Enquiry Response
Applicant Registration	
Applicant Num	0 = OK
Applicant Name and Address	1 = Applicant exists
Applicant Telephone Number	2 = Invalid skill type
Skill (repeating item)	
Applicant to be Matched	
Applicant Num	0 = OK
	3 = Applicant missing
	4 = No Vacancies found
Interview Arrangement	
Applicant Num	0 = OK
Employer Name	5 = Applicant missing
Vacancy Number	6 = Vacancy missing
Interview Date	7 = Interview already exists

Note that a UIMS usually makes no distinction between events and enquiry triggers. For example, designers using Motif would regard both as 'events'.

26.10 **Products of logical dialogue design**

In logical dialogue design, the I/O data structure(s) already documented for an on-line user function are taken forward to become the dialogue structure. The main products of logical dialogue design are as follows (these are comparable with, but a little different from, the products of the equivalent technique in SSADM4).

A **dialogue structure** is the basic structure of the external procedure component of an on-line user function. In addition to the dialogue structure for each dialogue, there are other products to do with the entry to dialogues and the movement between them. These products may be documented in text form (logically) before they are implemented in a physical form. A **command structure** is a list for one dialogue showing the various dialogues which may be directly invoked from this dialogue, thereby allowing dialogues to be connected in complex networks.

The **user role/user function matrix** records who is supposed to (or allowed to) carry out each user function. The **menu structure** is a hierarchical diagram showing the choice of user functions or dialogues available to the users; note that one dialogue can appear at the bottom of different legs of the hierarchy.

26.11 **Menus for the selection of dialogues**

It is convenient at this point to move from logical design to physical design, to look at how the menu structure will be implemented. The user will normally initiate a dialogue by selecting the desired user function from a list or menu. In a GUI, when activated by the user, a **Pulldown** menu displays a list of command buttons. The starting point for a Pulldown menu is normally the menu bar displayed along the top of an applications main window. This menu bar is normally visible to the user.

For example, chapter 25 shows a top-level Data Flow Diagram, showing the main functions of the Hi-Ho system. The list of functions is short enough to be displayed in a single Pulldown menu.

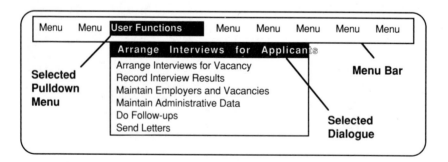

The most frequently accessed dialogues are invoked from a high-level or even top-level menu. Less frequently accessed or subordinate dialogues may be invoked from further **cascaded** Pulldown menus.

Suppose for example we allocate the system functions to three different kinds of user. The user roles may appear in the top-level menu, with functions at a lower level as shown below.

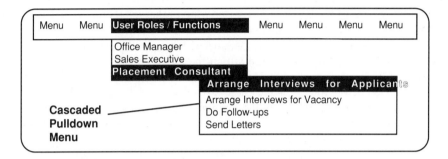

Access controls

Pulldown menus may be context insensitive, that is appear the same whatever dialogue is going on at the time. To make them context sensitive, menu items (which may be viewed as a variety of button) may be **activated** or **disabled** and their appearance altered to highlight this. Typically, buttons which are not applicable at a certain point during a dialogue are disabled and displayed in grey rather than black.

A simple way to implement the access controls implied by the user role/user function matrix is to implement the user roles as the top level of the Menu Structure, with all but one of them disabled for a given terminal.

26.12 Why not use JSP for dialogue design?

The technique closely resembles the beginning of JSP. We might imagine completing the definition of the input and output data structures, merging these to form a program structure, allocating programmable operations and conditions, and transforming the program structure into structured pseudocode (in the manner of JSP).

This *is* a possible implementation path. It would mean mapping the dialogue procedure onto single program. But the reasons for this approach seem (at the moment anyway) to be outweighed by the reasons against.

Reasons for JSP approach

It would be a rationale, teachable and methodical approach. It would provide a complete and machine-independent specification of the dialogue processing. It would enable us to embody the user's notion of a user procedure directly in one corresponding program, with the attendant advantages of understandability and amendability.

Reasons against JSP approach

First, the notion of a dialogue procedure runs against the grain of the way most UIMS expect code to be written (see the end of chapter 27).

Second, the JSP method would need to be supplemented with guidance on separating out reusable components, error handling components and so on.

Third, the JSP method isn't very designer-friendly in handling common features of on-line programs such as aborts and reverts, for which relatively complex 'backtracking' may be required in the program structure.

Fourth, the appearance of an event or enquiry response at the user interface may vary according to the user function within which the event or enquiry is invoked (being different say, on a screen and a report). Some throw-away user interface prototyping is probably needed before the event and enquiry responses can be specified with certainty. Much the same reasoning applies to the input and output data flows of a dialogue. The effect is that designers get some way down the path of physical design in building a prototype, and cannot be hauled back from it.

We'd like to be proved wrong on all these counts, but in the meantime we have to present a less structured way of taking the dialogue forward into physical design and implementation. Chapter 27 describes a step-by-step approach to completing the physical dialogue design, which may also prove helpful in user interface prototyping.

Chapter 27

User dialogue design (physical)

This chapter addresses dialogue design and implementation problems including guidance of users between windows in one dialogue, the storage of dialogue context data and elaboration of the dialogue to include errors, aborts and reversions. A seven step technique is introduced, leaning in places on earlier techniques for support.

27.1 **Summary of physical dialogue design**

The purpose is to specify the exceptional dialogue navigation beyond that shown by basic dialogue structure, and implement the user dialogue design in physical window designs and code. The principal inputs are the dialogue structure, events and enquiries from logical dialogue design. The outputs are a dialogue flowchart, windows, command buttons, code, etc.

What we mean by *physical* dialogue design is that the designer embodies the logical dialogue design in a specific implementation environment, though this may be only a prototype environment. The physical dialogue design technique is arranged in six steps, but these steps do not have to be done in the sequence shown. In fact it is very likely that steps 1 and 2 will be done in parallel.

Step 1: Design the dialogue navigation
Step 1.1: Design the commands for moving forward
Step 1.2: Design the commands for aborts and reversions

Step 2: Design windows for each logical exchange
Step 2.1: Design windows to accommodate events
Step 2.2: Design windows to accommodate enquiry triggers
Step 2.3: Design windows to accommodate event responses
Step 2.4: Design windows to accommodate enquiry responses

Step 3: Specify parallel dialogues
Step 3.1: Identify parallel dialogues to help the user
Step 3.2: Specify how data transfer occurs
Step 3.3: Design extra commands

Step 4: Specify error handling
Define for each error which may be detected, the error message to be displayed and the consequent user dialogue, using a parallel dialogue where possible.

Step 5: Define the dialogue state vector
Define the data items which are automatically passed forward within the data entry dialogue, rather than being reinput by the user, along with dialogue identity and state information.

Step 6: Code the dialogue management

Step 7: Assemble the system

27.2 **Step 1: Design dialogue navigation**

Given the basic dialogue structure, the designer has to specify with users the windows, the commands for navigating between windows, for aborts, reversions and so on. Later this navigation has to be programmed by the system builders.

One way to specify the extra navigation paths is to develop the dialogue structure using the Jackson notation, and using stereotype components for 'early death' and 'reversion' structures. This will provide documentation of the logic, but not of the user commands. Alternatively the GUI designer may employ a flowchart notation of the kind shown below. This is designed to sit half-way between the dialogue structure and the design of individual windows.

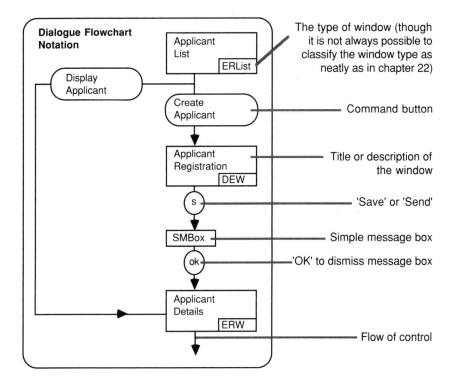

Given the unstructured nature of flowcharts, we find it helpful to follow some conventions, such as entering a box at the top and leaving at the bottom. Further research should be carried out into the best notation to be used at this point in a GUI design. There are a number of questions, such as whether the windows themselves can be represented (perhaps annotated in the data entry and display boxes). However, the notation is adequate for our example dialogue.

Step 1.1: Design the commands for moving forward

The dialogue flowchart below is a straightforward transformation of the basic dialogue structure shown earlier. We've added components for entering the dialogue, and explicitly named the navigation commands.

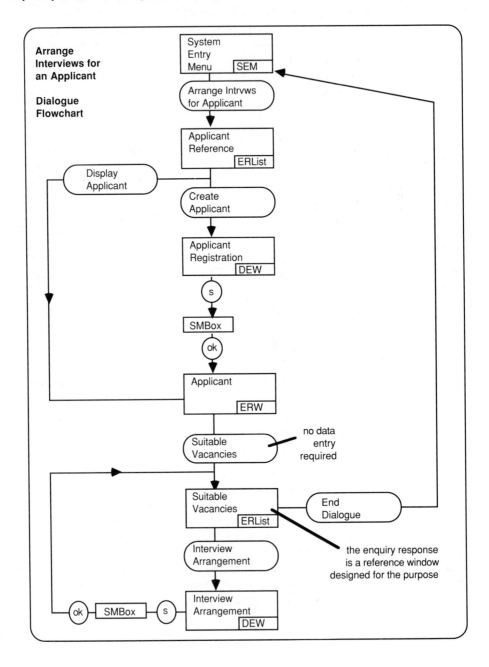

Step 1.2: Design the commands for aborts and reversions

It is impossible to specify a formal syntax for expressing sequence, selection and iteration using this flowchart notation, because of the need to design aborts and reversions into the structure. In the next flowchart, aborts and reverts have been added to the previous diagram. The © symbol stands for 'Cancel'.

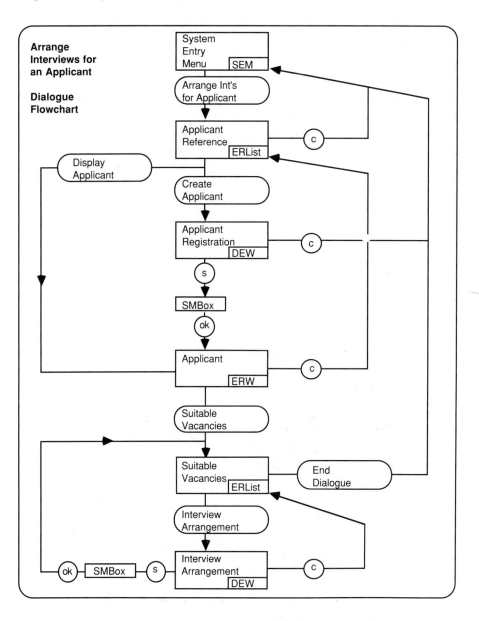

27.3 **Step 2: Design windows for each logical exchange**

Given a specification of the navigation paths through a dialogue, the analyst should specify the essential windows for the dialogue. This step may be partly redundant if an entity event system is built as described earlier. Chapter 23 has already provided some guidance on how window designs may be developed.

Returning to the example given earlier, we might see on the screen at one time windows involved in three of the logical exchanges.

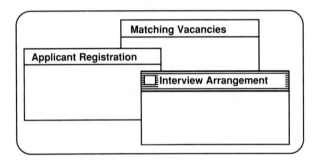

Of the logical exchanges, perhaps the most interesting example is the Interview Arrangement. Chapter 23 showed that some of the input data for the event (the Employee and Vacancy identifiers) may be selected by the user from the list on display, rather than entered in a separate window. However, this chapter considers only the Application Registration logical exchange.

Step 2.1: **Design windows to accommodate events**

A window may be designed for the input of one or several events. Given the standards in chapter 22, the window for an Applicant Registration event is shown below.

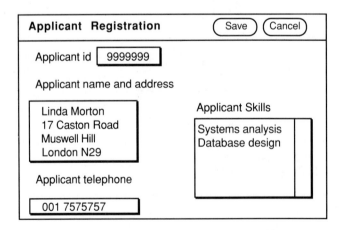

This window handles just one event (though a rather large one). The design of single and multi-event windows was discussed in chapter 23.

Step 2.2: Design windows to accommodate event responses

To begin with, dialogue design may proceed on the basis that the response to each event is always 'OK'. An OK response might not be made visible to the user at all. Using a *modeless or null response*, the dialogue may be left in exactly the same state, and the user may be able to alter the data and commit all over again. This is rather too modeless, the design should lead the user onwards through the dialogue.

In general, we recommend a *modal response* where the commit of an input event is made visible to the user. It was suggested in chapter 22 that the response should be:

- display a success message box
- close the event data entry window
- display an updated 'home' entity reference window.

Given these standards, the event response may be shown as below.

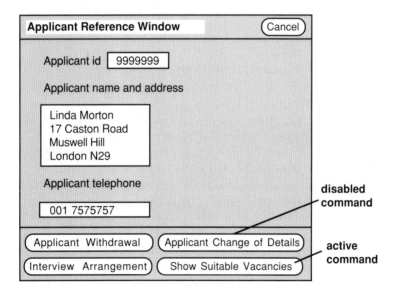

Compare this with the general purpose response to the applicant enquiry in chapter 22. Within the context of this specific dialogue, all the commands other than the next one in the dialogue should be disabled.

Step 2.3: Design windows to accommodate enquiry triggers
Much the same may be said for enquiry triggers as for events, except that while users may want to commit several events in one window, it is hard to imagine them ever wanting to submit more than one enquiry at once. So, it is normal to design a data entry window for the input of only one enquiry trigger at time.

In the example, the data for the enquiry trigger (the Applicant key) is available from the Applicant Registration data, so no additional window is needed for the enquiry parameters. There are two possible designs for the enquiry trigger:

- show it as a command button in the event response window (see above)
- let the 'save' button in the previous event window double as the enquiry trigger.

This second option is highly optimised, probably too far. The users may be confused by the sudden appearance of suitable vacancies following the registration of an applicant. It does no harm to make the users press an explicit command button.

Step 2.4: Design windows to accommodate enquiry responses
It seems natural to design a distinct window for an enquiry response, showing the main enquiry data in one or more text boxes, scrollable where necessary.

27.4 Step 3: Specify parallel dialogues

A big advantage of a GUI is the opportunity it gives for both simplification and reuse of dialogues. We recommend the dialogue is first constructed to provide a means of directly inputting the events and enquiry triggers. If it happens that some of the input data can be collected from the system, then instead of elaborating the dialogue with extra enquiry components, this data can be collected from a parallel dialogue.

Step 3.1: Identify parallel dialogues to help the user
The relevance of this to dialogue design, is that extra command buttons may have to be introduced into the relevant windows, sometimes in the form of a Popup action box. The example in chapter 23 shows that when a placement consultant registers a new applicant and all his/her skills, each skill must be checked against the range of valid skills. It seems natural for the placement consultant to copy the skills from a defined list, rather than enter them afresh, which means the user must be given a command button to call up the list.

One reference window used in many dialogues
The reference window of skills may be shared between the two Arrange-Interviews-For-Applicant dialogues. It seems natural to do this, rather than open a new reference window for each one, but this possibility is restricted to reference windows, rather than data entry windows (see chapter 24).

Step 3.2: Specify how data transfer occurs

Several ways to transfer values between windows involved in one dialogue were discussed in chapter 24:

- Manual Copy and Paste
- Automatic Copy and Paste
- Drag and Drop
- Point and Grab
- Batch Transfer of Multiple Items.

Step 3.3: Design extra commands

Having identified parallel dialogues the user may find helpful in the course of a given dialogue, the designer has two options. First, make the user abort the given dialogue and return to the main menu of functions. Second, add command buttons to reach parallel dialogues into windows of the given dialogue, which means extending the dialogue flowchart to show these commands.

Here we have added the Popup action box for displaying the Skill list, and a further command for reaching the Entry of a New Skill dialogue. These commands are placed on sideways arrows, jumping out of the given dialogue into parallel dialogues.

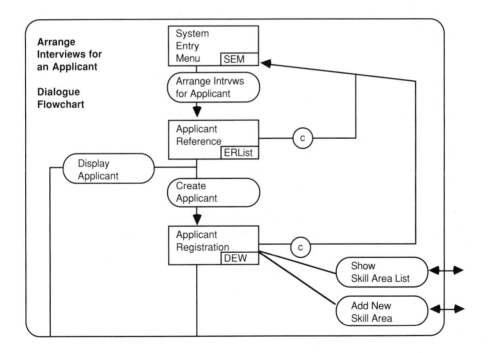

Any command represented on the flowchart should be added in the relevant window, though not necessarily in the form of a conventional button.

27.5 **Step 4: Specify error handling**

User-oriented and system-oriented views of error detection and reporting are discussed in chapters 22 and 29. This section looks only at the need for dialogue state management and the prevention or detection of 'dialogue state errors', where the user tries to do something which is invalid at the current point in the dialogue.

'Dialogues should be modeless' may be a well-established principle of interface design, but it is untrue that any action is possible at any point in a dialogue. Given that a dialogue progresses through a sequential series of defined states, the designer must implement the constraint that some things (some input events) are allowable in one state and not in another. Dialogue design implies controlling the sequence in which commands and windows are used in one dialogue.

The same point has been made by others. Antony Courtney (1991) opens his paper with this 'principal lesson': *'The style of programming enforced by the event callback mechanism (in the X Window System) is inadequate for large applications. This paper describes how and why we implemented centralised state management'*.

The dialogue structure or dialogue flowchart is the design document which specifies the valid state transitions. There are two ways to implement the state management.

By designing modality into the user interface
The state of a dialogue may be managed by designing the windows such that the relevant command button is not available to the user until the valid point in the dialogue.

For example, the command button for 'Show Matching Vacancies' cannot be used until the Applicant identity has been created or entered, because it depends upon this context data being available. So the system must reject any attempt to press the button (or in other examples, open a window) until the dialogue has reached the correct state.

By program design
Whether it is possible in all cases to design this amount of modality into a user interface is an open question. What if the standard application style (the one the user expects) allows the user to roam over the screen, returning at random to any of the windows which have been left open from any earlier stage of any dialogue? In the context of a specific dialogue, returning to input data via a previous data entry screen may not make sense; it may be something that the user should be prevented from doing.

If the user should be prevented from returning to input data via a previous data entry screen, and this modality is not designed into the user interface, then the sequence of conceptual events must be controlled by a process which understands the valid state transitions in a dialogue. This idea is developed at the end of this chapter.

27.6 **Step 5: Define the dialogue state vector**

As a user progresses from window to window through a dialogue, the application must save what might be called the dialogue's working storage or **state vector**. In the general case, the dialogue state vector will be composed as follows:

```
01      Dialogue state vector
        02      Dialogue Identity
        02      Dialogue State Variable
        02      Dialogue Context Data
                        (local variables, including running totals,
                        attributes of master entities and such like)
        02      Dialogue Currencies
                        (pointers to current rows of database tables)
```

For a specific dialogue, not all these variables may be needed.

The need for context data to be stored

It is clear that several windows may be involved in one dialogue. In the example given earlier, some data is carried forward from one window to the next, via context data.

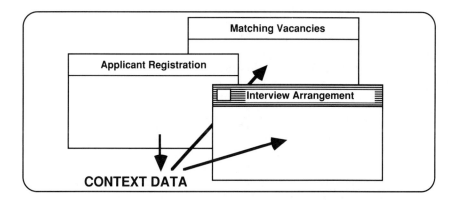

This 'context data' might be identified and documented by redrawing the input structure to include data items which form part of an event or enquiry trigger, but need not be input at the relevant moment, since they have been input earlier. An example is shown on the next page.

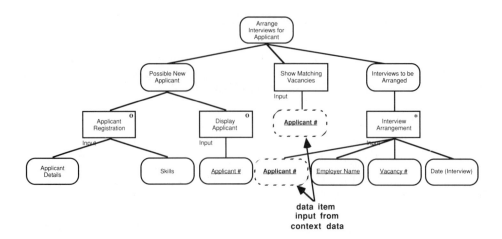

data item
input from
context data

Having input the applicant details or located him/her by enquiry, the user will not want to reenter the applicant identity when making the enquiry for vacancies which match the applicant's skills, or arranging an interview.

Further, having displayed the matching vacancies, the user will not want to reenter the employer name and the vacancy identity in order to arrange each interview. However, this data must be obtained by one of the mechanisms described earlier (such as 'copy and paste' or 'point and grab') rather than by retrieval from context data, since there are many vacancies to choose from.

Dialogue design is all about helping the user to progress through the dialogue with the least effort, without needless repetition of data entry. This implies the need to save context data for each user dialogue.

So far we have identified one variable which must be stored in the context data of an Arrange-Interviews-For-Applicant dialogue, Applicant Num.

The need for dialogue identity to be stored

The possibility of opening many windows on one terminal means that two quite independent functions or dialogues may be carried out on that terminal. We've already introduced one example, the parallel entry by a placement consultant of an Applicant Registration and Entry of a New Skill. For a more complicated example, consider two dialogues of one type (Arrange-Interviews-For-Applicant) being carried out on the same terminal.

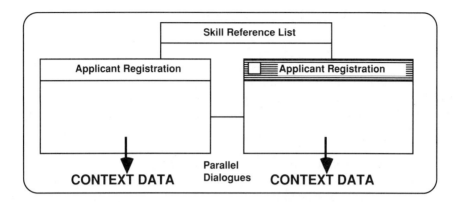

Suppose the placement consultant starts an Applicant Registration in one window, then starts another Applicant Registration in another window, then decides to back out the original Applicant Registration. Is the second Applicant Registration backed out also? The answer must be no, because these are independent dialogues.

This should not be a problem if the dialogues are truly independent. The only difference between this and a traditional multi-user system is that the two threads are active on the same end-user terminal.

In the general case, this means that several sets of context data (one per dialogue) may have to be saved for one terminal. However, theory can all too often be simpler than practice. It may be that there are problems with doing this using specific implementation-level products.

So now we have identified a second variable which must be stored in the context data of an Arrange-Interviews-For-Applicant dialogue, the **dialogue identity**, to distinguish one dialogue from another. In practice, what should we use as the dialogue identity? The Applicant Num is not sufficient to identify an Arrange-Interviews-For-Applicant dialogue, since other parallel dialogues might use the same key, but there are two other possibilities.

Assuming we rule out the possibility of a dialogue crossing from one terminal to another, the dialogue identity might be composed of the terminal identity plus a sequence number allocated by the software we design.

In a specific UIMS, it is probable we can identify a dialogue by the unique reference number given by the UIMS to the first data entry window in the dialogue. It is likely we can then create each subsequent window in the dialogue as a 'child' of this first window. We assume here that either each child carries the 'parent' reference number, or there is a function to find the 'parent' of any window.

The need for a state variable to be stored

Given that a dialogue progresses through a sequential series of defined states, the designer must implement the constraint that some things (some input events) are allowable in one state and not in another. There are two ways to do this:

- by designing modality into the user-interface
- by program design.

If the first is impossible, then the sequence of conceptual events must be controlled by a process which understands the valid state transitions in a dialogue. So now we have identified a third variable which must be stored in the context data of an Arrange-Interviews-For-Applicant dialogue, that is, a **state variable** enabling us to test what state the dialogue has reached.

The same design problem from the viewpoint of JSP

In terms of JSP there is a 'multi-threading clash' in any multi-user environment, and it can be seen that we have developed a state vector, much as JSP proposes. The standard JSP solution to this problem proceeds as follows.

Design a process to handle a single thread

At this stage, the process maintains the thread's variables in its 'local data' or 'state vector'. In our example, the local data for a single-threaded dialogue is:

```
01      Dialogue state vector
    02      Dialogue Instance Variables
        03      Applicant Num
```

Invert the process so that it processes only one input message at a time

At this stage, the process also maintains the thread's state variable in its 'local data' or 'state vector'. For example:

```
01      Dialogue state vector
    02      Dialogue State Variable
    02      Dialogue Instance Variables
        03      Applicant Num
```

Generalise the process so that it processes all entities

At this stage, the process must store/retrieve the thread's variables in/from a table or file, using the thread's identity as a key. For example:

```
01      Dialogue state vector
    02      Dialogue Identity
    02      Dialogue State Variable
    02      Dialogue Instance Variables
        03      Applicant Num
```

27.7 **Step 6: Code the dialogue management**

Implement the dialogue in piecemeal fashion

Most UIMS do not provide a means for the designer to preserve the concept of a user dialogue in the code. Most seem to work on the basis that each window is a dialogue in its own right. It is not always obvious how a UIMS makes provision for managing a dialogue of the kind we are concerned with, which links several windows in a sequential pattern.

The designer is usually forced to implement the dialogue management in bits and pieces, probably in the many routines designed for the various buttons in the windows which the dialogue uses.

Implementing the dialogue as a dialogue procedure

If the designer can build a dialogue procedure to manage the dialogue, the navigation between windows, the invocation of database routines and so on, then this dialogue procedure is the right one to store a state variable to record how far a dialogue has progressed. There are three ways to implement the dialogue procedure and its state variable testing.

Using a program inversion-like technique

We can design the dialogue procedure based on the dialogue structure, apparently reading input messages from a serial file, then implement this program using the 'program inversion' technique. To implement program inversion, the dialogue procedure needs code 'at the top' which examines the state variable before doing anything else, and code to mechanically assign values to the state variable at each point where a fresh input is required.

The serial file of valid input data is already represented in dialogue structure. This dialogue structure may be elaborated to show all the error possibilities as 'out-of-sequence events', so that there are places in the program which detect these errors and reject the erroneous inputs. The trouble is, elaborating the dialogue procedure to detect and handle dialogue state errors usually means enlarging the dialogue structure by a factor of two or three times.

Using an ECD-like technique

The dialogue procedure may test each input event against the state of the state variable. If there are 3 input events, and 6 values of the state variable, then there are potentially 18 possible permutations (though many will simply be error rejections). These 18 possible permutations might be implemented as 18 distinct cases or rules in the dialogue procedure.

Using a distinct error detection process

Instead of elaborating the dialogue procedure, the designer may introduce some kind of event manager program, which tests for a dialogue state error and either calls the dialogue procedure, or calls an error handling process to display an error message in a modal message box. This is the way we recommend. There is such scope for standardisation in the error processing that much of it may be treated as outside the scope of the dialogue procedure; it can be designed and implemented in entirely separate routines.

Implement the dialogue state vector

The users of a system may have many dialogues open at once, but only one can be active at one time. This means that it must be possible to store the state vector of an inactive dialogue somewhere while the active one is being processed, then retrieve this state vector when the user reactivates the first dialogue.

TPMS environment

Traditionally, programmers have stored the dialogue state vector in a working storage or 'scratch area' associated with a terminal, but it is not quite so simple in a windows-based environment where many dialogues may be current on one terminal. Strictly, we ought to store the dialogue state vector quite separately from the database and terminal. However, if we rule out the possibility of a dialogue crossing from one terminal to another, then the terminal provides the natural place to store local variables for a dialogue.

The dialogue state vector may be stored in other ways. It can be stored in a simple array held in main store. It can be stored in a directly accessible file stored on a disk, in which case it is necessary to add read/write statements to connect/disconnect the dialogue procedure with the correct state vector for a given input. These read/write statements might be placed at the top and bottom of the dialogue process, or in a distinct file handling process.

UIMS environment

Though it may be clear how the designer is to handle concurrent windows, it is often much less obvious how concurrent dialogues are to be handled. Some UIMS cannot handle concurrent dialogues at all, a failing which may be presented as though it is designed for the benefit of the user! For those UIMS which can handle concurrent dialogues, we have to find somewhere to store the dialogue state vector.

In a specific UIMS it is probable we can identify a dialogue by the unique reference number given by the UIMS to the first data entry window in the dialogue. It is likely we can then create each subsequent window in the dialogue as a 'child' of this first window. We assume here that either each child carries the 'parent' reference number, or there is a function to find the 'parent' of any window. If the UIMS provides a way to store user-defined attributes (or rather designer-designed attributes) along with a window, then the dialogue state vector may then be implemented as attributes (not displayed on the screen) of the parent window, that is, the first data entry window in the dialogue.

Otherwise the state vector for a single dialogue may be stored in an 'invisible window' created just for the purpose of storing the local variables of a dialogue. This 'invisible window' will be created when a dialogue starts and deleted when it finishes. In the worst case imaginable, it might be necessary to store for one dialogue, an invisible copy or phantom image of every window which has been used thus far in the dialogue. To connect any event in the user interface with the relevant 'invisible window', each input event must be labelled with the identity of the dialogue it belongs to. In general this can be done by labelling each data entry window with an 'invisible attribute', Dialogue Identity, composed as described above.

27.8 **Step 7: Assemble the system**

Since the External Design has to invoke the Conceptual Model with the relevant events and enquiry triggers, and has to process the responses, the two schemas must be designed in harmony, sharing a common interface. But the processing of the Conceptual Model should be hidden as far as possible from the processing of the External Design, in sub-routines or co-routines.

Sub-routines

It is usually easy to separate the database processing from user interface processing. As long as all the data for an event can be input in one input message (or one record of an input file), the obvious strategy is to implement each database procedure as a self-contained sub-routine invoked from the dialogue procedure (or input program).

Co-routines

There are three reasons to consider implementing one event across several exchanges, only the last of which requires some kind of co-routine solution.

Physical design reason

The data for an event may be so large that it cannot be accommodated in one window or record. This problem is unlikely, and is easily solved by storing the event data in the Context Data, until all the data for an event has been collected.

Implementation constraint

Some implementation environments construct their own database update programs, but scatter the parts of what we would regard as a single database procedure around the input/output programs. We are not concerned with implementation environments which do this, since they prevent the separation of concerns we are interested in.

User-oriented reason

Despite our earlier advice, the user may insist on seeing some integrity errors reported before entering all the data for an event, especially simple integrity errors of the kind 'this entity is missing'. This means implementing the event across several exchanges. Such a 'structure clash' between events (database processing) and exchanges (window processing) needs careful attention.

Ways to implement one event across several exchanges

Event and enquiry procedures are logical commit units. If a single event must be processed across several exchanges, then there are two implementation strategies: one modifies the design, the other doesn't.

Insert a pre-event enquiry before the event procedure

Before an event is input, a pre-event enquiry may be carried out. This may be used to test for some if not all of the possible integrity errors in the data to be updated. Later, when the event has been completely input and confirmed by the user, the event procedure can be invoked.

This means inserting an enquiry procedure into the dialogue before the event procedure on the same data. Assuming we do not lock all the data which might be updated in the course of a dialogue, from the first read to the last write, there are three approaches:

A   postpone all integrity tests until the event procedure
B   repeat all integrity tests within the event procedure
C   design manual record locking, say using an indicator in database records.

Whatever approach may be used, it is difficult to accept the notion that a pre-event enquiry procedure is a program which is logically distinct from the consequent event procedure.

In approaches A and B, the pre-event enquiry is partly or completely redundant. It duplicates part of the event procedure, yet the event procedure must still be implemented as a whole. A means duplicating code, B means repeating processing as well. This duplication may lead to maintenance and performance problems.

Approach C, since it joins the enquiry procedure and the event procedure together in one success unit, clearly points to the fact that these are really part and parcel of what is logically a single database procedure.

Implement the dialogue and event procedures as co-routines

A better design strategy is to run the dialogue and event procedures as co-routines. In this way the event procedure can be maintained as a distinct module. To overcome any locking problem, approach C is recommended.

The implemented code may resemble that of the pre-event enquiry solution above, but the integrity of the logical design documentation will be maintained in the physical implementation, and no additional enquiry program need be designed or implemented.

Chapter 28

Off-line function design

This chapter gives reasons why a function may be identified as appropriate for implementation in off-line mode, and introduces a step-by-step approach to off-line function design. It looks at the design questions raised by data collection before a function and data distribution after it, including the possible separation of input and output sub-systems. It outlines guidance on the decomposition of an off-line function into programmable units, and develops the specific function model for the case study function.

28.1 The trouble with off-line functions

Most modern methodologies lead naturally to an on-line implementation. They tend to be less good at defining how *off-line* input and output processes are derived from a logical design. This chapter outlines a rational and methodical framework for the design of off-line functions, presenting the major design questions which have to be answered. However, it should be noted that this method cannot be as prescriptive as the method we have presented for developing on-line functions, for reasons which will become clear.

The ideal function is on-line

In an ideal world, each event or enquiry would be input as it happened or occurred to a user; immediately afterwards the resultant output would be presented to any interested user. Many, perhaps most, user functions are naturally implemented on-line.

At one time, network databases and on-line interfaces were considered complex and difficult to implement. But it is now recognised that an on-line database system is a natural and straightforward implementation. On-line input has greatly simplified the detection and correction of input errors. Databases have largely freed us from the tyranny of the sort program.

Off-line functions are often unsatisfactory

Not so long ago, most system functions were implemented off-line; they processed batches of input data against 'flat' master data files. But it can now be seen that flat master data files are a distorted implementation of a network database structure, and that off-line input is a clumsy and unsatisfactory device, leading to delays and difficulties in validating and processing input data.

Every off-line update function must (by definition) impose a delay between the occurrence of an event or enquiry, its input to the system, and the presentation of the event response to the user. The batching of input data weakens the ability of the system to respond to real-world events as they happen,

The sorting of input data raises the possibility that the sequence in which events truly happen is altered before they are processed, and makes it harder to interpret the consequent processing of the main database.

The storage of data in input and output sub-systems obscures the clear picture we have presented of a 3-Schema Architecture, and puts a barrier between the user and the main database of the system.

The recycling of erroneous inputs to the next running of a function means that old events get mixed up with new ones (perhaps input because the old events had apparently disappeared without trace).

Nevertheless, we shall see there are still reasons to implement functions in an off-line mode, and guidance on their design is needed.

28.2 **Steps of off-line function design**

We present seven steps of off-line function design which may reasonably be followed in the sequence given.

Step 1: Identify the off-line function
A function may be defined using the techniques in chapter 25, without necessarily committing it to either on-line or off-line implementation. This chapter gives reasons why a function may be identified as appropriate for implementation in off-line mode, introduces a step-by-step approach to off-line function design, and the case study example.

Step 2: Plan data collection and distribution
This chapter outlines the design questions raised by data collection before a function, and data distribution after it, including the possible separation of input and output sub-systems. It is important to consider these questions before completing the detailed design of the input and output files, partly because they are related to user procedure design and must be agreed with users.

Step 3: Design the I/O files
In papers not included in this book, we have considered the detailed physical design of input and output files, using as an example the data flows for the case study function.

Step 4: Decompose the function into programmable units
This chapter offers guidance on the decomposition of an off-line function into programmable units, and develops the specific function model for the case study function.

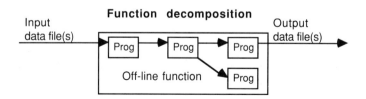

Step 5: Design each of the programs

In papers not included in this book, we have outlined a step-by-step program design method (akin to JSP), and apply it to one of the programs in the case study function.

Step 6: Combine the programs in the function

In papers not included in this book, we have explained the basic techniques for combining programs together into larger programs, run units, and systems. We show how a 'user function' is composed from co-operating programs and routines, and define design and coding rules for sub-routines and co-routines.

Step 7: Organise the running of the function

In papers not included in this book, we have outlined how functions are organised for running off-line, and the role of the operator.

Some off-line functions may be triggered from the work station of an ordinary user. Other off-line functions, usually because they consume expensive or limited resources (user time, computer time, special stationery, an expensive printer, etc.) may be restricted to be run only by a special user or a small group of users. The special user role might be called a 'system administrator', but we shall use the term '**operator**' to mean the user role with special responsibility for running off-line functions and distributing off-line output to the interested parties.

This chapter goes on to say a little more about steps 1, 2 and 4. The other steps are not defined in this book, but in other papers we have written (Model Systems, 1993).

28.3 Step 1: Identify the off-line function

At the beginning of this chapter we said that the ideal function is on-line; every off-line update function raises problems. So why introduce any off-line update function at all?

Suppose the user who inputs an event or enquiry is interested in seeing the output, but the output is too large for immediate presentation on the user's screen. The obvious solution is to present the output in the form of a paper report, printed out at the user's work station. Despite the use of a printer, this is really still an on-line function. But it is only a small step from here to a function for which the user's output request is placed into a queue within some kind of off-line function schedule, to be run from some other work station, by an operator.

Reasons to implement a function in off-line mode

There are several general reasons to do with timing, organisation structure, ergonomics, system efficiency and end-user input output device technology, and one very specific reason.

The natural input user is unable to run the function
If the user has insufficient time, authority or equipment, the function may have to be run by an operator who has access to these resources.

The trigger is a date or time
If the off-line function is triggered by a date or time event, and there is no ordinary user whose job it is to run functions according to a calendar or clock, then the function may have to be run by an operator who has this responsibility.

The logical commit unit is too large for on-line processing
If a logical commit unit for an event or enquiry is so large that to run it on-line would lock out too many users for too long a time (often true of a date or time events, and so-called table maintenance events) then the function may have to be run by an operator when no on-line user is connected to the system.

System efficiency must be improved
If efficiency is important (it isn't always), an off-line function may provide a faster or otherwise more practical way to process data (it doesn't always).

The data files are to be reused
A big advantage of off-line functions over on-line functions is that the input, output and intermediate data streams are permanent, so they can be used for purposes other than the immediate running of the function, such as security, recovery, audit, testing and subsequent input to other off-line functions.

The input arrives from distributed or remote sources
It may be impossible to establish a real-time connection between the system and the real world in which the input events arise. (This is true of the case study example which follows).

The output destinations are distributed or remote
If the user who runs the function is not the only one interested in the output, and it is impossible to send it immediately to all the other interested parties because:

- they are not connected 'on-line' to the system
- they are connected but cannot be interrupted
- the software to broadcast outputs is not available

then the function may have to be run by an operator who has the responsibility for distributing output to the other interested parties.

The input arrives in batches

Looking at the input to off-line functions, it can be seen that off-line enquiry functions usually process just one enquiry, but off-line update functions usually process a **batch** of events. Off-line update functions are used where the system only gets to hear of events via the postal system, or some other off-line mechanism, and these events arrive in batches which are ready for processing (this is true of the case study example which follows).

Case study

In the case study introduced in earlier chapters, an obvious candidate for off-line implementation is the function F3 which processes the data flow carrying Interview Results. First, here is the DFD.

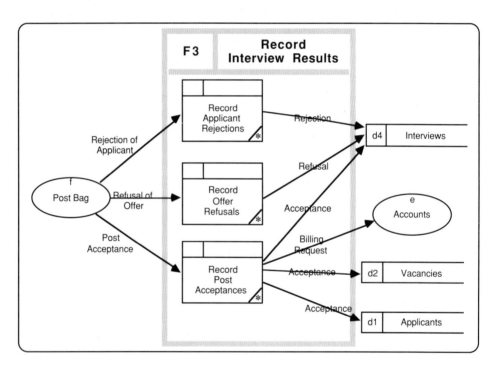

This is not in any way meant to be a formal specification of the function. Having identified the need for an off-line function during the relatively informal process of analysing the system using DFDs, the designer should then start to draft the specific function model for this function.

The first step is to draw what might be called a function boundary diagram, showing the data flows which the function consumes and produces.

Function boundary diagram

Input
data flow(s) → Off-line function → Output
data flow(s) →

As is not unusual, the function boundary diagram for the case study function is significantly different in appearance from the DFD. After further thought we have decided to send the 'billing requests' (following successful interview results or 'post acceptances') in the form of 'skeleton employer invoices', onto which the accounts department can type extra data, such as an invoice number.

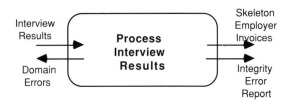

28.4 **Step 2: Plan data collection and distribution**

It is hard to prescribe a method for designing data collection and distribution; not only because these things are dependent on balancing the concerns we listed earlier (timing, organisation structure, ergonomics, system efficiency and end-user input output device technology) in ways which cannot be methodically prescribed, but also because there are design questions inherent in the design of off-line functions, which counter any attempt to be completely rational and methodical. These are to do with defining the scope of a function, and the system which contains it.

Any off-line function may be represented in an overview as shown below.

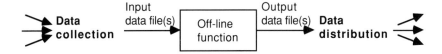

Data collection: design questions

Before an off-line function is run, it is necessary to collect the input data. The designer should answer design questions about the input source, input batching and the possible separation or integration of the input sub-system.

Input source

Who will provide the output? How will it arrive - by data network, post, verbal communication or other means?

Input batching

In collecting events for one running of an off-line function, or dividing up the processing within one running, events may be batched. The designer may usefully ask whether the input naturally arrives in batches identified with:

- a place: local business unit, office, site, field operation unit
- a person: data gatherer, stock auditor, input clerk
- a period: day, week, month, other business cycle or operation cycle.

The implications of this for off-line function design are mainly to do with its effect on how often the function is run, and how the outputs (including error reports) will be distributed. If there is a requirement to process the output before the next time period is complete: then running the function once per period is the natural thing to do. (See also output batching below).

Separation of input sub-system versus integration of input data

Very often, off-line input data has to be stored for archive or audit purposes, or to assist the correction and reinput of mistaken inputs.

This may mean extending design of the input file(s) to the point where some kind of database structure is required. In which case the designer may choose to regard this as the database of a distinct sub-system. On the other hand, there may be reasons to do with keeping track of all changes to stored data, to integrate the input data within the data model of the main system.

Data distribution: design questions

After an off-line function has been run, it is necessary to distribute the output reports to all the interested parties. The designer should answer design questions about the output destination, output batching and the possible separation or integration of the output sub-system.

Output destination

Who will use the output? How will it get to users - by data network, post, verbal communication or other means?

Output batching

The designer may usefully ask whether the output should be produced in batches identified with a place, person or period of time. These batches may not correspond to the input batches. If output must be directed back to the source from which the input came, then processing each natural input batch separately should help the designer to direct the output to the right person or place. Otherwise some kind of sorting may be required.

Separation of output sub-system versus integration of output data

Off-line output data may have to be stored for archive or audit purposes, or to assist the reuse, recycling or other processing of the output, after it has been generated from the main database.

In which case the designer may choose to treat the output data as the database of a distinct sub-system. On the other hand, there may be a need, perhaps to do with keeping a history of all outputs, to integrate the output data within the data model of the main system.

After reviewing a case study example and discussing error handling, later sections expand on the separation of input/output sub-systems, and the integration of input/output data within the data model.

Case study: data collection design questions

Input source

Who will provide the input? Employers will. How will it arrive? By post. A pre-printed reply-paid postcard is enclosed with each Interview Arrangement, so that the Employer can return Interview Results, needing only to tick the result and perhaps enter a date.

Business Reply Service	**2**		Employer	4569	CFC Inc
			Vacancy	62	Data manager
Hi-Ho Recruitment Ltd			Applicant	74849	Linda Morton
7 Dwarves Road			Interview Date	01 / 04 / 93	
Mirror-on-the-wall			Interview Result		
			Applicant Rejection ☐		
			Refusal of Post ☐		
			Post Acceptance ☐ Start Date		

Input batching

Input naturally arrives in batches identified with a period of time. Interview Results are collected from the post-bag and keyed daily onto a serial file via a key-to-disc system.

Separation of input sub-system versus integration of input data

Should the designer either break off an input sub-system, or integrate the input data within the data model of the main system? It may be helpful to do the former. The Interview Results file might be regarded as the database of an input sub-system, not connected to the main data model, but perhaps stored using the same database management system. We shall return to this later.

Case study: data distribution design questions

There are three output reports, to which we can apply the standard design questions.

Skeleton Employer Invoices report

Output destination

Who will use the output? The accounts department are interested in the report, because they must invoice the employers. How will it get to users? By internal mail. The system need not report any interview results to applicants, since it is assumed that employers will inform successful applicants, and cancel any consequent interviews, outside of the scope of the system.

Separation of output sub-system versus integration of output data

There is no need to integrate the output data within the data model of the main system. But the designer might break off the output data as the database of a distinct sub-system, as we shall discuss.

Domain error report

Output destination

Who will use the output? Missing data items and domain errors are cleared up by the input clerks, who call the Employer directly. How will it get to users? Error messages will be displayed on the screens used by input clerks.

Separation of output sub-system versus integration of output data

There is no need to either separate the output data as the database of a distinct sub-system, or integrate the output data within the data model of the main system.

Integrity error report

Output destination
Who will use the output? The input clerks responsible for the original input must investigate (perhaps by calling employers or applicants on the telephone) why an error has occurred. They may as a result have to reinput one or more of yesterday's interview results on today's file. How will it get to users? By internal mail to the input clerks' manager, who allocates the processing of the report to one or more of his staff.

Separation of output sub-system versus integration of output data
There is no need to integrate the output data within the data model of the main system. There could be a need to treat the output file as the database of a distinct sub-system, since the output data may be recycled after it has generated from the main database. Later however, we elect to store and re-process the original inputs instead.

28.5 Separation of an input sub-system

There are many cases where data collection becomes sufficiently complex that it is best regarded as a system in its own right.

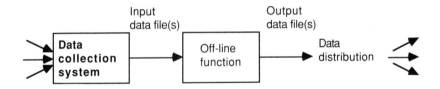

There are four questions to be answered:

- Why break off an input sub-system?
- How is the division between systems made?
- Is SSADM suitable for the design of sub-systems?
- If or when SSADM is not suitable, what is?

Why break off an input sub-system?

In general, a business may require input data to be stored, before processing against the main database, in a data structure which is readily accessible and modifiable. This data structure need not be connected to the main data model, but may be stored using the same database management system, to take advantage of facilities such as recovery, user access control, usage accounting, etc.

The need to keep input data separate from the main database may be clear where part of the function of a business is to collect data and assess it before the data is formally 'approved' or 'rejected' for registration in the main database. For example, to support the investigation of an applicant (person or organisation) applying for some kind of 'membership' of the business at hand. Alternatively, off-line input data may have to be stored and processed away from the main database in order to meet archive or audit requirements, or assist the correction and reinput of mistaken inputs.

Moving away from these clear-cut cases, the designer may find that even a trivial requirement (say to remove domain or syntax errors) justifies regarding the input processing as a sub-system.

How is the division between systems made?

Having decided to treat the input as a distinct sub-system, then the next and fundamental step is to define the interface between the input sub-system and the main system. Is it possible to offer any guidance as to what will be in this interface? Yes.

Assuming the Conceptual Model of the main system has been defined, then as far as the main system is concerned, what it 'wants' (to be anthropomorphic) is an input data stream of clean events and enquiries. The main system does not want to be concerned with batch totals, data item domain errors, or anything but events and enquiries ready for processing against the main database.

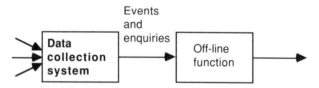

Is SSADM suitable for the design of input sub-systems?

It may turn out that the input sub-system requires considerable design effort. Once the decision is made to treat data collection as a distinct input sub-system, then it is possible that the input data structure is non-trivial enough to require data modelling. SSADM could be applied to the sub-system.

Note that the entity data model of the sub-system will store the events of the main system. Also, the events of the sub-system may not exactly match the events of the main system. It may turn out that a simpler, possibly more generic, view of input events should be taken.

However, an input sub-system is more of a physical system than a logical one. The sub-system is not directly connected to the real world by outputs which seek to control it, so the entity data model of the input sub-system is not so clearly a model of the real world as that of the main system.

If or when SSADM is not suitable, what is?

If the events of the main system are simply stored as entities in the sub-system, and they are input one at time into this sub-system, then rapid application development, using an application generator, will probably be sufficient for the development of the sub-system.

28.6 **Integration of input data within the data model**

Taking the opposite approach to that of the last section, there are cases where input data (the events of the entity event model) must be stored within the main database, more or less closely related to existing stored data, before these events are processed against the main database. There are two questions to be answered:

- Why integrate input data within the main data model?
- Does SSADM adequately cover these cases?

Why integrate input data within the main data model?

There may be a requirement to keep track of all changes to stored data, to connect the audit trail of input events to the entities which they update. This kind of requirement may be simply stated as 'keep a history of all changes made to the stored data', but it is very difficult to meet.

Does SSADM adequately cover these cases?

Yes and no. On the one hand, this kind of situation may be viewed as a merely complex entity data modelling problem. On the other hand, the requirement 'keep a history of all changes made to the stored data' may double or triple the size of a system and it turns out that there are many difficult problems to resolve.

Some specific questions include how to:

- link events to entities (especially entities yet to be created)
- store events with missing or invalid key values
- distinguish real-world changes from corrections of mistakes
- store changes or corrections to events, before they have been processed
- store invalid or mistaken events
- delete the invalid entities created by invalid events.

Warning

In general we advise against this approach. It is not at all obvious how to build an entity data model which includes the events which update it. This is something of a 'black hole' in current methodologies, not just SSADM.

28.7 **Separation of an output sub-system**

There are cases where data distribution becomes sufficiently complex that it is best regarded as a system in its own right.

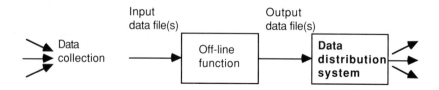

There are several questions to be answered:

- Why break off an output sub-system?
- How is the division between systems made?
- Is SSADM suitable for the design of sub-systems?
- If or when SSADM is not suitable, what is?

Why break off an output sub-system?

An output data store may need to be treated as a database in its own right when output data must be processed in reasonably elaborate ways after it has been generated from the main database. What does 'reasonably elaborate' mean? It probably means that the business requires that off-line output data must be stored for one or more of:

- history
          archive
          audit
- reinput
          recycling for input to the same function
          reuse by other functions of the system
- a further stage of output
          transmission across a network to many users.
          transfer into a different system (spreadsheet, word processor)
- different forms of output
          reformulation into different user views
          further processing before delivery to the user
- better performance for 'enquiry only' mode functions
          faster access to data
          reduction of multi-user conflicts.

How is the division between systems made?

Having decided to treat the output as a distinct sub-system, then the next and fundamental step is to define the interface between the output sub-system and the main system. Is it possible to offer any guidance as to what will be in this interface? Yes.

Assuming the Conceptual Model of the main system has been defined, then as far as the main system is concerned, what it 'wants' (to be anthropomorphic) is to output a data stream of simple responses to events and enquiries. The main system does not want to be concerned with page headers, control totals, or anything to do with the presentation of data in a two-dimensional report.

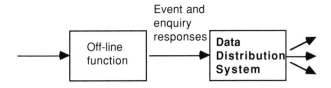

Note however that the response to an event or enquiry may be large and complex. See the next paper for examples.

Is SSADM suitable for the design of sub-systems?

Once the data distribution system is viewed as a distinct sub-system, then it seems unlikely that SSADM will be very helpful. Some of the 'entities' to be modelled in the output sub-system are likely to be system-oriented things such as:

- function scheduling points (person, place, point in time)
- end-users to whom output is directed
- query programs which may be run.

Other entities in the sub-system may be unnormalised aggregates of entities in the main system, so entity data modelling is inappropriate. And since it is doubtful that these things can be updated, entity event modelling will be inappropriate.

If or when SSADM is not suitable, what is?

It seems likely that JSP techniques will be more appropriate for the development of an output sub-system.

28.8 **Integration of output data within the data model**

Taking the opposite approach to that of the last section, there might be cases where output data must be stored within the main database, more or less closely related to existing stored data, after this output has been generated from the main database. If so, there would be two questions to be answered:

- Why integrate output data within the main data model?
- Does SSADM adequately cover these cases?

Why integrate output data within the main data model?

There may be a requirement to keep a history of all outputs, connected to the stored data of the main system. But it is hard to imagine realistic requirements, except at very low levels of detail, where a single entity represents a single output from the system.

Output reports usually contain higher level aggregates of data. They are unnormalised, so it would be difficult and probably unwise to consider them within the main entity data modelling and database design activities. In any case, there would presumably be no need to provide any update functionality for such data.

Does SSADM adequately cover these cases?

If there are cases where output data has to be included within the entity data model, then it is doubtful that SSADM will be helpful. It has nothing to say about how to store output data in a database, or how to design the processing of this data. It seems likely that the designer will be thrown back upon JSP techniques.

28.9 Step 4: Decompose the function into programmable units

Function decomposition strategies

Having defined the input and output files, their structure, record contents, and so on, the designer must define the programs to process them. It may be possible to write one program for each function, but it is usually better to decompose a function into distinct programs which can be designed and coded separately.

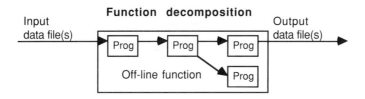

Function decomposition

This chapter offers guidance on the decomposition of an off-line function into programmable units. Readers may find it helpful to read Jackson (1975) on how to compose a function by combining programs, especially the sections on how programs communicate via intermediate data streams, or notional files.

Separation of concerns

The general criterion for dividing an off-line input function into distinct programs is 'separation of concerns'. This phrase covers a number of overlapping reasons and techniques for dividing an off-line function into programs. We propose a four step approach to decomposition of a function into programs:

4.1	Apply the 3-Schema Architecture
4.2	Separate the processing of input and output data
4.3	Establish I/O correspondences and resolve clashes (after JSP)
4.4	Design for consecutive runnings of the function

Case study

The function outline is shown below.

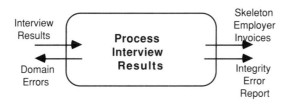

Step 4.1: Apply the 3-Schema Architecture

The 3-Schema Architecture was in the mind of the methodologist who developed the standard SSADM4 template for user function definition, called the 'universal function model', which is why the two ideas can be mapped onto each other as neatly as this diagram shows.

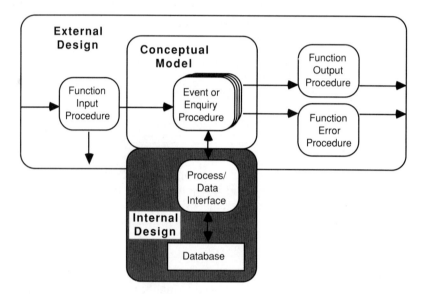

It can be seen that the separation of concerns expressed by the universal function model is no more than a pictorial expression of the 3-Schema Architecture. According to both, the designer would expect to separate:

- the user interface from the database
- domain rules from integrity rules.

For any specific user function, this universal model is always wrong. The specific function model for a user function may resemble the universal model closely, or barely resemble it at all. However, there are several points in favour of starting a user function definition with the universal function model in mind. It provides the designer with a general model which covers all kinds of user function, and helps the designer to:

- analyse and specify complex user functions
- suppress detail at the early stages of specification
- design cohesive, loosely coupled, modules.

Let us consider these points in turn.

Helping the analyst to analyse and specify complex user functions

Looking in more detail at the data streams between procedures, the universal function model helps the analyst to analyse and specify complex user functions by thinking about the content of each data stream in turn. In the case of an update user function, the input procedure may be elaborate, dealing with a large amount of input data, representing several events and enquiries, and there may be a complex error reports to produce, beside the main output of the user function.

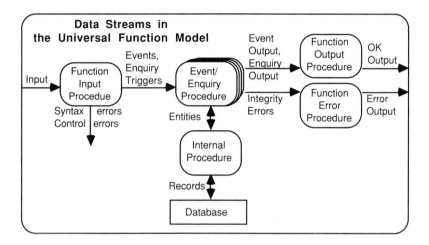

Helping the analyst to suppress detail at the early stages of specification

The model may help the analyst at the beginning of defining a user function to concentrate on what matters (events and enquiry triggers and the conceptual procedures they trigger) and to suppress less important detail (error reports, especially syntax errors) until later. So the analyst should specify the important parts first.

Helping the analyst to design cohesive, loosely coupled modules

Each user function is viewed as a series of external procedures (with no access to database) and conceptual procedures (with no access to user interface), communicating via intermediate data streams.

The separation of a user function into different procedures to deal with different kinds of system requirement gives obvious benefits in terms of system robustness and amendability. The modules should be cohesive, containing code concerned with the same area of user functionality and loosely coupled, easily separated from other modules and reusable in a different context.

Case study

Using SSADM's universal function model as a template, but turning it on its side, the designer may draft the following specific function model. We have used a DFD style notation, for the want of any more universal standard notation ('UPM' here is the SSADM term for an event procedure).

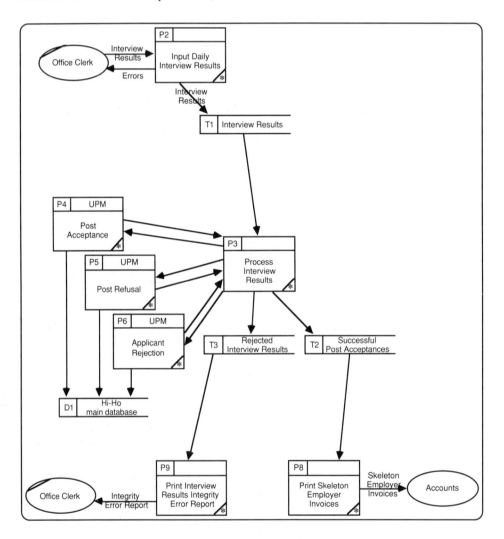

There is no Internal Design, because it is assumed that each entity becomes a record in the database, and no Process/Data Interface is necessary.

P2: Input Daily Interview Results

The input program detects and reports any domain and control errors in each input event/record. An example of a domain error in an input event/record might be 'Applicant id not numeric'. An example of a control error might be 'Total Interview Results for Vacancy not = Total on Vacancy Batch Trailer'.

P3: Process Interview Results

For each input event/record at a time, the program P3:

- invokes the relevant database update routine
- if it finds an integrity error, rejects the input and reports it
- if it finds no integrity error, processes the input
- produces an output file of valid Post Acceptances (for dummy invoices).

An example of a integrity error might be 'Vacancy Withdrawn', showing an entity in the wrong state for the input event type.

P4, P5 and P6

For the Conceptual Model, it is assumed in this chapter that the event procedures for the events Post Acceptance, Post Refusal and Applicant Rejection are implemented as database update routines as directly as possible.

P8: Print Interview Results Error Report

Picking up the intermediate file of interview results which have failed because of an integrity error, P8 prints the error report.

P9: Print Skeleton Employer Invoices

Picking up the intermediate file successful interview results or 'post acceptances', P9 prints 'skeleton employer invoices', onto which the accounts department can type extra data, such as an invoice number.

Step 4.2:   Separate the processing of input and output data

The office clerks need to be able to create, update and delete (CRUD) the input data via an on-line interface. Both the output reports might have to be reprinted, for example because of some kind of paper wreck in the printer, without running the database update routines again. So there is a need for distinct input and output sub-systems.

Step 4.3:   Establish I/O correspondences and resolve clashes

In dividing an off-line function into distinct procedures, communicating via intermediate data streams, JSP techniques make a large contribution. The first thing to learn from JSP is that there must be sufficient correspondence between output and input for the former to be generated from the latter. If there is not, then either more input data has to be provided, or there is a 'structure clash' of some kind.

The designer may separate programs in order to deal with structure clashes, notably separating different processing sequences (order clashes) and different groupings of data (boundary clashes). Elsewhere, we review four kinds of structure clash and standard solutions to them, in the light of off-line functions. The four kinds of clash are:

- order clashes
- boundary clashes
- multi-threading clashes
- scheduling clashes.

You might imagine scheduling clashes would not be found within a function, since we began by defining a function as processing which occurs together, rather than at separate times. But of course it may turn out there is a reason to divide an off-line function into processing stages, with outputs produced at different times.

This may arise during physical design, when it is discovered that there is a physical limit on the number of input and output devices (e.g. only one printer). Or the production of outputs may have to be timetabled separately to resolve an order clash in one part of the function. In our example, it is clear that processes P1, P2, P3, P8 and P9 all run at different times, and might be regarded as five distinct **system functions**, all supporting the one user function.

Case study

P3 receives only error codes and has insufficient input data to generate the error reports. This is rectified by connecting it to the error message database and passing error messages through the intermediate file to P9.

 P8 and P9 have insufficient employer data, and so we need to add P7 (an enquiry procedure designed to be reusable by both programs) for them to retrieve employer details from the database. Finally, there is an order clash, because to print one dummy invoice per employer, all of the Post Acceptances have to be sorted by employer. This is resolved by writing the Post Acceptances into a transient data store which can be read in employer sequence.

Step 4.4: Design for consecutive runnings of a function

So far we have only considered one running of the function. Finally, we must define by whom, when and how the function is to be run, taking into account the fact that the function will be run repeatedly. The final specific function model is shown below. Changes made at step 4 are annotated 4a, 4b, 4c, and 4d.

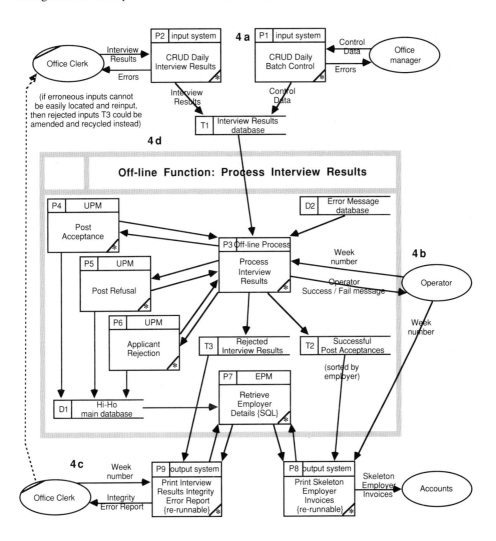

P1: Create Update Delete (CRUD) Daily Batch Control

In order to control the data entry on a daily basis, some kind of data management function may be designed to enter authorisations, dates, batch controls and so on. Let us say that office clerks are not allowed to enter any interview results into the system until the office manager has created a slot in the database for today's interview results, and entered a batch control total. P1 is the on-line function which enables the office manager to do this. We do not fully define this function in this chapter.

The operator role

The designer must design how the running of the main parts of the off-line function will be triggered. This might be automatically, by date or time, or from an automated operating schedule, but more likely the responsibility will be handed to an operator.

Since this function runs once per week, let us say that on a Friday night the operator triggers each of P3, P8 and P9 in turn, by entering the week number. At the end of each, a message will be returned to the operator. Since P3 can only be run once, if the operator tries to run it a second time, it should return an error message to the operator. To do this, knowledge of how many times it has been run must be held in some kind of control database, perhaps one designed to support the operating schedule as a whole: this database is not shown here.

Notice that each part of the function may be run separately from the others. One reason for this is to facilitate the rerunning of P8 or P9 should there be some problem with the printer.

Reinputting events/input records

In off-line function design, there is no avoiding the need for users to correct and resubmit individual inputs. These may be processed in a special error correction running of the function, or added to the next normal running of the function.

It is always possible to input corrected data as though from scratch. But since the input data has already been collected once, and it may require only a minor correction, it may be helpful to design automated assistance for the reinput of data. There are many ways to do this.

Reprocess the output data

The output error report may be (or be accompanied by) a file of rejected inputs, so that these can be amended and reinput (perhaps merged with the next normal input file).

Reprocess the input data

Off-line input data may be stored, both for archive or audit purposes, and to assist the correction and reinput of mistaken inputs. This may mean extending design of the input file(s) to the point where some kind of a database structure is required

In an input database, designed to record all of the input data, the designer may extend the input file specification so that it is be possible to mark inputs as accepted or rejected, and to copy and amend rejected inputs from one part of the database to another.

Is an input database to be supported by entity data model, as though it were the

Conceptual Model of a distinct system? Or is to to be treated as a transient data store, within the External Design of the overall system? These questions were considered earlier. At least three error processing strategies are possible:

1) a mechanism may be designed for copying corrected inputs from one 'input file' to the next, so that they are processed in the next running of the input function
2) the function may be designed to process two or more inputs files, selecting corrected inputs from previous input file
3) the function may be run on an *ad hoc* basis to process corrected inputs from any previous input files.

Extra functionality may be needed to report on errors which have not been corrected after a certain time limit, and kill off errors which cannot be corrected.

Organisations may find it helpful to set standards for how this kind of input sub-system will work, rather than permit a wide variety of more or less equally effective designs to be used.

Footnote
Reinputting data which has been rejected from an off-line input file is bound to disturb the natural sequence of data input and increase the number of events processed out of sequence. Inserting the corrected input data at the start of the next input file won't necessarily help, since the input may fail again and have to be resubmitted the time after next, and so on.

28.10 Further steps of program design and implementation

The central process, Process Interview Results, is used as an example of program design in other papers we have written (Model Systems, 1993).

Implementing an off-line function using co-routines
In implementing a function, the designer should remember that an intermediate data file, connecting two programs, may be replaced by direct communication between the programs. The main advantage is increased processing speed. The main disadvantage is the loss of the intermediate file, which might have uses beyond the immediate purpose of the function.

The design of two communicating programs should always be completed as though the intermediate file is a physical file. Jackson (1975) showed how to make the two programs into co-routines, using the technique of program inversion to modify the code produced.

Chapter 29

Error testing
and handling

This chapter looks at how rules and constraints should be classified, specified and tested, and how contravention of the rules will be reported and corrected.

29.1 **Business rules and business policies**

Business rules

In part four we had a great deal to say about business rules, or constraints as they are sometimes called. We specify these rules in the entity event model and code them in the conceptual procedures or database update routines.

There is a big advantage to specifying a business rule in this way. The rule is specified and coded only once. It will always be applied within the Conceptual Model, wherever or however the event appears in the External Design. You can design as many different on-line dialogues and off-line functions as you like; you don't have to do anything to specify the rule within them. If the rule changes, you only have to change one piece of code.

Avoidance of redundancy

It is clearly against the philosophy of maximising reuse to code two or more system components to do the same job. And yet there are many designers who do replicate business rules unnecessarily. It is very common to find that a business rule for an input event is tested by two different sets of code, one External and one Conceptual.

Consider the rule that an Applicant must be registered with at least one Skill. One designer may write some code to validate the input event within the External Design, as a validation rule on an input window. Another may write some code to test the same the rule in the Conceptual Model, as an integrity check made when updating the database. We strongly recommend against this duplication, not because it slows down system performance but because it leads to nightmares in system maintenance.

Business policies

There is however a disadvantage to implementing a business rule in the Conceptual Model. The rule is invariant. Often, what the analyst at first thinks is a mandatory rule to be applied to every case, turns out to be optional in exceptional cases.

In Hi-Ho for example, is it really true that every Applicant must have at least one Skill to be registered on the system? What if the users say that every now and then they do register the odd Applicant without any Skills. They do this where they have good reason to believe that an Employer will waive the requirement for formal matching by Skill Type because of the exceptional personal qualities of the Applicant.

There are a number of possible design strategies here. You could say the odd Applicant must be handled outside of the system being designed. Or you could insist that the odd Applicant was registered as having a Skill they don't really have. Or you might relax the 'at-least-one-detail' rule to handle exceptional cases like this.

The problem with the last approach is that the rule is useful for the majority of cases. It seems a shame to throw away the rule altogether. What we need is a way of implementing this as a **business policy** rather than a rule. We are currently toying with the idea of using an expert system for this kind of rule, however it is also possible to transfer the rule from the Conceptual Model into the External Design, so that it is applied on one or more routes into the system, but not all.

29.2 **Classifying rules or constraints**

The designer may begin designing a system under the assumption that all data is input correctly and business rules are automatically maintained. But sooner or later the designer must design how the system will detect contravention of these rules, and respond to errors. A classification of rules is needed, and one follows:

- Domain rule (usually tested in the External Design)
  predefined data type
  user-defined data type
  local data type

- Integrity rule (must be tested in Conceptual Model)
  referential integrity error
  non-referential integrity error

- External rule (must be tested in External Design)
  control item error
  dialogue-state error.

  The classification is a rough one. The three main headings are not entirely mutually exclusive. You might wish to argue against the classification, but we find it helpful. First, it helps designers to divide error detection in the methodology between rules which may be tested in the External Design and rules which should be tested within the Conceptual Model. Second, it helps designers to assess how far an application generator can generate the necessary code, more or less automatically.

Domain rule (or 'syntax error')

A domain rule is a rule which defines the valid range of values for a data item. A domain rule can be tested at the user interface without reference to the database, but it may instead be treated as an integrity rule, as discussed below. Domain rules were illustrated in chapter 21; this section recaps the definitions without examples.

  Implementation tools usually expect a domain rule to be attached to a data item, and triggered by an attempt to enter a data item on a screen. A typical implementation tool may offer three ways to specify a domain rule, which we name as follows. A **predefined data type** is a domain provided by the implementation environment, such as text, number and date. A **user-defined data type** is a domain defined by the analyst, either as an alternative to the predefined data types, or as a sub-type or extension of one of them. A **local data type** is the range of values for a data item allowed by the context of its input, a local refinement of a predefined or user-defined data type, not specified in the central repository or data dictionary.

  A fourth kind of domain rule, an **inter data item error** where the value of one input data item conflicts with another on display, can be treated as a local data type. So you might declare the validation rule 'Promotion Grade > Employee Grade', assuming both are on external display. But where one or both data items have to be retrieved from the database, it may be better to treat such an error check as an integrity rule.

Integrity rule

An integrity rule is a rule applicable to an event, which is tested by comparing the event data with the state of database. It may also be called a 'semantic error', 'business rule', or 'constraint'.

In several places we have suggested that integrity rules should be attached to events, not to entities or record types. The methodology specifies an integrity rule in terms of the 'valid prior states' of an entity when an event occurs, tested by a fail condition in the event procedure. However, application generators usually expect an integrity rule to be attached to a record type in the database, and to be triggered by any kind of event which stores or deletes a record instance. Integrity rules may be divided into two kinds.

A **referential integrity error** is a constraint which can be specified in terms of the mandatory nature of a relationship in the entity data model or database. Most application generators expect the stored data to be specified in the form of relational database; from this they can automatically impose constraints defined by the mandatory nature of a relationship in the entity data model; for example, there must be a master entity before a detail entity can be created.

A **non-referential integrity rule** is a constraint which cannot be defined in terms of the mandatory nature of a relationship in the entity data model or database. An application generator may provide both procedural and declarative mechanisms for implementing these.

Some integrity rules, especially inter data item errors, may be declared as domain rules attached to data items in database records. Some integrity rules, especially 'cascade' and 'restrict' deletes, may be declared as validation rules attached to records or relationships between records; these are often, but wrongly, included under the title of referential integrity error. Some integrity rules may be coded in a sub-routine which is hooked to a data item or record type in the database. We suggest it is best not to use any of these mechanisms, but to code all integrity rules in event procedures or the OO equivalent as described in chapters 17 and 18.

On distinguishing domain rules from integrity rules

The distinction between domain rules and integrity rules may be blurred. Consider for example the data item Country Name, which has a restricted but lengthy range of values. Should you define the valid range of Country Names as a data item domain in the External Design? Or should you specify country as an entity type in the Conceptual Model, so that an invalid Country Name is an integrity error? You need an analysis question to help you to sort this out. The analysis question we propose is:

- May the end-user introduce a new domain value while the system is running?

If yes, then the domain should be made an entity type in the data model, under the control of the users, and the rule becomes an integrity rule. If no, then the domain is better defined as a domain rule, which can only be altered by some kind of recompilation of the system.

Having said this, any domain might be represented in the database, as an operational master entity. And some implementation environments may force the designer to specify domain rules as integrity rules, because the entity data model is the only place they provide for recording knowledge of valid data types.

External rule

An external rule is a rule which should clearly be tested at the user interface without reference to the database. Unlike a domain rule there is no reasonable way to test it within the Conceptual Model.

A **control item error** occurs where the value of a data item, input by the user only as a double check, does not match the parts from which it is calculated. This category includes items such as batch totals, hash totals and check digits. An application generator may allow a control item error to be treated as a domain rule, declared by including an expression in the validation rule of the control data item.

A **dialogue-state error** occurs where the user is attempting an action which is impossible at this stage of the dialogue. Most of these errors can be prevented through skilful GUI design, by hiding or disabling data entry boxes and command buttons until the right time, but for further consideration of dialogue state errors see chapter 27.

29.3 **Error testing**

For every error which may occur, the designer must specify how the system detects the error condition and how it reports it. While error reporting clearly belongs in the External Design, as discussed at the end of this chapter, it is not possible to place error detection so easily within one of the three schemas. Some errors seem naturally detected within External Design, some can only be detected by Conceptual Model and then reported via the External Design. Reasonable generalisations are given below.

Where to test external rules?

It is obvious that external rules (control item errors and dialogue state errors) ought to be specified in the External Design.

Where to test domain rules?

Domain rules might be tested in the Conceptual Model, but they are better tested in the External Design (c.f. 'obligations' in chapter 9). They are usually specified as properties of data items in windows, exactly how will vary between implementation environments.

Where to test integrity rules?

We recommend that all integrity rules are coded and tested in the Conceptual Model (as fail conditions within event procedures), not in the External Design.

The External Design processes will invoke the Conceptual Model processes. If a

Conceptual Model process fails for any reason, it will return an error code. All the External Design has to do is detect whether the Conceptual Model process has succeeded or failed and display the relevant error message.

We recommend that integrity rules are not tested in the External Design, even if it seems possible to do so. For example, consider these two rules:

- on a Promotion event, Promotion Grade must be > Employee Grade
- on an Application Registration event, the Applicant must have at least one Skill.

These rules *must* be embodied in the Conceptual Model. It is true that the rules might also be built into the External Design (for example, users can be prevented from entering an Applicant with no Skills, by disabling the Save button until the Applicant Skills text box has some data in it), but this is not desirable. Not only is it generally impossible to do all the validation (test all the business rules and the state of all stored data) without calling a database procedure, but it is anti-reuse and anti-amendability to specify and code the validation twice.

29.4 **Error reporting**

Having detected an error, error handling comes in two parts: error report and error correction. We suggest that the report of any error is a feature of the External Design, not the Conceptual Model. It should be possible to modify any error message without inspecting or amending the code of a routine in the Conceptual Model.

So we recommend that every event and enquiry procedure will return a reply parameter indicating whether it has succeeded or failed, but that this reply is simply an error or failure code. Routines should be written within the External Design to control any event procedure, and to retrieve any error message from an error message database.

The error message database
Here is a suggested structure for an error message database, in which an error message is identified by a hierarchical key of two elements, event name and event failure code.

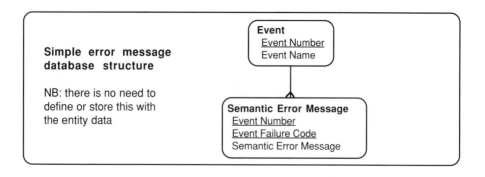

We have assumed that each event failure will trigger a distinct, user-friendly and specific message. It is possible to generalise error messages (say, 'this event is invalid because the entity owns active details'), so that several failures may trigger the same error message. This will require a more elaborate database structure.

Some of the event failures which are detected (say, 'this event is invalid because the master entity is missing') may indicate not so much that the input event is a mistake, but that the database has somehow become corrupted; perhaps because someone has been using a data fixing system to delete what they think is unwanted data. However, there seems no way for the system to know the difference between an integrity error and a database corruption (though note that we haven't given this much thought).

The event control routine

Within the External Design, a simple reusable routine should be written to manage the invocation and reply of the event procedure from and to the user interface. This routine may be attached to a 'button' in the user interface, or invoked from off-line functions, and may look something like the pseudocode shown below.

```
Event  control  program
  Invoke event procedure [with event parameters]
    If  error-code  =  0  then
    set  success  message in event response window
    If  error-code  >  0  then
    invoke  error  message  program  [event name, error number]
    set  error  message  in  event  response  window
  Return to user interface [with event response window]
```

The error message routine

Also within the External Design, another simple reusable routine should be written to retrieve the error message appropriate to the error code. This routine may look something like the pseudo-code shown below.

```
Error  message  program
  Read event type [using event name]
  Read error type [using error number]
  Return to event control program [with  error  message]
```

What error reports may look like in a GUI interface was illustrated in chapter 22.

29.5 **Error correction**

Can errors be avoided?

You may think that erroneous database updating can be avoided by very thorough testing of the input data. But imagine the case where two Post Acceptances are entered for the same Interview (let us say there has been a typing error in one of them) in two executions of an off-line function. Which Post Acceptance is the mistake?

If the second Post Acceptance is incorrect, then the system will behave perfectly. It will reject the second Post Acceptance. On investigating this error, the input clerks will be able to correct it and resubmit it. But if the first Post Acceptance was a mistake, then the system could not recognise this in the first execution of the off-line function, and the database will be processed wrongly.

Would it help to treat a whole function as one commit unit?

No. The users might repeatedly correct and resubmit the input data to the running of a function until all the input data seems to be error free. But not only does this waste time, since it delays the processing of valid events, but it cannot eliminate all errors. For example, a mistaken Post Acceptance event may not be detectable as an error until the next running of the function.

Would it help to test for integrity errors in the input data alone?

No. It would be possible to detect and reject multiple Post Acceptances for the same Interview within the one input file, but such a check would be arbitrarily limited to the scope of one day's post. In any case this is a redundant process, since any second or subsequent Post Acceptance for one Interview will naturally be rejected by the system as an integrity error when it is applied to the database.

So, the effects of processing mistaken events must be investigated and handled.

What are the effects of an error?

The effects of an error event are the same as effects of a valid event, except that they are mistaken, so the system will get out of step with the real world.

Output data will be produced, which is wrong

The mistaken Post Acceptance will have triggered the accounts department to bill the employer. This won't matter much if only the Applicant number is wrong, but it will matter very much if the Employer number is wrong. Further, it may cause the needless cancellation of other Interviews for the Applicant and other Interviews for the Vacancy (if there are no more posts on offer).

The stored data will be updated, but 'corrupted'

The mistaken Post Acceptance will have triggered all manner of database processing, so the database will be left in a state inconsistent with reality (though consistent within itself).

Future input data will be accepted or rejected, wrongly
If not corrected in time, the mistaken Post Acceptance will cause the rejection of the real Post Acceptance when it arrives.

How should the effects of an error be handled?

Whenever an error report is produced, someone must investigate and do whatever is necessary to put things right. A mistaken event may trigger processing which is:

- beneficial: later proves to have been useful
- neutral: later proves to have been unimportant
- intolerable: has to be undone or handled by remedial action.

For example, the rejection of the second Post Acceptance is a beneficial side-effect. It helps us to discover the error in the first Post Acceptance. Unfortunately, in systems design (as opposed to program design) most of the effects fall into the category of intolerable effects; they must be undone or avoided.

There are three things to do in handling intolerable side-effects:

- erase the effect of mistaken outputs (see paragraph below)
- restore stored data to the correct state (see section below)
- reinput events/input records which have been rejected (see chapter 28).

Erasing the effect of mistaken outputs

It is hard to generalise about this. Designers must find out whether users:

- do not care about small errors in the output they receive
- will find the errors for themselves and handle them without further help
- will require a kind of 'amendment notice'
- will require the output to be redone from scratch
- can be mollified by advance warning of possible error.

As an example of the last, consider the message often printed on reminder letters you receive, 'if you have already paid this bill, please ignore it'.

29.6 **Restoring stored data to the correct state**

Consider the case where by mistake two Applicant records have been created for the same real-world Applicant. Let us call the first record the 'real Applicant' and the second record the 'fake Applicant'.

It is clear you must delete the 'fake Applicant'. But the designer will have to think about the knock-on effects of accepting a mistaken event, and what to do to recover from the situation. This may involve the deletion and re-entry of a considerable amount of data, depending on how long the error has gone unnoticed. For example, you may have to:

- switch several Interviews from the 'fake Applicant' to the 'real Applicant'.

There are four ways to 'fix up' the database:

- Reversal events
- Deliberate abuse of proper events
- Data fixing system
- Special fix-up transactions.

These are discussed below.

Reversal events
Within the scope of the Conceptual Model, using entity event modelling techniques, it is possible to conceive of designing reversal events which back out the processing of an event. So to back out the effects of a mistaken Applicant Registration, you might try to design an 'Applicant Deregistration' event.

It is difficult to design such events (for reasons which are made clear below) but worse, they are likely to be of limited use. There will come a point in time, or an event such as the deletion of a master entity, which moves the system into a state which can no longer be reversed. Given the limits of automated error correction, manual error correction procedures must be designed, using one of the following three mechanisms

Deliberate abuse of proper events
The user may invent a fake Vacancy, fake Interview Results, award the fake Vacancy to the fake Applicant, archive all these entities, then arrange new Interviews for the real Applicant.

The trouble with deliberate abuse of proper events is that they produce unwanted side-effects. The system will generate a spurious invoice to the Employer with the fake Vacancy. This may be torn up, but what about the management reports which now overestimate the number of Applicants, Vacancies and Interviews which have been processed? What about the accounting system which includes the spurious invoice?

Data fixing system

Chapter 21 suggests that, outside the scope of the main systems development, you may use the facilities provided by the database management system or application generator to modify the database directly.

A facility to realign a database with the real world, by deleting or creating data, is usually necessary, but it is a dangerous facility, and should be controlled. First, the authority to use this facility must be restricted, perhaps to a database management team, or other team with intimate knowledge of the database. Second, programs to test the database integrity (beyond the scope of referential integrity) must be written, and run immediately after anyone has tampered with the database directly.

Special fix-up transactions

Rather than allow direct database manipulation, but outside of the scope of the entity event modelling techniques, the designer may specify special-purpose fix-up transactions. For example, you might design one to delete the 'fake Applicant', and to switch Interviews from the 'fake Applicant' to the 'real Applicant'.

Such a facility, to realign a database with the real world, may be used by naive users, because these special fix-up transactions will be designed to ensure that database Integrity rules are maintained.

29.7 The difference between events and fix-up transactions

We have reached the edge of our theory. We have suggested that database update routines may be designed to represent:

- events acting within an entity event model
- fix-up transactions restoring a 'corrupt' database.

Sometimes the difference between these is obvious. Consider the database update routine which switches all the Interviews from one Applicant to another. This is a fix-up transaction, not an event. It does not correspond to anything which happens in the real world. It means breaking the rules by changing the key of an Interview (assuming this includes the Applicant identity).

But consider the database update routine which updates an Applicant's address. Is this a real-world event? Or is it a correction of a mistake? Although the same database update routine may be used for both purposes, in fact the purposes are quite different, as would be revealed if you had to keep track how many times an Applicant has moved house.

It is normal in systems development to fail to completely separate events from fix-up transactions. However, ideally they should be separated, and the consequences of not separating them should be considered during design.

Including deletes in the real-world model

Delete transactions are used in two ways; first, to save space and clutter by removing old and uninteresting data from a database; second, to remove mistaken data. The first is a physical data storage optimisation process. The second is a fix-up transaction. Strictly, deletion is not part of the real-world model; there is no such thing as a deletion event.

However, if an entity is never deleted, then its entity behaviour model should be extended to include all kinds of events which may hit the entity after its death. To put this another way, when an event hits the system, it has to navigate its way through a lot of dead data before it finds the entities which are currently active and of interest to the users.

Actually, this reflects a real problem in system design. It is easy to specify how a database will be populated with data, but much harder to specify a controlled way of removing data when it is no longer of interest. Entity behaviour modelling can be useful here.

The development of a deletion strategy can be taught as a third analysis pass (we have described two passes in part four). A delete operation may be allocated underneath the final event in an entity behaviour model, though an apparently bizarre side-effect of mixing up the real-world model with the physical system, is that the delete operation may have to be allocated under the *penultimate* event where the final event is a restricted or controlled death event. This and other implications of including the delete operation in the entity event model are covered in our training material.

Part Six:

Further Issues

Chapter 30

Putting the
SE into CASE

Most current CASE tools are little more than graphical front-ends to data dictionaries. They are too sluggish and unfriendly to do as their name promises, to 'Assist Software Engineering'. This chapter (partly based on Robinson, 1992) looks at several ways a CASE tool can be developed to support the methodology described in this book, and examines how qualitative improvements in the way CASE tools are used can be made.

30.1 **Introduction**

In a pair of articles published recently in the computer press, Rosemary Rock-Evans ('bad users blame their tools') said that methodology must come before tool: and Martin Ford ('the bubble bursts') debunked the current crop of upper CASE tools. Both authors make valid points, but fail to explain why these CASE tools are so bad and what can be done about it.

Too many CASE tools are designed to support the documentation of a completed system, but not to support the analyst during the process of analysis and design. Many are little more than graphical front-ends to data dictionaries. Analysts may, with some difficulty, use them to document what has already been decided and designed, but not to help in the process of deciding and designing.

A comment in a recent issue of the SSADM Users Group newsletter seemed to suggest that CASE tools should not be used by analysts doing a systems development job, but should be used only for documenting the system! This is worrying. The rather primitive tools in use today have lowered user expectations about what CASE tools should be able to do. This chapter is a modest attempt to raise user expectations, to set ambitious but realistic levels of expectation.

In this chapter CASE is taken to stand for:

C Computer
A Aided or Assisted
S Systems or Software
E Engineering.

Two key ideas giving two benefits
The two key ideas a CASE tool should be providing are:

CA   computer assistance in software development and/or maintenance
SE   an engineering approach to software development and/or maintenance.

But the use of a CASE tool as merely a graphical front-end to a data dictionary seems to deliver neither of these ideas. If an engineering design tool isn't being used by an engineer while he/she is actually doing the engineering, it isn't really helping. The two key ideas (of CA and SE) should translate into two benefits:

Faster development and maintenance
Low defect solutions.

Is there anyone out there getting these benefits from CASE tools? Our guess is that there are very few.

What is the evidence of benefits?

Of course people are getting advantages from the use of 4GLs. And to the extent that a CASE tool may be a way of programming a 4GL, it may appear to give a development advantage. But is it the CASE tool or the 4GL which really delivers the advantage?

What good, controlled experiments have been done? Who has actually developed the same system twice, once using no tool, and again using a tool? And if they had, wouldn't the second development have profited from end-user and analyst experience to such an extent as to make the comparison meaningless?

If the perceptions mentioned above are widely shared, then few believe CASE tools are helping them in faster development. Maybe some use a CASE tool for documentation, in the hope that this will make maintenance easier. But this is an act of faith; few people if any have measured maintenance savings. Our own (uncontrolled) experience is that automated diagrams which were hard to construct are even harder to maintain.

There is much better experience of translating pictures into code. The advantage of automated transformation is that a more understandable and uncluttered representation can be reviewed for errors; we then have some assurance that the generated system accurately represents the requirements. But where CASE currently helps in this process is more or less at the back end. The situation is similar to that in conventional programming at the beginning of the 1980s, when we had good methods for constructing programs from specifications, but no way of guaranteeing that we were producing good specifications.

What can be done?

Some of things needed to bring CASE tools within the grasp of the systems and software engineers are just to do with usability. Others are to do with theory; unless we really understand what the job is, it's very difficult to help people do it.

A system is a large and complex piece of work; it needs to be split up for development, implementation and maintenance, but it needs to be split in a way that maximises the independence of the components. Of course, full independence of components cannot be achieved; the system, after all, is a *system.*

We need better ways of working through the implications of one piece of knowledge gained from the perspective of one component, ways of deducing its effect elsewhere. And we need better ways of transforming knowledge as we move down the design path.

We might summarise these requirements as:

- Enabling analysts and designers
- Better theoretical underpinning
- Better modularisation
- Better knowledge acquisition
- Better transformations.

In some of these areas we should be able to measure what happens. In others we may still be left with an act of faith, but we should have a better idea of how and why our expectations are reasonable.

30.2 **Enabling analysts and designers**

The first requirement is that the designer should want to use the tool. It should support the way the designer thinks. It should support the way the designer works. It should be faster and easier to use the tool than not. One way of assessing a tool's usability is to let its user choose it. Few organisations do this; if they did they'd get better productivity.

All of these things can be measured to some degree. It is clearly possible to know whether it is faster to draw a diagram using one particular tool rather than another or whether it is faster to use pencil and paper than a particular tool. And believe it or not, small-scale experiments have shown advantages of some tools over pencil and paper.

If you watch how a designer works, you see lots of things going on which give you some insight into the thought processes. Sometimes a designer is just trying out some new idea. Sometimes a designer is evaluating or making some catastrophic change to previous ideas (maybe about 90% of the pictures a designer draws get thrown away). Sometimes a designer is trying to customise something developed for another purpose. Sometimes two designers who have developed separate pieces of a solution are trying to bring them together. Sometimes a designer is checking that all of the ideas hang together. One thing you will see is that very little time is actually spent on the finished product. What this means is that a truly usable CASE product must be able to support all these modes of working. It must:

- be faster than pencil and paper
- be usable in sketch mode (that is not force consistency between diagrams)
- have intelligent cut and paste facilities
- have global rename, delete and merge capabilities
- provide selectively enforceable cross-checking capabilities.

Let us pick up the 'intelligent cut and paste facilities' item. The designer should be able to copy part of a data model, such as the part shown below.

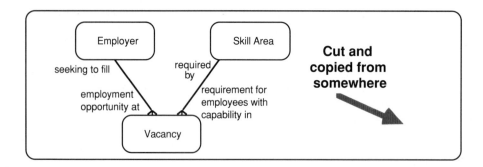

The designer should be able to paste the diagram above into the one below.

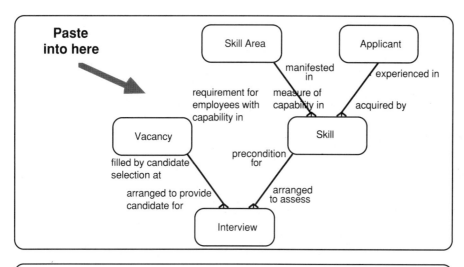

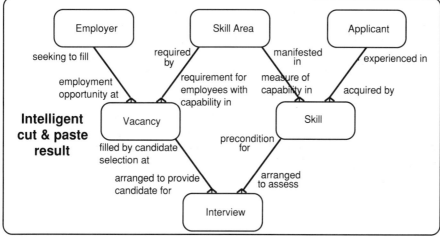

30.3 **Better theoretical underpinning**

A CASE tool's purpose is to assist in the engineering of an end-product. In order to do this, it must have some 'understanding' of the purpose of that end-product, and of any intermediate purposes relevant to the achievement of the ultimate purpose. An engineering process which designed part of a car on the basis that turning one particular wheel around its axis should cause two other wheels to turn around their vertical diameters and didn't 'know' that this was part of a steering system would be unlikely to result in a good design.

CASE tools are limited here by the fact that there is no generally accepted theory of what data processing is. Maybe this isn't surprising for a profession which is only about thirty years old. But the fact remains that we are doing to ourselves what we recommend users not to do to themselves, namely automate a system without analysing what it is about.

In these circumstances it's not surprising that people look for CASE tools which are uncommitted to any methodology. But we believe this is even worse than going for a methodology; at least with a methodology-based tool there is some underlying theory that people have tried to make consistent. We exclude from criticism here what we might think of as 'platform' tools (such as IPSYS and VSF) which can be used to construct methodology-specific tools.

What agreement about theory is there? Most people seem to agree on something like a 'logical' before 'physical' (or 'what' before 'how') approach to development. Most methodologies seem to agree that some kind of data modelling is desirable. Most methodologies seem to use some form of data flow diagrams, but the purposes they put them to can be surprisingly different. Relational systems are very popular and they're fine for retrieval; but we believe they're flawed for updating. Most CASE tools are based on some or all of these ideas.

Missing - the event

Picking up the theme started in chapter 5.6, events are necessary to understanding what a system is about. We can see this from a number of perspectives.

First, we need to model the atomic changes in reality which correspond to commit units. Second, DFD-based methods which don't take into account how activity is triggered, notoriously have difficulty in providing systematic ways of deciding how to move from data flow representations to program-like representations. Recall from chapter 6, the cartoon where the designer explains how this gap is filled with '..... and then a miracle occurs.' Third, attempts to model reality without events seem to fail. One such attempt is to hang activities directly on data. You can try this non-procedurally using some relational integrity constraints such as **cascade** and **restrict**, or you can provide data base procedures. Either way there are some problems for which the approach fails. Let us recount the moral tale mentioned in chapter 5.

A moral tale

A designer specifies a RESTRICT rule on the deletion of a Customer record, so that all the Customer's Contracts must be deleted before the Customer. So when a Customer walks in the door and says he wants to stop dealing with us, the user must say 'Wait a minute. We have to work through your contracts one-by-one and close them down first.'

But suppose the Customer says 'I haven't got time for that', turns away, walks out of the door, and steps under a bus. Perhaps the designer should have specified a CASCADE rule after all!

And what if the Customer is not to be deleted in either of these cases, but simply updated to a 'dead' status. Then whatever rule is specified on deletion, (RESTRICT or CASCADE) won't be fired at the time it is needed.

MORAL: rules should be attached to events, not records.

Where will a better theory come from? There are at least three possibilities. First, the Euromethod project is going to have to find a theoretical framework in which all of the popular European methodologies fit. Second, some of the AD/Cycle Information Model is likely to become a de facto standard; there are enough people active in this field who will want to expand its coverage. Finally there is user-led research. This is the approach we believe most likely to bring useful new theories, and is the one behind the development of this book.

Bob Brown of the Database Design Group, Newport Beach, California, has proposed a historic view of Information Processing theory as ascending up a series of slopes and plateaux. The last major plateau is defined by the emergence of data-centred design. His view is that the next plateau must be an object-centred one which will integrate things like data modelling, object-oriented design, event analysis, window-based operating environments and knowledge-based processing. This can't be developed by theorists alone, but by end-users and theorists co-operating in solving real problems.

30.4 **Better support for modularisation**

The best modularisation of a system is one which enables changes to be localised. We propose that the 3-Schema Architecture provides a useful framework of modularisation. It suggests how upper and lower CASE tools might modularise systems, how methodology-independent tools might be built, and where prototyping and animation are useful.

Modularity of systems
It ought to be possible to construct the implemented system from programs quite clearly belonging to one and only one schema. However, some current CASE tools and implementation products do not allow such modularisation. A designer might be forced to either structure his/her conceptual processes in terms of implementation objects, or to restrict his/her choice of implementation objects.

A further difficulty is with systems like CICS which have no concept of a whole dialogue of several input and output messages, and which force commits to take place at the screen in/screen out level. Someone designing for a CICS environment may feel that they are forced to dismember their conceptual processes and distribute them around their screen-handling processes. A good CASE tool here would take data and processing descriptions from each of the three schemas and automatically perform the dismembering and recombination to form screen-based programs. No such tool yet exists.

Methodology-independent tool
Methodologies like IE address the documentation of the Conceptual Model, but not its discovery. Cultural methodologies like Mumford's address mainly the performance and acceptability of the External Design. A CASE tool which supports the different schemas separately should be portable between such different methodologies.

Prototyping

The discussion in chapter 2 suggested the External and Internal Designs must be designed not discovered. Heuristic approaches like prototyping clearly have a strong role to play here. We can create first-cut designs for dialogues and improve them through prototyping. CASE tools clearly have a role to play here, although that role might be best carried out on the implementation product. CASE tools could also provide performance analysis capability for improvement of Internal Design prototypes.

Animation

How can we validate the discoveries in the Conceptual Model? At present all we do is show the end-users data models and data flow diagrams. Future CASE tools should be able to *animate* the conceptual processes. At first the animations will be crude, such as highlighting the path an event takes through an effect correspondence diagram, showing what actual values lie behind a particular entity and how they are changed. But maybe in twenty years time we'll be using moving icons to show pictures of lorries arriving at warehouses, unloading and loading, stock piles depleting!

30.5 **Better support for knowledge acquisition**

One of the advantages of the diagrammatic representations that we use is that they contain information, not just about what the designer told the tool, but also about possible implications of that information. This information is also available manually, but the advantage of a CASE tool is that it can bring that information to the designer's attention.

For example, in an entity data model, the presence of a 'double-V' structure suggests there may be a relationship between the two entities at the bottom of the 'V'.

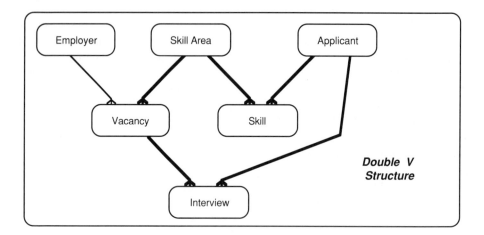

There should be a direct relationship between Interview and the Applicant's Skill which led to it.

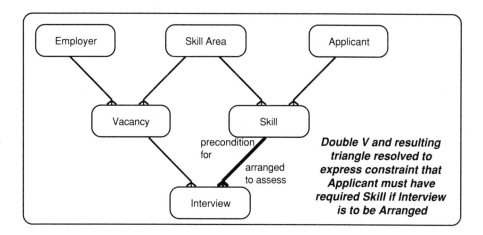

Again, a common mistake in the construction of entity behaviour models is to represent what should be a selection of two sequences as a sequence of two selections.

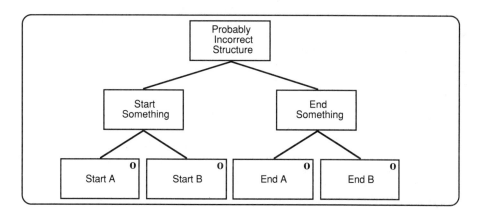

The above diagram should normally be redrawn as a selection of two sequences. The above structure is so rarely correct that a tool could make a point of detecting and querying it, perhaps proposing to the designer the revised structure shown below.

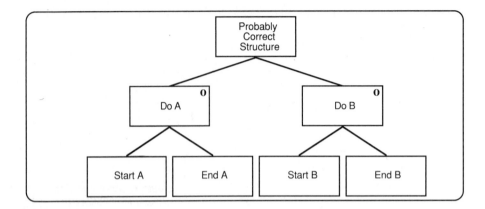

Finally (and there are lots more), a tool could be proactive in propagating the event-effects equivalent to RESTRICT and CASCADE rules around the entities in a data model as shown on the next page.

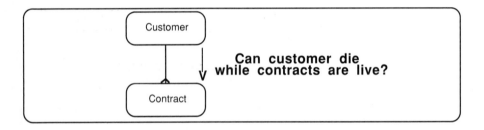

30.6 **Better support for transformations**

Most of the methodology techniques combine three elements in varying degrees:

- analysis: requiring the discovery of new facts
- design: requiring judgements and decisions based on facts and rules of thumb
- transformation: of inputs into outputs.

Those techniques which require little or no discovery, and require few or no decisions to be made, are the best candidates for automation.

The transformations and techniques listed below have already been mostly or completely automated in current CASE tools, and ought to be supported to some extent by any CASE tool claiming to support the methodology:

an I/O structure	-> a set of TNF relations
a set of TNF relations	-> a partial Logical Data Model
two partial LDMs	-> a single Logical Data Model
a Logical Data Model view	-> an Enquiry Access Path *
an Enquiry Access Path	-> an Enquiry Process Model *
LDM + its set of ELHs	-> the set of Effect Correspondence Diagrams *
LDM + its set of ELHs +an ECD	-> an Update Process Model *
LDM + volumetrics	-> the universal first-cut database design.

The biggest productivity gains result from automation of the techniques marked *. We've already discussed earlier how forward engineering transformations could be used to take products representing the separation of concerns in a 3-Schema framework and repackage them for a hostile environment such as CICS.

Sideways transformations can be used for example to take a data model, extract a subset hit on a particular access path and transform that access path into a skeleton enquiry procedure. For example, from the Hi-Ho data model shown above you can cut the access path shown below.

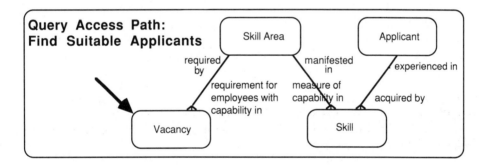

and transform the access path automatically into a processing skeleton:

```
Find Suitable Applicants
    Process Vacancy & Skill Area
        Get Suitable Applicants
        Read Vacancy, On Error Set Vacancy ` Sv = Null
        Read Skill Area, On Error Set Skill Area ` Sv = Null
        Read Skill, On Error Set Skill ` Sv = Null
        DO WHILE   Skill ` Sv ≠ Null
            Process Skill & Applicant
                Read Applicant, On Error Set Applicant ` Sv = Null
                Read Skill, On Error Set Skill ` Sv = Null
```

30.7 **Conclusion**

The criticisms we make here are real ones and so are the suggestions for improvement. This book is a substantial way up Brown's slope to the last plateau. Parts four and five present a theory for combining data modelling, object orientation and so on. This theory can be used in CASE tools.

Just about everything we've talked about is being done to some degree somewhere. Our own CASE tool satisfies the usability criteria we're talking about. People are using the 3-schema processing architecture. There are tools which address the Conceptual / External Design separation to some degree or other. People are working on animation systems. Some CASE tools, ours for example, provide ways of encoding new knowledge.

30.8 **Testing an upper CASE tool**

Part of the problem is that CASE tool purchasers are still too naive, they have failed to test the important features of a tool before they buy it. For medium to large projects, performance and user-friendliness are *paramount* considerations in selecting a CASE tool. Analysts *must* be able to use the screen like a whiteboard, to express ideas quickly and then reshape them.

We cannot emphasise enough how important performance and user-friendliness are to end-users. Unfortunately, the people who choose CASE tools are usually not the end-users, and they have little feel for these issues. The less prominence they give to performance and user-friendliness, the less vendors will try to provide it.

Next, to take up Rosemary Rock-Evan's point that methodology must come before tool, a CASE tool *must* actively help your analysts to apply your systems development methodology: it should integrate different diagrams, maintain cross-references and automate techniques.

What can be done? We suggest there are seven things a CASE tool should be doing, and can do for you. These are things you should try to measure before you buy a CASE tool.

Swift manipulation of diagrams

Practical experience of a CASE tool soon teaches you how important it is that the tool actively helps the analyst to draw diagrams and to change them. Some tools are unusable because to create any diagram is so laborious that analysts are thrown back to using paper and pencil to record what matters to them during day-to-day work.

User-friendliness inevitably means implementing a 'tidy-up diagram' function. This is useful for all system modelling diagrams, but essential for those which employ strictly hierarchical structures. So does the tool have an effective 'tidy-up diagram' function for all the diagrams in your methodology? And are the various objects overlaid on the basic diagram (such as relationship names, operations, state variable values) preserved in their correct position by the tidy-up function?

To compare ease of diagram manipulation

Play about with an entity data model thus.

Start a new entity data model (A).
Create four entity boxes.
Name each of them.
Connect the entities by relationship lines.
Alter the optionality of relationship lines.
Draw an exclusion arc.
Erase the exclusion arc.
Move an entity around the screen.
Regenerate (tidy up) the diagram.
Copy a sub-set of entity data model A (say three entities) into entity data model B.
Rename all but one of the entities in entity data model B
Merge the two entity data models into one.

Immediate access to related diagrams and objects

A CASE tool should 'understand' the system model. It must have intelligence about the objects in the diagrams, how they relate to other objects within the same diagram, and how they relate to objects in other diagrams. It is vital for practical use that a CASE tool can automatically ensure that related analysis products are compatible, whether by maintenance of a cross-reference or by generating one from the other.

Examples of immediate access to related diagrams / objects

Take a data flow diagram:
look inside a process at its lower-level decomposition
look inside a data store at the entities stored in it
look inside a data flow at the data items within it.

Take a data flow (in a data flow diagram):
show the grouping of data items into third normal form relation(s)
show the transformation of the data flow into a screen/report design
show the grouping of input data items into events and enquiry triggers.

Take an entity (in an entity data model):
look at its attributes or data items
look at the events which update it
look at the state-transitions caused by events
look at the operations triggered by an event.

The diagram on the next page shows more connections which may be made.

Navigating between the objects in a system specification

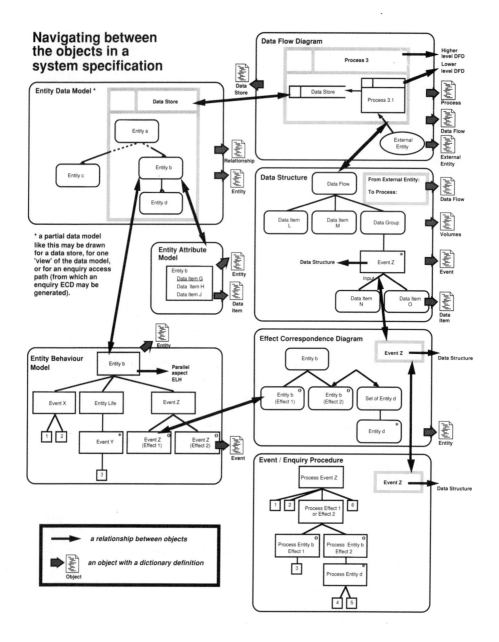

* a partial data model like this may be drawn for a data store, for one 'view' of the data model, or for an enquiry access path (from which an enquiry ECD may be generated).

Immediate access to dictionary description of an object

It is a vital requirement for practical use that a CASE tool automatically maintains the cross-references between an object and its dictionary definition (as illustrated above) and enables both global and local changes to be made to object names.

Immediate access to dictionary description of an object

Take a data item (appearing as an attribute of an entity):
look at its dictionary definition
list all the places the data item appears.

Do likewise for:
    a data store, in a data flow diagram
    an external entity, in a data flow diagram
    a process, in a data flow diagram
    an entity, in an entity data model
    a relationship, in an entity data model
    an event, in an entity life history.

For all the objects recorded in the dictionary, the CASE tool should automatically maintain the cross-reference between the object and its dictionary definition. It should enable three kinds of object update.

Global Change: it must be possible to rename or delete the object globally in all the diagrams and products in which it appears.

Local Change: it must be possible to rename or delete the object locally in only one diagram or product, leaving all other references to the object unaltered.

Global Merge: it must be possible to rename the object to completely merge its definition with another object, so the two objects become one.

Validation of diagram syntax - enforced by tool

Given the syntax rules of a specific methodology, the tool should ensure that these rules are never broken. This kind of validation should be on-line.

Three simple examples of on-line syntax validation

    Taking a data flow diagram, check that:
    annotation of bottom-level processes is automatic
    annotation of duplicate data stores is automatic
    data flows cannot be drawn from external entities to data stores.

Unfortunately, many tools go beyond enforcement of syntax rules and impose semantic checks on the analyst. These should be executed only under the control of the analyst.

Validation of diagram semantics - controlled by user

A CASE tool must not prevent analysts from breaking the integrity rules of their methodology. This makes the tool unusable. Analysts *want* to build diagrams which conflict with existing documentation; they knowingly contradict themselves while they are playing about with design ideas and they want to be in control of validation.

**Three kinds of off-line semantic validation
(not to be enforced until the user requests it).**

Validate data flow diagrams: report where they are incorrectly levelled,
an entity (from the entity data model) appears in more than one data store, etc.

Validate access paths: report all entities in the access paths which are
missing from the entity data model.

Validate entities: report all entities without attributes defined for them.

Import to and export from other software tools

Perhaps one day an upper CASE tool will be developed which incorporates every feature of every other software development tool. Before this halcyon day, it is helpful if tools are built to facilitate communication with other tools.

**Two examples of data which might have to be exported
from an upper CASE tool to a lower CASE tool**

List the entities and their attributes in a serial ASCII file.
List the process definitions in a serial ASCII file.

Automation of methodology techniques

The real benefits of a CASE tool lie in improving productivity by automation, not just in meeting 'conformance criteria'. Productivity from automation was discussed earlier. Some tests to apply are suggested below.

Relational Data Analysis

Take a data flow diagram:
look inside a data flow at the I/O structure
perform First Normal Form analysis
perform Second Normal Form analysis
perform Third Normal Form analysis
consolidate TNF relations
generate a TNF data model
compare the TNF data model with the entity data model.

From Data Model to Enquiry Procedure

Take the entity data model:
cut an access path from it
transform the access path into a process structure (EPM in SSADM)
translate the process structure into a pseudo-code (Action Diagram in IE).

From Data Model to Event Procedures

Take the entity data model:
develop a set of entity life histories, one per entity
generate a set of effect correspondence diagrams, one per event
transform an effect correspondence diagram into a process structure (UPM in SSADM)
translate the process structure into a pseudo-code (Action Diagram in IE).

Support for system implementation

This is not something to worry about in testing an upper CASE tool. If you need the system implementation functions provided by a lower CASE tool or 4GL, then it is unwise to buy an upper CASE tool for this purpose.

There is only a limited amount that an upper CASE tool can do in the way of system implementation, without getting so far into bed with the manufacturer of a specific implementation environment that the tool ceases to be a distinct and general purpose tool. Beware also that many claims for 'code generation' by 4GLs have been exaggerated.

However, there are tasks in physical design which an upper CASE tool may assist.

Three tasks in Physical Design which may be supported

Paint a screen / report from a data flow definition.
Set up the data definitions in a database management system.
Generate compilable COBOL code from structured pseudo-code.

Chapter 31

Software reuse
issues and ideas

One way to reduce the development and maintenance costs of large database systems is to make greater reuse of software components. The methodology in parts four and five is designed with this in mind. But there is more to be said about reuse and we can take a broader perspective. So this chapter develops a wider framework for issues and ideas in maximising software reuse, and places the methodology within this framework.

31.1 **Introduction**

It has long been realised that the development of an information system is a difficult and time consuming task, prone to error and delay. What is particularly frustrating to end-users is the need to develop more or less from scratch a system to support a new business service, when they can see that new service resembles existing services already supported by automated information systems.

We need the ability to develop an information system as a by-product of defining the business services it is to support. This is being solved by modelling techniques. Then what we need is the ability to define that system in terms of components that already exist. This is the new dimension made possible by the analysis design techniques in parts four and five.

The hope is that the designer can build systems by pulling together components which have already been defined in other programs or systems. Clearly this should help us to build systems quicker, as well as better, since the components should already be tried and tested.

More than this, the hope is that the user can define a new system by saying 'it's like system A, except without this feature, and with the addition of this feature and this feature which are in system B', and that the designer can work directly from such a definition to build the new system from existing objects which implement those features.

To a large degree, the methodology described in parts four and five has already given us the means of satisfying these hopes, but this chapter takes the widest possible view of reuse, to make sure no other avenue is overlooked.

Roles in achieving reuse

In creating and using reusable components, there are two kinds of role for the application designer. There is the reactive role of looking for something which can be reused. More importantly there is the proactive role of developing something so that it can be reused at a later date.

Above the level of the application designer there are many other kinds of proactive role in setting out techniques and standards which are designed to encourage the likelihood of reusable components. People who can play these proactive roles include:

- systems managers
- IT quality departments
- IT strategy planners
- suppliers of application generators
- suppliers of CASE tools
- suppliers of methodologies.

This book itself plays a proactive role in offering guidance on different strategies for achieving reuse, and introducing techniques which can be added to popular systems development methodologies like Information Engineering and SSADM.

Areas in which systems development managers seek guidance

Systems development managers who want a coherent plan for maximising software reuse may look for guidance in many different areas. Some of the questions they may ask are listed below.

OO ideas

How should we use object-oriented ideas and techniques in systems analysis? In part four we showed how object-oriented ideas can be added to entity data modelling and entity event modelling techniques, and how significant benefits can be achieved.

CASE tools

Where should CASE tools offer support? In chapter 30 we showed where object-oriented analysis and design techniques can be supported by current CASE technology.

Corporate strategies

What needs to be done outside the application development life cycle, at the strategic and management levels? Chapter 32 discusses the development of:

- corporate models for connected systems
- generic designs for similar systems
- standards and style guides for constraining design.

Libraries

Can we develop component libraries for conventional information systems development? Meyer (1988) has said that 'the ability to reuse libraries of 'canned' software components is one of the major benefits of the OO approach'. Chapter 32 considers the possibilities.

Limits to reuse

Where are the limits to the amount of reuse which is achievable? Chapters 9, 10 and 12 discussed limits to the usefulness of object-oriented ideas within large information systems. There are also irreconcilable conflicts between different directions in systems development. In this chapter we shall have something to say about two specific conflicts:

- 'composition' versus 'reuse'
- 'suppression of detail' versus 'helpfulness'.

It is important that system development managers are not led by object-oriented programming enthusiasts into false expectations about what can be achieved in the way of software reuse within or between systems. It is just as valuable, perhaps more valuable, to understand why some things are impossible as it is to understand why other things are possible.

31.2 **Basic kinds of reuse**

Taking the widest interpretations of 'reuse', this section classifies the variety of ways in which reuse can work and points to the main emphases of this book. To begin with, let us say the component or feature which is to be reused might be almost anything to do with an information system, any kind of logical model of a system or any kind of physical component of a system.

Tailoring reuse, copy reuse and true reuse

Tailoring reuse means adapting an old component to make a new one. This is indirect reuse: it is more widespread, but much less effective, than direct reuse.

Direct reuse means using a component without amending it. The hope is that the component can be implemented without any design or testing effort, because it is already tried and tested. There are two kinds of Direct reuse, Copy and True.

Copy reuse means replicating an old component in a new place (that is new environment, function or system). 'Cloning' is another word for copying a component for use in another system and plugging it in there.

True reuse means extending the use of an existing component, without creating a new component. Extending a component is only possible within the scope of one system. The main emphasis of this book has been on true reuse.

Reuse between systems and within a system

The scope of one system can be defined in terms of the scope of its stored data. In logical design, a system is a collection of processes which provide input to and generate output from a single coherent entity data model. In physical design, a system is a collection of programs which provide input to and generate output from a single coherent database, governed by a single database or file management system.

If the stored data of two physical systems can be described in a single entity data model, then these are two parts of one logical system.

To increase reuse *within a system*, it is now clearer where object-oriented ideas can be applied within a systems development methodology such as Information Engineering or SSADM, and how object-oriented ideas can help us to generate reusable components. Some of these ideas do give us true reuse; so although they are narrow in scope, they do give immediate and significant benefits.

To increase reuse *between systems*, there are many things which can be done at the strategic level in terms of techniques, at the high level in terms of corporate and generic models, at the low level in terms of stereotype models, standards, libraries and so on. Most of these ideas do not give us true reuse, only tailoring reuse or at best copy reuse. So while there is a wide scope for things to be done, they are not always of great benefit.

The main emphasis of this book, in parts four and five, is on true reuse within a system, whether this be a physical system or a logical system which links several physical systems.

Reuse of whole systems

Of course it is possible to reuse an entire system. Here we are talking only of implemented systems. We deliberately exclude the specifications of systems, where the issue is clouded by different possible levels of abstraction.

Tailoring reuse of an existing system means adapting it to your purposes. For example, UNISYS generate specific packages such as their Courts Information System by tailoring a generic package called LINC.

Copy reuse of an existing system means installing your own copy of it. For example you may buy a 'packaged system' such as PRINCE for project management. Of course you must be prepared to live with the fact that a package may not be designed to meet your specific requirements.

True reuse of an existing system means extending it by entering your own data. For example, you may discover the system you want is already being used by someone in a neighbouring department, but dealing with different population of data.

Reuse of system components

Much more commonly, people will want or need or find a chance to reuse a small part of an existing system. This is the kind of reuse we are mainly concerned with in this book, the reuse of system components.

Tailoring reuse of old components is what analysts and programmers do all the time, whether they are told to or not. They borrow a file definition, program or routine from someone else and modify it for the job in hand. In practice, this indirect kind of reuse is the most common kind of reuse. Even though it clearly lacks the advantages of direct reuse and it requires the new component to be tested as though it had been built from scratch, it can save considerable design effort.

Copy reuse of old components is most profitable at the level of data items, small data groups, and small routines dealing with very few data items. Copy reuse is rare above this level. One reason is that trivial differences in data item definitions prevent direct copying; so one way to increase copy reuse is to impose design standards. Another reason is that composition is the enemy of reuse, as discussed later in this chapter.

True reuse of existing components is perhaps the most ideal and profitable kind of reuse. The main emphasis of this book, in parts four and five, is on true reuse of existing components.

31.3 Ideas about information systems as tools for reuse

Reuse is a pervasive idea, too pervasive to be easily summarised. It invades almost everything you can think of to do with information systems development. Some of the ideas which were introduced in chapter 4 are relevant and helpful in thinking about reuse; notably the ideas about 'the primacy of data' and 'abstraction'.

Primacy of data: external view of process components

For a new process to be implemented by reuse of an old one, the first and only criterion is that it must produce exactly the same output from the same input. In this sense, what goes on inside the process is irrelevant. This is the other side of the coin to the principle known as 'information hiding'.

Primacy of data: reuse of input data structures

Different outputs may be produced from one input data structure, that is, the input structure may be reused for different processes. For example, many different SQL enquiries may be run against a database, or many different COBOL programs may read the same input file. The more a data structure is reused in this way, the greater the evidence that the data structure is an accurate model of something in the world, something which people are interested in.

Abstraction: towards the real world

The idea of abstracting a conceptual model from an implemented system is a very powerful tool for increasing reuse, taken up in chapter 32 under the headings of 'reverse engineering'.

Abstraction: by generalisation

The various elements of databases and programs can be described as instances of types which are designed to be reusable. Arguably the most important job of the software engineer is to identify the types which can be reused most widely and most efficiently. Earlier chapters discuss ways in which generalisation (notably of super objects, super-events, and reusable GUI components) can be used in systems development.

In chapter 32 we use generic design to mean that a positive step is taken to design data and process objects in a way that extends their possible reuse wider than the specific application being designed. It implies that there is a family of related systems (or system components) of which the current system (or system component) is only one example.

In part four, we saw how *super-type objects* can be used in entity data modelling and database design to minimise redundant data and processing and maximise reuse. We also saw how *super-type events* can be used to separate the cause of an event from its effects on a database, which helps us both to identify and to generate reusable database update code.

There is one more kind of generalisation, abstraction of a machine-independent specification from a product-specific component. This has been discussed earlier.

Abstraction: by suppression of detail

When looking at a high-level specification, the definition of the lower level components may be taken for granted, so we can suppress detail from the high-level specification. This suppression of detail gives a limited opportunity for reuse.

The higher we abstract a systems description, the more we suppress the detail of lower levels, the easier it is to make it generic. At a sufficiently high level a family of related systems (say, order processing systems) can be made to look the same. Thus a high-level specification may provide a plan which can be reused for many similar systems.

On the other hand, suppression of detail is the enemy of helpfulness. Although a high-level specification may prove to be reusable, the suppression of detail which is required makes the specification less helpful. The higher level a specification, the more must be done in the way of adding meaningful detail before it can be used for anything.

31.4 Composition as the enemy of reuse

Composition is not a tool for reuse, in fact it runs counter to it. While generic objects are (by definition) more reusable than specific objects, composite objects are far less likely candidates for reuse than the base objects of which they are composed.

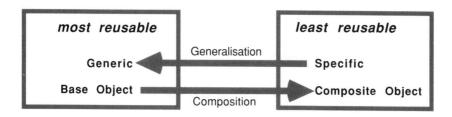

At the *bottom level*, systems are composed of relatively few types of base object (data item and executable programming operation). These are intentionally designed by production software engineers to be generic, to be reused by composition in many different ways. It is clear that data items may be reused by aggregating them into many different data groups and record types. Moving to a higher level, data groups can be reused in different record types, and record types can be reused by copying them into data structures.

At the *highest levels* of composition (above the level of individual record types) data structures are rarely reusable between systems. Graham (1991) says 'In fact, reusable data structures have proved an elusive goal even where OO methods have been used'. Some reasons for this are explored in chapter 12, but one simple reason is that composition is the enemy of reuse. Large composite objects are naturally specific and rarely reusable. Data structures and programs are complex composites of base objects which are tuned to carry out a specific function. There are an enormous variety of ways to composite data items and program statements to meet a specific user requirement. The larger and more complex the composite object, the less chance it will prove useful to another user, or in another circumstance; it is bound to differ in at least small ways from the object which is required elsewhere.

By making a conscious effort to design large components more generically, we could at least provide stereotypes for reuse by tailoring if not direct copying. But as Ian Graham points out, what has been missing so far is the time to do it, and the motivation. If the aim is to build a new application system, there is simply not enough time or will to make large composite objects more generic.

What about the *middle ground* between base objects and large composite objects, that is objects at not-too-high-a-level of composition? There are indeed many opportunities to reuse middle-level objects (data groups, record types, windows and the routines which operate on these), but designers need guiding towards these opportunities.

One aim of the methodology in this book is to raise the level at which true reuse of system components is commonly achieved, to ensure that opportunities for reuse at this middle level are detected and taken advantage of.

31.5 A framework for approaches to increasing reuse

There are several obstacles to successful reuse of system components, some physical and some logical. To identify three: the components of physical systems are limited to use in the implementation environment they are defined in; designers do not generate logical or physical components in a way which facilitates reuse; designers do not yet have enough logical models to copy. These and other obstacles can be overcome, at least in part, by encouraging designers to:

- follow universal models and stereotype components
- follow corporate models and standards
- build new systems to fit the corporate model
- build new systems with generic components
- follow existing generic designs
- use design techniques to factor out common elements during design.

Designers who do these things should generate components (both logical and physical) which are reusable. What these things mean in detail will be explained in chapter 32, but first we can place them within an overall context by using two of the ideas about abstraction to develop a framework for classifying approaches to software reuse.

First, there is a scale from generic to specific. This is only a rough categorisation, not a smooth or regular scale. Notice how the various people mentioned at the beginning of the chapter can be fitted to the categories.

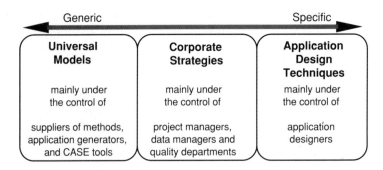

Generic		Specific
Universal Models	**Corporate Strategies**	**Application Design Techniques**
mainly under the control of	mainly under the control of	mainly under the control of
suppliers of methods, application generators, and CASE tools	project managers, data managers and quality departments	application designers

By adding another dimension, very roughly indicating a range from high-level outline to low-level detail, we can develop a framework to organise the approaches which are discussed in the various parts of this book. Chapter 32 concentrates mostly on the central column of this framework.

A framework for approaches to software reuse

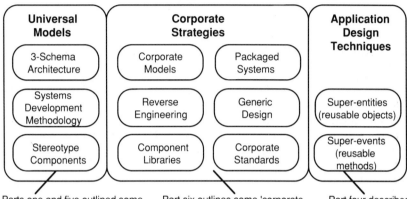

Universal Models	Corporate Strategies		Application Design Techniques
3-Schema Architecture	Corporate Models	Packaged Systems	
Systems Development Methodology	Reverse Engineering	Generic Design	Super-entities (reusable objects)
Stereotype Components	Component Libraries	Corporate Standards	Super-events (reusable methods)

Parts one and five outlined some 'universal models' for systems development, that is to say, models which are not specific to any corporation or implementation environment.

Part six outlines some 'corporate strategies', looking at areas in which a corporation, or organisation, may develop models and standards and urge them upon its analysts and designers.

Part four described these 'application design techniques'.

Chapter 32

Corporate strategies for achieving software reuse

Earlier parts of the book concentrated on design techniques for discovering and designing reusable components during the development of one system. This chapter looks at corporate-wide strategies for increasing software reuse between systems, and between generations of systems.

32.1 Corporate strategies

Taking the framework from the end of chapter 31, the three major headings name three different ways to avoid redundancy in systems specification:

- Universal models (covered in parts one and five)
- Corporate strategies
- Application-specific design techniques (covered in parts four and five)

For all kinds of commercial, theoretical and practical reasons it is difficult to develop or impose universal models on system specification, however this book makes an attempt to present some universal stereotypes. We have also said a lot about application-specific design techniques. The main target we haven't hit so far is the middle one, corporate strategies. Corporate strategies fall under two main headings:

- Extending the use of old systems
  The corporate model *
  Reverse engineering
  Incremental re-engineering
  The corporate component library

- Making extendible systems
  Generic design *
  Corporate standards.

* Notice that these two key strategies are entirely separable as ideas. In the language of chapter 4, a **corporate model** is an 'composition' of distinct application system models, whereas a **generic design** is a 'generalisation' or super-type for a family of similar systems. Composition and generalisation need not necessarily be linked in corporate modelling. Designers should be aware of this, though in practice the strategies are often confused (accidentally) or combined (on purpose).

Amongst other ideas, we shall look in this chapter at the evolution by re-engineering of existing systems into a form which can more easily be extended by reuse.

32.2 The corporate model

It almost goes without saying that large organisations are always seeking to be more efficient, to reduce duplication of development and maintenance effort across their more or less distinct application systems, to migrate from old systems to new systems more readily. To do this, they need a corporate model.

What the corporate model is not

Many organisations have developed some kind of corporate model, but there have been misunderstandings about what it means to create and use a corporate model, and there are blind alleys to be avoided.

... not the start of a top-down development strategy

A corporate model is not the start of a top-down development strategy. A weakness of several object-oriented methodologies is to assume that it is possible or advisable to start from a top-level model, showing relatively few highly generic objects, and then develop distinct systems which instantiate more specific variations of those object types.

This is not to say that high-level specifications are unhelpful. They are, and there are many ways to suppress detail in presenting a corporate data model. The problem here is with the notion that highly generic object types are powerful and helpful design tool. They are not.

... not a model of highly generic objects

Generalising across application areas, it is all too easy to waste time developing a model which contains entity types generalised to the point where they become meaningless, such as person, location, event and money transaction.

Users do not say, 'we want a system which contains variations of the generic objects person, location, and so on'. They say 'we want a system with objects like the specific ones already instantiated in system A and other objects like those in system B, with some differences we'll tell you about'.

At the end of the day, a model of highly generic objects does not turn out to be very helpful, except insofar as it might help to focus attention on common requirements. However, of course some degree of **generic design** is useful, and we shall return to this point later.

... not a common requirement specification

It is undeniably true that system developers do keep reinventing the wheel. For example, almost every system contains a significant amount of functionality devoted to storing and maintaining names and addresses, often those of customers.

The building of a model, and ultimately a system, to handle requirements common to several applications of a business is a valuable activity. The model/system may become a cornerstone of the business, but it is not what we mean by a corporate model, and it is not especially dependent on or relevant to object-oriented ideas.

Note that the key to successful implementation of a common requirements system is to carry the users with you. It is no use building a model in which all users use the same address format, unless you can persuade users to do this.

What the corporate model is

A corporate model covers several or all of the application systems of an organisation. It is potentially the start of an attempt to create a single corporate system out of these distinct application systems.

Too often, a high-level model is developed by managers, perhaps over a weekend in some retreat, then presented to application designers as though it will solve all their problems and enable them to integrate systems. While this may be a way to get things started, a corporate model requires far more development effort, management and attention than this. It should be developed and extended by reverse engineering from existing systems wherever possible. In areas where there are no existing systems, the corporate model should be extended by using all of the normal application-specific techniques, including Relational Data Analysis of input and output requirements.

Perhaps most importantly of all, the corporate model is not worth a candle if it is left on the shelf. It must be used and maintained. It requires just as much attention as the application-specific data structures which it seeks to embrace.

The corporate model as a Conceptual Model

Since different application systems and different generations of one system may be implemented on different machines, the corporate model must be a machine-independent specification. To this end, the main idea brought forward in this book is that of the Conceptual Model, that is, a machine-independent specification of the essential data and processes of a system.

As a Conceptual Model, the corporate model may be viewed as a model of the real world, but this is not a necessary starting point for planning to increase software reuse. It is enough to view the corporate model as a machine-independent specification. As a Conceptual Model, the corporate model must cover both data and processes.

Corporate data model

A corporate data model takes the form of an entity data model, which integrates the data structures of the various application systems of an organisation, assuming they have at least some data in common.

An entity data model already uses 'suppression of detail' by hiding the aggregates of data items which are the attributes of each entity. Further suppression of detail can be applied to a corporate data model by:

- Rolling detail entities into their master entity
- Rolling sub-types into their the super-type
- Rolling many-to-many link entities.

These are illustrated below.

Rolling detail entities into their master entity.

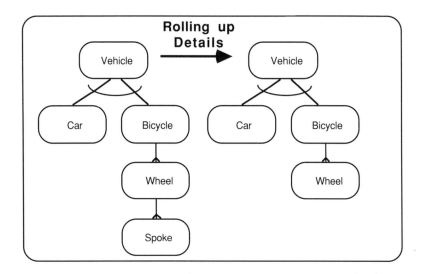

Rolling sub-types into their the super-type, leaving only the top of a class hierarchy.

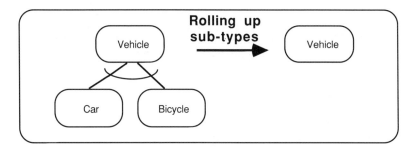

Rolling many-to-many link entities, showing a direct relationship instead.

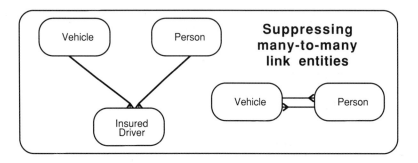

The point about all of these transformations is that they enable a *direct correspondence* to be maintained between entities in the corporate data model and the more detailed entity data models. If the corporate data model is to be useful, such a mapping must be specified and maintained.

Suppression of detail may be useful in presenting a high-level specification, but like all composite objects, a corporate data model is not helpful unless the base objects of which it is composed are also specified and implemented, just as in chapter 1 we pointed out that the sets of a tennis match are not meaningful and cannot be completed without playing each point.

Corporate process model

The corporate system model, or simply 'corporate model' should be composed of both a corporate data model and a corporate process model.

The corporate process model must be clearly and inextricably tied to the corporate data model. It follows that the corporate process model must be to do with the conceptual model, rather than the external design. So (rather than some form of data flow diagram or process hierarchy), we propose that a corporate process model takes the form of an entity event model, which is clearly tied to the corporate data model.

It is possible to suppress detail from a corporate process model by using a diagram notation of the kind employed by several object-oriented authors.

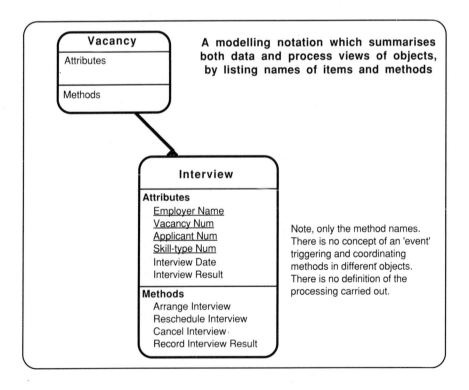

The point about this kind of model is that it can be seen as a transformation, by suppression of detail, from the more detailed entity event models described in part four. If the corporate model is to be useful, such a mapping must be specified and maintained.

There have been other views of what it means to create and use a corporate process model. Some people have taken it to be a top-down approach, using data flow diagrams or the like, but we do not take this line.

Like the corporate data model, the corporate process model is not worth a candle if it is left on the shelf. It must be used, and it must be maintained. It requires just as much attention, probably more, than the corporate data model.

Trust in the corporate model

People generally have less faith in a corporate model than in an application-specific specification, because they know the latter has been or can be proven by implementation. How can they be sure that the corporate model works, or is up-to-date with current user requirements? The longer a model is not implemented, the less people will be inclined to trust it or even look at it.

One solution to this is to work at maintaining the corporate model in parallel with each application system. Another solution is not to build or reverse engineer a corporate model until you have a plan to implement it in some way.

The corporate model as a tool for reuse

The corporate model is not a practical tool for reuse until it is implemented. To do this means adding the other two schemas of the 3-Schema Architecture.

How the corporate data model is stored in a physical database should be invisible to any application which wishes to access the corporate data. This implies building an Internal Design (a physical database design and a Process Data Interface) via which part or all of the corporate data is implemented in a physical environment.

Each application system to make use of the corporate data may impose its own External Design views upon this data. This is entirely a matter for judgement within the design of an application system. However, it is also possible and probably desirable for different application systems to share or reuse the same external views of the corporate data.

As each existing system is modified, it can be revised and rebuilt in line with the 3-Schema Architecture. This will make it possible to implement the corporate model and to develop systems by extending this model in the future. To separate the concerns of the Conceptual Model from the Internal and External Designs, some kind of reverse engineering must be carried out.

32.3 **Reverse engineering**

Existing systems can be very hard to understand. They are usually defined in ways incompatible with the ways that new systems are to be defined. If we are to make use of existing systems, we need some way of extracting reusable components from them. Reverse engineering means abstracting a machine-independent specification from an existing system.

Reverse engineering helps designers to understand the existing systems and detect reusable components within them. But reverse engineering does not automatically reveal the components you are looking for; it must be managed. Two conclusions which may be drawn from this book are that for reverse engineering:

- the main goal is specification of the Conceptual Model
- this specification should comprise entity data and entity event models.

The relationship between forward and reverse engineering

Forward and reverse engineering must be closely related. Good candidate techniques for reverse engineering are the reverse of those which are the best candidates for forward engineering by a CASE tool (see chapter 30). For those software engineering activities which have already been automated as forward engineering steps in CASE tools, it is best to start by studying what has already been achieved here and how it was done, rather than starting from scratch with new proposals.

Automatable forward engineering techniques in SSADM4

Most SSADM4 techniques combine three elements in varying degrees: *analysis*, requiring the discovery of new facts; *design*, requiring judgments and decisions based on facts and rules of thumb; and *transformation* of inputs into outputs. Those SSADM4 techniques which require little or no discovery and require few or no decisions to be made are the best candidates for automation.

There are several forward engineering techniques in SSADM4, already all or partly automated in current CASE tools, which might usefully be reversed:

a Logical Data Model view	-> an Enquiry Access Path
an Enquiry Access Path	-> an Enquiry Process Model
LDM + its set of ELHs	-> the set of Effect Correspondence Diagrams
ECD + its set of ELHs + LDM	-> an Update Process Model
LDM + volumetrics	-> physical database design.

There are several more SSADM4 techniques, already all or partly automated in current CASE tools, which are designed for engineering a data model out of I/O descriptions. Whether these are best called forward or reverse engineering depends on your point of view.

an I/O screen or report	-> an I/O structure
an I/O structure	-> a set of TNF relations
several sets of TNF relations	-> consolidated set of TNF relations
a set of TNF relations	-> a partial Logical Data Model
two partial LDMs	-> a single Logical Data Model

Relational Data Analysis is especially useful as a tool for extracting entity data models from existing systems, it is a good reverse engineering technique. This analysis suggests five chains of SSADM4 activities which might be automated as reverse engineering steps.

Automatable reverse engineering techniques in SSADM4

Only a few links in the five chains of activities listed below are considered in current reverse engineering methods and tools:

	Input	Reverse engineered product
1	An I/O screen or report	-> an I/O structure
	an I/O structure	-> a set of TNF relations
	several sets of TNF relations	-> consolidated set of TNF relations
	a set of TNF relations	-> a partial Logical Data Model
	two partial LDMs	-> a single Logical Data Model
2	Physical Database / File Design	-> Universal first-cut database design
	Universal first-cut database design	-> Physical Data Model
	Physical Data Model	-> Logical Data Model
3	Physical code of programs	-> FCIM
	FCIM	-> Specific Function Models
	Specific Function Model	-> Function Definition
4	Database enquiry routine	-> Enquiry Process Model
	Enquiry Process Model	-> Enquiry Access Path
	Enquiry Access Path	-> a Logical Data Model view
5	Database commit unit	-> Update Process Model
	Update Process Model	-> Effect Correspondence Diagram
	Set of Effect Corresp. Diagrams	-> Entity Life Histories

Integration with other systems via the corporate model

Reverse engineering goes hand in hand with corporate modelling. Both corporate modelling and reverse engineering of an existing system should produce entity models, so the results can be compared and contrasted. One or both of these models should be revised in the light of the other until they match.

32.4 **Incremental Re-engineering**

Reverse engineering can be used to rebuild systems in line with the corporate model. This process is more accurately called 'Incremental Re-engineering'. It means that as an existing system is modified, it is re-engineered to separate the code which deals with the separate concerns of the Conceptual Model, External and Internal Designs. Having done this, the system can be reimplemented in different ways.

Making use of an existing physical database

If the existing database does not match the structure of the corporate data model, but contains the essential data, then a Process Data Interface can be built to present the existing database as though it is a corporate data model. Other systems (old and new) can now be interfaced to the existing database. Their logical database processes can be designed using the techniques in chapter 18, and directly implemented.

Making use of an existing user interface

If the existing user interface captures the essential input data (events and enquiry triggers), then it can be retained as an interface to new systems which provide more sophisticated processing of these inputs against a more sophisticated database. Note however that more sophisticated processing of the Conceptual Model may involve improved error reporting, leading to some redesign of the interface.

32.5 **The corporate component library**

Suppose a designer is asked to build a new software component, and is expected to consider first the possibility of reusing or extending an old system component.

(By 'designer' we probably mean either the 'systems analyst' or the 'programmer' though there are now more job titles for these roles than you can shake a stick at. By 'component' we probably mean a record definition or a processing routine.)

If reuse is to be planned and managed properly, components must be stored in some kind of 'library'. For now we use this word in the loosest of senses as just a collection of components, not necessarily implying any kind of computerised storage and retrieval system, nor even a proper manual filing system. If the component library is to be successful, someone (or several people) must play the role of 'librarian'. This is not necessarily a job title, just the role of someone who 'knows' what is in the library, and 'catalogues' the entries in it.

Graham (1991) has said 'there is a lack of commercially available libraries. Without such libraries... the benefits of true reuse cannot be delivered in volume'. We agree that outside of very narrow areas of software engineering, libraries have to date delivered little of any kind of reuse (true or not) to information systems developers. Why have component libraries not worked very well to date? How can we make them more effective?

Why component libraries haven't worked very well to date

Reuse has always gone on in an informal way. Experienced designers build up a library of components which they use over and over in various ways. Sometimes a designer will plunder someone else's library. Informally this approach can be very successful. Where each designer is his/her own librarian it is clear that the designer will swiftly recognise opportunities for reuse, and will barely need to catalogue the library at all.

The classical approach to reusability is to try to formalise this approach by building a library of common components: data definitions, routines, procedures, functions, subroutines, modules or whatever. These attempts have not been very successful, at least for information systems design.

For many years the hopes of software developers have centred on the reuse of common modules. It was hoped that by keeping chunks of code small they could be independently tested, and that those validated chunks could be recombined easily into new programs. This approach, using conventional technology, is generally agreed to have failed. As Jackson once observed:

'a subroutine library is the only kind of library where everyone wants to put something in but no-one wants to take something out'.

To understand why modularity is not enough on its own, imagine a designer who seeks to retrieve and use components from a library. Consider in detail the steps he/she has to go through.

Assessment of the new component

The designer may be under instruction *always* to look for an old component before building a new one. This has pros: the designer is forced to become well acquainted with the library; the maximum amount of reuse will be achieved. But it has cons: an unsuccessful search for a reusable component is a waste of time; a successful search may take longer than building the new component from scratch.

The alternative is that the designer must first assess the new component, to decide whether or not a search for a reusable old component will be cost effective. It is not at all obvious how the designer should assess whether the search is likely to succeed.

Searching for the old component

If the designer is also the librarian, then this is rarely a problem, he/she might for example simply flick through the relevant pile of documents at the bottom of a filing cabinet. But in accessing someone else's library the designer is faced with two problems.

First, finding the best or correct search key: it is difficulty for a programmer or designer to identify the component they want, perhaps looking for a label, or a few key words, in the catalogue of the library.

Second, selecting the best or correct component: there might be many (say twenty) components which match the search criteria. It is a laborious task is to examine each one to see if it does the right job.

Using the old component

The next difficulty is how to use the component when you've found it. There are three possibilities:

- the component does exactly what is wanted and no more
- the component doesn't quite do what is wanted
- the component does what is wanted, but does other things as well.

The last two of these mean the designer must in effect create a new component, which must be fully tested before implementation. It may take longer to eliminate bugs caused by modifying an old component than to develop new special-purpose code. This raises one more question.

Adding the component in the library

If the designer creates a new component from an old one by copying and tailoring it, should the new component now be added into the library? Even if the new one is only slightly different from the old one?

How to make component libraries work?

There are things which can be done to improve the way libraries are maintained and used. First, we suggest maintaining separate libraries for components of the Conceptual Model, External and Internal Designs. For the Conceptual Model, we have further suggestions.

Effective cataloguing of components in the Conceptual Model library

Of course the library will be useless if the designer cannot find what is required. We suggest that for the Conceptual Model library, the catalogue should be the corporate data model. Thus it will be easier to:

- find the appropriate code because of the way in which object types are organised in a (more or less) hierarchical taxonomy
- customise code by declaring new object types as variations on old ones
- produce code that can often avoid the need for customisation because of the ability to define processing generically without being aware of the kind of data being processed
- avoid unpredictable side-effects because of the way the internal workings of one object are hidden from another object, and the way you are encouraged to define new classes to objects to define processes specific to those new classes.

The techniques in part four naturally associate essential routines with objects in an entity data model.

Limiting the scope of the Conceptual Model library

Should the Conceptual Model library cover one application or all of the application systems owned by one organisation? Should it cover hard components (tested and implemented) or soft components such as untested components and design documents?

We suggest limiting a library to components of those application systems which are covered, or potentially covered by a single corporate model.

Appointing a librarian for the Conceptual Model library

The role of librarian, whose job it is to 'know' the catalogue (in the same way that the designer knows his personal library of past work) is a difficult one:

- the role is very taxing in the fast moving world of software design
- it is hard to find someone both qualified and willing to take on the role
- it is difficult to retain them for the length of time needed to do the job well.

Our answer is to appoint someone in charge of the corporate model. This is no mere librarian's job, but the senior system design role. It has to attract a highly skilled person.

32.6 Generic design

Abstraction by generalisation was introduced in chapter 4. This section is about making wider use of this idea in systems design. Where a family of related systems or system components is to be developed, a proactive approach to reuse is to develop generic models and components which can with little effort be instantiated as a specific system or component, or else extended with features specific to the system required.

Generic design is a compromise. The more generic a model or component, the more widely reusable it is, but the less closely it is likely to fit the development of a specific system and the more likely it will require tailoring or adaptation to the specific case; consider for example the Universal Function Model of chapter 28. The less generic a model or component, the narrower the scope of its potential reuse, but the more likely it can be reused directly or requires only extension with a few specific details.

Packages as generic applications

Many generic application systems are already in use. These systems are usually called 'packaged systems' or simply 'packages'. Their development is driven by commercial demand.

The functions which are best supported by packages tend to be in the area of what might be called administrative support (payroll, order processing, invoicing). This is not just because so many businesses require similar administration functions. It is because businesses do not set out to gain a competitive advantage in these areas.

Where businesses share the same functions and do not seek to be better than their competitors in carrying out those functions, there is clearly a commercial gain to be made by building and selling a package to carry out these functions.

There are many areas of business which seem like they ought to be candidates for the development of packages (say the management of savings accounts in banks and building societies) but where packages are much harder to build and to sell, because each organisation is trying to outdo its rivals, and their information system is a vital weapon in this struggle for supremacy. Anyone with the expertise to develop a better system sells their services to one organisation rather than to all.

It is not our concern here to suggest candidate applications for the development of further packages. Anyone who detects a good opportunity in the market-place is well advised not to tell everyone about it!

Generic models

We are concerned not with packages, rather with the development of generic models by large organisations who can benefit from reuse between overlapping systems. For example, this is very much the idea behind the development of the Common Basic Specification (chapter 2) being developed within the National Health Service.

What is a generic model? The Oxford Reference Dictionary includes the following definitions:

generic - characteristic of or applied to a genus or class; not specific or special

model - a representation in three dimensions of a proposed structure

Consider for example a hospital record keeping system in which there are two forms, one describing the activity of a nurse on a ward, the other the activity of doctor in a clinic. These are specific models.

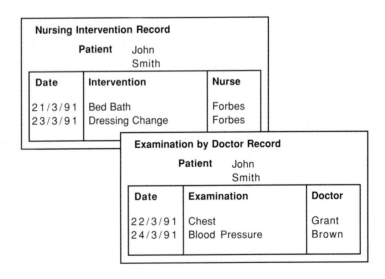

If we wish to build a system encompassing the work of all clinical staff, we may attempt to classify activity such that both points of view may be accommodated, and still allow for the detailed occurrences of activity to be correctly identified. The above two record types can be generalised into the one shown below.

Patient Activity Record

Patient   John Smith

Date	Activity	Activity Type	Staff Member	Staff Type
21/3/91	Bed Bath	Int	Forbes	Nur
22/3/91	Chest	Exm	Grant	Doc
23/3/91	Dressing Change	Int	Forbes	Nur
24/3/91	Blood Pressure	Exm	Brown	Doc

Note how the generic design in this example is fully specific and detailed. Although it is a generalisation, it does not involve suppression of detail; these were identified as separate ideas in chapter 4.

Why produce a generic model?

A base for systems with wider applicability: generic systems are by definition more widely applicable than specific systems.

A platform for integration: to accomplish any form of integration between systems, an understanding of what is common between systems must be achieved. The existence of a generic model should accelerate this process.

A base for comparison: a generic model can be used to help in the comparison of two or more specific models, developed at lower levels of abstraction. This provides a check on the scope and integrity of the specific models, and leads to a clearer understanding of the specific models.

A base for less costly systems: a generic model is usually smaller than the collective base of models from which it is an abstraction.

A base for more stable systems: generic models are more stable than specific ones. Changes in terminology, organisational structures and practices can be more readily accommodated at the abstract level. The concepts which are most subject to change may be stored and processed in a generic system.

Having quoted this, there are reasons to be sceptical about how much is achievable using a generic design approach. These reasons were outlined in chapter 12.

32.7 **Corporate standards**

A very important contribution towards software reuse can be made by developing standards which impose constraints upon the way software components are designed. Where the choice between design options is more or less arbitrary, standards are especially helpful.

Implementation-led standards and constraints
Implementation tools can themselves impose some consistency on the design of data and process components. Whereas a 3GL may permit a needless variety of design options, the use of a specific application generator or 4GL can help by limiting design options. Having said this, popular application generators are now being extended with procedural programming languages in a way which gives the designers far more design choices to make. And the trouble with standards imposed by any implementation tool is that they may make it harder to move from one tool to another.

Organisation-led standards and constraints
If an attempt is to be made to achieve reuse between systems, then the organisation should set out standards which constrain the design of system components, ensuring that needless variations in design of components are less likely.

Conceptual Model documentation standards for:
- use of a specific methodology
- use of a specific CASE tool
- use of a specific data dictionary.

External Design standards for:
- use of a specific GUI
- standard I/O formats * and procedures
- standard on-line service structure
- style guides for user dialogues (see chapters 22 to 24).

Internal Design standards for:
- use of a specific DBMS
- design and coding of a process/data interface (PDI).

* Mismatches between data item lengths and types are a common source of problem. If a telephone number is defined as 30 characters long in an old system and 32 characters long in a new one, then any attempt to reuse a routine which uses a fixed length field for the name (say, displaying it in a window on a screen) may fail. Likewise, if the telephone number is defined to be of a text data type in one system and of a numeric data type in another, then this will also prevent true reuse of system components.

32.8 **Design techniques for avoiding redundancy**

Finally, decisions about what design techniques to use must be taken at the corporate level. Despite some of the claims which have been made, methodologies like Information Engineering and SSADM do not offer much help to the analyst in detecting reusable components or specifying them.

Our main concern in parts four and five was to develop application-specific techniques for discovering and designing reusable components. In looking at where object-oriented ideas might be useful, we showed how to discover and record reusable objects (or super-entities) and more importantly reusable methods (or super-events).

32.9 **Framework for software reuse within SSADM4**

We can reshape and extend the framework developed at the end of chapter 31 to show where the ideas discussed in chapters 31 and 32 impact on stages and steps of SSADM4.

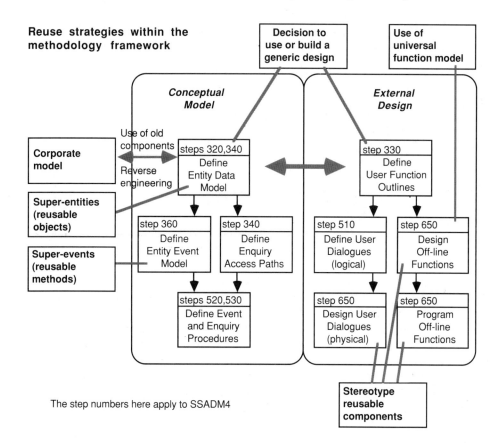

32.10 **Where next?**

This book has covered several reasonably prescriptive techniques for achieving software reuse, ones which can be applied more or less immediately by analysts and designers, without reference to any corporate strategy. It has also pointed towards wider corporate strategies. We have more to say about setting out to design distinct systems so that they can be bolted together relatively easily at a later date.

We have much more to say about entity event modelling, and there are many other topics which might be integrated into the theory. The diagram below, adapted from Robinson and Berrisford (1993), shows the extent to which we have *not* covered information systems development in this book.

Information System Development Matrix

	Strand of IS Development					
	Conceptual model					
Level of IS Specification	Object data	Object behaviour	External design	User roles	Distri-bution	Require-ments
Scope description						
Enterprise model						
Informal						
Formal System specification		Main focus of OO SSADM				
Physical design						
System components		Coded software				

Some people are trying to use OO ideas at row two, the level of business or enterprise modelling. We think that formal computer system specification techniques are not the best tools here, and prefer a 'soft systems' approach. You have to accept that between rows two and three you will flip between informal and formal specification languages.

In addition to the subject areas indicated by this diagram, and the topics mentioned in the preface, the impact of client-server architectures may be of interest. The most naive interpretation of a client-server architecture maps perfectly onto the division we draw between External Design and Conceptual Model. Taking another view, one might say that each object can take client and server roles within the processing of different events, or even one event.

All these subjects must wait for a book with sufficient room to explore them properly.

References

Alexander J. [1992]
'The ISTEL Application Architecture' in
'CASE Current Practice Future
Prospects' John Wiley & Sons

Bergland G. D. [1981]
'A Guided Tour of Program Design
Methodologies'
Bell Labs, Computer & IEEE

CCTA [1990]
'SSADM Version 4'
NCC Blackwell, 1990

Checkland P. [1984]
'Systems Thinking, Systems Practice'
John Wiley & Sons

Conway M.E. [1963]
'Design of a Separable Transition-
Diagram Compiler' Communications of
the ACM vol. 6 pp. 396-408

Dahl, O-J. [1966]
'Simula - an Algol-Based simulation
language' Communications of the ACM
9, 9, pp. 671-4678

Dahl, Dijkstra and Hoare [1972]
'Structured Programming'
Academic Press

Duschl R. and Hopkins N.C. [1992] *
'SSADM / Grapes Comparison'
Springer Verlag

Ford M. [1992]
Article in *Computer Weekly*,
June 18th.

Goldberg A. [1981] *
'Smalltalk-80, The Language and its
Implementation' Addison Wesley

Graham I. [1991] *
'Object-Oriented Methods'
Addison Wesley

Griethuysen J. J. Van [1987]
'Concepts and Terminology
for the Conceptual Model
and the Information Base'
ISO report ISO TC97-TR 9007
ISO Geneva

Hopcraft J. and Ullman J. [1969]
'Formal Languages
and Their Relation to Automata'
Addison Wesley

Hughes J. G. [1991]
'Object-Oriented Databases'
Prentice Hall

IOPENER [1992]
Newsletter of the IOPT club, Nov.
(the club for the Introduction Of Process
Technology)

Jackson M. [1975] *
'Principles of Program Design'
Academic Press

Jacobson I. [1992] *
'Object-Oriented Software Engineering'
Addison Wesley

Johnson D. [1993]
'The Tower of Babble'
The Veteran Neophyte, March

Kieras and Bovair [1984]
'The role of a mental model in learning to
operate a device' Program in Technical
Communication, College of Engineering.

University of Michigan, Ann Arbor, MI
48109

Kleene S.C. [1956]
'Representation of events in nerve nets
and finite state automata' Automata
Studies, Princeton University Press

Martin J. and Finklesteen C. [1981]
'Information Engineering'
Prentice Hall

Meyer B. [1988]
'Object-Oriented Software Construction'
Prentice Hall

Miller G.A. [1956]
'The magical number seven, plus or
minus two: some limits on our capacity
for processing information' *The
Psychological Review* Vol. 63 March

Model Systems Ltd. [1993a]
'Aut2 User Manual'

Model Systems Ltd. [1993b]
UBS papers 30 to 38
Union Bank of Switzerland

Naur P. [1963]
'Revised Report on ALGOL 60'
Communications of the ACM vol. 6 pp.
1-23

Robinson K. [1977]
'An entity/event data modelling method'
Computer Journal Vol. 22 no. 3

Robinson K. [1979]
'Infotech Systems Technology'.
Infotech International

Robinson K. [1990]
'Two paradigms of OO design, or,

OOPS, it's an entity'
Proceedings of GUIDE 74, Toronto

Robinson K. [1992]
'Putting the SE into CASE' in
'CASE Current Practice Future
Prospects' John Wiley & Sons

Robinson K. and Berrisford G. [1993]
'The ISE Product Framework' in
BCS CASE Newsletter October

Robinson K. and Hall J. [1989]
'An Entity's Life History'
Proceedings of GUIDE 73, Anaheim

Rock-Evans R. [1992]
Article in *Computer Weekly* June 18th.

Rochfield A (1987)
'MERISE, an Information System Design
methodology' in 'Entity Relationship
Approach' S Spaccapietra (Editor).
Elsevier Science Publishers B.V.

Rumbaugh *et al.* [1991] *
'Object-Oriented Modelling and Design'
Prentice Hall

Tsichritzis D.C. and Klug A. [1978]
'The ANSI//X3/SPARC DBMS
Framework: Report of the Study Group
on Data Base Management Systems'
Information Systems 3

Smith *et al.* [1982]
'Designing the Star Interface'
Byte Magazine, April

Vonk R. [1988]
'Prototyping' Prentice Hall

* relevant further reading

Index

The references below are to chapters or
sections within chapters.